British Architectural Theory 1540–1750

An Anthology of Texts

Edited by Caroline van Eck
with contributions by
Christy Anderson

Routledge
Taylor & Francis Group
LONDON AND NEW YORK

First published 2003 by Ashgate Publishing

Reissued 2018 by Routledge
2 Park Square, Milton Park, Abingdon, Oxon OX14 4RN
711 Third Avenue, New York, NY 10017, USA

Routledge is an imprint of the Taylor & Francis Group, an informa business

Publisher's Note
The publisher has gone to great lengths to ensure the quality of this reprint but points out that some imperfections in the original copies may be apparent.

A Library of Congress record exists under LC control number: 2002074720

ISBN 13: 978-1-138-71072-6 (hbk)
ISBN 13: 978-1-138-71067-2 (pbk)
ISBN 13: 978-1-315-19920-7 (ebk)

Typeset in Palatino by Manton Typesetters, Louth, Lincolnshire, UK

BRITISH ARCHITECTURAL THEORY 1540–1750

British Architectural Theory 1540–1750 shows the variety, scope and originality of architectural thought in early modern England. This is the first collection of English writing on architecture from this period to be published in a modern, accessible edition. The texts included here offer practical advice on how to build a country house, farm or fortress, how to select building materials and how to draw or survey, but they also discuss the nature of architecture, the sense of the past, church building, and the social, political and religious meaning of architecture. They also reveal a very independent spirit of inquiry into the principles of classical design. Authors include well-known writers such as Inigo Jones, John Evelyn, or Sir Christopher Wren, but also some writers who are not usually associated with architectural theory, such as John Donne, Henry Hawkins or Walter Montague, who nonetheless have a lot to tell us about the ways in which architecture was perceived.

The transmission of ideas through illustration is an important feature of architectural theory and the book is illustrated with 30 seminal images. All fragments are introduced and annotated. Substantial endnotes and an extensive bibliography for further reading complete the book providing an invaluable resource for students and teachers as well as equipping the general reader with an accessible introduction to the key issues of British architectural theory in this period.

Caroline van Eck is a Senior Research Fellow at the Vrije Universiteit in Amsterdam, where she directs a research program on the role of rhetoric in the visual arts and architecture funded by the Dutch Foundation for Scientific Research (NWO), and an Honorary Visiting Fellow at the University of York. She has published widely on architectural theory of the nineteenth century and the Renaissance. Publications include *Organicism in Nineteenth-Century Architecture: An Inquiry into its Theoretical and Philosophical Background* (Amsterdam 1994); *The Question of Style in Philosophy and the Arts* (Cambridge 1995), and articles on Renaissance architectural theory for *Renaissance Studies* and *The Journal of the Society of Architectural Historians*. With Ashgate she has also published the first English edition of Germain Boffrand's *Book of Architecture* (2002).

British Architectural Theory 1540–1750: An Anthology of Texts
is published in the series
Reinterpreting Classicism: Culture, Reaction and Appropriation
Edited by Caroline van Eck, Vrije Universiteit, Amsterdam

IN THE SAME SERIES

Producing the Past
Aspects of Antiquarian Culture and Practice 1700–1850
Edited by Martin Myrone and Lucy Peltz
Preface by Stephen Bann

Sir John Soane and the Country Estate
Ptolemy Dean

Building on Ruins
The Rediscovery of Rome and English Architecture
Frank Salmon

Allan Ramsay and the Search for Horace's Villa
Edited by Bernard D. Frischer and Iain Gordon Brown

The Built Surface, Volume 1
Architecture and the Pictorial Arts from Antiquity to the Enlightenment
Edited by Christy Anderson

The Art of Building
From Classicism to Modernity:
The Dutch Architectural Debate 1840–1900
Auke van der Wond

Germain Boffrand
Book of Architecture Containing the General Principles of the Art and the Plans, Elevations and Sections of Some of the Edifices Built in France and in Foreign Countries
Edited and introduced by Caroline van Eck
Translated by David Britt

Contents

List of figures ix

Acknowledgements xiii

Introduction 1

1 **The nature of architecture** 7

Introduction; John Dee, from his Preface to Euclid's *Elements of Geometrie* (1570); Francesco Colonna (attr.), from *Hypnerotomachia*, trans. 'R. D.' [Robert Dallington] (1592); Guglielmo Grataroli, from *The Castel of Memorie*, trans. William Fulwod (1572); John Willis, from *Mnemonica; or, the Art of Memory* (1661); Robert Stickells, two texts on design (1597); Paolo Giovanni Lomazzo, from *A Tracte containing the Artes of Curious Paintinge Carvinge & Buildinge*, trans. 'R. H.' [R. Haydocke] (1598); Inigo Jones, from his 'Roman Sketchbook' (1615); Sir Henry Wotton, from *The Elements of Architecture* (1624); Thomas Hobbes, from 'Answer to Davenant's Preface to *Gondibert*' (1650); Sir Roger Pratt, from 'Certain Short Notes Concerning Architecture' (1660); Nicholas Barbon, from *An Apology for the Builder* (1685); Roger North, from 'Of Building' (1690s) and 'Of Unity and Variety' (*c.* 1695–96); Joseph Addison, from 'Essay on the Pleasures of the Imagination' (1712); Nicholas Hawksmoor, from a letter to Lord Carlisle at Castle Howard (7 January 1724); Robert Morris, from *Lectures on Architecture* (1734); James Ralph, from his Preface to *The Builder's Dictionary* (1734); Batty Langley, from *Ancient Masonry* (1736)

2 **Building** 53

Introduction; Andrew Boorde, from *The Boke for to Lerne a Man to be Wyse in Buyldyng* (1540); Leonard Digges, from *A Boke named Tectonicon* (1556); John Shute, from *The First and Chiefe Groundes of Architecture* (1563); Richard More, from *The Carpenters Rule* (1602); Charles l'Estienne [Stevens], from *Maison Rustique*, trans. Richard Surflet (1606); David Papillon, from *A Practicall Abstract of the Arts of Fortification and Assailing* (1645); Sir Balthazar Gerbier, from *The First Lecture touching Fortifications* (1649); Roger Pratt, from 'Rules for the Guidance of Architects' (1665; published 1672); Sir Balthazar Gerbier, from *Counsel and Advise to All*

Builders (1663); Sir John Evelyn, 'Londinium Redivivum' (1666); Stephen Primatt, from *The City & Country Purchaser & Builder* (1667); Joseph Moxon, from *Mechanick Exercises* (1678); Sir H. Shere, 'Some Directions for my Lord Nottingham's Building' (1695); Andrea Pozzo, from *Rules and Examples of Perspective Proper for Painters and Architects*, trans. John James (1707); John Webb, from 'Memoirs Relating to the Life and Writings of Inigo Jones, Esq.' (1725); Richard Holt, from *A Short Treatise of Artificial Stone* (1730)

3 **Architecture and religion** 105

Introduction; From the Book of Kings, in the Authorized (King James) Version of the Bible (1611); John Donne, from his *Sermons* (1630 and 1625); Henry Hawkins, from 'The House', in *Partheneia Sacra* (1633); R. T., from *De Templis* (1638); Walter Montague, from *Miscellanea Spiritualia* (1648); Sir George Wheler, from *An Account of the Churches* (1698); Sir Christopher Wren, 'Letter of Recommendation to a Friend on the Commission for Building Fifty New Churches' (1711); Commission for Building Fifty New City Churches, from 'Rules for the Fifty New Churches' (1712); Sir John Vanbrugh, 'Mr Van-Brugg's Proposals about Building ye New Churches' (1712); Charles Wheatly, from *The Church of England Man's Companion; or a Rational Illustration of the Book of Common Prayer* (1710)

4 **The sense of the past** 143

Introduction; George Hakewill, from *Apologie or Declaration of the Power and Providence of God* (1627); Inigo Jones, from *Stone-Heng Restored*, and dedication 'To the Favourers of Antiquity' by John Webb (published 1655); Sir Christopher Wren, from 'Design for Repairing the Old Ruinous Structure [of Saint Paul, 7 May 1666]' (1666); Roger North, from 'On Gothic Architecture' (*c.* 1696); Sir John Vanbrugh, 'Reasons Offer'd for Preserving some Part of the Old Manor [at Woodstock]' (1709); Robert Castell, from *The Villas of the Ancients Illustrated* (1729); John Wood, from *The Origin of Building* (1741)

5 **Following the example of Antiquity** 177

Introduction; John Shute, from *The First and Chiefe Groundes of Architecture* (1563); From Sebastiano Serlio, *The first Booke of Architecture* (1611), dedication and 'To the Lovers of Architecture' by Robert Peake; Inigo Jones, from his notes written in his copy of Andrea Palladio, *I quattro libri dell'architettura* (1613–18); Sir Henry Wotton, from *The Elements of*

Architecture (1624); From VIGNOLA: *or, the Compleat Architect* (1655), dedication 'To the Ingenious Artists' by Joseph. Moxon; Sir Balthazar Gerbier, from *A Brief Discourse Concerning the Three Chief Principles of Magnificent Building* (1662); From Andrea Palladio, *The first Book of Architecture* (1663) (based on the French translation and abridgement by Pierre Le Muet), Preface and Book I, Chapter XX from the translation by G. R. [Geoffrey Richards]; From *The Architecture of Palladio; in Four Books* (1715) (a translation by Nicholas Du Bois, published by Giacomo Leoni after the French version of Roland Fréart de Chambray), 'Preface' by Nicholas Du Bois and extract from Book I, Chapter XX; From *Andrea Palladio's Architecture in Four Books*, translated and edited by Edward Hoppus (1735), Book I, Chapter XX; Sir John Evelyn, from *A Parallel of the Antient Architecture with the Modern* (1664); From Vincenzo Scamozzi, *The Mirror of Architecture* (1676) (based on Joachim Schuym's Dutch edition), 'To the Lovers of Architecture' by William Fisher; Sir Christopher Wren, 'Tract I' and extract from 'Tract IV: Observations on the Temple of Peace, built by the Emperor Vespasian' (both written after 1680); Roger North, from 'The Origin and Development of Regular Architecture' (*c.* 1690); Anthony Ashley Cooper, Lord Shaftesbury, from 'A Letter concerning Design' (1712); Colen Campbell, from the Introduction to his *Vitruvius Britannicus* (1715); James Ralph (attr.), from *A Critical Review of the Publick Buildings, Statues and Ornaments, In and About London and Westminster* (1734)

Notes 237

Bibliography 245

Index 261

List of figures

1 **The nature of architecture**

1.1 John Willis, *Mnemonica; or, the Art of Memory. Drained out of the pure Fountains of Art and Nature* (London, 1661), plate 1; photograph reproduced with permission of the Beinecke Rare Book and Manuscript Library, Yale University

1.2 Frontispiece to *The Builder's Dictionary: Or, Gentleman and Architect's Companion* (London, 1734); photograph reproduced with permission of the Yale Center for British Art (New Haven), Paul Mellon Collection

3 **Architecture and religion**

3.1 Frontispiece to Henry Hawkins, *Partheneia Sacra, or The Mysterious and Delicious Garden of the Sacred Parthenes …* (Rouen, 1633); photograph reproduced with permission of the Beinecke Rare Book and Manuscript Library, Yale University

3.2 'The Embleme' and 'The Poesie' from 'The House', in Henry Hawkins, *Partheneia Sacra* (p. 172); photograph reproduced with permission of the Beinecke Rare Book and Manuscript Library, Yale University

3.3 'The Device' (or 'impresa') and beginning of 'The Character', from 'The House', in Henry Hawkins, *Partheneia Sacra* (p. 163); photograph reproduced with permission of the Beinecke Rare Book and Manuscript Library, Yale University

3.4 George Wheler, *An Account of the Churches, or Places of Assembly, of the Ancient Christians from the Churches of Tyre, Jerusalem and Constantinople …* (London, 1698), plate 5; photograph reproduced with permission of the Beinecke Rare Book and Manuscript Library, Yale University

4 **The sense of the past**

4.1 Inigo Jones, *The most notable antiquity of Great Britain, vulgarly called Stone-Heng, on Salisbury plain, restored* (London, 1725), plate 1; photograph reproduced with permission of the Yale Center for British Art (New Haven), Paul Mellon Collection

4.2 Inigo Jones, *The most notable antiquity of Great Britain, vulgarly called Stone-Heng, on Salisbury plain, restored* (London, 1725), plate 3; photograph reproduced with permission of the Yale Center for British Art (New Haven), Paul Mellon Collection

4.3 Inigo Jones, *The most notable antiquity of Great Britain, vulgarly called Stone-Heng, on Salisbury plain, restored* (London, 1725), plate 4; photograph reproduced with permission of the Yale Center for British Art (New Haven), Paul Mellon Collection

4.4 Inigo Jones, *The most notable antiquity of Great Britain, vulgarly called Stone-Heng, on Salisbury plain, restored* (London, 1725), plate 5; photograph reproduced with permission of the Yale Center for British Art (New Haven), Paul Mellon Collection

4.5 Inigo Jones, *The most notable antiquity of Great Britain, vulgarly called Stone-Heng, on Salisbury plain, restored* (London, 1725), plate 7; photograph reproduced with permission of the Yale Center for British Art (New Haven), Paul Mellon Collection

4.6 Wenceslas Hollar, engraving of Old Saint Paul's seen from the west, from William Dugdale, *History of Saint Paul's Cathedral* (London, 1658); photograph reproduced with permission of the Yale Center for British Art (New Haven), Paul Mellon Collection

4.7 Wenceslas Hollar, engraving of Old Saint Paul's, interior of the nave, from William Dugdale, *History of Saint Paul's Cathedral* (London, 1658); photograph reproduced with permission of the Yale Center for British Art (New Haven), Paul Mellon Collection

4.8 Frontispiece to Robert Castell, *The Villas of the Ancients Illustrated* (London, 1729); photograph reproduced with permission of the Beinecke Rare Book and Manuscript Library, Yale University

4.9 Robert Castell, *The Villas of the Ancients Illustrated* (London, 1729), plan of Laurentinum; photograph reproduced with permission of the Beinecke Rare Book and Manuscript Library, Yale University

4.10 Robert Castell, *The Villas of the Ancients Illustrated* (London, 1729), the Cryptoporticus of Laurentinum, plan and elevation; photograph reproduced with permission of the Beinecke Rare Book and Manuscript Library, Yale University

5 Following the example of Antiquity

5.1 John Shute, *The First and Chiefe Groundes of Architecture used in all the auncient and famous monymentes* (London, 1563), illustration of the Doric order; photograph reproduced with permission of the Prentenkabinet of the Universiteit Leiden

5.2 *VIGNOLA: or, the Compleat Architect*, translated into English by Joseph Moxon (London, 1694; 4th edn), illustration of the Tuscan order (p. 17); photograph reproduced with permission of the Beinecke Rare Book and Manuscript Library, Yale University

5.3 *The first Book of Architecture, by Andrea Palladio. Translated out of Italian … by P^R le Muet. Translated out of French. By G. R. [Geoffrey Richards]* (London, 1663), illustration of the Ionic order (p. 77); photograph reproduced with permission of the Beinecke Rare Book and Manuscript Library, Yale University

5.4 *The first Book of Architecture, by Andrea Palladio. Translated out of Italian … by P^R le Muet. Translated out of French. By G. R. [Geoffrey Richards]* (London, 1663), illustration of Ionic column (p. 72); photograph reproduced with permission of the Beinecke Rare Book and Manuscript Library, Yale University

5.5 *The first Book of Architecture, by Andrea Palladio. Translated out of Italian … by P^R le Muet. Translated out of French. By G. R. [Geoffrey Richards]* (London, 1663), illustration of the Corinthian order (p. 99); photograph reproduced with permission of the Beinecke Rare Book and Manuscript Library, Yale University

5.6 *Andrea Palladio's Architecture in Four Books … Carefully Revis'd and Redelineated by Edwd Hoppus, Surveyor* (London, 1735), illustration of the Corinthian order (p. 44); photograph reproduced with permission of the Beinecke Rare Book and Manuscript Library, Yale University

5.7 John Evelyn, *A Parallel of the Antient Architecture with the Modern* (London, 1664), Doric profile at Albano (p. 21); photograph reproduced with permission of the Yale Center for British Art (New Haven), Paul Mellon Collection

5.8 John Evelyn, *A Parallel of the Antient Architecture with the Modern* (London, 1664), illustration of the Doric order according to Palladio and Scamozzi (p. 25); photograph reproduced with permission of the Yale Center for British Art (New Haven), Paul Mellon Collection

5.9 John Evelyn, *A Parallel of the Antient Architecture with the Modern* (London, 1664), Doric profile at the Baths of Diocletian (p. 19); photograph reproduced with permission of the Yale Center for British Art (New Haven), Paul Mellon Collection

5.10 John Evelyn, *A Parallel of the Antient Architecture with the Modern* (London, 1664), perspective elevation of an Ionic profile at the Baths of Diocletian (p. 43); photograph reproduced with permission of the Yale Center for British Art (New Haven), Paul Mellon Collection

5.11 *The Architecture of Palladio; in Four Books. Containing a Short Treatise of the Five Orders, and the most necessary Observations concerning all Sorts of Building … Revis'd, Design'd, and Publish'd by Giacomo Leoni* (London, 1715), 'Temple of Peace', Rome [now thought rather to be the Basilica of Constantine or Maxentius], sections and façade (plate 13 in vol. 4); photograph reproduced with permission of the Beinecke Rare Book and Manuscript Library, Yale University

5.12 *The Architecture of Palladio; in Four Books. Containing a Short Treatise of the Five Orders, and the most necessary Observations concerning all Sorts of Building … Revis'd, Design'd, and Publish'd by Giacomo Leoni* (London, 1715), 'Temple of Peace', Rome [now thought rather to be the Basilica of Constantine or Maxentius], illustration of its Composite order (plate 14 in vol. 4); photograph reproduced with permission of the Beinecke Rare Book and Manuscript Library, Yale University

5.13 Colen Campbell, *Vitruvius Britannicus or the British Architect …* (London, 1715), façade of the Banqueting House, Whitehall; photograph reproduced with permission of the Yale Center for British Art (New Haven), Paul Mellon Collection

5.14 William Marlow, *Whitehall* (c. 1775), oil on canvas, 71.1 × 91.1 cm, Yale Center for British Art, Paul Mellon Collection; reproduced with permission of the Yale Center for British Art (New Haven), Paul Mellon Collection

Acknowledgements

This book was originally conceived as a joint project with Christy Anderson at Yale. Unfortunately she was unable to continue working on it after its initial stages, but I am very grateful to her for her contributions, and for opening some doors at Yale. The earlier stages of the research were carried out at the Yale Center for British Art and the Beinecke Library. I am very grateful to the BAC for giving me a Visiting Fellowship, and to the staff of both institutions for their support. In particular, I would like to thank Susan Brady, the Head of the Reference Library at the BAC for her keen interest in the progress of this book. Both institutions were very generous in providing images. Andrew Drabkin gave much time and effort at a crucial phase of the preparations at Yale. The staff of the Warburg Institute, British Library, Royal Institute of British Architects, Royal Library in The Hague and the Print Room of the University at Leiden were very helpful in providing illustrations and finding rare material, both published and in manuscript.

Without Eileen Harris and Nicholas Savage's *British Architectural Books and Writers 1556–1785* and Howard Colvin's *Biographical Dictionary of British Architects 1600–1840* this book could not have been written. David Watkin offered very thorough criticism of an earlier version. Lucy Gent made me question all my assumptions about architectural theory and classicism in England, and was uncommonly generous in her searching criticism of earlier stages of the book. I profited very much from conversations with Anthony Geraghty, Vaughan Hart, Lex Hermans, Derek Matravers, Sophie Ploeg, Nicholas Savage, Edward Winters, Richard Tucker, Auke van der Woud and Chris Wood. My colleagues and students at the Vrije Universiteit in Amsterdam offered a very stimulating environment in which to test out the ideas and arguments behind this project.

The Dutch Foundation for Scientific Research (NWO) generously supported this project. At Ashgate, Alan Bartram, Helen Hodge, Maureen Street and Kirsten Weissenberg took great care over design and copy-editing. Maureen Street in particular has greatly improved the consistency, clarity and user-friendliness of the book. Pamela Edwardes, Ashgate's commissioning editor in art history, took great interest in the project from its earliest stages and watched over its completion in every possible way, providing astute comment and very generous support at every stage.

Every effort has been made to trace all the copyright holders, but if any have been inadvertently overlooked the publishers will be pleased to make the necessary arrangement at the first opportunity.

Introduction

British architectural theory before 1750 consists of a large body of writing on architecture in a variety of genres, such as the letter, the essay, the poem, the sermon or the manual offering practical instructions, but it rarely adopted the format of the classical treatise. Authors addressed a wide scale of topics ranging from the practicalities of church building to the representation of national identity, from the handling of materials to the staging of architectural experience, and from surveying to the appreciation and conservation of the mediaeval heritage. With a few exceptions such as *Vitruvius Britannicus* or the writings of Roger North and Sir Christopher Wren these works have not been reprinted recently. The aim of this anthology is to give some idea of the variety, scope and originality of British thought about architecture, which is distinguished by a mixture of the practical and the contemplative; a very independent spirit of enquiry about the principles of classical design; and a concern about the meaning of architecture and its effect on the beholder.

On the Continent architectural theory had modelled itself, with only a few exceptions, on the only book-length treatment of classical architecture that had survived from Antiquity, Vitruvius' *Ten Books on Architecture*, written in the first century BC. Architectural theory was presented as a book-length, discursive statement of the first principles of classical architecture, aspiring to the status of a liberal art, and treating the topics included in Vitruvius' book: the classical orders of architecture, proportion, sacred and secular architecture, fortification, hydraulics and war machines. The first Renaissance treatise, Leon Battista Alberti's *On the Art of Building* (substantially completed in the 1450s and first published in 1486), opens with a eulogy of architecture as the most useful and ennobling among human arts and sciences, and a statement of the author's intent to give the first, general principles of the art. This is followed by chapters on planning and design, sacred and secular building types, public and private building, the orders, aesthetics and the restoration of buildings. Although the scope and approach of Renaissance treatises may vary, they all offer conceptualizations of practice, and they all set out to give an authoritative, preferably complete, statement of the universally applicable principles governing correct building in the classical way. These principles were formulated with the help of the liberal arts, in particular geometry, and to a lesser degree rhetoric.[1]

Renaissance treatises were based on a view of the architect as the intellectual author of the design and the sole authority on how it was to be executed by craftsmen whose role was merely to act as his hands. These treatises were part of a humanist culture and evolved as part of a larger scientific or scholarly genre, which included treatises on rhetoric, poetics, music, mathematics and astrology. But before the 1750s, which saw the publication of Isaac Ware's *Complete Body of Architecture* (1756) and Sir William Chambers's *Treatise of Civil Architecture* (1759), very few extensive pieces of writing on architecture were published by British authors that aspired to the general, authoritative pretensions of Italian treatises, and those that were published did not fit into the Italian formal mould. Evelyn's *Parallel*, for example, resembles a Bible concordance, and Colen Campbell's *Vitruvius Britannicus* is a visual statement of architectural and nationalist norms.

The great variety of topics and treatments in British writing on architecture raised a number of questions about the procedure to be adopted in editing this anthology. One possible reaction is to include only those texts that in some way belong to the Vitruvian tradition: translations of Serlio and Palladio and other disseminations such as Inigo Jones's annotations to Palladio that show the process of learning to design in the classical manner, and British contributions to that tradition, such as Campbell's *Vitruvius Britannicus*. This would mean, however, that a large quantity of unique, sometimes highly idiosyncratic but always interesting and challenging thought about architecture would remain unread except by the most specialized architectural or literary historian.

I have therefore decided to adopt another approach, in which the decision to include a text is based on a much wider definition of theory as both the knowledge or principles that guide a practice, and the reflections on or contemplation of a given subject or topic. Etymologically 'theory' is derived from the Latin *theoria*, which in its turn is derived from the Greek *theaomai*, to look at something with amazement or admiration, or to contemplate with the mind's eye. In England 'theory' became current at the end of the sixteenth century (it is for instance included in Florio's *Worlde of Words* of 1598), but initially the sense of sight, spectacle or contemplation prevailed. In a sermon delivered in 1638 Lancelot Andrewes spoke of the Passion as a sight to be contemplated: 'Saint Luke calleth the Passion *theorian* a Theory or Sight ... of our Blessed Saviour's Whole life or death, there is no part but a Theorie of itself, well worth our looking on.' But 'theory' could also be used to refer to that part of an art or technical subject which consists in the knowledge or statement of the facts on which it depends, or of its principles or methods, as distinguished from its practice. In his *Table Alphabeticall of English Wordes* of 1613 Robert Cawdrey defined 'theorie' as the 'contemplation, or inward knowledge of any art', thereby neatly uniting both aspects of theory.[2]

Accordingly both varieties are represented here: writings that are concerned with rules and principles governing the practice of building, and more contemplative texts concerned with the nature and meaning of architecture. To the first category belong the textbooks on surveying, such as Leonard Digges's *Tectonicon*, which are among the first published writings on architecture in English; the very practical advice by Andrew Boorde and Sir H. Shere on how to build a house; the translations of the chapters from Palladio, Vignola or Scamozzi on the orders; and Joseph Moxon's *Mechanick Exercises*, which was one of the very first publications of the knowledge of craftsmen that could be afforded by tradesmen. The contemplative variety of architectural theory is represented by fragments from Sir Henry Wotton's *Elements of Architecture*. That book was addressed to aristocratic patrons of architecture, not craftsmen. Its aim was to present architecture in such a way that it became acceptable as a gentleman's pursuit, and Wotton achieved this by drawing on a wide range of learning in his definition of architecture and by concentrating on aesthetic aspects instead of the practicalities of design and its execution. Although writings on religious architecture are sometimes concerned with very practical matters such as the location of pews or the admission of women or non-conformists, they also offer some conspicuous examples of meditations on architecture's religious meaning, such as Henry Hawkins's devotional emblems or Walter Montague's presentation of the sumptuous architecture of the Court of Charles I as a figure of Heaven.

Two strands may be distinguished in British writing on architecture, which sometimes interact. One is a native tradition consisting of both practical instruction in the crafts involved in building and contemplative writing on the nature and meaning of architecture and its impact on the beholder. The other strand is that of the assimilation of Vitruvian theory. The earliest stages of this process can be observed in Inigo Jones's annotations to Palladio, John Shute's incomplete treatise on the orders, and the translations of the more practical parts of the treatises by Palladio, Serlio and Scamozzi. Roger North and Sir Christopher Wren integrated parts of Vitruvian theory in their own writings. But with the exception of Evelyn's translation of Fréart de Chambray's *Parallèle* and John James's English edition of Claude Perrault's *Ordonnance*, complete translations of Vitruvian treatises only began to appear after 1715. It took until the 1750s before the first full-length English Vitruvian treatises were published, those by Ware and Chambers. At first sight this process may look like a linear progression from the records of Jones's struggle to understand classical design via (partial) translations to independent contributions. But the actual situation is more complex. Some of the earliest texts, Wotton's *Elements of Architecture* of 1624 and the anonymous *De Templis* of 1638 (published under the initials 'R. T.'), offer quite sophisticated and original statements of Renaissance architectural theory. Their authors possessed a profound knowledge of classical, mediaeval and Renaissance thought on the arts: Alberti's *On the Art of Building* was clearly a model, but so were Aristotle, Quintilian, Saint Gregory, Cusanus and Sir Thomas More. Compared with their intellectual richness, the early translations of Vitruvian treatises are much more restricted in scope and intellectual ambition. This suggests that we should distinguish between the English reception of Vitruvianism from the second half of the seventeenth century onwards and that of European thought on the arts in the early decades of the same century.

The picture of the assimilation of the Vitruvian tradition in Great Britain is further complicated because the English added some original elements from the outset: George Hakewill for instance argued in 1630 for the superiority of the Moderns over the Ancients in his *Apologie or Declaration of the Power and Providence of God in the Gouernment of the World*, declaring that he thought None-Such Palace in no sense inferior to the Pantheon. Sir Christopher Wren observed in the final decades of the seventeenth century that the absence of a corona in the cornice of the Temple of Peace in Rome (now identified as the Basilica of Maxentius or Constantine) significantly affected the impression that façade made on the viewer. Thereby he addressed not only one of the essential aspects of the aesthetics of the classical style, but also one of its most elusive, and a topic that had rarely been discussed in Vitruvian treatises; he also investigated the ways in which buildings can convey a particular impression with architectural – as opposed to verbal, pictorial or sculptural – means:

> But shall I accuse Antiquity for want of Skill in Opticks, of which every where it shews such admirable Proofs? since particularly here the Architect hath given great Testimony of it in the Contrivance of his Cornice, wherein he hath left out the *Corona*, or Hanging-square, by an unusual Example. The *Corona* seems an essential Part in all Cornices, as that which gives Denomination to the whole, and is necessary to the Beauty of a Cornice; because, by its Projecture, it shadows all the lower Members, receiving upon its plane Surface a terse Light from above; this gives the Eminence and distinct Appearance which we see in the Parts of a Cornice at distance; but the Artist here ingenuously apprehending that his Lights in this Fabrick stood level with his Cornice, and therefore it would want the Effect for which it is used, and that the Hanging-face of it would be fore shortened to nothing, to the Eye which beholds it from beneath, wisely left out this Member … .
>
> It was not therefore Unskilfulness in the Architect that made him chuse this flat Kind of Aspect for his Temple, it was his Wit and Judgment. Each Deity had a peculiar Gesture, Face, and Dress hierogryphically proper to it; as their Stories were but Morals involved: and not only their Altars and Sacrifices were mystical, but the very Forms of their Temples. No language, no Poetry can so describe Peace, and the Effects of it in Men's Minds, as the Design of this Temple naturally paints it, without any Affectation of the Allegory. It is easy of Access, and open, carries an humble Front, but embraces wide, is luminous and pleasant, and content with an internal Greatness, despises an invidious Appearance of all that Heighth it might otherwise justly boast of; but rather fortifying itself on every Side, rests secure on a square and ample Basis.

If a wide definition of theory as both the principles guiding a practice and the reflection on its meaning or nature is adopted – which comes much closer to views of the nature of theory held in the seventeenth and early eighteenth centuries than the restricted definition of theory as a Vitruvian treatise – a large amount of writing on architecture before the publication of Isaac Ware's and Sir William Chambers's treatises in the 1750s qualifies as architectural theory. The problem is not that there is not enough material, but that there is far too much to include in a reasonably sized and affordable book. To keep the book's size within limits, while at the same time attempting to offer a representative selection that would at least attempt to do justice to the great variety and richness in themes, genres and treatment, I have decided to give precedence to texts that cannot be found easily: thus Sir H. Shere's advice on how to build a country house is included because it only exists in manuscript, instead of Roger North's equally valuable thoughts on house building, because these have been published by Howard Colvin and John Newman in 1981. For similar reasons I have not included well-known statements of Neo-Palladian doctrine such as Pope's 'Epistle to Burlington'; neither are chapters included on the city, landscape or the garden. Readers interested in these topics are referred to Elizabeth McKellar's *The Birth of Modern London: The Development and Design of the City 1660–1720*, Sir John Summerson's *Georgian London* and *The Genius of the Place: the English Landscape Garden 1620–1820*, edited by John Dixon Hunt and Peter Willis.

A very persuasive case could be made, particularly if one adopts a wide definition of what counts as architectural theory, that those writings should be included in which architecture is used as a metaphor or allegory: to characterize the state, the education of man, the activities of the human mind, various aspects of Christianity, or the way a text, discipline or body of learning is organized. Such texts, even though they do not address architecture itself in a literal sense, do matter because they are about architecture, albeit only metaphorically, because they inform the way people look at and think about architecture. For reasons of space such texts have not been included, with a few exceptions in the domain of architecture and religion and the art of memory. These exceptions were made because the texts involved all offer particularly rich clues to the ways in which people looked at architecture and what kinds of conceptual systems they used to make sense of what they saw. John Donne's use of architectural metaphor to describe Christian doctrine, or Walter Montague's typological description of Charles I's Court as a figure of Heaven, do not simply use the metaphor of architecture to put across a particular opinion or doctrine, but also presented their public with instruments to go beyond simply registering what they saw when looking at a building.

The entries have been organized into five chapters: 'The nature of architecture', 'Building', 'Architecture and religion', 'The sense of the past' and 'Following the example of Antiquity'. Within each chapter entries are printed in roughly chronological order of actual writing, except in cases where there is a very close relationship between texts produced at different times, as in the various translations of Palladio and Vignola, and the extracts from two treatises on the art of memory, one of which, though written much later than the other, offers a very good illustration of what is discussed in the other. Each chapter is preceded by an introduction that sets out the main issues involved and offers some general background information; individual entries are preceded by a short biography of the author (except for the best known, such as Sir Christopher Wren), suggestions for further reading and, where needed, additional background information. The suggestions for further reading are presented in chronological order, not in order of (perceived) importance; they are intended not to present the reader with a complete bibliography of all possible related aspects of their entry, but to open up avenues of enquiry and discussion. In reprinting the extracts the original spelling and typography have been respected, with the exception of ligatures and the occasional use of italics to distinguish a preface or dedication from the main body of a text. Entries are listed by short title and date. Full titles can be found in the 'Primary sources' section of the Bibliography.

Caroline van Eck
The Hague
June 2002

1

The Nature of Architecture

Introduction

In the texts included here architecture is variously defined as a craft, as a science, as the result of the cooperation of reason and fancy, as one of the arts based on design, as an activity that is essential to the social and economic well-being of society and the happiness of its practitioners, as a source of great wonder and overpowering visual delight and also as a reminder of the transitory nature of human life. Only a few of the authors included here have not turned to other disciplines to define the nature of architecture. From the late sixteenth century onwards most attempts to characterize architecture were influenced by one of the Continental traditions of thought about the nature and classification of all human activities, including what we now call the visual arts and architecture.

From Antiquity until the end of the eighteenth century, two main classifications of all human activities and pursuits were current. One classification was introduced by Aristotle, and was based on a distinction between doing, making and knowing. Architecture was a productive art, as was music and poetry, but mathematics belonged to the theoretical sciences. The other was the division into the mechanical and liberal arts, codified by Martianus Capella in the fourth century AD in his *De Nuptiis Philologiae et Mercurii*. To the mechanical arts belonged all the activities which we would now call crafts, concerned with the practical aspects of human survival: for instance shoe making, house building or medicine.[1] The seven liberal arts were concerned with scientific knowledge and contemplation, reasoning and language: geometry, music, astronomy and physics (which made up the quadrivium), and grammar, logic and rhetoric (which made up the trivium). In all these classifications, the arts were grouped in the lowest category. However, in the Renaissance it was often argued that painting, sculpture and architecture should really be counted among the liberal arts because they were based on general theoretical principles, and these principles were based on one of the liberal arts. Alberti for instance made a very influential case that the principles of painting were based on geometry, particularly in its use of linear perspective, and he made the case for architecture by showing its connections with mathematics, music and rhetoric.[2] Vasari argued that painting, sculpture and architecture belong to the liberal arts because they are all three based on *disegno*, abstract design in the mind of the artist.[3]

In all of these ways of looking at the arts, the arts and sciences were not separated, as they are in modern thought. Architecture, mathematics, poetry and painting were considered to be much closer than they are now. For instance John Dee's Preface to a translation of Euclid published in 1570 (often referred to as his 'Mathematical Preface') argues that the activity of the architect is intellectual in nature, unlike that of the craftsman, who merely obeys the directions of the architect. Architecture is based on the first principles of mathematics, and requires a great deal of learning in all the disciplines that deal with the natural world and the ways in which man interferes with it. Dee thus presents to the English public what was by then the standard argument of Italian architectural theorists to demonstrate that architecture is not a craft but a science.[4] This marks a watershed between traditional English views on building as the expedient, skilled practice that was often transmitted orally and by example and the Italian Renaissance view of architecture as primarily an intellectual activity, based on a theory formulated with the help of the liberal arts, in particular geometry. In the Neo-Platonic view which Dee represents, geometry is much more than measuring and 'creeping on the ground [that is, surveying] but lifting the heart above the heavens, by invisible lines, and immortall beames [it] meteth with the reflexions, of the light incomprehensible'.

By separating design from practice, and by defining architectural design as a mathematical activity, architecture could be presented as one of the liberal arts instead of a mechanical art or craft, the status it had generally been accorded in the Middle Ages. One of the most powerful varieties of this tradition was the view that the architect should use the proportions of the human body in his designs, because these reflect the hidden mathematical order of the universe. Accordingly, the human body can be considered as a microcosm which reflects the divine order of the macrocosm.[5] In Paolo Giovanni Lomazzo's *Tracte* painterly proportions, derived from the human body, are applied to architecture on the basis of this analogy.

What are now called the humanities, and in particular rhetoric and poetics, also offered important paradigms for thought about the nature of architecture. The doctrine of the Sister Arts goes back to a statement by the Greek poet Simonides (*c.* 556–476 BC) that painting is mute poetry and poetry is speaking painting, and to the famous Horatian tag 'ut pictura poesis', which was taken to mean that poetry is like painting.[6] This became one of the central tenets of teaching at the Academies of Art which had been founded in Europe from the end of the sixteenth century onwards, because it provided the basis for the use of the principles and concepts of poetics and rhetoric to formulate theories of the visual arts. The painter for instance had to be like a poet or orator in that he had to move, teach and delight the public in order to persuade it of the message his painting was to get across. The passage by Roger North 'Of Unity and Variety' applies to architecture another important Academic principle based on the doctrine of the Sister Arts, namely the tenet that paintings should have the same three unities of time, place and action (or plot) as tragedies should have.

Rhetoric was the source for one of the most widespread ways of looking at architecture, namely in the art of memory, which offered a way of training the memory by teaching the student to select a building, scrutinize its layout carefully and place all the parts of the speech he wanted to memorize on a conspicuous part of the building. The two extracts from Guglielmo Grataroli and John Willis reprinted below are only a few of a vast and widely read series of handbooks on the art of memory. But rhetoric also offered the view that the chief aim of works of art, like speeches, is that they delight, instruct and move the spectator, and thereby persuade. It was a storehouse of stylistic strategies by which that aim could be achieved, ranging from the use of figures of speech to that of gesture and dress. These could be transferred from speech to the visual arts; perhaps the clearest case is the transposition of the figure of speech of *antithesis* or opposition to the visual arts in the guise of *contrapposto*.[7] But rhetoric also offered a general theory of both verbal and visual persuasive communication. Because of the central place of rhetoric in the curriculum every educated person in Europe was familiar with it, and because of its inclusive nature it could be used in the visual arts and architecture.[8] A few examples of its use in thinking about the design process are included below: Inigo Jones for instance listed the emotional effects of ornament as delight, amazement, laughter, contemplation or even horror. He reminded himself in his 'Roman Sketchbook' that architectural design, like the writing of a speech, should be ruled by decorum. The influence of rhetoric is less explicit, but nonetheless present, in the stress on vividness and the suggestion of life in the passages by Robert Stickells and Francesco Colonna here, because imparting the illusion of life was considered in classical and Renaissance rhetoric as one of the most important stylistic strategies the artist or orator possessed for moving an audience. The public becomes fascinated and cannot turn away. Similarly, a building can overwhelm the spectator by its vivid and lifelike form.

Thomas Hobbes presented an analysis of the arts and sciences in terms of fancy (or imagination) and judgement, the mental faculties that are involved in the creation of works of art. Time and education result in experience; memory is the storehouse of experience, and fancy and judgement are the daughters of memory. In this philosophy of artistic creation memory is not only the storehouse of knowledge, but an image of the world, providing the materials for the creations of fancy. By showing how the visual fluency of fancy is guided by the discretion of judgement in artistic creation Hobbes not only formulated a view of artistic creation in which the rational and imaginative aspects of design are balanced, he also presented the rudiments of a system of architectural criticism. His statement that 'All that is defensible in building, or marvellous in Engines and Instruments ... is the workmanship of Fancy, but guided by the Precepts of true Philosophy' was echoed in the next century by Nicholas Hawksmoor's advocacy of strong reason and good fancy. But in stressing the effects of the right combination of fancy and judgement Hobbes also made room for considerations of another aspect of architecture: the visual and emotional impact of a building on the spectator.

Hobbes's analysis of both the creative process and the rhetorical or poetical view of the nature of the visual arts and architecture focused on the relation between a building and its beholders. A different approach was taken by architects and critics who were influenced by Continental academic discourse. Both Inigo Jones and James Ralph presented architecture as an art of design, and as such close to painting.[9] Jones for example stressed the similarities between the procedure of the painter when composing a scene by starting from the limbs of the figures and that of the architect when decking out the functional parts of a building with ornaments based on the Orders.

A different approach was taken by Nicholas Barbon and Roger North, who considered the economic and social relevance of architecture. They both wrote apologies for architecture, defending it against detractors by pointing out how greatly it contributed to the well-being of its practitioners and users and the prosperity of the nation. Other apologists argued that good building, because of its concern for order and decorum, contributed to the virtue of the state and reflected the moral stature of the owner or architect. Drawing on the ancient tradition of speaking of the human mind in terms of architecture, Hobbes described fancy as the architect of moral philosophy when ethical precepts have failed, thereby taking away much of the flightiness often associated with that mental faculty and instead suggesting systematic and productive thought that leaves lasting results.

All these wide-ranging attempts at grasping the essence of architecture, drawing from so many disciplines, show that in the period 1540–1750 architecture was certainly not considered as simply the art or craft of building. By defining architecture in certain ways, all the extracts included here present hidden or explicit aesthetic and ethical canons. Jones's musings on ornament, for instance, present the reader with a very strict system of architectural decorum, underpinned with a very pervasive codification of proper male behaviour, which by its exclusive focus on masculinity excludes women from being the designers or patrons of decorous classical architecture. Architecture possessed a wide range of social, cultural and religious meanings. In its turn it served as a powerful source of metaphor and allegory in other disciplines such as literature and politics. For reasons of space no examples of this have been reprinted below, but some are included among the suggestions for further reading.

Further reading:
Primary sources: Sir Thomas More, *Utopia* (1516); Edmund Spenser, *The Faerie Queene*, Book II, Canto IX, stanzas 21–23 ('Arithmological Stanza', 1590); Sir Philip Sidney, *An Apologie for Poetry* (1595); Michael Drayton, *To the Reader of the Barron's Warres* (1603); Sir Francis Bacon, 'Of Building', in *The Essays or Counsels Civil and Moral, newly enlarged* (1625), and his *New Atlantis* (1626); Thomas Lord Strafford, Viscount Wentworth, 'Speech when He First Sate Lord President of the North' (1628) and 'Strafford's Last Speech in his Defence' (1641) (ed. Kenyon, 1986); Andrew Marvell, 'Upon Appleton House' (*c.* 1650–52); Isaac Browne, *On Design and Beauty* (1734).

Secondary literature: Fowler (1964); Summers (1981), pp. 76 ff; Vickers (1988); Howard (1990); Farago (1991); Fumaroli (1994); Johnson (1994); Gent (1995a); Howarth (1995); Evans (1995); van Eck (1998a); Hazard (2000); van Eck (2002); Eriksen (2001).

John Dee, from his Preface to Euclid's *Elements of Geometrie* (1570)

John Dee (1527–1608), mathematician and astrologer, was educated at St John's College, Cambridge, and travelled in Europe in 1548–51. His Preface to Euclid's *Elements*, which was widely read, introduced the Vitruvian view of the architect as a mathematician, who because of his knowledge of mathematics and all its applications in mechanics, hydraulics, astrology and music is able to supply designs and direct their execution by means of the exertions of craftsmen (or artificers). The architect's designs are not actual drawings, but geometrical diagrams (or lineaments, outlines, as Alberti called them) conceived in the mind of the architect and subsequently put on paper to serve as instructions for the builders. Dee's view of the architect as the director and judge of building did not at all correspond with contemporary practice; it would take almost 150 years before it became generally accepted as a result of the revolution in taste imposed by Lord Burlington and his followers.[10]

Further reading: Dee, *Private Diary*; Yates (1966), which includes a reprint of Dee's text; Bennett (1993); Sherman (1995); Harkness (1999).

Architecture, to many may seme not worthy, or not mete, to be reckoned among the *Artes Mathematicall*.[11] To whom, I think good, to give some account of my so doyng. Not worthy, (will they say,) bycause it is but for building, of a house, Pallace, Church, Forte, or such like, grosse workes. And you, also, defined the Artes Mathmaticall, to be such, as dealed with no Materiall or corruptible thing: and also could demonstratively procede in their faculty, by Number or Magnitude. First, you see, that I count, here, *Architecture*, among those *Artes Mathematicall*, which are Derived from the Principals:[12] and you know, that such, may deale with Naturall thinges, and sensible matter. Of which, some draw nerer, to the Simple and absolute Mathematicall Speculation, then other do. And though, the *Architect* procureth, enformeth, and directeth, the *Mechanicien*, to handworke, and the building actuall, of house, Castell, or Pallace, and is chief Iudge of the same: yet, with him selfe (as chief *Master* and *Architect*,) remaineth the Demonstrative reason and cause, of the Mechaniciens worke: in Lyne, plaine, and Solid: by *Geometricall, Arithmeticall, Opticall, Musicall, Astronomicall, Cosmographicall* (& to be brief) by all the former Derived *Artes Mathematicall*, and other Natural Artes, hable to be confirmed and stablished. If this be so: then, you may thinke, that *Architecture*, hath good and due allowance, in this honest Company of *Artes Mathematicall* Derivative. I will, herein, crave Iudgement of two most perfect *Architectes*: the one, being *Vitruvius*, the Romaine: who did write ten bookes thereof, to the Emperour *Augustus* (in whose daies our Heavenly Archemaster, was borne): and the other, *Leo Baptista Albertus* a Florentine: who also published ten bookes thereof.[13] *Architectura* (sayeth Vitruvius) est Scientia pluribus disciplinis et variis eruditionibus ornata: cuius Iudicio probantur omnia, quae ab caeteris Artificibus perficiuntur opera.[14] That is, *Architecture*, is a Science garnished with many doctrines and diverse instructions: by whose Iudgement, all workes, by other workmen finished, are Iudged. It followeth. Ea nascitur ex Fabrica, et Ratiocinatione. &c. Ratiocinatio autem est, quae, res fabricatas, Solertia ac ratione proportionis, demonstrare atque explicare potest. *Architecture*, groweth of Framing, and Reasoning. &c. Reasoning, is that, which of thinges framed, with forecast, and proportion: can make demonstration, and manifest declaration. Againe. Cum, in omnibus enim rebus, tum maxime etiam in Architectura, haec duo insunt: quod significatur, et quod significat. Significatur proposita res, de qua dicitur: hanc autem Significat Demonstratio, rationibus doctrinarum explicata. Forasmuch as, in all thinges: therefore chiefly in *Architecture*, these two thinges are: the thing signified: and that which signifieth. The thing propounded, whereof we speake, is the thing Signified. But Demonstration, expressed with the reasons of diverse doctrines, doth signifie the same thing. After that. Ut literatus sit, peritus Graphidos, eruditus Geometriae, et Optices non ignarus: instructus Arithmetica: historias complures noverit, Philosophos diligenter audiverit: Musicam sciverit: Medicinae non sit ignarus, responsa Iurisperitorum noverit: Astrologiam, Caelique rationes cognitas habeat. An Architect (sayeth he) ought to understand Languages, to be skilfull of Painting, well instructed in Geometrie, not ignorant of Perspective, furnished with Arithmetike, have knowledge of many histories, and diligently have heard Philosophers, have skill of Musike, not ignorant of Physike, know the aunsweres of Lawyers, and have Astronomie and the courses Caelestiall, in good knowledge. He geueth reason, orderly, wherefore all these Artes, Doctrines, and Instructions, are requisite in an excellent Architect. And (for brevitie) omitting the Latin text, thus he hath, Secondly, it is behofe for an Architect to have the knowledge of Painting: that he may the more easilie fashion out, in patternes painted, the forme of what worke he liketh. And Geometrie, geueth to Architecture many helpes: and first teacheth the Use of the Rule, and the Cumpasse: whereby (chiefly and easilie) the descriptions of Buildinges, are despatched in Groundplats: and the directions of Squires, Levells, and Lines. Likewise, by Perspective, the Lightes of the heaven, are well led, in the buildinges: from certaine quarters of the world. By Arithmetike, the charges of Buildinges are summed together: the measures are expressed, and the hard questions of Symmetries, are by Geometricall Meanes and Methods discoursed on. &c. Besides this, of the Nature of thinges (which in Greke is called *physiologia*) Philosophie doth make declaration. Which, it is necessary, for an Architect, with diligence to have learned: because it hath many and divers naturall questions: as specially, in Aqueducts. For in their courses, leadinges about, in the levell ground, and in the mountinges, the naturall Spirites or breathes are ingendred divers wayes: The hindrances, which they cause, no man can helpe, but he, which out of Philosophie, hath learned the originall causes of thinges. Likewise, who soever shall read Ctesibus, or Archimedes bookes, (and of others, who have written such Rules) can not thinke, as they do:[15] unlesse he shall have receaved of Philosophers, instructions in these thinges. And Musike he must nedes know: that he may have understanding, both of Regular and Mathematicall Musike: that he may temper well his Balistes, Catapultes, and Scorpions, &c. Moreover, the Brasen Vessels, which in Theatres, are placed by Mathematicall order, in ambries,[16] under the steppes: and the diversities of the soundes (which the Grecians call *echeia*) are ordered according to Musicall Symphonies and Harmonies: being distributed in the Circuites, by Diatessaron, Diapente, and Diapason. That the convenient voyce, of the players sound, when it came to these preparations, made in order, there being increased: with the increasing, might come more cleare & pleasant, to the eares of the lookers on. &c. And of Astronomie, is known the East, West, South, and North. The fashion of the heaven, the Æquinox, the Solstice, and the course of the starres. Which thinges, unleast one know: he can not perceive, any thyng at all, the reason of Horologies. Seying therefore this ample Science, is garnished, beautified and stored, with so many sundry skils and knowledges: I thinke, that none can iustly account themselves Architectes, of the suddeyne. But they onely, who from their childes yeares, ascendying by these degrees of knowledges, beying fostered up with the atteynyng of many Languanges and Artes, have wonne to the high Tabernacle of Architecture. &c. And to whom Nature hath given such quicke Circumspection, sharpnes of witt, and Memorie, that they may be very absolutely skillfull in Geometrie, Astronomie, Musike, and the rest of the Artes Mathematicall: Such, surmount and passe the callyng, and state, of Architectes: and are become Mathematiciens. &c. And they are found, seldome. As, in tymes past, was Aristarchus Samius: Philolaus, and Archytas, Tarentynes: Apollonius Pergeus: Eratosthenes Cyreneus: Archimedes, and Scopas, Syracusians.[17] Who also, left to their posteritie, many Engines and Gnomonicall workes: by numbers and naturall meanes, invented and declared. Thus much, and the same wordes (in sense) in one onely Chapter of this Incomparable Architect Vitruvius, shall you finde. And if you should, but take his boke in your hand, and slightly loke thorough it, you would say straight way: This is *Geometrie, Arithmetike, Astronomie, Musike, Anthropographie, Hydragogie; Horometry.* &c, and (to conclude) the Storehouse of all workmanship. Now, let us listen to our other Iudge, our Florentine, Leo Baptista: and narrowly consider, how he doth determine of Architecture. *Sed anteaque ultra progrediar.* &c.[18] But before I procede any further (sayth he) I thinke, that I ought to expresse, what man I would have to bee allowed an Architect. For, I will not brying in place a Carpenter: as though you might Compare him to the Chief Masters of other Artes. For the hand of the Carpenter, is the Architects Instrument. But I will appoint the Architect to be that man, who hath the skill, (by a certaine and mervailous meanes and way) both in minde and Imagination to determine: and also in worke to finish: what workes so ever, by motion of waight, and cuppling and framing together of bodyes, may most aptly be Commodious for the worthiest Uses of Man. And that he may be able to perfome these things, he hath nede of atteynyng and knowledge of the best, and almost worthye things, &c. The whole Feate of Architecture in buldyng, consisteth in Lineaments, and in Framing. And the whole power and Skill of Lineamentes, tendeth to this: that the right and absolute way may be had, of Coaptyng and ioyning Lines and angles: by which, the face of the buildyng or frame, may be comprehended and concluded. And it is the property of Lineamentes, to prescribe unto buildynges, and every part of them, an apt place, & certaine number: a worthy maner, and a semely order: that, so the whole force and figure of the buildyng, may rest in the very Lineamentes &c. And we may prescribe in mynd and imagination the whole formes[19] all material stuffe beyng secluded.[20] Which point we shall atteyne, by Noting and forepointyng the angles, and lines, by a sure and certaine direction and connection. Seying them, these thinges, are thus: Lineamente, shalbe the certaine and constant prescribyng, conceived in mynde: made in lines und angles: and finished with a learned minde and wyt. We thanke you Master Baptist, that you have so aptly brought your Arte, and phrase thereof, to have some Mathematicall perfection: by certaine order, number, forme, figure, and *Symmetrie* mentall: all naturall and sensible stuffe set apart. Now, then, it is evident (Gentle reader) how aptly and worthely, I have preferred Architecture, to be bred and fostered up in the Dominion of the pereles *Princesse, Mathematica*: and to be a naturall Subiect of hers. And the name of Architecture, is of the principalitie, which this Science hath, above all other Artes. And Plato affirmeth, the Architect to be Master over all, that make any worke.[21] Whereupon, he is neither Smith, nor Builder: nor, separately, any Artificer: but the Hed, the Provost, the Director, and Iudge of all Artificiall workes, and all Artificers. For, the true Architect, is hable to teach, Demonstrate, distribute, describe, and Iudge all workes wrought. And he, onely, searcheth out the causes and reasons of all Artificiall thynges. Thus excellent, is Architecture: though few (in our dayes) atteyne thereto: yet may not the Arte, be otherwise thought on, then in very dede it is worthy. Nor we may not, of auncient Artes, make new and imperfect Definitions in our dayes: for scarcitie of Artificors: No more, than we may pynche in, the Definitions of *Wisedome*, or *Honestie*, or of *Frendeshyp* or of *Iustice*. No more will I consent, to Diminish any whit, of the perfection and dignitie, (by just cause) allowed to absolute Architecture. Under the Direction of this Arte, are the principall, necessary *Mechanicall* Artes. Namely, *Howsing, Fortification*, and *Naupegie*.[22] *Howsing*, I understand, both for Divine Service, and Mans common usage: publike, and private. Of *Fortification* and *Naupegie*, straunge matter might be told you: But perchance, some will be tyred, with this Bederoll,[23] all ready rehearsed: and other some, will nycely nip my grosse and homely discoursing with you: made in post hast: for feare you should wante this true and frendly warnyng, and tast giuyng, of the *Power Mathematicall*. Lyfe is short and uncertaine: Tymes are perilouse: &c. And still the Printer awayting, for my pen staying: All these thinges, with farder matter of Ingratefulness, give me occasion to pass away, to the other Artes remainyng, with all spede possible.

Francesco Colonna (attr.), from *Hypnerotomachia*, trans. 'R. D.' [Robert Dallington] (1592)

The *Hypnerotomachia Poliphili* was first published in Venice in 1499 by Aldus Manutius. The identity of its author is uncertain, but is generally assumed to be Francesco Colonna. Written in a mixture of Italian, Latin and Greek, it tells the story of the journey made by a young man called Poliphilo to find and marry his beloved Polia. A large part of the text consists of descriptions of gardens, sculptures and buildings, often based on the treatises by Alberti and Filarete. These were the first two Renaissance books on architectural theory. Alberti's was substantially completed in the 1450s and published in 1486; Filarete's was written *c*. 1460–65 and remained in manuscript until the twentieth century. Their use in the *Hypnerotomachia* suggests considerable inside knowledge of architectural theory on the part of its author. It had little direct influence on architects at the time of its publication, but was very popular with emblematists and designers of devices. Its popularity is also attested by the English and French translations that were made in the sixteenth century. Robert Dallington travelled in Italy and was also the author of *A Survey of the Great Dukes State of Tuscany in the year of our Lord 1596*, published in London in 1605.

Further reading: Colonna, *Hypnerotomachia*; Lefaivre (1997); Chaney (1998), pp. 148–59.

[p. 26] Poliphilus entring a little waye in at the described porch, with great delight he there also beheld how it was garnished and adorned, and after as he was coming out he met with a monstrous dragon whereat he was extreemlie afraide, and compelled to runne backe into the building, and at last getting foarth with much adoe hee came into a fertile place.

A Great and commendable thing without dout it shold be, trulie to discribe, & point to point, to set down the incredible work, and unimagined composition, of so vast a frame, and huge bignes, of so great a buildinge with the excellencie of the entrance, in a conspicuous and sightly place, conveniently situated, where of my delight to behold them, did exced the greatnes of my admiration breeding in me such a conceit so as I perswaded my self that Iupiter durst not undertake the like to the rest of the gods, & cortainly beleeving that no workman or human witt could compase so huge a frame, expresse so notable conceits, or imagine and invent so rare devises and so gorgiousle to garnishe them, in so singuler an order and simmetry, to dispose them, and without supplement or correction perfictlye to finishe them. A rare and insolent pride in a building. Upon which occasion I was in some doubt and that not a little if the naturall historiographer had seene or heard of this, he woulde have scorned that of Egipt, and the cunning and industrie of the woorking thereof, for that heerein the sundrie and divers woorkes effected by many severall woorkmen seemed in the perfections, of their dewe proportions as if they had been performed by one himselfe.

Guglielmo Grataroli, from *The Castel of Memorie*, trans. William Fulwod (1572)

Guglielmo Grataroli (1516–68) was a physician. He studied in Padua, and left Italy after accusations of heresy which led to a trial in Venice. He settled in Basel, where he became professor of medicine at the University and befriended Calvin and other prominent reformers. *The Castel of Memorie* is a translation by William Fulwod of his *De memoria reparanda, augenda, conservandaque, ac de reminiscentia*, which had first been published in 1553. William Fulwod (or Fullwood) (fl. 1562) was a poet, whose chief claim to fame is his *The Enemie of Idlenesse* (1568), a manual on letter writing which included excerpts from Cicero and Renaissance authors such as Poliziano, Ficino, Pico della Mirandola and others. His translation of *The Castel of Memorie* was dedicated to Lord Robert Dudley (*DNB*).

Further reading: Yates (1966); Carruthers (1990); Bolzoni (1991).

The Seventh Chapter treateth in a fewe wordes of locall or artificiall Memorie
Artificiall Memorie is a disposing or placing of sensible thinges in the mynde by imagination, whereunto the naturall Memorie having respect, is by them admonished that it maye be hable to call to minde more easily and distinctly suche thinges as are to bee remembered: and (as *Cicero* sayth in hys seconde to *Herennius*) it consisteth of places as it were of waxe or tables, and of Images or of figures and letters. For so it cometh to passe that such thinges as we have heard or learned, we reherse agayne even as though we reade them. [...]

I will put forth the example of tenne [...][24]

And therefore I take or choose a great and emptie house, to the which you muste not go often but seldome, and appointe or sette the fyrste place which is at the doore, three foote distant from the doore. Let the seconde place be twelve or sistenne foote distant from that, or for example let them bee one corner or angle. Let the thyrd place be distant from the seconde even as many as twelve foote, that there may be perchance another corner, or a middest betweene the fyrste and the seconde corner. The fourth shall be a corner. The fyfth, shall be a corner distant by as muche. The sixte lykewyse: and the hall bying finished, you shall enter into one chamber, and immediately with the doore you shall note or appoynte the seventhe, and afterwardes in the firste corner of the chamber be the eyght, and in the seconde corner the nyenthe, and in the thyrd, the tenthe wyth hys distance. And if you will have any more places, goe oute of the chamber, and so marke or note the other chambers proportionally.

John Willis, from *Mnemonica; or, the Art of Memory* (1661)

John Willis (d. 1628?) was a stenographer and mnemonician. He invented the first practical and rational scheme of modern shorthand founded on a strictly alphabetical basis. His Latin *Mnemonica; sive Arte Reminiscendi* ... (London, 1628) was translated into English for a wider readership by Leonard Sowersby. It is distinguished by a particularly clear illustration of the actual room the student was to imagine as a mnemonic aid, and how the topics of his speech should be located in it (see Figure 1.1) (*DNB*).

Preface
[A3V] [...] Now if men deal impartially, they will easily find, that the *Art of Memory* by *Places* and *Idea's* or *Images*, doth very nearly resemble *Writing*. The *Places* in artificial *Memory*, are as it were *Leaves*; the *Idea's*, *Letters*; the distribution of them in *Places* representeth *Writing*; lastly, the repetition of them, *Reading*: which thing *Cicero* in his *Partitiones*, but more copiously in his Second Book, *De Oratore*, doth elegantly declare.

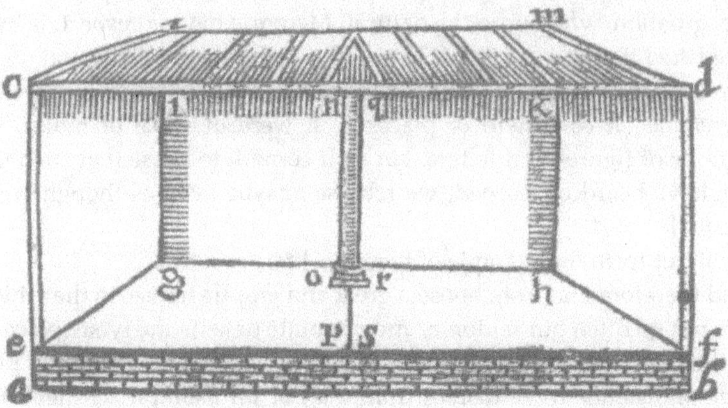

1.1 John Willis, *Mnemonica; or, the Art of Memory. Drained out of the pure Fountains of Art and Nature* (London, 1661), plate 1, illustrating the imaginary theatre where things to be memorized are situated in certain places, indicated by the letters a–s

The third Book

[p. 52] The Art of *Memory*, which we now treat of consisteth of *Idea's*, and places, wherein we will first handle the *Reposition* of *Idea's*, and afterwards their *Disposition*.

Reposition of *Idea's* is, when things to be remembred are charged upon *Memory* by *Idea's*, disposed in certain places of a *Repository* [...].

A *Repository* is an imaginary fabrick, fancied Artistically, built of hewen stones, in form of a *Theater*, the form whereof followeth; suppose the Edifice to be twelve yards in length within the walls, in breadth six yards and in height seven yards [i.e. six], the roof thereof flat, leaded above, and pargeted underneath, lying wholly open to view, without any wall on that side supposed next to us: let then be imagined a *Stage* of smooth gray Marble, even and variegated with a party coloured border, which *Stage* is to be extended over the whole length and breadth of the building, and raised a yard high above the *level* of the ground on which the said Edifice is erected: let all the walls, that is, the opposite wall, and two ends be wainscotted with *Cypresse* boards, so artificially plained and glewed, that the joynts be indiscernable; suppose also a *Groove* or *Gutter* cut in the middle of the *Marble Stage*, then made broad, extended from the opposite wall to the other side of the *Stage*, whereby it is exactly divided into two equal parts, and that upon the further end of the said *Groove*, there is erreared a *Column*, a foot and half thick, arising up to the *Roof* of the building, almost touching the opposite wall, and deviding it into two equal parts, as the *Groove* divideth the *Stage*, so that by the *Groove*, and the *Pillar*, the whole Representation is parted in twain, and consisteth of two *Rooms* siding each other, each of them being six yards long, six yards broad, and six yards high. For the better understanding this invention, I have caused a *Type* of the *Representation* to be here delineated, the explanation whereof immediately followeth.

The letters *a, b, c, d,* shew the length of the Edifice, *a, c, b, d,* the height, *a, e, b, f,* the height of the *Stage g, i, k, h,* are boundaries of the opposite wall, *e, c, i, g,* the side wall upon the left hand, *h, k, d, f,* the side wall of the right hand, *c, l, m, d,* designs the *Roof; g, i, r, p* [*g, i, n, o*], the opposite wall of the first *Room*, *e, g, o, p* [*r, q, k, h*], the opposite wall of the second *Room*, *s, r, h, f,* the *Stage* of the second *Room*, *n, a* [*n, o*], the *Pillar* dividing the opposite wall, *o, p,* the *Groove* wrought into the *Stage*.

A *Representation* according to this fashion, is to be represented before the eyes of our minde, whensoever we are, as oft as we intend to practise this Art; supposing ourselves to stand about two yards distant, against the midst thereof.

Chapter III. Of Idea's in General

[p. 58] An *Idea* is a visible representation of things to be *remembred*, framed by a strong imagination, by help whereof the minde by reflection caleth to *memory*, together with the *Idea*, the thing represented. *Idea's* are to be united with their proper circumstances, according as their natures require, for like as *Writings*, the fairer they are, are more forcibly read, so *Ideas*, the more aptly they are conceived, according to the exigency of their nature, are more speedily recalled to minde, and also consequently the things by them signified. [...]

After this manner *Idea's* of Edifices, Machines, and all Artificial things whatsoever, ought to be signalised; property of form, and splendor of colours, must be attributed to *Pictures*; grace, liveliness to letters; to *Writings*, glory and excellency of *Workmanship*, to *Engravings*; Finally, every *Idea* must have such illustration as may render it most notable and conspicuous, and seem principally coherent to its nature.

Robert Stickells, two texts on design (1597)

Robert Stickells was a naval engineer, joiner and architect. In 1597–98 he became clerk in the Queen's Works, designing a hunting lodge at Richmond and providing drawings for country gentlemen, including a design using the Doric order for Sir Thomas Tresham. In a letter to Tresham, probably accompanying a drawing, Stickells wrote that 'I have mayd the ordnance accordinge to Request, and have mayde them by the Simetry or mean agreinge withe the Doricke Architrave frees and corniche.' Stickells died in 1620. The first passage looks like a series of questions or problems that an architect might be asked so that he could show his expertise; but the first statement in it is rather intriguing because it associates ancient architecture with truth and life. If a building's design is based on Vitruvian proportions it will be true and alive; if – like many buildings of Stickell's age – it is not, it is lifeless. This identification of life, truth and proportion may reflect the Renaissance view that the creation, including man, was endowed with proportion by God, just as God gave life to it; proportion thus becomes a symbol of the divine, life-giving spark which distinguishes all living creatures from dead, unformed matter. The passage about the dimensions of floors and rooms in a house combines practical advice with a statement of the Renaissance doctrine that architectural proportions should reflect those of man, based on divine reason. A classical building is rational because its design is based on *ichnographia*, the on-site use of compass and rule to lay out a plot to scale (see Vitruvius, *Ten Books on Architecture*, I.ii.2); modern building design (that is, traditional English practice as current in the late sixteenth century) is not, because it is based on the use of a circle, and hence, according to Stickells, it will always result in uneven or unproportional numbers.

Further reading: Summerson (1957); Anderson (1995); Hazard (2000).

Foirst, it wold be known [whether] the woorkes, moddarn; or the woorkes Antiques, is of most effecte, & which of them, Contayn most Truthe; They both consest in all thinges Liuinge, & being seprated; the one is sencable, the other insencable; no sencles thinge can be perfect, before by lif it be maid perfet:

Secondle, ther is Apece of ground, to build A manner house, upon; which contayneth in Length. 107 foot & in Breadth, 84. Foot, nowe it wolde be known, howe high I might, I Build upon that ground, that I Build not to high, nor, too loe;

Thurdle, the Roumes or offices for that house upon the ground (before Reherced), being contrived by just p[ro]porction; then, By the Breadth of the Roume to geue the heayth, that the heayth be no mor, nor no les then just p[ro]portion doth Requi^{re}.

Forthle, havinge the Just heayth of the Storis then to shewe, how Beige [big] or howe thick the storie post or wauls, shalbe that theay benot too beige nor too Letell;

Lastle, A shipe is too be Builte, of 300 Tones in Burden, searvesable in all seas; now it wold be knowne howe Beige, her kelle, Reibes, or Tembers, Beames, wayles or Bendes shalbe that no won part of them be to Beige nor to letell;

I shewe thes propoc[i]tions to the ende I wolde have them Exzamond, proved, & tryed, by the Learned & Skilfull; & for thes p[ro]poc[i]tions I'll make perfect demonstraction; fore that I see all Buildinges, grownded upon the emperfect sence, [of] the bookes of Architecture, Victrivces[25] & all thoos Authers have, taken the wronge sense; ther in wardes woorkes are dead when theay shewe no Lif in ther outward Doweinges.

Robert Stickelles

For the byldinge of an howse of state, then to shewe by the quantite of the grownd delyevred, howe hie I may bylde that I byld not to hie, nor to loe, &c.

And that by that quantite of grownd before rehearsed, the offices or Roumes beinge contrived by due preporction, then by the breadthe, the heathe may be geven that the lyght, shalbe no more, nor no less then nede shall Require, &c.

Then havenge the heathe of the storries, to showe how greate or howe thicke the wales or postes shalbe, that the shall be not too begge, nor to lettell &c.

Thes thinges consisteth in man hime self, for that man is the proportionall & resonable Creature, & therfor whatso is done witheowt thes Rules [...] is but unsearthen matter, the seartayn have ther true quantites & measueres, & the unsearten, ar delivered throwe Ignorance, &c.

Thear ar too sortes of byldenges, the on in sence; the other withowt sence; The antikes in sence; the moddarn witheout sence; Because it is from cirkler [circular] demonstraction, withowt sence: for that no cirkell Riseth in evenness of nomber, the antikes allwayes in evenness of nombre be cauese hthe [they] ar derived from an Ichnographicall ground; it the unevn may be broght into proporctions as well as the even, &c.

There is no mor but Right & wronge in all things whatsoever, The squear Right the cirkell wronge, &c.

Rob Stickells

Paolo Giovanni Lomazzo, from *A Tracte containing the Artes of Curious Paintinge Carvinge & Buildinge*, trans. 'R. H.' [Robert Haydocke] (1598)

Giovanni Paolo Lomazzo (1538–1600) was a Milanese writer, painter and draughtsman. His *Trattato dell'arte della pittura* was published in 1584, and *Idea del tempio della pittura* in 1590. In both he tried to create a great unified theory for the principles and practice of art within a strongly Neo-Platonic cosmological framework, in which beauty and goodness are equated, both have their origin in God, and beauty consists 'wholly in due proportion'. The *Trattato* is divided into seven books, the first of which deals with natural and artificial proportions as the harmonious basis of art. It was the first theoretical treatise on the arts to be translated into English. At the time of its English publication, the chapters in Book I on the proportions of the five orders, intercolumniation and temples, illustrated by three engraved plates added by 'R. H.', Robert Haydocke, to the unillustrated original, were, together with John Shute's *First and Chief Groundes* of 1563, the only Renaissance architectural theory then available in English. Haydocke's translation did not attempt to provide a literal translation of the original. Haydocke wanted to 'divulge to all' Lomazzo's treatise. To achieve this aim he added images, subdivided the dense and long chapters, added marginal notes and also added contrary advice on fluting taken from Hans Blum's *Quinque columnarum* (1601), a translation of which appeared in 1608. Haydocke also removed all controversial religious statements of Counter-Reformation doctrine. The translation was one of the first books to be presented to the Bodleian Library in Oxford (Harris, 1990).

Further reading: Gent (1979); Höltgen (1984); Cassimatis (1985); Peacock (1990), pp. 162–3; Severi (1991); Turner (1996), entry on Lomazzo.

Of the Vertve and Praise of Proportion. Chapter III.

[p. 25] Svch is the importance and vertue of *Proportion*, that nothing can any way satisfie the eie, without the helpe thereof. So that whosoever worketh any pleasure or delight in vs, doth therefore content vs, because the grace of Proportion, consisting in the measure of the partes, appeareth therein. Wherefore all the inventions of men carry with them so much the more grace and beauty, by how much more ingenuously they are proportioned. Whence *Vitruvius* saith, *that whosoeverwill proceede in his workes with iudgement, must needes be acquainted with the nature and force of proportion:*[26] *which beeing well and kindly vnderstoode, will make him not only an excellent iudge of ancient and late workemen, but also an inventor and performer of rare and ancient matters, himselfe.*

Now the effectes proceeding from the proportion are vnspeakeable: the principall whereof, is that *maiestie and beautie*, which is founde in bodies, called by *Vitruvius, Eurithmia.*[27] And hence it is, that vvhen wee beholde a well-proportioned thing, wee call it *beautifull*; as if wee shoulde saie, indued with that exact and comely grace, whereby all the perfection of sweete delightes belonging to the sight, are communicated to the eye, and so conueyed to the vnderstanding.

But if we shall enter into a farther consideration of this beauty, it will appeare most euidently, in things appertaining to Ciuile discipline.[28] For it is strange to consider, what effects of *piety, reuerence*, and *religion*, are stirred vp in mens mindes, by meanes of this sutable comelinesse of apte proportion: A pregnant example whereof we haue in the *Iupiter*, carued by *Phidias* at Elis, which wrought an extraordinary sense of *religion* in the people.[29] Whereupon, the ancient and renowned *Zeuxis*, well knowing the excellencie and dignity thereof, perswaded *Greece*, in her most flourishing estate, *that the pictures wherein this maiesty appeared, were dedicated to great Princes, and consecrated to the Temples of the immortall Gods*; so that they held them in exceeding great estimation; partly because they were the workes of those famous Masters, who were reputed as Gods amongst men; and partly because they not onely represented the workes of God, but also supplied the defects of Nature: euer making choise of the flower and quintessence of eie-pleasing delights.[30]

Neither yet is this proportion proper vnto painting alone, but extendeth it selfe, even vnto all other arts;[31] insomuch as it is drawne from mans body, which as the painter chiefely proposeth to himselfe (as *Vitruvius* noteth)[32] so doth the *Architect* much imitate it, in the conveiance of his buildings, and without which, neither the caruer, nor any handcrafts man, can performe any laudable worke: because it was the first patterne of all Artificiall thinges; so that there is no arte, but is in some way beholding to Proportion. Yet notwithstanding, the Painter (as *Leo Baptista Albertus* affirmeth)[33] insomuch as he considereth mans body more specially, is iustly preferred before all other Artisans, which imitate the same: because Antiquity meaning to grace painting aboue all the rest (as being the chiefe Mistresse of this proportion) hath named all the rest *Handicraftsmen*, exempting only Painters out of that number. [...]

Of the necessitie and definition of proportion. Chapter IV.
[p. 27] It is apparent then, that a picture lacking [proportions], is like a peece of Marble groslie wrought, without rule or measure: or to *Columns*, which although they be too slender or too grosse, too shorte or too long, yet are called *Columns*, as dwarfes and deformed creatures are named men. Now this first booke shal containe the generall proportions of the principall things alone, from whence the rest are derived: of which before I beginne to speake, I holde it convenient to consider the definition of *proportion* and the partes thereof.

Proportion is a correspondencie and agreement of the measures of the partes betweene themselves, and with the whole, in every worke. This correspondencie is by *Vitruvius* called *Commodulation*:[34] because a *modell* is a measure which beeing taken at the first, measureth both the partes and the whole. And this is that (to omitte the severall kindes thereof, which shalbe distinguished in their due place) which for so longe space having bin lost, was the cause why the exact and true proportion of mans body was not vnderstood: by occasion whereof there never came any workemanly peeces abroad, although the matter were never so costly; & consequently that the Painters being ignorant of that they had in hand, in steede of proportionable men, made *lame* pictures, as the *architecture, temples, images, & pictures* made throughout the whole world (but especially in Italy) about the time of *Constantine the great*, vntill *Giotto* in *Tuscany, & Andrino di Edesia Pavese in Lombardy*, can sufficiently witnes.[35] And this (in a word) is that, the knowledge whereof so satisfieth the iudgement, that it maketh vs not onelie able to make whatsoever wee list, but also teacheth vs to iudge of Images & picturs, aswel ancient as new; & without this a Painter (besides that he is not worthy the name of a Painter) is like one which perswadeth himselfe he swimmeth aboue water, when indeed he sinketh. To conclude then it is impossible, to make any decent or well proportioned thing, without this symmetricall measure of the partes orderly vnited.

Inigo Jones, from his 'Roman Sketchbook' (1615)

The first part of this long note in Inigo Jones's 'Roman Sketchbook' recalls the advice Alberti gave in §§36–40 of *On Painting* (1436). In pictorial design one should start with the limbs of the figures and their parts, composing the figures into a *historia* or narrative scene. In executing the design, the painter should first paint the skeleton and muscles, next the skin and finally the clothing of the figures. The second part of Jones's note applies the rhetorical theory of decorum, with all its moral connotations of socially acceptable behaviour, to the design of ornament. The use of ornament is not simply a matter of aesthetic preference or an expression of the desire to imitate architecture *all'antica*. Instead ornament guided by decorum reflects both the owner's public face and his private, personal imagination in a way that is regulated by the principles ruling correct classical design and social conventions.

Further reading: Peacock (1990); Higgott (1992); Cast (1993); Anderson (1997); Tucker (2000).

Thursday ye 19 January 1614 [1615 in current reckoning]

As in dessigne first on [one] sttudies the parts of the boddy of man as Eyes noses mouthes Eares and So of the rest to bee practicke in the partes Sepperat ear [before] on comm to put them togeathear to maak a hoole figgure and cloath yt and consequently a hoole Storry wth all ye ornamentes. So in Architecture on must studdy the Partes as loges Entranses Haales chambers staires doures windoues, and then adorrne them wth colloms. Cornishes. Sfondati. Stattues. Paintings. Compartimentes. quadraturs. Cartochi. tearmi. Festoni. Armes. Emprese. Maskquari. folliami. Vasi. Harpis. Puttini. Scarfinye Stratsi. Scroules, bacementes. Balustri Rissalti. Lions, or eagles clawes, converted in to folliami. Sattires. Serpentes victories or angels. Anticke heads in shells. Cherubins heads with winges. Heades of beastes. Pedistals. Cornucopias. Basketes of fruites. Trofies. Juels. Medalie. Draperies. Frontispices Broken. And Composed [fol. 76v]

[January 1615]

In all inuencions of C[a]ppresious ornaments on must first designe ye Ground, or ye thing plaine, as y^t is for youse, and on that, varry yt, addorne yt. Compose yt wth decorum according to the youse, and tye order yt is of. And to saie trew all thes composed ornaments the wch Proceed out of ye aboundance of dessigners and wear brought in by Michill Angell and his followers in my oppignion do not well in sollid architecture and ye fasciati [façades] of houses, but in garden loggis stucco or ornaments of chimnies peeces or in the inner parts of houses thos compositions are of necessity to be yoused. For as outwardly every wyse man carrieth a graviti in Publicke Places, whear ther is nothing els looked for, yet inwardly has his immaginancy set free, and sumtimes licentiously flying out, as nature hirself doeth often tymes stravagantly, to dellight, amase us sometimes moufe us to laughter, sumtimes to contemplation and horror, so in architecture ye outward ornaments oft to be sollid, proporsionabl according to the rules, masculine and unaffected. [fol. 76r]

Sir Henry Wotton, from *The Elements of Architecture* (1624)

Sir Henry Wotton (1568–1639) was a diplomat, collector and writer. He spent much of his life as English ambassador in Venice, where he was involved in the acquisition of works of art for the Stuart Court. The *Elements* were written after his return to England in 1623 to support his application for the position of Provost of Eton College. Although Wotton assumed a pose of modesty and wrote in great haste, his book was the fruit of extensive, first-hand study of classical and Renaissance sources, both built and written, and of his acquaintance in Italy with important theorists and patrons such as Daniel Barbaro, for whom Palladio built the Villa Maser. The *Elements* were read widely, and also published both in a Latin edition which appeared in 1649 as part of Johannes de Laet's edition of Vitruvius and in a Spanish version published in 1698. A 'contracted' version of the first part (called 'The Ground-Rules of Architecture') was added by William Fisher to the second edition of his *The Mirror of Architecture* of 1670, a practical pattern-book on the orders based on Scamozzi's *Idea dell'Architettura Universale*, which went through eight editions, the last in 1752. It was also reprinted as an addition to the 1722 and 1733 editions of John Evelyn's *Parallel* (see below, Chapter 5) and was even published in Oakley's *Magazine of Architecture* in weekly sixpenny instalments in 1732–33, and thus this extremely learned treatise, written for discerning patrons, came within the reach of even the poorest workmen (Harris, 1990).

Further reading: Pearsall Smith (1907); Nugel (1980), pp. 113–18; Harris (1990); Mowl and Earnshaw (1995), p. 66ff.

[p. 1] In Architecture as in all other Operative Arts,[36] the end must direct the Operation. The end is to build well. Well building hath three Conditions. Commoditie, Firmenes, and Delight. A common division among the Deliverers of this Art, though I know not how, some what misplaced by Vitruvius himselfe lib. 1 cap. 3. Whom I shalbe willinger to follow, as a Master of Proportion, than of Methode.

Now, For the attayning of these Intentions, wee may consider the whole Subiect, under two generall Heads.

The Seate and the Worke.

Therefore first touching Scituation.

The Precepts thereunto belonging, doe either concerne Totall Posture, (as I may tearm it) or the Placing of the Parts: whereof the first sort, howsoever usually set downe by Architects as a piece of their Profession: yet are in truth borrowed, from other Learnings: there being betweene Arts and Sciences, as well as betweene Men, a kinde of good fellowship, and communication of their Principles.

For you shall finde some of them, to be meerely Physicall, touching the qualitie and temper of the Aire: which being a perpetuall ambient, and ingredient, and the defects thereof, incorrigible in single Habitations (which I most intend) doth in those respects, require the more exquisite caution; That it be not too grosse, nor too penetrative; Not subject to any foggy noysomnesse, from Fenns or Marshes neere adioyning; nor too Mineral exhalations, from the Soile itselfe. Not undigested, for want of Sunne, Not unexercised, for want of Winde: which were to live (as it were) in a Lake, or standing Poole of Aire, as Alberti the Florentin Architect, doth ingeniously compare it. Some doe rather seeme a little Astrological, as when they warne us from Places of malign Influence: where Earthquakes, Contagions, Prodigious Births, or the like, are frequent without any evident cause: whereof the Consideration is peradventure not altogether vaine: Some are plainely Oeconomical; As that the Seate be well watered, and well fewelled, That it bee not of too steepie and incommodious Accesse to the trouble both of friends and familie. That it lie not too farre, from some navigable River or Arme of the Sea, for more ease of provision and such Domestique notes.

Some againe may bee said to bee Optical? Such as I meane as concerne the Properties of a well chosen Prospect: which I will call the Royaltie of Sight. For as there is a Lordship (as it were) of the Feete, wherein the Master doth much joy when he walketh about the Line of his owne Possessions: So there is a Lordship likewise of the Eye which being a raunging, and Imperious, and (I might say) an usurping Sence; can indure no narrow circomscription; but must be fedde, both with extent and varietie. Yet on the other side, I finde vaste and indefinite viewes which drowne all apprehension of the uttermost Objects, I condemned, by good Authors, as if thereby some part of the pleasure (whereof we speake) did persist. Lastly, I remember a private caution, which I know not well how to sort, unlesse I should call it Political. By no meanes, to build too neere a great Neighbour; which were in truth to bee as unfortunately seated on the earth, as Mercurie is in the Heavens, for the most part, ever in combustion, or obscuritie, under brighter beames then his owne. (…)

[p. 102]: And let thus much summarily suffice, touching the choice and vse of these adorning *Arts*. For to speake of garnishing the *Fabrique* with a *Row* of erected *Statues*, about the *Cornice* of euery *Contignation*[37] *or Story*, were discourse more proper for *Athens* or *Rome*, in the time of their true greatnesse, when (as *Plinie* recordeth of his own *Age*) there were neere as many carued *Images*, a liuing *Men*; like a noble contention, euen in point of *Fertility*, betweene *Art* and *Nature*; which passage doth not onely argue an infinite abundance, both of *Artizans* and *Materials*; but likewise of *Magnificent* and *Majesticall* desires, in euery common person of those times; more or lesse according to their *Fortunes*. And true it is indeed that the Marble *Monuments & Memories* of well deseruing Men, wherewith the very high wayes were *strewed* on each side was not a bare and transitory entertainement of the *Eye*, or onely a gentle deception of *Time*, to the *Travailer*: But had also a secret and strong *Influence*, euen to the aduancement of the *Monarchie*, by continuall representation of vertuous examples; so as in that point *ART* became a piece of *State*.

Thomas Hobbes, from 'Answer to Davenant's Preface to *Gondibert*' (1650)

Thomas Hobbes (1588–1679) was a philosopher; his main work is *Leviathan*, a treatise on political philosophy (1651). Sir William D'Avenant (1606–68) was a Royalist poet, who had met Hobbes in Paris in 1646. He had invited Hobbes to reply to his Preface to his verse epic *Gondibert* on the subject of imagination and the art of poetry. Hobbes's 'Answer' to D'Avenant, together with the original Preface, was published in 1650, a year before the publication of the first three sections of the poem. In this extract Hobbes offers a solution for the problem of reconciling judgement and fancy. For Hobbes this issue was important because such a conjunction would help to produce a persuasive moral or civic philosophy, in which soundness of argument (based on judgement or philosophy) would be enhanced by the persuasive effect of figures of speech (supplied by fancy). For architectural theory this passage is of great interest because it offers a concept of good architecture as the result of the collaboration of judgement and the imagination. While this is a significant departure from the traditional Vitruvian view which presents architecture as a science, and the architect as a scientist. It is also significant because Hobbes explicitly acknowledges the rhetorical aspect of architecture. As in moral science, beautiful architecture is a result of the conjunction of sound judgement and persuasive ornament.

Further reading: Skinner (1996), pp. 241, 332–3, 363–75.

[p. 59] Time and Education begets experience; Experience begets Memory; Memory begets Judgement and Fancy: Judgment begets the strength and structure, and Fancy begets the ornaments of a Poem.[38] The Ancients therefore fabled not absurdly in making memory the Mother of the Muses. For memory is the World (though not really, yet so as in a looking glass) in which the Judgment, the severer Sister, busieth her self in a grave and rigid examination of all the parts of Nature, and in registring by Letters their order, causes, uses, differences, and resemblances; Whereby the Fancy, when any work of Art is to be performed, findes her materials at hand and prepared for use, and needs no more then a swift motion over them, that what she wants, and is there to be had, may not lie too long unespied. So that when she seemeth to fly from one *Indies* to the other, and from Heaven to Earth, and to penetrate into the hardest matter and obscurest places, into the future and into her self, and all this in a point of time, the voyage is not very great, her self being all she seeks; and her wonderful celerity consisteth not so much in motion as in copious Imagery discreetly ordered & perfectly registred in the memory, which most men under the name of Philosophy have a glimpse of, and is pretended to by many that, grosly mistaking her, embrace contention in her place. But so far forth as the

Fancy of man has traced the ways of true Philosophy, so far it hath produced very marvellous effects to the benefit of mankinde. All that is beautiful or defensible in building, or marvellous in Engines and Instruments of motion, whatsoever commodity men receive from the observations of the Heavens, from the description of the Earth, from the account of Time, from walking on the Seas, and whatsoever distinguiseth the civility of *Europe* from the Barbarity of the *American* savages, is the workmanship of Fancy but guided by the Precepts of true Philosophy. But where these precepts fail, as they have hitherto failed in the doctrine of Moral vertue, there the Architect, *Fancy*, must take the Philosophers part upon her self. He therefore that undertakes an Heroick Poem, which is to exhibite a venerable & amiable Image of Heroick vertue, must not only be the Poet, to place and connect, but also the Philosopher, to furnish and square his matter, that is, to make both Body and Soul, colour and shadow of his Poem out of his own Store [...].

Sir Roger Pratt, from 'Certain Short Notes Concerning Architecture' (1660)

Sir Roger Pratt (1620–85) was the son of a lawyer; he was educated at Magdalen College, Oxford, and the Inner Temple. The outbreak of the Civil War forced him to travel in France, Italy and the Low Countries in the years 1643–49. In 1666 he was one of the Commissioners who advised on the rebuilding of Old Saint Paul's Cathedral; after the Great Fire that same year he became a member, together with Christopher Wren and Hugh May, of the King's Commission for rebuilding the City. He built four great houses: Coleshill (*c.* 1658–61); Kingston Lacy (1663–65); Horseheath (1663–65) and Clarendon House, Piccadilly (1664–67). Only Kingston Lacy survives, but remodelled. The systematic and didactic form of his writings suggest that he intended to publish a treatise, but he never saw them in print (Turner, 1996).

Further reading: Summerson (1983), pp. 151–5; Silcox-Crowe (1985); Mowl and Earnshaw (1995), p. 27.

[p. 18] [...] I conceive Architecture to be an art teaching us to build as we ought, both in regard of the person for whom the building is made, as also for the use for which it is chiefly intended.

Of this Architecture there are chiefly these four parts

1. Precognition. 2. Edification. 3. Finishing. 4. Restoration.

As to the first, Architecture being no one single science, there is requisite a competent knowledge at the least of 1. *Arithmetic*, as to the calculation of all expenses and the content of the areas of all figures which by accident may probably be offered to us etc.

Secondly of *Geometry*, as to the drawing of perpendiculars, parallels, making of all regular polygons, circles, ovals, etc.

Thirdly of *Designing*, as to the Ichnography, orthography, scenography and perspective of any building,[39] to the which may like wise be added the most clear and satisfactory way of framing all kind of modules, as likewise a perfect insight in all forms of building.

Nicholas Barbon, from *An Apology for the Builder* (1685)

Nicholas Barbon, MD (d. 1698) was also the author of two treatises on money, and the originator of insurance in Great Britain. He was born in London, and although he studied medicine in the Netherlands at Leiden and Utrecht he never practised as a physician. Instead, he became one of the first and most considerable speculative builders of the City of London after the Great Fire of 1666 (*DNB*).

Further reading: North, *Autobiography*, pp. 54–7; Summerson (1978), pp. 38, 44–51, 59, 68; Harris (1990); Colley (1992), pp. 55–101; Lubbock (1995), pp. 96–100; McKellar (1999).

[p. 1] To write of Architecture and its several Parts, of Scituation, Plat-forms of Building, and the quality of Materials, with their Dimensions and Ornaments: To discourse of the several Orders of Columns, of the Tuscan, Dorick, Ionick, Corinthian, and Composit, with the proper Inrichments of their Capitals, Freeze and Cornish, were to transcribe a Folio from *Vitruvius* and others; and but mispend the Readers and Writers time, since we live in an Age and Country, where all the Arts belonging to Architecture are so well known and practised: And yet at the same time and place to write an Apology for the Artist, may seem a greater trifling; In a time when since the Grecian greatnes their Arts were never better performed. In a place where Buildings are generally so well finish'd, that almost every House is a little Book of Architecture; and as the ancient Artists made Athens and the rest of their Cities famous by their Buildings, and still preserve the Memory of the Places by the Ruins of their excellent Arts; so the Artists of this Age have already made the City of *London* the Metropolis of *Europe*, and if it be compared for the number of good Houses, for its many and large Piazzaz, for its richness of Inhabitants, it must be allowed the largest, best built, and richest City in the world.

But such is the misfortune of Greatness to be envied. The Citizens, nay, the whole Nation is astonished at the flourishing condition of this Metropolis, to see every year a new Town added to the old one; and like men affrighted are troubled with misapprehensions, and easily imposed on by the false suggestions of those that envy her Grandeur, and are angry with the Builders for making her so great.

The Citizens are afraid that the Building of new Houses will lessen the Rent and Trade of the City. The Country Gentleman is troubled at the new Buildings, for fear they should draw away their Inhabitants, and depopulate the Country, and they want Tenants for their Land. And both agree, that the encrease of Building is prejudicial to the Government, and use for Argument a simile from the Rickets,[40] fancying the City to be the Head of the Nation, and that it will grow too big for the Body.

This is the Charge that is laid on the Builders: Therefore the design of this Discourse is to answer these Aspersions, to remove these fears and false conceptions, by confuting these Popular Errors, and shewing that the Builder ought to be encouraged in all Nations as the chief promoter of their Welfare.

This is done by shewing the Cause of the increase of Building, and the Effects; as they relate to the City, to the Country, and to the Government.

Of the Cause.

The Cause of the Increase of Building is from the *natural Increase of Mankind*, that there is more born than die. From the first Blessing of Creation, *Increase and multiply*, in a good Government, where Property is well secured. There are three things that man by nature is under a necessity to take care of, to provide food for himself, Cloths and a House. For the *first*, all the rest of Creation as well as man is under that necessity to take care of: for life cannot be maintained without *food*.

The second belongs only to man, and it is a question by some, whether it is required of him by nature, or custom, because in some Countries (and those cold) men go naked. But as to the *last*, it is most certain, that Man is forced to Build by nature, as all those Creatures are, whose young are born so weak (like the offspring of Mankind), that they require some time for strength after their birth, to follow their Parents, or feed themselves. Thus the Rabbit, the Fox and Lyon make themselves Burrows, Kennels, and Dens to bring forth, and shelter their young; but the Mare, Cow, Sheep, &c., bring forth in the open field, because their young are able to follow them as soon as folded. So that the natural cause of Building a House, is to provide a shelter for their young; and if we examine man in his Natural condition without Arts, his Tenement differs little from the rest of Natures Herd: The Fox's Kennel, though not so large, being a lesser creature, may yet for its contrivance in its several apartments be compared with any of his Cottages: Earthen walls, and covering, are the manner of both their Buildings, and the Furniture of both their Houses alike: Now as the Rabbits increase, new Burrows are made, and the Boundaries of the Warren are enlarged. So it is with Man, as he increaseth, new Houses are built, and his Town made bigger.

When Mankind is civilized, instructed with Arts, and under good Government, every man doth not dress his own Meat, make his own Clothes, nor build his own House. He enjoys property of Land and Goods, which he or his Ancestors by their Arts and Industry gained. These Possessions make the difference among men of rich and poor. The rich are fed, clothed, and housed by the labour of other men, but the poor by their own, and the

Goods made by this labour are the rents of the rich mens Land (for to be well fed, well clothed, and well lodged, without labour either of body or mind, is the true definition of a rich man.)

Now as men differ in Estates, so they differ in their manner of living. The rich have variety of Dishes, several suits of Clothes, and larger Houses; and as their riches increase, so doth their wants. For Trade is nothing else but the making and selling all sorts of Commodities to supply those wants. And there are more hands imployed to provide things necessary to make up the several distinctions of men; things that promote the ease, pleasure and pomp of life, than to supply the first natural necessities from hunger, cold, and a house only to shelter their young. Now the Trader takes care from time to time, to provide a sufficient quantity of all sorts of Goods for many occasions, which he finds out by the Market: That is, By the quick selling of the Commodities, that are made ready to be sold. And as there are Butchers, Brewers and Cooks, Drapers, Mercers and Taylors, and a hundred more, that furnish him with food and clothes; so there are Bricklayers, Carpenters, Playsterers, and many more Traders, that build houses for him; and they make houses of the first, second, and third rate of building, in proportion to the increase of the several degrees of men, which they find out by the Market, that is, by letting of houses already built: so that if it were not throughly believed, that Mankind doth naturally increase; this Miracle of the great increase of Houses would cease: It is therefore necessary to shew, that man doth naturally increase.

Of the Effects of New Buildings as they relate to the Country.

New Buildings are advantageous to the Country: I. By taking off the Commodities of the Country.

The Materials of these Houses, as Stones, Bricks, Lime, Iron, Lead, Timber, &c., are all the Commodities of the Country. And whatsoever the Inhabitants of these New Houses have occasion for, either for food, Apparel, or Furniture for their Houses, are at first the growth of the Country; and the bigger the Town grows, the greater is the occasion and consumption of these Commodities, and so the greater profit to the Country.

II. New Buildings provide an habitation and livelihood for the Supernumerary and useless Inhabitants of the Country. The younger Sons of the Gentry, the Children of the Yeomen and Peasants are by these means provided with Callings, Imployments, and Habitations to exercise them in; which should they have continued in the Country, would have been burdensome, & chargeable to their Friends for want of Imployments. For there is always Inhabitants enough left in the Country for the imployments of the Country. For if the Country wanted people, there would be a want of their Commodities, for want of hands to provide them.

Now there is as much Land Plowed, and all sorts of Grain sown, and reaped every year, as there is occasion for; and sometimes more: For the Crown in some years hath been at charge to Export it. And there is as much Wooll provided and made into Clothes and Stuffs, as the Market can take off, and so for all other Commodities of the Country. Nay, there are more of all the Country Commodities every year made than formerly [...]. For there are more people in the City to be fed; so that there must be more hands in the Country to provide this greater quantity of Commodities: and the Country does increase as well as the City, as hath been already observed from the *Doomsday-Book*.

Therefore if the Rents of the Lands fall in the Country, it must not be ascrib'd to the *New Buildings draining their Inhabitants*, but to some other occasions; Which probably may be from the great improvements that are made upon the Land in the Country, either by draining of Fens; improving of Land by *Zanfoin;*[41] or other profitable Seeds; inclosing of grounds, or disparking and plowing of Parks, by which means the Markets are overstock'd and furnished at a cheaper rate than those Lands can afford, who have had no advantage from improvements: Or else the Market is removed at a greater distance, and the Lands are forced to abate in their price for the carriage; The Town perhaps is decayed, that they used to furnish, and the Trade removed to some other flourishing place at a greater distance; occasioned some times by the death or removal of some great Clothier or Trader; or some other natural obstruction of the place; as the choaking-up of some Haven, and the forsaking of the Sea, which is the reason of the decay of the CinquePorts. These or some other occasions may make some particular mens Farms fall in value; but there is never a County in England, where the Land of the whole County doth not produce a third part more in value than it did within a 100 years, and whosoever will compare these present Rents, with what they were then, will find them generally increased. Therefore the New Buildings of this City cannot prejudice the Country, but are greatly advantageous to it.

Of the Effects of the New Buildings, as they relate to the Government.

New Buildings are advantageous to the King and Government. They are instrumental to the preserving and increasing of the number of the Subjects; And numbers of Subjects is the strength of a Prince: for Houses are Hives for People to breed and swarm in, without which they cannot increase; And unless they are provided for them from time to time in proportion to their increase, they would be forced to go into the Plantations and other Countries for habitations; and so many times become the Subjects of other Princes; but at the best, the Country loseth the profit of feeding them; for they that live in a City are unskilfull and unfit for a Country-life; and this is the reason why so many *Scotch* Citizens are wandring Pedlars; and that every Town in *Europe* hath a *Scotch-man* for an inhabitant.

And that this will be the Effects, will appear plainly by examining the growth of the City of *London*, since the Buildings have flourished, with its condition, when the Buildings were prohibited; and we cannot make a better discovery of it, than by the Bills of Mortality, for it is reasonable among such a number of Mankind, such a number should die; [...] but it is a certain demonstration, That if the Burials have increased, the number of Citizens hath increased, though the proportion may be uncertain. [...]

This is sufficient to shew, that a Nation cannot increase without the Metropolis be inlarged, and how dangerous a consequence it may be to obstruct its growth, and discourage the Builders. It is to banish the People, and confine the Nation to an Infant Estate, while the Neighbouring Nations grow to the full strength of Manhood, and thereby to render it an easie Conquest to its Enemies.

For the Metropolis is the heart of a Nation, through which the Trade and Commodities of it circulate, like the blood through the heart, which by its motion, giveth life and growth to the rest of the Body; and if that declines, or be obstructed in its growth, the whole body falls into consumption: And it is the only symptome to know the health, and thriving of a Country, by the inlarging of its Metropolis; for the chief City of every Nation in the world that flourisheth, doth increase. And if those Gentlemen that fancy the City to be the Head of the Nation, would but fancy it like the heart, they would never be afraid of its growing too big. To conclude, it was upon these Considerations, That by the building and inlarging of a City, the People are made *Great*, *Rich*, and *easily Governed*: That those ancient and famous Governments, *Thebes*, *Athens*, *Sparta*, *Carthage*, and *Rome*, began their Dominions, and inlarged them with their Cities; and of late the States of *Holland* have followed these Examples.

The Citizens of *Amsterdam* have thrice flung down their Walls to inlarge it; so that from a little Fisher-Town within less than 200 years it is become the third or fourth City of *Europe*; and the rest of their Cities have followed their Pattern, and made Grafts and Streets at the Charge of the Government; endeavouring to outvie one another by giving Priviledges to incourage the Builders and Inhabitants. And these States have found the effects of it; for by this means they have changed their Style from the Poor Distressed States (as they wrote to Queen *Elizabeth*) to the High and Mighty States of the United Provinces.

And if the City of *London* hath made such a Progress within this five and twenty years, as to have grown one third bigger, and become already the Metropolis of *Europe*, notwithstanding the Popular Error the Nation have been infected with, and the ill censures and discouragements the Builders have met with; had they been for this last hundred years encouraged by the Government, the City of *London* might probably have easily grown three times bigger than now it is.

And if we consider what the natural effects of so great a City must have been; To be furnished with such large provisions for War suitable to its greatness; Such a vast number of Ships; being Scituate on an Island and Navigable River; filled with innumberable Inhabitants, of such natural courage as the English are; and to be so easily transported on a sudden with all things necessary for War, it would long before this time have been a Terror to all *Europe*; and now would have had the opportunity with much ease, to give a check to the growth of *France*, might be made the Metropolis of the World, and cause *England's* Monarch to be acknowledged Lord of all the Navigable Cities, and Sea-port Towns in the World; might make an universal Monarchy over the Seas: an Empire, no less Glorious, and of much more profit, than of the Land; and of larger extent, than either *Caesar's* or *Alexander's*.

Roger North, from 'Of Building' (1690s) and 'Of Unity and Variety' (*c.* 1695–96)

Roger North (?1653–1734) was educated for the Bar and practised as a lawyer. His interests ranged from optics, music and botany to architecture and painting. He played an important part in the negotiations with Nicholas Barbon, who was the 'undertaker' of the rebuilding of the Temple, destroyed by fire in 1678/79. This excited his interest in the theory and design of architecture. He designed the Great Gateway leading from the Temple into Fleet Street; this has traditionally been attributed to Wren, who in fact only offered advice. North did not build much, but some of his designs are preserved with his papers in the British Library (Colvin, 1995). The first extract from 'Of Building' reprinted here is an apology for building based not on the intrinsic excellence of architecture, but on its moral and social beneficence; the second is a discussion of the question whether beauty is an inherent, objective property of objects or a matter of taste or familiarity. In another British Library manuscript North identifies his interlocutor: 'I had once some discourse with Sir Christopher Wren on this subject, who for argument sake, held that there was that distinction in Nature, of gracefull and ugly; and that it must be so to all creatures that had vision.'[42] Wren's 'Tract I', which argues that there are two kinds of beauty, one based on geometry and one caused by familiarity, is reprinted below, in Chapter 5.

Further reading: Colvin (1995); Mowl and Earnshaw (1995), p. 27; Soo (1998), pp. 119–20.

'Of Building'

[p. 3] This title leads forth an expectation that I should discourse at large of Architecture and the rules or laws derived from antiquity, for creating beauty as well as strength in fabricks to be undertaken. But this hath bin so copiously effected by authors especially of Italy, whose just works have long since bin deniz'd in English, that it is fondness to pretend to add or much inlarge them. Nor are the termes, as in other sciences, abstruse, so that it might be worth while to open the science of building by explaining them. Therefore it is not my aim to treat the subject in a formall way but onely hint some observations I have made, as much to refresh my owne memory, as to advise my friends, if any such happen on these papers, and thinck them worth their perusall.

It may be inquired, what should make me so much a pretender, as above, considering my small beginnings, and imployment another way, demanding as much time as life can spare to attend duely. To which I must answer, that inclination hath bin too hard for prudence; and made me robb my profession, for pleasure, which was ever to me very great in the speculation, as well as the practise of mechanicks; and the consummate use of them is had by building. I name not other arts, all of which that I have knowledge of, and indeed all the force of humane understanding and conduct have their share in that business; so that it may well be sayd, that nothing more shews a man, than his building; as I may demonstrate hereafter.

But in the mean time, let me owne it a weakness to be propence as I am, to building; the nicety of which is little or no improvements to life; say luxury what it will, a retirement to warmth and safety, is all that nature cares for. Pomp and ornament, are but fancy and chimera of the imagination, and lean on pride, ambition, and envyous comparison. Ostentation draws company and that vice; and the monster devours familys, by the enormous charges, that are before, in, and after it. So much for blame.

It is bad cause which cannot be palliated, therefore let us see if the vanity of building will be defended.

Whatever vanity it is, it doth not terminate in our persons, nor draw the censure of self conceipt, as dressing, discoursing, &c. doth. That boast it hath, is of the judgment, and contrivance, whereof it is lawfull to boast. And the end or aim is, the accomodation of freinds with ease and delight. And if envy and vicious comparison be absent, litle or no immorality remaines.

It is a sober enterteinment, and doth not impeach but defend health. Other pleasures which are less despised, as wine, women, gaming, &c. have a sting, which this hath not. And it is also an exercise of the mind, as well as of the body, and a pratique of manage and conduct greatly usefull in all civil life. For what habits ought to be imprest with more efficacy than those of providing materialls, foreseeing occasions, snatching opportunities, waylaying prises, and making bargaines? Then for the forme, conceiving in your mind things not existent but in *potentia*; and comparing them with your occasions, and your scituation; take further deliberation, lateration and amendment. And in doing this, which a builder should do, or want great part of his pleasure, he practiseth, and under that learneth geometry; and after all making workmen understand, laying out the ground, perpetuall overseeing, ordering, and resolving doubts and querys, setting right, and amending the beginnings of error; are a full imploy, and fill the mind. These exercises goe alone, inclination actuates them, and are much beyond assumed diversions or exercises as by prescription for health sake, while the intervening doubts and fears of success knaw and deprave nature, more than the formall exercise helps it. A builder is so full, it must be an inundation, and not a flood, that concernes him.

Building is very beneficiall to the publick, and in truth the best sort of charity, for much the greater part of the charge is mony paid to poor people. The very materialls, except timber, are the product of men's labour. And the publick hath not a more effectuall means of maintaining the lower order of men, out of rich men's purses, than this. I am sure superfluous mony cannot be better imployed. To maintaine idly mean men and their familys, is to nourish vice and imorality, as will happen if their time be not filled with drudgery for a lively hood. Nay the master himself, not having some diversion that is agreable, and harmeless, seeks company and finds his ruin. What then is it, to maintaine men, not onely idly but as ministers or at least partakers of gluttony and sottishness, to say no worse, such as wee mean when we talk of living well. So farr mistaken are comon notions of things, for better it were that the mony were hurled into the sea, that nothing might succeed from it, rather than a pestilence. But when it falls to labouring men and their familys, they are kept in order, maintained, and the product of their labour remaines for the comfort of the present age and posterity.

It may be objected, that these men may be better imployed in husbandry, planting, and other real improvements. I answer, it is possible, that wee have more than may be so imployed, but grant it other wise, that the riches of the nation would be so increast. I demand, what is the end of riches? Not gluttony, lust, and drunkenness, but plenty without excess, neatness and elegancy of living, charity to the poor, and liberality to inferiors. Mony hoarded is not riches, but earth, and barren earth, sent abroad and imployed, is wealth, which is either for increase or injoyment. The former is not to be endless, but tends to and terminates in the other. And surely of all injoyments, in the way of magnificence, building, with its appendage furniture, gardens, &c. are the most great and usefull; for the owner is honestly exhalted, and injoys a plenty with vertue, and the exercise of business and arts, and the poorer sort participate in their way a competent share. Which is an ordonnance of affairs in the world, that God and nature intends; and the wicked onely labour to prevent or destroy. And this point I may conclude with an observation, that in most countrys and ages, the prime and most exalted spirits, have bin declared lovers of building. And the greatest statesmen, and favorites of fortune, after proof of all the envyed grandure upon earth, have chosen, either upon disgrace or to voluntary retiredment, to imploy their time, in designing fabricks and executing them. I shall add, that designing and executing is not onely a lawfull, but a very great pleasure; and hath somewhat I cannot describe, but is more lofty and aspiring than any other injoyment upon earth, and savours of creation, the knowne act of an almighty power. This ambition is not discouraged, but excited by religion; for wee ought to follow devine example, as farr as our groveling state will allow. But to abate these flights, and come to the matter, that is the pleasure that builders have. I read not that wee are sent into the world to be tormented, and to encrease the paines of life, but on the contrary, to be joyous and happy, as farr as wee can contrive, by our owne regiment. This all agree in: but wee differ in methods. Some are for the sences, and mistake their way thro vice and intemperance. Others, and so our religion engageth, seek comfort by doing reall good to themselves, and their fellow mortalls. The pressing arguments, wee often hear against pleasure, mean the vicious and unlawfull; not that which is had from the best use of fortunes with respect to our health, private and nationall, such as among other ways, comes by peace, justice, charity and temperance. Perhaps some lawfull injoyments, in strictness of rule, may be disswaded, (they cannot be forbid,) it is on account of danger, and flattery tending to worse, and in prudence, though lawfull, not to be used. Otherwise lawfull pleasures are the guift of heaven, and intended to be used as expedients to releive the meer paines of life, which at best is bitter enough, and it is enthusiasme and madness to decline them.

Lastly wee must consider the real usefullness of building, which furnisheth a true plenty of what is good, that is safety from force and fraude, by the orderly disposition, receipt in, and delivery out of our goods; latitude of place, for accomodating ourselves, freinds and family, variety and ornament, for the diversion of all. Relief from the clamour, occasioned from the want of fitting convenience, which often is a perpetuall rack to a master of a family; nay all disorders and abuses, though moving from stupidity, carelessness or perfidy, shall be charged upon that. It is not a litle, that things are not onely sufficient for use, but pleasant and aggreable to the eye, rather than abrupt and deformed. In short he that hath no relish of the grandure and joy of building, is a stupid ox and wants that vivacity of sence and spirit, that seasons humane life, and make[s] it less insipid. And if there be high and low in honest injoyment of pleasure, that by building is the supream. Which concludes this appology, (as I must stile the foregoing excuses for my owne vanity,) and I proceed next to some matters relating, tho but circumstantially, to the present subject.

It is manifest infelicity that happens to building; all men pretend to judge, and thinck themselves masters of it, and very few have an idea so just as to satisfie either themselves or others, with what is done. And I know not which sort is most dissappointed, those who invent and execute for themselves, or such as, (for invention at least) imploy others. It is not amiss to inquire the reason of this unhappyness. No man is a stranger to habitation, or structure; but every one is well aquainted with some sort or other. So none is without prejudice, and you cannot charge any with ignorance, or unacquaintedness with the matter, as if there were an art to be acquired, such as geometry or algebra; but the way of living every man hath, gives him a gusto to what he hath by use happened to approve of, and that he calls well and others he calls not well. And this sort of projudice once attach't, is hard to be removed, and tho some are inquisitive and curious, the generality goe on in an assurance of their owne understanding, hate to be corrected even by themselves, but shoot their bolts, determine, and declare themselves wise; and as the errors or prejudices in the mind proceed and are seen more or less in all the outward actions, nothing more exposeth them than building. I can shew you a man's caracter in his house. If he hath bin given to parsimony or profusion, to judge rightly or superficially, to deal in great maters or small, high or low; his edifices shall be tincted accordingly, and the justness or imperfection of his mind will appear in them. [...]

[p. 10] In discourse with [Wren] on the subject of beauty, I urged, that in nature, the distinction of handsome and ugly had no place, but arose by use and the reason of things. He (for argument sake), held the contrary, that there were things naturally handsome or deformed, which were so to all eys, learned or unlearned. And instanct't in tryangles, that all approved an equilater, and disliked a scalene; and so the comon demensions of columes, which were aggreable to all. I thought even those instances proved my side, as may appear anon; but first I would know why wee are pleased, or displeased with any thing. And here I medle with no appetites nor gross sensations, for that which gratifies or hurts us corporally cannot be thought aggreable, but in things more indifferent as objects of sight, which touch us but lightly.

Wee find by effect that things which conforme and agree together please, and such as thwart and clash, the contrary. This holds in most things, especially sounds. For now it is proved to the eye it self, that discord is from opposed and crossing movements, and concord from such as co-operate and agree. It is found also, that movements in unequall and uncertein periods, as the clapping of a door, and any sound, not a musicall tone, which consists of equall timed pulses, are intollerable; but any regular movement, as the sound of a bell, pendlum clock, dropping of water, and the like, are not unpleasant, but so much the contrary, as to induce repose, and sleep. There is some cause in nature of these differences, which I take lys in this.

That which is most understood, or brings more to our knowledge, and comprehension, is pleasing, and things not understood nor comprehended are painefull, that is ugly and offensive. Againe things understood, or appearing to be just and fitt for the use intended are handsome, and others unfitt or unequall for the occasion, are blameable, and therefore ugly. These 2 rules, will determine all questions of beauty and ornament. 1. As to the former, I have no proof but an universall assent of mankind. The effect springs from a sence of imperfection all of us have, and cannot avoid; wee dayly find novelty, which speaks our ignorance, and that is a trouble; so wee, desiring to have ease, makes us [*sic*] ambitious to know, and comprehend more than wee doe, and thence is curiosity and inquisitiveness, the gratifiing which is ever a pleasure. For the perception that wee have of the least advance towards perfection, must needs be gratefull; and this is so setled in our natures, that as in other instances, wee are often pleased, when there is this reason for it, tho wee doe not immediately reflect upon it; wee are not so much philosofers to understand the causes of our passions and opinions, it's enough that they are, and wee discover them by signes, which are an approbation with joy at some things, and aversion with paine at others; and such as no naturall appetite is concerned with, as musick, building &c.

Granting then that whatever is comprehended is pleasing, and the contrary offensive; and that altho wee doe not advert to that reason but onely find the effect in ourselves, I shall apply it so some instances; as first that of regular or equall timed movements, as a clock, water dropping, and, (most eminently) musicall sounds. These are aggreable, because by the past wee know the future, and are not surprised or doubdtfull what follows, and imediately the movement[s] of our parts fall in with the measure, as the keeping time with a drum, or musick, and all jog on in harmony together. [...]

'Of Unity and Variety' (*c.* 1695–96)

[p. 56] These wee hear of in the discourse of plays, poetry, and painting.[43] The first casts it into a devision by time, place, and fable. And in that and the epick poetry, demand unity, yet allow for variety by plotts and episodes, which yet must hang upon the main. So the painters will not have a clutter, but some principall thing, at first view eminently cheif, to which all the other figures must relate. It is the same for building, and, to say truth, all things of delight in the world. The rule is not from men's invention, but from nature, and truth, as it is found the best and most experienc't senses will dictate. The reason is what I hinted at first, that pleasure from without consists in exercising the understanding without pain, and not in tormenting it, without any, or hard-gained satisfaction. If a play be double, that is 2 storys without dependance on each other, the audience is distracted which to attend, and when one comes, it breaks off the attention to the other, and hath the same disturbance at every transition. So 2 pictures in one is unlike nature, for wee cannot look at 2 things at once. So in building, 2 differring manners and ranges in one house, as if two houses came together, and justled, is disagreable. And yet this doctrine of unity must not exclude variety, but artists must find out such as will divert, and not devide, and that is consummate height of art.

In the gothick times, structures of great pomp and strength were made, but failed in the way of setting off their fronts and views. They continued ranges of the same height and order into great length, not breaking the course, or intermixing any great in the way of ornament; I say great, for of small ornaments, which I esteem trifles [of which] they had enough and too many. But those take not the eye at any distance, where a building should be viewed. (…) It is certein that no true beauty is found in the out-line of a Gothick building, and cheifly because they used no breaks for variety in their ranges. A long building, consisting of bays of the same invention continually repeated, is a dull object. A long walk however well planted, is not compleat without opening, and crosses, to interrupt the sameness of it, by new views. The dullest road I ever saw was a fenbank, where for 5 or 6 mile the landscape had no change; and was like traveling in a trunck, seing only a small hole at the end. Of the moderne fabricks, Hampton Court, hath this fault conspicuously. It is new built, but the old had a better view, for that had gate towers, and some risings, but this is all of an height: balustred, flatt, which looks like combs stuck at the topp, and a series of round windoes, like the ports of a ship. […]

Of the ancient fabricks, there are 2 sorts, which seem to contradict this doctrine of variety, that is their temples, and amphithetres, both of which had no variety of parts, but went thro with one and the same order and manner. I must needs grant, that the danger of introducing variety is great, least trifling be the consequence. And singleness and plaineness where the order is great and good, is a vertue, and if a fault, the best of errors. The temples were single things, which spoke but one single use, that is sacrifising. To what end should that be broken? Why should hipps and valleys and gutters be made in a roof, to gaine no good, but onely to make a figure without, and imply no sort of advantage within? So also in a small dwelling house, what needs breaks? One pile and one covering is sufficient; if a porch be in the middle, to wether the door, it is enough and justifies an ornament, as a lofty pediment, to sett it off. And where countrys are warme, an open walk in the midle. This plaineness is without question comendable. But what is that to a greater extent of building, such as Bedlam, Chelsea Colledge, or Hampton Court, which speaks a provision to be made for various and numerous sorts of people; and is rather a compound than a simple fabrick. Wherefore singleness doth not become it, as it doth a church or small house.

The amphitheaters were all of a peice without, and I beleeve they were content with a moderate beauty, where there was such vast magnitude and strength to be provided. I beleeve it will not be controverted, but if those buildings instead of 3 or 4 orders one above another, had bin composed with one order onely, carrying a stately intablature, with fitt apertures, and broke forewards ornamentally on each quadrant, they had bin more beautifull; and if prime and perfect beauty had bin the aim, as it was in the building temples of the gods, they had not bin sett off as they were, tale quale. And this argues for breaking the height into severall others. The whole was made for seats and staires, which staires were in the hollow under the seats, and it was fitt to make walks and windoes, upon severall landings, for the people to spread and evacuate by. Which severall ranges of windoes, or arches, did not so well consist with one great order, which should have had but one aperture in the height, because more ranges of apertures speak severall storys, and single columns but one, so that there was reason to break the orders. But the strickt rule of beauty is not to be taken from them; nor is there any thing exquisite in the proportions, however artists have given themselves the trouble to describe them.

Joseph Addison, from 'Essay on the Pleasures of the Imagination' (1712)

The Spectator, in which this essay was published in serial form in several instalments, was a periodical edited by Richard Steele and Joseph Addison from 1 March 1711 to 6 December 1712. It appeared daily, and was very popular with an emergent middle-class readership. Most of the essays were written by Addison or Steele, but other contributors included Alexander Pope and Lady Mary Wortley Montagu. *The Spectator* was mainly concerned with manners, morals and literature but, as this essay shows, it also played an important role in the dissemination of aesthetic theories outside the treatises and their professional readership.

Further reading: Brewer (1997), pp. 1–201.

[no. 411, 1907 edn, vol. III, p. 276] Our sight is the most perfect and most delightful of all our senses. It fills the Mind with the largest Variety of Ideas, converses with its Objects at the greatest Distance, and continues the longest in Action without being tired or satiated with its proper Enjoyments. The Sense of Feeling can indeed give us a Notion of Extension, Shape, and all other Ideas that enter at the Eye, except Colours; but at the same time it is much streightned and confined in its Operations, to the Number, Bulk, and Distance of its particular Objects. Our Sight seems designed to supply all these Defects, and may be considered as a more delicate and diffusive kind of Touch, that spreads its self over an infinite Multitude of Bodies, comprehends the largest Figures, and brings into our reach some of the most remote Parts of the Universe.

It is this sense which furnishes the Imagination with its Ideas; so that by the Pleasures of the Imagination or Fancy (which I shall use promiscuously)

I here mean such as arise from visible Objects, either when we have them actually in our View, or when we call up their Ideas into our Minds by Paintings, Statues, Descriptions, or any the like Occasion. We cannot indeed have a single Image in the Fancy that did not make its first Entrance through the Sight: but we have the Power of retaining, altering, and compounding those Images, which we have once received, into all the Varieties of Picture and Vision that are most agreeable to the Imagination; for by this Faculty a Man in a Dungeon is capable of entertaining himself with Scenes and Landskips more beautiful than any that can be found in the whole Compass of Nature.

[...] by the Pleasures of the Imagination, I mean only such Pleasures as arise originally from Sight, and [...] I divide these Pleasures into two Kinds: My Design being first of all to discourse of those primary Pleasures of the Imagination, which entirely proceed from such Objects as are before our Eyes; and in the next place to speak of those Secondary Pleasures of the Imagination which flow from the Ideas of visible Objects, when the Objects are not actually before the Eye, but are called up into our Memories, or formed into agreeable Visions of Things that are either Absent or Fictitious. [...]

[no. 412, 1907 edn, vol. III, p. 279] I shall first consider those Pleasures of the Imagination which arise from the actual View and Survey of outward Objects: And these, I think, all proceed from the Sight of what is *Great*, *Uncommon*, or *Beautiful*. There may, indeed, be something so terrible or offensive, that the Horrour or Loathsomeness of an Object may over-bear the Pleasure which results from its *Greatness*, *Novelty*, or *Beauty*; but still there will be such a Mixture of Delight in the very Disgust it gives us, as any of these three Qualifications are most conspicuous and prevailing.

By *Greatness*, I do not only mean the Bulk of any single Object, but the Largeness of a whole View, considered as one entire Piece. Such are the Prospects of an open Champaign Country, a vast uncultivated Desart, of huge Heaps of Mountains, high Rocks and Precipices, or a wide Expanse of Waters, where we are not struck with the Novelty or Beauty of the Sight, but with that rude kind of Magnificence which appears in many of these stupendous Works of Nature. Our Imagination loves to be filled with an Object, or to grasp at any thing that is too big for its Capacity. We are flung into a pleasing Astonishment at such unbounded Views, and feel a delightful Stilness and Amazement in the Soul at the Apprehension of them. [...]

[no. 415, 1907 edn, vol. III, p. 287] Having already shewn how the Fancy is affected by the Works of Nature, and afterwards considered in general both the Works of Nature and of Art, how they mutually assist and compleat each other, in forming such Scenes and Prospects as are most apt to delight the Mind of the Beholder, I shall in this Paper throw together some Reflections on that Particular Art, which has a more immediate Tendency, than any other, to produce those primary Pleasures of the Imagination, which have hitherto been the Subject of this Discourse. The Art I mean is that of Architecture, which I shall consider only with regard to the Light in which the forgoing Speculations have placed it, without entring into those Rules and Maxims which the great Masters of Architecture have laid down, and explained at large in numberless Treatises upon that Subject.

Greatness, in the Works of Architecture, may be considered as relating to the Bulk and Body of the Structure, or to the *Manner* in which it is built. As for the first, we find the Antients, especially among the Eastern Nations of the World, infinitely superior to the Moderns.

Not to mention the Tower of *Babel*, of which an old Author says, there were the Foundations to be seen in his time, which looked like a Spacious Mountain; what could be more noble than the Walls of *Babylon*, its hanging Gardens, and its Temple to *Jupiter Belus*, that rose a Mile high by Eight several Stories, each Story a Furlong in Height, and on the Top of which the *Babylonian* Observatory? [...]

We are obliged to Devotion for the noblest Buildings that have adorned the several Countries of the World. It is this which has set Men at Work on Temples and Publick Places of Worship, not only that they might, by the Magnificence of the Building, invite the Deity to reside within it, but that such stupendous Works might, at the same time, open the Mind to vast Conceptions, and fit to converse with the Divinity of the Place. For every thing that is Majestick imprints an Awfulness and Reverence on the Mind of the Beholder, and strikes in with the Natural Greatness of the Soul.

In the second place we are to consider *Greatness of Manner* in Architecture, which has such force upon the Imagination, that a small Building, where *it* appears, shall give the Mind nobler Ideas than one of twenty times the Bulk, where the Manner is ordinary or little. [...]

Let any one reflect on the Disposition of Mind he finds in himself, at his first Entrance into the *Pantheon* at *Rome*, and how his Imagination is filled with something Great and Amazing; and, at the same time, consider how little, in proportion, he is affected with the Inside of a *Gothick* Cathedral, tho' it be five times larger than the other; which can arise from nothing else but the Greatness of the Manner in the one, and the Meanness in the Other.

[...] Among all the Figures in Architecture, there are none that have a greater Air than the Concave and the Convex, and we find in all the Ancient and Modern Architecture, as well as in the remote Parts of *China*, as in Countries nearer home, that round Pillars and Vaulted Roofs make a great Part of those Buildings which are designed for Pomp and Magnificence. The Reason I take to be, because in these Figures we generally see more of the Body, than in those of other Kinds. There are, indeed, Figures of Bodies, where the Eye may take in two Thirds of the Surface; but as in such Bodies the sight must split upon several Angles, it does not take in one uniform Idea, but several Ideas of the same kind. Look upon the Outside of a Dome, your Eye half surrounds it; look up into the Inside, and at one Glance you have all the Prospect of it; the intire Concavity falls into your Eye at once, the Sight being as the Center that collects and gathers into it the Lines of the whole Circumference: In a Square Pillar, the Sight often takes in but a fourth Part of the Surface, and, in a Square Concave, must move up and down to the different Sides, before it is Master of all the inward Surface. For this Reason, the Fancy is infinitely more struck with the view of the open Air, and Skies, that passes through an Arch, than what comes through a Square, or any other Figure. The Figure of the Rainbow does not contribute less to its Magnificence, than the Colours to its Beauty, as it is very poetically described by the Song of *Sirach*: *Look upon the Rainbow, and praise him that made it; very beautiful it is in its Brightness; it encompasses the Heavens with a glorious Circle, and the Hands of the most High have bended it.*

Having thus spoken of that Greatness which affects the Mind in Architecture, I might next shew the Pleasure that rises in the Imagination from what appears new and beautiful in this Art; but as every Beholder has naturally a greater Taste of these two Perfections in every Building which offers it self to his View, than of that which I have hitherto considered, I shall not trouble my Reader with any Reflections upon it. It is sufficient for my present Purpose, to observe, that there is nothing in this whole Art which pleases the Imagination, but as it is great, Uncommon, or Beautiful.

Nicholas Hawksmoor, from a letter to Lord Carlisle at Castle Howard (7 January 1724)

In 1724 Sir John Vanbrugh and Nicholas Hawksmoor, who had been involved in the design and building of Castle Howard since 1699, each submitted a design for a Temple of the Four Winds in the grounds of the Castle. In this letter Hawksmoor comments on Vanbrugh's design.

Because of its identification of the 'rules of the Ancients' with 'strong reason and good fancy' this passage may be compared to the empiricist position of the Royal Society, and especially of Sir Christopher Wren. The Royal Society was founded in 1660, the year of the restoration of King Charles II to the throne, by Wren and a group of fellow scientists from Oxford. Supported officially by Charles II, its aim was the scientific investigation of nature, based on observation and by means of mathematical reason, to provide practical and reliable knowledge. The Society's project was based on the assumption that this reliable knowledge can only be acquired by means of sense perception. Wren advocated a combination of reason (in particular mathematical reasoning) and experiment as the basis for architectural design. But Hawksmoor's use of the term 'fancy' recalls the terms Thomas Hobbes had used to discuss design, and introduces the elements of imagination and pleasing ornament into the rationalist equation: judgement is needed to give structure and strength to a poem, but fancy is needed to invent ornament (see above, pp. 27–8).

Further reading: Downes (1959), pp. 33–48; Saumarez Smith (1997), pp. 142–6, 163–4.

[...] What Sr. John proposes is very well, and founded upon ye Rules of ye Ancients I mean upon Strong Reason and good fancy, Joyn'd with experience and tryalls, so that we are assured of ye good effect of it, and that's what we mean by following ye Antients, if we contrive or invent otherways, we doe but dress things in masquerade which only pleases the Idle part of mankind, for a short time. [...]

Robert Morris, from *Lectures on Architecture* (1734)

Robert Morris (1703–54) was the son of Thomas Morris, a joiner. He practised as an architect and surveyor, but is chiefly remembered for his prolific Neo-Palladian writings on architecture, in both poetry and prose. The form of his writings is original, but the ideas are not. He drew on a wide variety of sources, ranging from Alberti, Vitruvius and Evelyn (see Chapters 2 and 5, below) to Lord Shaftesbury, Addison (see Chapter 1, above) and above all Alexander Pope. His attempts to unite architecture, poetry and music, which were a continuation of the Renaissance tradition of architectural thought, did not fit in very well in the climate of scientific enquiry of the eighteenth century. No buildings survive that can be attributed to him with any certainty (Harris, 1990; Colvin, 1995).

[p. 47] REGULARITY and Proportion are the fine Parts of *Architecture*, and these are perform'd by stated Rules, handed down to us by the Care and Vigilance of preceding Ages, to whom we owe all our Knowledge, as well Historical as Architectural. I say Buildings are to be perform'd by stated Rules, as the several Parts of Musick in Concert are; in which, if one Instrument is illy tuned, or in a different Key, it immediately creates a Jarring and Discord, which is not to be remedied without setting aside that Instrument, or putting it in a proper Key with the rest: The same Rules perfect *Architecture*, and are essentially necessary in its Performance [...].

[p. 51] As Buildings, by Time, were beautied and regulated under certain Proportions allotted by the Antients, so they were adapted to the Strength requir'd in the Edifice to be erected; and under the Difference of these Proportions of Heights and Distances which the Antients made use of in each *Order*, are still preserv'd all the Beauties contain'd in *Architecture*, and are to be varied as extensively as the Mind can invent, differing only in the Form or *Modus*; as the Multitudes of Tunes are perform'd by only the seven Notes in *Musick*. [...]

[p. 73] NATURE has taught Mankind in *Musick* certain Rules for Proportion of Sounds, so *Architecture* has its Rules dependant on those Proportions, or at least such Proportions which are Arithmetical Harmony; and those I take to be dependant on Nature. The Square in *Geometry*, the Unison or Circle in *Musick*, and the Cube in *Building*, have all an inseparable Proportion; the Parts being equal, and the Sides, and Angles, *&c* give the Eye and Ear an agreeable Pleasure; from hence may likewise be deduc'd the Cube and half, the Double Cube; the *Diapason*, and *Diapenté*, being founded on the same Principles in *Musick*.[44]

James Ralph, from his Preface to *The Builder's Dictionary* (1734)

James Ralph (1705–62) spent his early years in America; he was a friend of Benjamin Franklin, with whom he came to England in 1725, and of Henry Fielding and William Hogarth. He assisted the latter in writing *The Analysis of Beauty*. Ralph was the author of *A Critical Review of the Publick Buildings ... In and About London* of 1734 (see Chapter 5, below). This introductory essay to the anonymous *Builder's Dictionary* (see Figure 1.2) was probably commissioned on the strength of his *Critical Review*, but the orthodox Vitruvian principles of the former are very different from the views Ralph expressed in the latter, such as his criticism of the architect Nicholas Hawksmoor.

The following sentence appeared above the names John James and James Gibbs at the beginning of the *Dictionary*: 'We have perused these Two volumes of the Builder's Dictionary, and do think they contain a great deal of useful Knowledge in the Building Business.'

Further reading: Harris (1990); Russell (1997).

The Preface.

Architecture is one of those Arts which Necessity has made universal: From the Time that Men first felt the Inclemencies of the Seasons, it had its Beginning; and accordingly it has spread wheresoever the Severities of the Climate demanded Shelter or Shade: It is to be traced in the Indian's Hut and the Icelander's Cave; and still shews, in those barbarous parts of the Globe, from what mean Original it rose to its present Glory.

As Distress was the Parent of it, so Convenience was the first Object it regarded: Magnificence and Decoration were the Result of long Refinement, and designed to flatter the Ostentation of the Owners: Politeness is but a more delicate Term for Luxury; and was it not natural for Men to grow wanton with Ease and Affluence, all the Sciences in general had laid inactive, nor ever started into Being.

'Tis easy to conclude from hence, That Convenience should still be the Builder's first View: Every Structure is raised to answer some particular End; and the most obvious and simple Means are always the best to obtain it. When such a Plan as this is uniformly and consistently laid; when all its Uses may be comprehended at a single Glance, and all appear undeniably reasonable and perfect, then the Artist is at Liberty to add Grandeur and Elegancy to Strength and Propriety, and finish the Whole with the full Splendor of Beauty and Grace.

1.2 Frontispiece to *The Builder's Dictionary: Or, Gentleman and Architect's Companion* (London, 1734), I. Devoto artist, Toms engraver.

By this Division of Architecture into Beauty and Use, it will be demonstrable to every Reader, that 'tis partly an Art, and partly a Science; that the first is mechanical, and the last the Result of Genius and superior Understanding: One calls in all the Aid of Fancy and Imagination, grows poetical in Design, and picturesque in Decoration; the other lays down fix'd and stated Rules, proceeds in the same invariable Track of Reasoning, and comes always to the same Conclusions. Hence it happens, that many an excellent Workman has proved himself a mere Mechanick, and many a surprizing Genius, that he was ignorant of the very Principles of the Art he made it his Profession to understand. To make a thorough Master, both must be united; for the Propriety of a Plan is seldom attended to, and seldomer understood; and a glaring Pile of Beauty, without Use, but mocks the Possessor with a Dream of Grandeur he can never enjoy.

After this short introduction, the author proceeds to point out what are the foundations of this noble art, and begins first with arithmetick as the first, as being the Ground-Work of Mensuration, either as Extent or Solidity, as being the Medium of all Calculations, and the only Road to any Degree of practical Knowledge in the Mathematicks [...]. *Geometry* follows in the next place, and is indeed the foundation that all students must build upon, since 'tis impossible to attain to any perfection in *architecture* without it: 'tis *geometry* that lays down all the first principles in building, that adjusts all bearings and proportions, and measures points, angles, and solidities. In short, there is no being perfect in all the parts of *geometry*; and he that is so, tho' he may err in decoration, can never do the same, either in strength or proportion.

Masonry, or the mechanical means of raising perpendiculars, turning arches, erecting bridges, and forming stair-cases, is another branch of this art, and must be understood with great accuracy and readiness; as being the execution of the whole which the student desires to learn.

Levelling and *Hydraulics*, are likewise of great importance to the builder: the first at once enabling him to understand good situations, or amend them if they are otherwise; and the last, of course, directing the conveyance of water, the draining of low grounds, and teaching the whole secrets of collecting reservoirs, or afterwards employing them to the best advantage. In short, on these depend both the necessary use of water for family supply, and also all the beautiful effects that can result from it in gardens, by basons, fountains, cascades, *&c.*

Mechanicks is another essential in this noble art. 'Tis by understanding their power and effect, that such machines are contriv'd, as alone are able to raise up the heavy materials to buildings of any considerable height, or empty waters from a bottom, or drain a level, or force them upwards, as art would direct, or necessity require.

These, with the art of *sketching* and *drawing*, are all the different branches of study which are necessary to form a compleat mechanical architect. But when he is thoroughly initiated in them all, so as not to err, even in principles or practice, if he cannot add as much knowledge more of his own, in their use and application, he will be fit for nothing more than the overseer of a work, or a judge of the mere methods to carry on, and finish the whole.

The Science of Designing is still wanting to form a Great Master, or produce such Plans as would vie with the antient Beauties of Greece and Rome. But if this is not in the Genius, it is never to be learned: To be able to enter into this Secret, the Student must have great natural Parts; a noble and fruitful Imagination, a thorough Insight and Acquaintance with Beauty, and Judgement sedate and cool enough to form a just and delicate Taste. Without Taste, even Genius itself wanders blindfold, and spends itself in vain. Genius is, indeed, the first Quality of the Soul; but Taste must be added, or we shall censure the Wildness, instead of admiring the Beauty; we shall be dissatisfy'd with the Irregularity, instead of being pleased with the Magnificence. But though Genius cannot be learn'd, it may be improv'd: And through the Gift of Designing is born with a Man, it may be methodized by Study and Observation. [...]

Batty Langley, from *Ancient Masonry* (1736)

Batty Langley (1696–1751) was the son of a gardener and seems to have started his career as a landscape gardener. In the 1740s he established a school or academy offering instruction in architecture and drawing. In an advertisement in the architectural periodical *The City and Country Builder's Treasury* of 1740 he offered to make designs for buildings, gardens, parks and hydraulic engines. He also manufactured artificial stone, from which he made statues and ornaments. As a practising architect he was not very successful. This may have prompted him to attempt to make a living by his numerous architectural publications, mainly manuals destined for craftsmen. From these he emerges as a zealous Freemason who was devoted to the education of his brother Masons (*Ancient Masonry* is dedicated to English and French Grand Masters of Freemasonry) and a pioneer of the Rococo. In his articles for the *Grub Street Journal* of 1734 and 1735 he attacked James Ralph's *Critical Review of the Publick Buildings, Statues and Ornaments In and About London and Westminster* (1734; see below, Chapter 5), praising Gothic architecture and the churches of Hawksmoor and criticizing the Italianate, Neo-Palladian architecture introduced by Inigo Jones, Lord Burlington and William Kent. He defended English craftsmen against the monopoly of foreign taste imposed by Burlington's 'Rule of Taste', whose key concepts were reason, common sense and rules derived from classical architecture. The wide range of sources for *Ancient Masonry*, from Hans Vredeman de Vries to James Gibbs, make it one of the most comprehensive English treatises on building (Harris, 1990; Colvin, 1995).

Further reading: Rowan (1975); White (1983); Harris (1990).

[p. 3] The number of books daily publish'd on Architecture, and the little use they are of to Workmen in their Practice, for want of a just Knowledge of those Sciences on which Architecture immediately depend, gives so sensible an Idea of the Advantage a Work of the following Nature would be to all concerned in Building, that a Society (who daily experience and practice the several Arts which lead to a general knowledge of Architecture) have concluded to demonstrate the same, in a plain and easy manner, throughout all its various Parts, for the Use of Artificers in general.

And, as everything which is necessary to make compleat Workmen, and good Architects, will be carefully and ingeniously handled in the following Work, it will contain more knowledge than all the other Books of Architecture. [...]

Learning, in all its Branches and Characters, may be properly said to distinguish us from one another, as well as from the rest of the Animal Creation, more distinctly than Speech: Birds acquire the Faculty of speaking, but it is for the most part misplaced; it is only the retaining Words and Accents, not knowing how to apply them: In short, they may be compar'd to an Engine justly performing its Rotation, and not knowing its own Use: And thus it is with many Workmen, who by Habit and Custom perform divers Operations, but know not the cause or Reasons thereof.

The natural Embellishments of the Mind, by Conversation and Society cultivated and improved, and by a Propensity to Knowledge rectified and regulated, soon acquires the Faculty of Learning; and in whatever Branch of Learning the Mind makes its progress, it attains its desired End. [...]

Learning is necessary for the sure Direction of Affairs in all Parts of human Life, but more particularly in making Laws, distributing Justice, Trade, Traffick, and Commerce; in discerning the Motion of the heavenly Bodies; in Weights, Measures, Travel; in short in every thing which concerns Society to be acquainted with. Without Reason and Wisdom, Laws were not first form'd modell'd and design'd; nor could Justice be impartially distributed. Without Navigation and Geography, Traffick and Commerce could not be; nor could we judge of, nor describe the Motion of the heavenly Bodies, without Astronomy; by Geometry, Weights, Measures, and the Power of Lines are preserved; and indeed we find no one Branch of Learning but is useful in some Part or other of the Oeconomy of human Nature. [...]

I must observe to you, as Buildings are requisite for private Houses, so publick Transactions require much Knowledge in the right Application of our Ideas: And to adapt them justly to the wants and Conveniences, is (tho' seldom regarded) what appears most requisite in our Taste and Executions. Courts, Palaces, Seats of Pleasures, &c. should be gay and airy; on the contrary, Tribunals, Courts of Judicature, Temples, &c. should be grave and solemn, to strike the Beholder with a majestick Awe of the Solidity and serious Purposes of the Design. Seminaries of Literature should have a little more Vivacity and Gaity. Much Temper is required in Productions of this Kind, and much Study necessary, to know where to apply rightly the different Ideas intended to be executed.

A Seat continually exposed to the Violence of the extream Seasons, or on a Hill unguarded by Woods, should have a Mixture of Solidity and Gaity at the same Instant. The Vallies require more Chearfulness, while the shady Rivulet, with the encircling Warmth of chearful Greens, and all the Pleasures of a rural Prospect, should be pleasing and serious, adorn'd with Sculptures and Festoons of the various Products of the Seasons, with an enlivening Variety and Regularity. The silent Gloom of Woods, and the desart and unfrequented Places, among winding Meanders, and a short bounded Prospect, requires most airy and beautiful Productions, mixing with the solemn Gravity of Nature, the most exalted Beauties and Gaiety of Art; such are the different Products which different Situations require, and such are the Necessities which should induce us to apply ourselves to the Study of a Science the most pleasing and various that the Art of human Invention could produce thro' every Age since the Beginning of Time.

As I believe it will be granted that the Ancients had this just Taste of Building peculiar to themselves, so our Endeavours should be used for the attaining those Rules of which the Ancients were possessed; whose Buildings, as well internal as external, so charm'd the Mind, and ravish'd the Eye, that the architects themselves were, by the Vulgar, often thought to be divinely inspired; when, in Fact, the Beauty and Pleasure their Works gave, were only the Effects of a well-chosen Symmetry, connected together according to the harmonick Laws of Proportion, which of necessity naturally produce that Effect upon the Mind thro' the Eye, as the Cords and Discords of Musick, please or displease the Soul thro' the Ear.

Building

Introduction

The term 'architect' was introduced into printed English by John Shute in 1563. Compared to practices on the Continent, this was relatively late, and reflected the continuing strength of the mediaeval organization of architectural practice in Britain. Until the revolution of taste introduced by Lord Burlington in the early decades of the eighteenth century, the architect in the Renaissance sense, that is, as the intellectual author of the design who supervises the work of all the craftsmen involved in its execution but is not himself one of them, was not known in Britain. Instead, building was directed by individual master workmen, mainly masons, bricklayers or carpenters, who had served an apprenticeship of seven years, then worked as journeymen, and finally became master craftsmen. The masters were, at least in London, members of City Companies who continued the tradition of the mediaeval guilds. The City Companies monopolized the building trade until the Great Fire of 1666, when in order to attract a greater work-force Parliament lifted the restrictions against foreigners working in the City. In addition to the knowledge and skills involved in their trade craftsmen possessed some ability to draw as well, and architects acted so frequently as measuring surveyors that in the early eighteenth century the two terms were almost synonymous. But in general the training and equipment of a craftsman was limited to his own craft, and this meant that the master builder of a project would have to subcontract to other craftsmen those parts of the process he could not execute himself.

Master builders provided designs for themselves and for others, but they also took existing structures as their models. The intellectual authorship, and degree of control, by the supervisor of the building was limited as well because highly experienced craftsmen often executed parts of the work without supervision. In Wren's City churches in particular the ceilings, altarpieces, pulpits and other furnishings were often designed and executed by the craftsmen without their submitting a design or model to the Surveyor-General.

All this changed when Lord Burlington and his circle managed to impose Palladianism and its working practices.[1] Here the architect was the sole intellectual author of the design; the craftsmen were merely the hands that served to execute it. As a result there was very little room for creative input by the craftsmen involved. This transformed the practice of building. The master builder was no longer in charge of both the design and the execution of a building; for the former he had to give way to the architect. But in Britain design did not become the absolute monopoly of the architect, because patternbooks by Halfpenny and Langley, and translations of Vignola, Vitruvius and Palladio offered relatively easy access to the new taste in architecture (see their entries in the Bibliography). Many manuals were intended not for architects in the sense of the term that had become accepted in the Renaissance in Italy and France, but for the patron, who often acted as the supervisor of the building process. The manuals were not, as were so many texts from the Continent, concerned with the scientific or artistic status of architecture, but rather with practical advice on how to build in a sound and economic fashion. This may perhaps explain the lack of attention to stylistic matters that is so striking in the texts by Charles L'Estienne and Sir H. Shere included here. On the Continent the authority of the architect as a scholarly professional specialized in an art that was the intellectual equal of painting and sculpture had been based in large part on the efforts of architects and writers such as Alberti, Palladio or Barbaro. By publishing treatises setting out the principles of their art, and showing their closeness to those of the seven liberal arts, they had demonstrated that architecture was a liberal art and not a craft. Their efforts were supported by the foundation of Academies which taught and supervised the visual arts and architecture and gave them a firm theoretical basis. In Britain, however, the introduction of the architect as the authority on building was not the result of such a concerted and sustained intellectual, educational and political effort, but rather the result of changing attitudes among patrons.

The British architect in the Renaissance sense of the word did not evolve from the master builder, but instead was often an outsider, called in by a patron desirous to build in the classical taste he had acquired through his knowledge of classical architecture on the Continent: John Shute and Inigo Jones were painters sent by their aristocratic patrons to learn about the most recent developments in architecture, Sir John Vanbrugh was a soldier and playwright, Sir Christopher Wren a mathematician and Colen Campbell a lawyer. Inigo Jones was the first architect who fulfilled this role, and it was the Stuart Court that provided the demand, the appreciation and the setting for it.

In fact the King's Works or Office of Works provided the organization for British architecture that on the Continent was offered by the Academies. This institution was a department of the royal household, with permanent central offices at Westminster and temporary offices at the site of each of the King's major building enterprises, each of which was headed by a surveyor. The central office was located at or near Scotland Yard from 1530 onwards, and consisted of a surveyor and a comptroller, purveyor, clerks, mason and carpenter. This became the administrative centre through which, from Elizabeth I onwards, royal building projects were executed. During the seventeenth and eighteenth centuries the Office of Works was the most important employer for the architectural profession because of the surveyorships and clerkships it offered, and it served as a forum for architectural training. Outside it, there was little continuity in experience or teaching; the system of pupillage was only introduced in the mid-eighteenth century, when James Paine (1717–89) and Sir Robert Taylor (1714–88) started to take pupils on a regular basis. Indeed, before the foundation of the Royal Academy of Arts in 1768, there were few opportunities for the study of architectural designs, or for architects to meet and socialize. Some architects, including Wren, William Kent and William Talman, were members of the Society of Virtuosi of St Luke, a painters' club; and they were well represented in the Society of Antiquaries and the Royal Society.

The extracts included in this chapter reflect the organization of building in Britain, its practical aspects, the changing role of the architect and the political constraints on it. Shute bases his claims for architecture as a liberal art on the traditional arguments taken from Vitruvius that had by then become traditional on the Continent; John Webb, in writing what is probably the first biography of an English architect, presents Inigo Jones as a well-educated gentleman and a courtier, the equal of poets, who saw the classical heritage in Italy and 'the politer parts of Europe' with his own eyes, and became the English Vitruvius; the extract from Stephen Primatt shows how closely the activities of design, planning and surveying had become related; Sir Roger Pratt gives an insider's account of what to look for in a good architect. The passage from the English translation of Andrea Pozzo's *Prospettiva*, with its formal approval by Wren, Vanbrugh and Hawksmoor, is a testimony to the evolution of the architect from the master builder to the designer, the *auctor intellectualis* of the building, whose designs, made with the help of perspective, are the blueprint for the actual work; the texts by Andrew Boorde, L'Estienne and Shere offer advice to the patron on the practical foundations of architecture. Also included here is John Evelyn's proposed plan for the rebuilding of London after the Great Fire on the pattern of Italian cities.

Further reading:
Primary sources: John Evelyn, 'Account of Architects' (1664); Roger North, *Of Building*; William Halfpenny, *The Art of Sound Building* (1725); James Gibbs, *Rules for Drawing the several Parts of Architecture* (1732); Knowles and Pitt, *History of Building Regulations* (1972), pp. 12–32.

Secondary literature: Colvin (1993); Crinson and Lubbock (1994), pp. 7–37; Colvin (1995), pp. 21–45.

Andrew Boorde, from *The Boke for to Lerne a Man to be Wyse in Buyldyng* (1540)

Andrew Boorde (or Borde), *c.* 1490–1549, was a cleric who became a physician through study and travel. Before 1528, when he set out to travel extensively around Europe, he spent many years teaching at Charterhouse in London, one of the first schools in England to teach the classical curriculum. The *Boke for to Lerne a Man to be Wyse in Buyldyng* is in fact the first part, published separately, of his *Dyetary of Helth,* which was written during his stay at the University of Montpellier in the early 1540s. The complete *Dyetary* is dedicated to the Duke of Norfolk whom Boorde had attended as a physician in 1530; at the time Boorde was writing the chapters on house building the Duke was engaged in building new town houses in Norwich. It was reprinted several times during the sixteenth century. The chapters on building reflect the best of contemporary English practice. They are based on practical concerns rather than theoretical architecture; their ultimate aim is one of promoting good health rather than beauty, suggesting the existence of a tradition of practical advice in which Vitruvius can be used as one authority among others. These chapters are the most substantial piece of writing on architecture in English before John Shute's *First and Chief Groundes* of 1563 (*DNB* Howard, 1988).

Further reading: Boorde, *Thoughts Before Building*; Howard (1988).

[aiir] The fyrste chapter dothe shewe where a man shulde buylde or set his howse or place for the helth of his body.

A man of honoure, or worshyp, or other estate, the whiche dothe pretende, to buylde a howse or any mansyon place, to inhabyte hymselfe: Or els doth pretende to alter his howse, or to alter olde buyldynge in to comodyous and pleasaunt buyldyng, not onely for his owne proper commodyte, welth and helth, But also for other men, the whiche wyll resorte to hym, hauynge also a respect to his posteryte. Fyrste it is necessary and expedyent for hym to take hede what connseyll god dyd gyve to Abraham, and after that to take hede what connsell God dyd gyve to Movses, and to hys chyldren of Israell, as it appereth in the .viii.chapter of Exodi And the.xx chapter of Numeri. And the vi. Chapter of Deutronomii. And also in the Boke of Leuites, sayeng fyrst to Abraham. Go thou forth of thy countre, & from thy cognacion or kynred, and come thou in to ye countre, the which I wyl shewe to the[e] a countre, abundyng & plentyful of milke & hony. here is to be noted that where there is plentye of mylke, there is plentye of pasture, and no skarsyte of water. And where there is plentye of hony, there is no skarsyte, but plentyfulnes of wodes. For there be moo bees in woddes, and so consequently abundauce of hony, than there be bees or hony, or wax in the hyves in gardynes, or orchardes. Wherfor it apereth that whosoever that wyl buylde a ma[n]syon place or howse, he must sytuat and set it there where he must be sure to have both water and wod, except for pleasure, he wyl buylde a howse in or by some cytie or great towne, the whiche be not destytude of such comodytes. But he the whiche wyll dwell at pleasure, and for profyte and helthe of his body, he must dwell at elbowe rome hauynge water and wod anexed to his place or howse. For yf he Be destytuted of any of the pryncipalles, that is to saye, fyrste of water for to wasshe and to wrynge, to bake and to brewe, and dyvers other for petyll the which myght fall By fyre it were a great discomodyous thynge. And better it were to lacke wodde, than to lacke water, ye premysses cosyderyd althoughe that wod is a necessary thynge not onely for fewell, but also for other urgent causes specyallye consernynge buyldyne and reperacyons.

The seconde chapter, doth shewe a man, showe he shulde buylde his howse or Mansyon, that the prospecte be fayre, and good for the conseruacion of helthe.

After that a man haue chosen a conuenyent soyle and place accordynge to his mynde and purpose to buylde his howse or mansyon on he must haue a fore cast in his mynde, that the propecte to and fro the place, be pleasaunt, fayre, and good to the iye, to behold the woddes, the waters, the feldes, the vales, the hylles, & the playne grounde. And that euery thynge be desent and fayre to the iye not onely within the presynct of the place apoynted to buylde a mansyon or a howse to the comodyties about it, but also it may be placable to the iyes of all men to se and to beholde whan they be a good dystaunce of from the place, that it doth stande comodyously. For the comodyous buyldynge of a place doth not onely satyssfye the mynde of the inhabytour, but also it doth co[m]forte and reioyseth a mannes harte to se it, specyally the pulcruse[2] prospecte. For my conceyte is such that I had rather not to buylde a masyon or howse, than to buylde one without a good prospecte I[n] it to it, & from it. For & the iye be not satysfyed, the mynde can not be cotended, the harte can not be pleased, yf the herte and mynde be not pleased nature doth abhorre. And yf nature do abhorre, mortyfycacion of the vytall and anymall and spyrytuall powers do consequently folowe.

Leonard Digges, from *A Boke named Tectonicon* (1556)

Leonard Digges (or Digge) was a landed gentleman of Barham in east Kent; he is best known as the inventor of the earliest theodolite. John Dee (see above, Chapter 1) was a close friend and taught mathematics to Digges's son Thomas, who became very distinguished in that field. The *Tectonicon* was the first treatise on surveying written in English for artisans; it was reprinted very often and remained the most important source of information about measuring until the Fire of London (Harris, 1990).

Further reading: Taylor (1954), p. 166.

L. D. vnto the Reader.

Although (gentle Reader) manye excellent in Geometry, vpon infallyble grounds haue put forth diuerse most certaine and sufficient rules, touching the measuringe of all maner Superfiecis: yet in that the arte of numbringe hath bene required yea, chiefely those rules hid, and as it were locked vp in straunge tongues (they do profite, or haue furdered very lytle the most parte: certes nothing at all, the Landemeater, Carpenter, Mason, wanting the aforesaide) for their sakes I am here prouoked not to hide, but to open, and so encrease the talent which I haue receyued, yea, to publishe in this our tongue very shortlye, if God geue life, a volume contayninge the flowers of the Science Mathematicall, largely applyed to our outward practise, profitablye pleasaunte to all maner men of this Realme. In the meane time I shall desire the Artificers abouenamed to be contented with this little Booke, a tast of my good will towards them, which I wishe euen so to forder the readers, as I know it sufficient for the true measuringe and reedy accompt of all manner lande Tymber, Stone, Borde, Glasse, Pavement &c.

Here mine aduise shalbe to these Artificers that will profite in this, or any of my bookes, now published, or that hereafter shalbe, first confusely to reade them thorow, then with more iudgement. Read at the thirde reading wittelye to practice. So fewe things shalbe vnknowen. Note, oft diligent reading, ioyned wyth ingeniouse practise, causeth profitable laboure.

Thus most hartely farewell (louinge Reader) to whom I wishe myselfe present to further thy desire and practise in these.

The pleasant profite, or content of this litleboke.
And in what it exceedeth all other published.

Other Bookes tofore put forth in o[u]r Englishe tongue contayned onely the bare measuringe of Lande, Timber, and Borde, howe agreable in al places to the rules of Geometry, let the learned iudge. Here (gentle Reader) thou shalt plainly perceiue throwe diligente reading, how to measure truly and very spedely all maner Land, Timber, Stone, Steples, Pillers, Globs, Bord, Glasse, Pauement, &c. without trouble, not payned with many rules, or obscure termes. Nor yet with the multitude of tables, as here before haue bene: in whiche not a fewe errours were committed: for that cause no iust accompt might any way be had: Further ye shal by this Booke vnderstand the whole making and comlye handelinge of the Carpenters Ruler, with the true measure &c. And his vse appointed to the readye measuringe of all kind of Timber, Stone, Borde &c. Also the leauelinge of groundes, taking of Heightes, is pleasauntly and diuersly practised by the ruler. Ye haue here not the common but the rare vse of the Squir applied to Heights, Lengthes, &c. and to the findinge of the iust houre of the day diuers wayes: throughe the ayde of pleasaunt tables, newly adioyned to my generall Prognostication, by the which the proportion of things direct or squirewise standing, are by their shadowes knowen. [...]

John Shute, from *The First and Chiefe Groundes of Architecture* (1563)

The writer and painter John Shute (d. 1563) was the author of the first treatise in English on classical architecture. It was published in 1563 and dedicated to Elizabeth I. Almost all we know about the book, its author and its background is derived from this dedication. Shute visited Italy in 1550, sent there by John Dudley, 1st Duke of Northumberland, 'to confer with the doings of ye skilful maisters in architectur, & also to view such auncient Monuments hereof as are yet extant'. *The First and Chiefe Groundes* was possibly intended as the first part of a much more ambitious, comprehensive theoretical treatise on architecture. These ambitions were probably cut short by the execution of his patron for conspiring against Mary Tudor. It is mainly based on Vitruvius and Serlio. Although Shute described himself as a 'Paynter and Archytecte' there is no evidence to suggest that he had been active as an architect, or had first-hand knowledge of the practical aspects of building. His book was in great demand, which is unsurprising as there was nothing available in English on proportion or on classical architecture in general until the appearance of Haydocke's translation of Lomazzo in 1598 (see Chapter 1, above) and of Hans Blum's *Booke of Five Collumnes* in English in 1608. Nevertheless only ten copies, all of the original edition, are known. In it, the words 'architect' and 'architecture' appear for the first time in printed English. Like Dee's 'Mathematical Preface' (see Chapter 1, above), the passage reprinted here is very much based on the catalogue of knowledge the qualified architect should possess that is listed in Vitruvius I.i (Harris, 1990).

Further reading: Summerson (1983), p. 56; Howard (1988) and (1990); Harris (1990).

What the Office and Duetie is of him that wyll be a Perfecte Architecte or Mayster of buyldings.

Architectur (by the common consent of many notable men) as Cesarius[3] sayth, ys of all artes, the most noble and excellent, Contayning in it sundrie sciences and knowlaiges wherwyth it is furnished and adourned, as full well Vitruvius doth affyrme and declare by his writinge. For saith he, an Architecte must be sharpe of understandinge and both quicke and apte to conceive the trewe instructions and meaninges of them that have written therof: and must also be a perfect distributor of the great misteries, that he hath preceved and experymented, that playnlye and briefly he maye discusse and open demonstrations of that which shalbe done or mete to those persones, that shalbe the fownders of any noble workes. Werefore he ought to be a very good Grammarian, then to have experte knowladg in drawing and protracting the thinge, which he hath conceyved, Nexte he must have a good sight in Geometrie, Consequently in Opticke and in such lyke sciences he must have good perceverance. Likewise in Arithmeticke, he must also besides all thise ben [be in] Philosophie, very experte. The causes why al thise science before names, ought to be in him that is a parfaict Architect and maister of buildinges be of Vitruvius in this sorte rehersed. If he have (saith he) learninge he shall strengthen his memory with all written bookes, and throughe drawing utter his fantasie and shewe the trike or fascion of the thing that he goeth about to make. And Geometrie teacheth us the order of rules, Compasses, Squiers, Quadrangles, and Iuste waterlevels with manie other knowlaiges that procedeth thereof as Euclide, and other authors & also Sebastian Serli,[4] in his first Chapter reherseth, Opticke sheweth us howe and by what meanes the lightes should be set into the House, And howe they should be brought from place to place, as to serve the hole house, and every place therein, which Optica, is properly called perspective, and is of a furder speculation, then therein can or nedeth to be exprest: which of Sebastian Serlius, in his second book first second and thirde Chapiter is partely declared. Arithmeticke, teacheth us innumerable poinctes most necessarily required to the parfaicte knowlaidge of this art, for without yt, we can neither know or yet discusse the measures and harde sentences or questions of Symetrie, neither howe to accompte the Coste and charges of our labores. An Architect must also have a knowlaige in hystories, There be moreover multitude of causes in buildinges, and very many ornatures and garnishinges of which he must nedes geve answere, from whence they come, and for what purpose they are made, As for an example, If a maister workman should make ymages, figures like women, clothed and garnished after a beautifull soarte, which are named Cariatides, and set them in his worke for pillers and make over their heade Mutilos, and Coronas, yf yt were demaunded of him to what purpose those ymages wer made, then he shuld answer that Caria, a towne in Peloponeso, trayterously conspired with the Persians, against the Grekes: But the grekes getting the victorie over their enemies, agreed with one accord, and beseiged Caria, and wan the citie, killed the men and toke the women, careing them as bond women not suffering them to put of their Ryche ornamentes and Iewells to the intent, that the showe of their triumphe, myghte be thereby the more glorious. So they subdued, weare brought into bondage.[5]

For this cause and other suche lyke, the chief maisters of Architecture made in their common places and pallaces such women to beare up the burthen of their buildinges, the whiche was a remembraunce and memorial of their punishmentes for their mallice against the Grekes, sustained by the Cariatides, that is to saye, by the women of Caria. [...] Many suche Histories an Architecte, ought of necessitye to know.

Richard More, from *The Carpenters Rule* (1602)

Very little is known about Richard More (fl. 1602–12). His book is the second on the subject, and was published by the publisher who had in 1599 taken over publication of Digges's very successful *Tectonicon* (see above, this chapter) (Harris, 1990).

Further reading: Taylor (1954), p. 50.

To the Worshipful, The Master, Wardens, and Assistants of the Company of Carpenters of the Citie of London: And to all other the curteous Readers.

After I had long considered, and that not without some griefe, the great losse that commeth to those of my Companie and others, by errors ordinarily committed in measuring of timber; I did often thinke with my selfe what might be the readiest course to redresse them. One while I thought to have declared to you the Master and Wardens, what errors I had observed in our ordinarie measure, and so to have desired you in all charity to have provided a remedie. But when I perceived, that custome had caused error to be received as a truth, and that therefore men would not forsake them, unlesse, they were plainly convinced to have erred: And when I did also see, that most men are very ignorant in true measure, though they seeme and professe to know much therein; and did also remember that not only Carpenters in this Citie doe in this sort erre, bot also Carpenters elsewhere, as also Shipwrights & others, and that throughout the whole land, for the most part: then this course seemed to me to be too private, and such as was like to doe but little good. The best course that I could thinke upon, was, to publish some booke, wherein not only true measure should be set downe, but also the common errors plainly laid open to the capacitie of the simplest, that so all men might take knowledge thereof.

My selfe I knew to be very unfit for this worke, both because of mine inabilitie, as also by reason of some exceptions that divers might take against me, to their owne hindrance and my discouragement. But when I saw none addressed hereunto, then remembring the saying of a Heathen, that men are not borne for themselves, but for their Countrey I did set aside all lets,[6] and both boldly and rudely have put out this my simple booke, in manner as you see.

The booke I have divided into three parts. In the first part I declare the errors most commonly committed, and taken for truth, in measuring of timber. In the second part I shew how ordinarie timber may be measured, both by sundrie plaine waies, as also by waies more artificiall. And in the third part I shew, how extraordinarie timber and sollid formes may be measured.

The errors ordinarily committed in measuring timber, are many. But of them all, especially two, bringeth losse to the buyer. The first is by buying of waynie[7] timber and measuring it as square. The other is by taking halfe the breadth and thickness of a peece being added together for the square thereof.

These errors are such, as bring apparent dammage: and therefore they are not to be respected lightly. I would they might not bee said to be a great cause, if not of the overthrow, yet of the impairing of some mens estates. [...]

[p. a4recto] I have heard some men wish, that wee had an act of Parliament procured for redresse of false measure. But truly that seemeth to be the law of our land alreadie, though not the statute law: for the law intendeth that the buyer should have that which he buyeth. And when we buy a load of timber, doe we not intend that we have bought 50. Foote of sollid timber, every foot being full 12.inches every way, that is, in length, breadth, & thicknes? Why then may we not require so much for a loade, and why is not the seller bound to deliver it? [...] Therefore let us either have iust measure, if we buy by measure; or els let us buy it by gesse. For it is a shame to pretend to measure truly, and yet doe nothing lesse.

If any man of knowledge shall except against me, for my rude writing and grosse demonstration: I pray them to understand, that I writ not for them, but for the simple; and therefore I demonstrate grossely, not being well able to doe better: Also, that I am not a scholler but a Carpenter, and therefore could not write but rudely. Unto such also I doe further say, that my desire is, that they would take knowledge, that this hath been one cause of my writing, even to provoke them (seeing our present error and losse, with which peradventure they were not so well acquainted as my selfe) to take some paines to reforme the same, in better sort then either I have or can doe.

Charles l'Estienne [Stevens], from *Maison Rustique*, trans. Richard Surflet (1606)

Charles l'Estienne or Estienne (*c.* 1504–64) was a member of an important French family of humanists and printers/publishers. He studied classics, botany and medicine in Paris, and wrote and published a number of dictionaries and grammars, as well as works on medicine, botany and agriculture. *Praedium Rusticum* (1554) was translated into French by his son-in-law Jean Liebault (1534–96), who was a physician and agriculturist. He added significantly to his translation, which was published in 1564 as *L'Agriculture ou la maison rustique*. This version was a great success. It remained in print until the end of the eighteenth century, and was translated into English, German and Dutch.

The book is a very extensive discussion of all aspects of farming, from building or 'good ordering of a Husbandsmans house or Countrey Farme', to the motions of the sun and moon, cures of man and beast, dress, how to plant or make gardens, and 'a brief discourse of the nature, maner of taking and feeding of the nightingale, Linnet, Goldfinch [...] and other such singing and melodious beasts'. The treatment of all these subjects is structured along the lines suggested by handbooks on memotechnics or arts of memory (see Chapter 1, above): the reader is asked to imagine a country farm in the mind's eye and to follow, with the author, the process of designing, building and taking care of it.

Further reading: Grente (1951), entry on Estienne; Giraud and Jung (1972), p. 310; Howard (1987).

The Second Chapter. *A briefe shew of that which shall more largely be described in that which followeth*

[p. 2] The better to helpe the memorie, and as it were by the way of pointing out of our French husbandrie, I will propound and set before you a champion place seated in such a coast or corner as you may finde, not as you could chuse, and there we will prepare without extraordinarie costs or charges, a house with all such appurtinances (or verie neere such) as are fit and requisite for our time [...].

At the one side of this house, euen iust in the place whereupon the sunne riseth, and in one part thereof we will place the houshold garden which neere vnto the borders of his quicke ser hedge shall containe a frame or railes in forme of an Arbor for vines to runne vpon for the furnishing of our houshold store with Veriuce[8] [...]. In the other part we shall make a garden for flowers and sweete smels [...].

Next to our gardens we must dresse some well defenced piece of ground or green plot for fruits [...].

The fifth Chapter. *The building and inclosing of our countrie farme.*

[p. 18] Peace being purchased, then builde thine house, said the wise and prudent householder; and the author of the Latine Georgickes[9] doth highly prize and valew those great farmes and houses, whose appurtenances and expences are great: but he counsaileth men to vndertake and deale with so little, as he knoweth well to do. For as great cages make the birdes neuer a whit the better, euen so it is not so safe and sure a course to have a costly and large building vpon the ground, neither yet to haue so faire and large fieldes, neither yet so great quantitie of groundes, as that they must be either all ill husbanded, or else if for the carefull tilling of one part of them, all the rest be left & let goe vntilled, as neither to couet greedily, or aspire to possesse other great & stately farmes, when he is not able to and till that which he hath already in possession [...].

Better therefore is a small house of good stuffe, not sumptuous, well seated and well fitted (but let it haue of euerie thing a little) than so costly a place and of such large roomes, as that eitherr they become enuied of their superiours for it, or else at length causeth the master to sell it againe [...].

[p. 19] The placing of such building as is made, is most fit to be on the edge of some great hill, vpon some small hill, or the top of the hill, if the countrie bee tempestuous and full of mountaines: for by this meanes he shall reape the libertie of the aire and a goodly prospect, he shall be safe from the annoyances of foggie mistes, he shall not be opprest with cold in winter by reason of ice, nor euer hot in sommer, and the water and floods which runne downe from the top of the hills shall not threaten, much less doe harme vnto the foundation of his dwelling place, as also he shall not bee too much subiect to the windes and raines of the whole yeere: he shall procure his principall lights to stand vpon the sunne-rising in the moneths of March and September: for the windes blowing from those quartes are drie, more hot then cold, but verie wholesome, as well for the bodie as for the spirit of man; and the sunne which commeth to enter betimes in the morning into the house, doth diminish and waste the darkenes and grosnes of the aire: adde further, that looke by how much his house shall be set vpon the saide eastern point, by so much the more easily it will be able to receiue that winde in sommer, and bee less beaten in winter with frosts. [...]

[p. 20] And although that euerie one build after his owne humour, yet the cause should so stand as that reason should rule euermore: & surelie such a man should be esteemed but of a slender iugment, which having a place and commodities belonging thereto, did not fit things in such sort, as that on one side of his chamber he haue a light open vppon the court and forepart of his farme by which they must enter that come to it, and another open vppon his gardens and principal grounds. Wherefore that he may know the more easily to prepare his buildings as it were anew, or else repaire it after his owne fansie, it will be meete and conuenient for him to doe in manner as followeth.

Draw a great court and wide, and that verie square every way, in the middest thereof cause to be cast two fishponds at the least, one for geese, duckes and other cattell: the other two to water, steepe or soften Lupines, Osiers, Roddes and such other thinges, as also for the rotting of your doung: and somewhat more to the further side, a well with two or three troughes of hewen stone to water your cattell and poultrie at, if you haue not the benefite of a running water or some neare riuer either great or small. [...]

[p. 21] This court containing two acres square shalbe compassed in with a wal of eighteene inches thicke, and tenne foot high from the ground, for the resting of your buildings vpon that are within: and to meete with the danger threatned by theeves, and ruynes procured by raine, it shalbe strenthened with chaines on those sides which lye next vnto waies, as also with good rafters, according to the greatness of the commodity of your place and other stuffe.

In the midst of the walle, and in the forepart, which is the part lying vpon the sun-set, you shall make your gates and their arch [...].

The farmers lodge shall be built neere to the side of the porch vpon the left hand, and shall haue the daylight coming in vpon the side toward the street, westward; notwithstanding that his windowes shall lie vpon that side of the court which is Estward. His kitchin shall be raised two or three steppes aboue the ground, to the end it may be freed of the moisture wherwith the court aboundeth in winter: it must also be high built & great, to the end that the floore lying next aboue may not be so subiect to the danger of the fire, and to the end that all his frindes and seruants may at all time easilie bestow themselues therein; the ouen shalbe set without the roome hauing the mouth in the inner side of the chimney of the said kitchin, and lower then the mantle-tree, not far aboue the hearth.

At the entrance of the said kitchin and in such place thereof as shalbe least subiect to the sun and most coole, you shall haue a dairie-house or small vaulted roome paued, and lying slope-wise and with a gutter, to serue for the huswifes dairie, and therein shee shall doe all her businesse about making of butter and cheese, and the said gutter or sinke shall serue for the auoiding and conueying of all such washingsas she is to make about her milke vessels. On the other side of the said kitchin she shal haue the like house or office or vaulted room, which shal also be for the huswifes vse and serue for a spence, to keepe her provision of victuals in: and vnderneath this a little cellar, and the place for the coming out shall be in steede of an vpright table, set as you go into the kitchen.

On the other side of the kitchin shall be the farmers bed-roome, and one other ioyning to it for his maide seruants and children, and a third ioyning close vnto it, for to keepe foule linnen. To the wals of which roome you shall goe forward to ioine a fourth which shalbe sufficient large, and the doore to goe into it shall stand in the court without, and it shall serue for sewell, working tooles, and other necessarie things. And the vpper part or loft of this roome shall serue for garners to lay fruits, al manner of pulse, corne, hearbes, and rootes in, that are to be kept. [...]

In the place right ouer the porch of the farme, shall open the doore of your owne house, which by a staire of eight steps at the most, shall bring you to the first storie of the same: the entrie whereinto shall be like vnto a plaine vacant alley of an indifferent widenes, with an outcast at the further end, vpon the garden, and that with a descent of a like paire of staires vnto those at the entrance. Vpon the right hand of this entrie shalbe your kitchin, storehouse, buttery, and a place of recourse or lodging for two or three seruing men. Betwixt which kitchin and butterie, there shall be a winding staire, which shall haue his foote into the kitchin and butterie, and thereby you shall go vp to the corne loftes there aboue: neere vnto your kitchin you shall make roomes to stampe and presse your grapes in. The first storie shall be of such length and bredth as your appointed platforme laieth out vnto you, borne vpon a raised vault from the ground, well staied vpon bearing pillars, and furnished with casements to take the aire at, vpon both sides, and that to the ende that you may haue an vnderstorie of like length and bredth to that aboue, which shall be a half-cellar, and a halfe-vault, which beside that it will preserue your lodging from earthquakes, will also serue you to couch your wines and cidres in, without any fear of rotting the hoopes, as also to hang your bacon and other powdred prouision, your oyles, candles, yea & your wood also: and your fruits likewise during the frost. Your lodging or mansion shall haue no more then this one storie, aboue which you shall raise no other saue onely your garners and galleries, keeping your house thereby of a lower pitch: and so lesse subiect to the rage of the windes, which will saue you a great deale of charges, when as you shall not be forced to vse the helping hand of tylers euery howre. Vpon the left hande of the saide ally or entrie shalbe your hall, through which you shall passe into your chamber, and out of your chamber into your wardrobe and inner chamber: and at the end heereof, if the bodie of your house shall haue compassed in place inough, you shall make a chamber to lodge strangers the way into, as also out of which, shall be by a turning staire on that side toward the court, that so such strangers may be at their libertie, not molesting or trobling you by their passing in or out: and this if so be that your good liking and inclination mooue you not rather to build for the entertaining of your friends and other strangers on the other side of your hall. You shall make your fairest lightes and frames towards the east vpon your garden, reseruing onely halfe windowes for the side lying vpon your court, seeing they serue for no other thing, but that you may hauve an eie vpon your folke, and to see who be commers and goers to your lodging, and at the end of euery such little chamber you shall make a priuie, for the necessarie vse of euerie of the two saide bodies of the house. Whatsoeuer roome shall be ouer head or aboue your alleyes, hall, chamber, wardrobe, and chamber for strangers, shall be for garners, that so you may lay apart and by it selfe, your Rie, Wheate, Pulse, and fruits and cast aside your foule linnen, and they shall all of them haue prettie windowes vpon the north side, for that quarter is most coole, and least moist: which two things are of great force long to preserue and keepe graine. At the end of your roomes for the treading and pressing of your grapes, you shall set vp your hen-house, and roomes for other fowles, fashioned fowre square like a towre, but yet more long then wide or broade, in such sort as that the lowest roome shall serue for water fowles, as for geese and duks by themselues; and the vpper for those of the yeard, together with their pearches and baskets to laie in: and you must make vnder the hen-loft, some prepared rome for turkie chickins and turkie cockes: and vpon high vnder the floore that is ouer them, you shall continue a close roome after the fashon of a lettuce therein to keepe your feasants. As for your peacockes you shall giue them libertie to roust euerie where. Neere vnto the same place you shall make your ground Doue-house (if the lawe will permit you such a one) in fashion like a round turret in the midst of your court. [...]

[p. 26] Notwithstanding all which, it my meaning is that your cost and course in building should be according to the reuenues of the grounds or value of the profits, and that (as saith *Cato*)[10] the dwelling house be not set after seeking of groundes, nor groundes caused to goe seeke houses and roomes: for great plots of building and inclosure of pleasure, cost much to build and maintaine: and buildings which are lesse then were requisite for the profits of the grounds, are a great cause of much losse in the fruites of the same.

David Papillon, from *A Practicall Abstract of the Arts of Fortification and Assailing* (1645)

David Papillon (1581–1655?) was an architect and military engineer who was born in France into a Huguenot family. He was educated in England, where he arrived in 1588. He had a flourishing career as an architect and military engineer and bought an estate in Leicestershire, where he built Papillon Hall. He fortified Gloucester for Parliament in 1646. He also wrote a moral and religious essay called *The Vanity of the Lives and Passions of Men* (London, 1651), and left in manuscript a philosophical essay on government: *Several Political and Military Observations. A Practicall Abstract* was dedicated to Sir Thomas Fairfax, who had been made commander of Parliament's army in January 1645 (*DNB*).

To the Reader

[...] these motives following, have therefore induced me to publish this Abstract.

1 To procure the common safetie.

2 To rectifie the deformities of our Fortifications.

3 To enlighten the meanest capacities, that delight in the practice of these Arts.

For the first, it is certaine and known to all men, that the insufficiencie of the works of our Garrisons, hath been the secondarie cause, that divers of them have been lost suddenly, and their Inhabitants brough to penurie. To prevent this evill for the future, I propose to our Counties foure different methods of Fortifications, that they may make choyse of the most sutible to their meanes and abilities, assuring them that the meanest of these foure Methods is stronger and safer than their Mounts[11] and winding Angles; so they observe the dimensions described here for everie one of them.

For the second, the deformitie of our Works is so great, and the errours in the setting out of them so grosse, that they serve only as an object of derision to Forrainers that see them: And these errours proceed from a self-conceitednesse inherent in some men of these dayes, that presume to have skill in those things, in which they have no skill at all: for the most mechanicall Artificers and Shop-keepers will be meddling with the spirituall Function, and controll Enginiers. And some Divines, in stead to feed their flocks, do take upon them to be Sub-Committees of the fortifications of a Garrison. And these disorders are permitted by the over-frugalitie of some Committees, to save an Enginiers pay: a destructive frugalitie to themselves, and to a whole Countie, as some have found by lamentable experience. Now to avoyd these errours for the time to come, I have in this Abstract set downe (without reservation) the proportions and dimensions they are to observe, and from whence they are to draw the Lines of their Flanks, and of their Line of defence to be convenient for the Cannon and the Musket-shot, without which observations no Fortification can be good, or serveable.

For the third, the Theoreticall writings of Mr. *Ward*, Mr. *Chrisso*, Mr. *Norwood*,[12] and of the Author of the *Enchyridion*,[13] have rather encreased the ignorance of meane capacities, then their knowledge in the practice of these Arts: For I have conversed with some, that had all their rules upon their finger's ends, that could not set out a Superficie in the field to any purpose, and that is the reason why I write more plainly then they; or that I should otherwise have done, if it had not been to enlighten the inexact capacities, that delight in the practice of these noble Arts. Therefore if these Essiyes [essays] of mine may any way be profitable to thee, I shall attaine to my wished end: If not, accept how ever my good will, since I can neither offer nor give more then I have received from above. And so committing thee to the gracious protection of God, I desire to rest Thy servant in the Lord David Papillon. From London the first of January, 1645.

Chapter IIII. Of the true use of the Art of Fortification

This Art was invented at the first, to preserve a handfull of men against the oppression and cruelty of a multitude; for according to the rules of it, a Garison Town is not sufficiently fortified, except one hundred men within it, can oppose a thousand assailants without [...]; but it is with this caution, that the place besieged be provided with a competent number of men, ordnance, ammunition, arms, victuals, and a Magazine furnished with all manner of fire-works, morter-pieces, engines of warre, ladders and pioneer's tools [...].

2. It was invented to preserve a small Army in the field, against a great and powerfull army, or of an army against three armies. [...] But we have shamefully been inforced sundry times to raise our sieges for want of an intrenched Camp, as at *Newark*, *Dudley Castle*, *Pomfret-Castle*, *Banbury-Castle*, and *Dennington-Castle*,[14] and in all these by an handfull of men; whereas if we had been in an intrenched Camp, an Army six times as great could not have forced us to a retreat. Therefore to besiege Towns or Castles of any moment, without an intrenched Camp, except we come to a generall and furious storme, the next day after our Army hath faced the same, it is properly to spin out this war wittingly; and for to receive rather an affront, then to obtaine a victorie, or honour and reputation.

3. It was invented to erect strong holds upon the Frontiers of a State or Kingdome, to prevent the incursions of a forraine Enemy, that might with a

great Army, come like a roaring floud, that throwes downe all the river banks, into the verie heart of a Kingdome, without opposition, and by meere activitie conquering the same [...].

4. It was invented to preserve mens habitations, and the Suburbs of Corporations, and not for to burne, or pull them downe, as many of our Enginiers have done in these dayes, to their shame and guilt of conscience. For if an Enginier, to comply with those in authoritie, or with the selfe-conceited men of a garrison, Assent to pull downe Suburbs, or small Hamlets that are joyned to their Corporations, except they are suddenly and certainly in danger of a Siege, it argues that hee is either unskilfull in his profession, or voyd of all Christian charitie, and naturall humanitie; for by the experience of his Art, or alteration of his method of Fortification, he may preserve these Suburbs or Hamlets, to the great advantage of the Town; or of another Fortification, and so dispose of his works, that he may secure them, and yet the Corporation shall rather need fewer men to man their works, then it would require when these Hamlets are pulled downe.

5. And lastly, it was invented to fortifie some places of refuge in the time of a Civill War, that a whole Countie be not ruinated by a roving and plundering Army: But in this, the Committees of such Counties are to be verie cautious in their election of a seat, for all the head-Towns of Counties are not convenient to erect Garrisons [...] all seats of Garrisons, if they may be found, are to be as neare the middle of the Countie as may be, that they may the sooner releeve all the parts of the Countie: And that by no means they assent to erect any more than one in one and the same Countie, that they may be the better to fortifie, man, and provide the same to some purpose; for pluralities of Garrisons in one and the same Countie, whether they are foes or friends, are destructive to a Countie.

Chapter V. Of the best, and the worst Seats for Garrisons

And first of the best Seats, as better deserving the precedency; a good Seat is to be freed of all sides, from hills or raising grounds that may command, or of all hollowes that may indanger the garrison it selfe, or the Workes of it; If the Towne hath walls, a good Enginier is not to regard them, specially if there be hollowes, and raising grounds within Cannon-shot of them; for it is not the lining of these walls, or the erecting of Mounts near or upon them, or the drawing of ill-lined and ill-flanked dikes within five or six yards of them that will secure the same. But a prudent Enginier is to let them stand, as a second weake defence, to obtaine a parley after all is lost, and yet not to rely on them, for they are rather destructive helps then profitable defences; But to draw this Line of Communication one hundred yards or more into the field beyond them, to take in those hollowes that will indanger, and hills or raising grounds that will command his Workes. Or if they be too farre distant from the walls, he is of necessity to erect well flanked Forts, or Redoubts to secure them, or all his Workes will not be worth a button; let his Workes be never so well carried up, or lined out. And these Forts are to have Corridors, or covered wayes to retreat into, for to be relieved from the main Line of Communication, out of danger of the assailists shot [...]. And as for Mounts errected neare or upon old walls, they are of no other service, then to hinder the assailants approaches, for a day or two; but when their approaches are made, they are of no defence at all, for having a raising ground within Cannon-shot, one may dismount all the Ordnance upon them in an instant of time; and for the musket-shot, they are also of no use, because the shot of the Musket doth not fly upon a levell line, if the bullet misse one, it will hit another, and what is said here of the musket-shot, it may be applied to the Cannon-shot, for if the assaylants had no raising ground to dismount the Cannons placed upon these Mounts, their Cannon-shot cannot offend them, when their approaches are within one-hundred yards of these Mounts, for it is the long distance that giveth a levell line to the Cannon-shot, when it is mounted so high. [...]

1. The best seat of all seats, is a Haven towne freed on the land side of the fore-said impediments, having a safe rode for ships, and a deep and broad chanell for the coming in, and such a one was *Tyrus* and *Rochell*,[15] for a Garrison so seated can hardly be reduced without a Sea Navy and a Land Army, and how inconstant the winds and seas are when winter is at hand, all ingenious men know. [...]

2. The second is a Towne, seated upon a raising hill in the midst of a Champion Countrey,[16] well provided with springs and cisternes of water, having an even flat top, and all the sides but one, of straight down and Rockey Clifts of some thousand yards Diameter, and such a one was *Beeston*-Castle in Cheshire, for such a place cannot be reduced but by famine.

3. The third is a Towne seated in a Champion Countrey, free of the aforesaid impediments having an unfordable river running in the middle or close to one side of it, and such another is *Newarke*, for it cannot be reduced without an untrenched Campt (if the Workes be high and strong) and two bridges traversing the river, that the one Army of one side may relieve the other on the other side, as occasion requireth.

4. The fourth is a Towne seated on the side of a hill having a deep river running in the foot of it; whose buildings and works extend themselves to the verie top of the hill, and her Fortifications unto the two sides of the river, and such a one is Nottingham, had it not as it hath a sandy soile, yet this defect may be remedied with art and charges.

5. The fifth is a towne seated upon a raising ground, in the midst of a marish, having but one coming to it, provided with wholsome springs, and such a one is *Pessaro* in Italy.

6. The sixth is a dry towne seated in a Champion Countrey that is of good soile, and in a place where divers Roads meet, and upon the borders of three or foure Counties, for this being regularly fortified, is of great defence, and of great advantage to the owners of it, and such a one is Cremona in Lombardia.

The worst seats are these: First, a Towne seated betweene two hills, within Cannon shot; Secondly, a Towne seated in the midst of a Marish, upon a flat and even ground; Thirdly, a Towne seated upon the side of a hill, the top of the hill commanding the same; Fourthly, a Towne seated upon a hill barren of water, and a rocky ground; Fifthly, a Town seated upon a sandy soile. Sixthly, a Towne seated in the midst, or on the side of a Forrest.

Sir Balthazar Gerbier, from *The First Lecture touching Fortifications* (1649)

Sir Balthazar Gerbier (1591/92–1667) was a painter of miniatures, architect, courtier and diplomat. He was born in Middelburg (Netherlands), the son of a Protestant refugee from France. He travelled to England in 1606 with the Dutch ambassador Noel de Caron and entered the service of James I's favourite George Villiers, subsequently Duke of Buckingham. He was active as a diplomat and art buyer for Charles I on the latter's accession. In 1648, in his *Interpreter of the Academie for Forrain Languages and All Noble Sciences and Exercises*, he proposed the foundation of an Academy, to give instruction to the sons of the gentry and nobility in all kinds of subjects, ranging from languages to drawing, riding and fencing. His academy opened in 1649 at his own house in Bethnal Green; many of his lectures given there were printed. As with many of the series that were announced, only the first lecture of the series here was delivered or preserved. His architectural activities fall into two periods, the first in the 1620s, when he was artistic advisor to the Duke of Buckingham, working mainly on alterations to York House in the Strand and New Hall in Essex. The second period was in the 1660s, when he designed a house for Lord Craven at Hampstead Marshall in Berkshire. In 1662 he published *A Brief Discourse* (see below, this chapter) and in the next year *Counsel and Advise to All Builders* (Colvin, 1995; *DNB*).

The Introduction

As by holy Writ it appears that God who is the Creator of Heaven and Earth is likewise termed the Lord of Hoasts, and Battels, so the Royal Prophet *David* sought him, that he might *teach his hands to warre, and his fingers to fight*. God permits men to finde out inventions, and engine to wage war withall: And that even since *Caine* brake the league of amity and brotherhood with *Abell*.

Experience is onely gotten by length of time, and not by birth, nor courage: For if so bee the first Rabins were wel grounded in what they affirme of *Caines* death, *Lamech* slew him with an Arrow, which time had taught men to make.

The severall pretences of waging War are various: Nature warrants the first, which is *Selfe-defence; Religion* the second, *Lawes* and *Liberties* the third. [...]

But before we enter into the field, display colours, and draw forth our Armies: as we finde God to be the Lord of Hoasts and Battells, preservation, the first Law of Man; the defence of Religion, the next strong tye; Lawes and Liberties the third grand interest and greatest concernment of Nations. Let us then take along with us the prescriptions of the Scripture concerning wars, *Deut.* 20.11, 12 *When thou comest nigh a City to fight against it, then proclaime a peace unto it, and it shall be, if it make thee answer of peace, and open unto thee, then it shall be, that all the people that are found therein shall be tributary unto thee, and they shall serve thee: But if they will make war against thee, then thou shalt besiege it.* [...]

[...] as for as ignorance is despicable, so its prejudiciall: Let not any Souldier then perswade himselfe, that it can any wayes suffice him to goe but just as far as the pronunciation of the Alphabet; for that it will availe them no more, when they shall come to be put to the practicall part, then it will to any Auditory when they shall onely be told, what followeth, *viz.*

That the *Orthography*, or *Purfile* [profile] of a Fortresse, is a section, or a perpendicular line, running eaven with the Horizon, and that which representeth unto our view the severall parts of a Fortresse.

That the *Scenography*, is an explaining of the Names and Temes properly used in the Art of Fortifying.

That a walled place, where store of houses are seated together, whose inhabitants are governed by a Civill Magistrate, may properly be termed a Towne.

That a Fort, is a place, environed with Motes, Ramparts, and with Bulwarks, wherein a few Men, may defend themselves against a greater number, and the assault of many.

That a Citadell is a Fortresse of foure, five, six, or more Bastions, which is joyned to a Town for to command, and keep it in awe.

That a Castle is an ancient kinde of building, with severall Towers or Turrets, and a Mote or Ditch about it, either dry, or full of water. [...]

So that for the present, wee will close this with a short Meditation fit for all good Christians; That if so be it necessary, to have so many qualities, and to take so much care for the preservation of a small compasse and parcell of clay, loam, and of a few houses within the circumference of a Wall or Bulwark: What care ought we then to have (but meer dust and ashes) for the preservation of our soules, placed in an habitation, continually beset by an Army, compassed by legions of Princes of the Ayre, by Spirits of darknesse and destruction, who are never to be tyred, who need neither to borrow or buy any Victualls, for their subsistance, who have numberlesse engines at hand, who have placed their Petards[17] and murdering peeces at all the gates of our Senses, and never run any danger themselves of being surprised, though they have millions of deceits, to ensnare the onely two Sentinels of our body, our Eies, by giving a world of false alarm; To surprise our Hearing; and who at the very first, strike at the maine Fortresse, the Heart, and Minde of Men: And it so be the gaining of all the World, be nothing, in comparison to the losse of one soule; O what a precious task must the preservation of that Soul be against the grand and common Enemy to mankinde; and what an honour is the preserving thereof! as it ought to be Mans sole blisse; who can never miscarry therein, so long as he fixeth on his strong Tower, and Fortresse of defence; and that he doth continually watch, pray, and manfully fight the good combate of Faith; hereby the greatest honour is to be acquired, for that by so doing, the grand Enemy will be forc't to break up his siege, and retire.

It was the fervent, zealous, and most pious prayers of the Royall Prophet *David, That Gods enemies might bee confounded and be put to flight;* And what can we desire more, then that by his unspeakable mercies (we that are the precious gems for which Christ Jesus hath spilt his most precious blood) have made the grand Enemy of our souls to retire, *&th.*

Roger Pratt, from 'Rules for the Guidance of Architects' (1665 and 1672)

(See the note on Roger Pratt in Chapter 1, above.)

From 'Rules for the Guidance of Architects' [7 December 1665]
[p. 82] It is the part of a good Architect not only to see his building truly laid out, and prosecuted by the Bricklayer, but also by the Carpenter, and daily to consider what trades are working there, what then in doing, and what worthy either of his observation or direction.

To determine anything without due premeditation, is rashness. Not to come to any determination in a convenient time, is an effect either of ignorance, or sloth.

To wittingly omit to do that at the first, which at the last we shall be forced to, to our great advantage, is the extremity of folly.

2. To be so forward in his premeditation as to make no trade at a stand for want of his directions, which will cause great repining etc and to be careful to see them exactly performed, for otherwise all trades will be at catch with him.

3rdly. To weigh what Trades are the most chargeable in a building, what proportion there is between them as to matter of expense, and what between the quantities of materials and the workeing.

An able Architect ought perfectly to understand these things:

1. To be able to design all sorts of buildings after the most useful, strong and beautiful manner, and that may be both in regard of the person, time, place, expense or any other circumstance proposed to him, as likewise to be able to adorn and repair etc.

2. To perfectly understand the natures, and qualities of all the most usual sort of materials, the best ways of acquiring them both as to their price, carriage, etc., and also of preparing them for the intended building, and how to take the due tale of them.

3. To know the best manner of working in all kinds of materials, the just dimensions, distances and whole method of them, the usual frauds, or errors in it, the true value of it, which must proceed not from any guess, but from a most clear demonstration of the progress of every particular in it, all proved by a most diligent, and reiterated observation of how much of each can be done by a sufficient workman per diem, at such wages as most usually is given to them, as likewise to be assured of what is necessary as to the quantity, of any desired undertaking.

4. To contrive all things with the most orderly thrift, and longest duration.

5. Somewhat nearly to calculate the expense of any designed building; wherein yet that he may not err, and so the builder be surprised, it is good adding about one fourth part more for things probably forgotten amongst so great a diversity of particulars, and for all other accidents, whereof there are usually many.

Whosoever desires to perfectly understand any trade, must labour diligently to inform himself from the very originals of it, through all the successive progresses, until he has traced it to its utmost perfection.

The first thing therefore that will fall under our consideration, is that of the materials, the qualities of which ought thoroughly to be known to us, so that everything may be employed to the use which is most proper for it, as likewise the quantities which are absolutely necessary for the effecting of any determinate work, wherein great care is to be had, that the least waste be possibly made.

But because no such material can be had, but that either it must be provided out of something of our own, or be bought of others; if we have it of our own, we must then procure such persons who have been the most versed, and who have the esteem of the most honest and able proficients in things of that nature, to set themselves about the preparing of it, at the most seasonable time, wherein we shall be sure to have a sufficient number of experienced workmen at the most reasonable rates, as likewise in the most convenient places, whereby much will be saved us in the price of carriages.

But if we must buy of others, then we must be sure to have it from those persons, who are the first owners of it, not to take it from the second, or third hand, all who will then first make their advantages out of it, as likewise from honest and sufficient men who in their dealings will have regard not more to their gains than to their reputations.

We must have a great regard to the time for one year a material is much cheaper, or dearer than it is in another, as likewise in the several seasons of that year, so as almost to make a difference of a fourth or a fifth part of the price of it.

We must very well consider the place, both in regard of the source, or accumulation of any material there, as likewise the convenience of transporting it thence to us; the cheapness or dearness of that country etc.

It: the manner of buying it; much better bargains are generally had when great quantities are bought and with ready money, than when otherwise.

The measure, for therein is the advantage so great, that in many things this is the chief gain of the retailer.

The main intention in every building to be chiefly observed, [which] is to keep the whole firm, tight and close against all injuries either of time, or weather; and to examine all things as to their bond, and joints, and how they stand as to the square, plumb-line, and level. Likewise as to the qualities of the materials etc.

The angles of a building in all sorts are most chiefly to be observed, that they be well bonded.

The form of building is to be chiefly observed, that there be a perfect correspondency of the like parts one to the other and that all apertures have their due dimensions, and stand in their right places, which will best be found out by comparing them with the parts next to them.

Certain general rules concerning building

What soever seems to be weak either in any foundation or walling, in regard of the weight above it, there to most strongly and reiterately arch over it; which arch will much defend it through the foundation upon which it is built be in itself but weak, for an arch being pressed flies out to the sides than directly downwards; especially a seeme one.

Not so to mix timber in our walls for binding them, as that the wood decaying, they must necessarily sink, viz. As when we lay thick lintels over the whole breadth of our walls, especially of the piers, which will have nought to support them; but perhaps they may be laid with advantage, about 4 or 6 inches both in their breadth and depth etc., so to run round the whole inside of the building; for the better tying of the walls, and the equal pressing of them by the several timbers.

To put rarely anything into any building which does not as well add to the strength, or safeguard as to the beauty of it.

Where we are in some doubt of the well doing of anything considerable, there not to trust only to the bare force of our imagination, or reason; but in things of small cost there to make trial first of some little part of it; in greater, by some model of it etc.

When we are to consider in a building how anything may be performed with the greatest perfection, then we ought first well to weigh what the inconveniences are to which it may be subject and that not only in regard of itself, but also to all other things near which it is placed and so to provide sufficiently against them: but chiefly we ought to have an eye to the uses of it, which being thoroughly looked into will best of all directions. In all designings to consider not only how things do look for the present, but also how for the future, and not only in regard of time, but also when ye ornaments shall be put into it etc: To search what of walling etc may be saved in our designing, the same conveniences still remaining.

How suddenly to comprehend all things in a Building [1672]
[p. 45] The first thing to be considered is that of situation; as to whether upon a plain ground, low or rising. And next the position of the house, in regard of the four winds, the conveniences about it, and the ways conducting to it. In both which if we find not what is best, we are not presently to blame it, but rather to seek after the occasion of it, which we may many times at length find to have so necessitated it. From thence we proceed to observe the length of the building, and also the height of it (which will be best taken one corner of it) and into how many parts each line has been divided by the windows in it. Which done, we mark in one perpendicular successively the several proportions, and ornaments of them, then the spaces including them, the bounding of each storey, and lastly the top finishing. From the end we remove to the middle of the front, the place of entering from whence the uniformity of the whole is most perfectly seen, and where if there be anything extraordinary it is there to be placed, and is accordingly to be noted. In a more curious enquiry we gently move our eyes through the whole length of each particular storey, and afterwards cross them down again in their perpendicular divisions, by which means the least fault will scarce want its discovery. After this we view the roof, of what pitch and slope, how bounded at the bottom, how covered at the ridge, what windows and chimneys appearing out of it, with their number, order, fashion, and all their dimensions. And having thus taken in such an idea of the whole, we are at length at leasure to consider the nature and quality of the materials, and the working, laying, jointing, and carving etc. of them, and we are afterwards to judge according to the rules of art each particular.

How to find out the expense of any designed building, and of the means to be used before the undertaking of it, and afterwards in the erecting and finishing of it.

As the hand is the instrument of all mechanical action, so is money the nerve whence it derives its motion, this therefore is most carefully to be regarded as the chief principal of all sensation, as upon any defect whereof the whole work languishes if not totally ceaseth, and upon its plenty on the contrary guided by a proportionate discretion, flourishes, and is most rigorously carried on to its utmost perfection. Now though it cannot well be supposed that any rational man should put himself upon building without having first made in his purse some competent provision, yet are the examples but too many of those who have not first laboured to make of their expenses some near calculation, so that men having been too large in their designs in the beginning, in the conclusion those of moderate estates have either been necessitated to give it over, and by that means to proclaim their folly to their perpetual derision, or else (which is most usual) being stimulated with the sense of so great a dishonour, have been carried on imperfectly to finish, to the high vexation of themselves, and thre almost continual and causeless teasing of their workmen [...] Hereupon they most commonly fall into the highest exclamations against the chargeableness of building, forewarn their acquaintance not to venture to put their fingers into the mortar, and so generally deter them, that by such means they do not only deprive them of one of the chief comforts of life, a handsome, sweet, and convenient habitation; but their country also of that ornament, which else it would have owed to them.

Sir Balthazar Gerbier, from *Counsel and Advise to All Builders* (1663)

Gerbier's descriptions in this text of building materials and their prices are among the earliest published in England; only Thomas Willsford's *Architectonice* of 1659 was earlier. (See the note on Gerbier earlier in this chapter.) Their importance to architectural history was already recognized in an article on the *Counsel and Advise* in the *Builder* of 1848 by the architect Sydney Smirke (Harris, 1990).

Further reading: Harris (1990); Mowl and Earnshaw (1995).

[p. 4] Whosoever is disposed to Build, ought in the first place to make choice of a skilful Surveyour from whose Directions the several Master work-men may receive Instructions by way of Draughts, Models, Frames, &c. For the better managing their intended work, since an ill built Palace leaves a perpetual reflection of Ignorance on the Builder; whereas a compact Building, whether City, Castle or House, like a stock of Children continue the Name and Memory of the Owner.

An exact Architect must have the Art of Drawing, and Perspective; ought to know what appertains to each Inhabitants Conveniency: Since there is a vast difference between the House of Prayer, and a Princes Palace, and meaner Inhabitations, nor is a Laboratorium for a Chymist fit for either Baking or Brewing.

Therefore he ought to know wherein is the use of Perspective, otherwise he will never rightly describe the dimensions of solid Bodies, which are to stand high; his Circles will seem Ovals in Breadth, and his Ovals Circles, and all his contrivances will be at randome; as it is said of some men, who first act, and afterwards consider, excusing their mistake, which they thought it otherwise.

The Surveyour must in the first place consider the ground whereupon the Building must be Erected, make a Distinction between a Plot in the Citty, and one in the Country; and then govern himself as the ground will give him leave; reflecting still on the Houses adjacent, and those which are opposite, if they be high to raise as high, if not higher, to prevent the smoaking of Chimneyes.

Secondly, He must place the Front of a Building in the Country towards the East, if the place giveth leave; by which means he may shelter his double Lodging Rooms from the Northwest: He must cause all the back of his Stone-work (which stands within the Brick) to be cut with a Rasat[18] three Inches broader then the breadth of his Iambes and Cornish; which will hinder the Rain (driven by a feirce North-west winde) to peirce into the Inside of the Wall, and through the meeting of the Brickwork and Stone; whereunto the Morter affords the passage of the Water. It may be some will carp at this free Expression, pretending that Surveyours and Master Workmen (in this refined Age, which abounds in Books, with the Portractures of the Out and Inside of the best Buildings) are not to seek the first Points of their apprenticeship: whom I ask the reason, why modern and daily Buildings are so exceedingly Defective? And whether it is not because many of them (if well considered) have been but Apprentices lately, and too soon become Journey-men; And that Surveyours (who either affect more the Building to themselves a strong Purse, or are blind in the faults which their Work-men commit) like careless Postillions, hasten with the Packet-Maile to the Post Office, be it never so ill girted, whereby it oft falls in the mid-way? [...]

[p. 9] The readiest way to try a Surveyour, is to put him to draw a ground Plot in the Builders presence, to make him describe the fittest place for a Seat, the ordering of Rooms, for Summer and Winter; to Contrive well the Staires cases, Doores, Windows and Chimneys; that the Staires may stand conveniently to the Stories, Doores and Windows; so placed, as that they may not be inconvenient to the Chimneys; the Bedstead place far from Doores and Windows, and of a fit distance from Chimneys.

And as for height of Seelings, the Surveyour ought to make a Distinction, between the height of a House, or Town Hall; of a Colledge and that of a Church, the Hall of a private house, serving for the most part, but for a Passage, the others for a Receptacle of a whole Body (consisting of number of Persons) who for an houre or two joyntly breath in one place, and the which may be Offensive.

Nature of Aire being to ascend, and when it meets (with a sudden opposition it spreads; Since the Nostrils (as the Pipes of Bellows) will attract to each Persons Braines the scent which is composed of that Steam.

The Surveyours skill and discretion will also be discovered by the well contriving of the respective feelings of common Rooms, and Closets for private use; For as rooms of State, ought to be of an equall height, the feeling of a Closet (ten foot square, lesse or more adjacent to a Bed-chamber of State (which may be Thirty foot wide, Fourty in length, and Sixteen or Eighteen foot high) would be Proposterous, Inconvenient; and like a Barbers Comcase;[19] Staircase, and Steeple-like to hang Bells in.

A good Surveyour sheweth his Art, both within the Building, as on its Front; and in the fit mixture of Materials, Morter, Brick and Stone, being Simpathike stuff.

Sir John Evelyn, 'Londinium Redivivum' (1666)

John Evelyn (1620–1706), was a virtuoso and diarist. His family's fortune was made by his grandfather, who introduced the manufacture of gunpowder into England. Evelyn was educated at the Middle Temple Bar in London and Balliol College, Oxford. He travelled extensively on the Continent after the outbreak of the Civil War, staying in Paris, Florence, Rome, Naples and Venice. He returned for good to England in 1659. Until the Restoration he devoted his life to private pursuits, including the arts and gardening. He was on intimate terms with the mathematician John Wilkins and the physicist Robert Boyle, and was elected a Fellow of the Royal Society in 1660, the year of its foundation. One of his main interests was the encouragement of the arts in England, and in particular to introduce Renaissance theory (hence his translations of Alberti and Fréart de Chambray) and Continental ways of organizing political support for the arts, such as the foundation of a royal academy of arts.

Evelyn's 'Londinium Redivivum' was never published during his lifetime. It started life as a discourse he sent to Wren on or before 11 September 1666, two or three days after the Great Fire; he presented it to the King on 13 September, and on 22 December a copy was sent to Henry Oldenberg, the Secretary to the Royal Society. A complete transcript is preserved in the Guildhall Library in London. From this a modern edition was made by E. S. de Beer, who added plans Evelyn drew for the rebuilding of London. (see also the entry on Evelyn in Chapter 5, p. 203)

Further reading: de Beer (ed.), *John Evelyn: London Revived*; McKellar (1999).

The pretences of the several Proprietors in the funds being first of all secured, and put into such a method, as by the wisdom of his Majesty and Parliament shall be found most conducible to the prevention of future suits and disturbances, interrupting the order of a new designation; the city of London might doubtless be rendered as far superior to any other city in the habitable world for beauty, commodiousness, and magnificence (the situation and other circumstances considered) as it has hitherto been somewhat inferior to many imperial cities in Europe, for want of improving those advantages, which God and Nature have dignified it withal above them.

In pursuance of this (if without offence, and with submission to abler judgements, I may with others be permitted to cast in my Symbol) I humbly conceive, that an exact plot, according to the geometrical scale of feet, ought in the first place to be taken by some able Artist, and in that accurately to be described all the declivities, eminences, water Courses &c. of the whole Area. The Gent. who performed that of Tangier (according to my conceptions of that plan) might, I suppose, be a very fitting person for that employment. After this I conceive there may be delineated some more particular iconographical plan of the whole city membratim, as it were, with the principal streets; where the piazzas, churches, hospitals, courts of justice, halls, markets, quay, exchange, magazines &c. shall be placed. And this ought to be the joint and mature contrivance of the ablest men, Merchants, Architects, and Workmen, in consort; and such as have a true idea what proprieties, and conveniencies, belong to so great a city, and which I therefore briefly, but fully, comprehend in these two transcendences, Use and Ornament.

The plan thus prepared and resolved on, hands must be employed for the speedy removal of the rubbish, which should be so disposed of, as might best signify to the carrying on of the work, by laying apart, and carefully separating all such materials, as may be useful for the several occasions of building, coving, filling up, and to be sifted for the mortar; cleansing and severing the whole bricks, bast, stones &c. every of which should be consigned to such void places, as by the draughts are so to be left, for avoiding after removals and confusion, and that the ground may be disencumbered, and fitted for the laying out, and digging of foundations. And in order to their future stability, and for that divers of them may be of singular use to the inhabitants, and save a world of charge in making new ones, there would also be drawn, and accurately measured, a subterranean plan of all the vaults, cellars and arched Meanders, yet remaining, thereby to consider how they may fall out, and accommodate to the new erections, what were fit to be filled and dammed up, and what to be reserved. It were therefore (I say) highly requisite, that this rubbish were perfectly cleared, that so the inequalities, and several affections of the surface might be more apparent. But *hic labor hic opus*, this will be found a work; of unimaginable difficulty, and require a multitude of hands; nor can it be effected to purpose, without infinite confusion (as it presents itself to my apprehension) till those several plans and types of the future city be first concluded on, and applied accordingly: and then they may stake it out, and deliver it to the owners of the ground; provided they exactly conform to the plot, to the shape of the front, and to such other directions for uniformity and solidity, as his Majesty's Surveyors or Commissioners shall appoint. In this work it might haply be thought fit to fill up, or at least give a partial level to someof the deepest valleys, holes, and more sudden declivities, within the city, for the more ease of commerce, carriages, coaches, and people in the streets, and not a little for the more handsome ranging of the buildings. For instance that from about the Fleet to Ludgate, which yet should be no more than might only afford a graceful and just ascent from thence up towards St. Pauls, the only spot in the whole city, where I would plot that ancient and venerable cathedral again. But here is to be considered the channel running thence through Holborn, which would be so enlarged as not only to be preserved sweet (by scouring it through flood-gates into the Thames on all occasions) but commodious for the intercourse of considerable vessels, thwart this position of the town, and which therefore should be accordingly wharfed on both sides to the very quay of the river, and made contiguous to the streets by bridges arched to a due lovel, as it might be easily be contrived (and with passage sufficient for lusty barges and lighters under them) were the valley so elevated as 'tis projected. There is only this care incumbent, that all foundations upon this new ground be searched to the old and more solid basis from whence they may also store themselves with vaults and collerage in abundance. The same might be considered in some sort from the descent of the hill towards Thames-street, so as to come down upon the future quay by a far less declivity, which would give those houses, that should be built fronting to the river, a more becoming aspect, and an easier footing to the ranges above them, which would peep over one another successively, with a far better grace, than those do at *Genoa*, where the ascent is too precipitous.

These considerations and employments would greatly forward the prompt and natural disposure of the more useless and cumbersome rubbish, unless it might be thought more expedient (if there should be not sufficient for both) to design it rather towards the enlargement of a new and ample quay, which I wish might run parallel from the very Tower to the Temple at least, and if it were possible (without augmenting the rapidity of the stream) extend itself even as far as the very low watermark; the basin by this means kept perpetually full, without slub, or annoyance, and to the infinite benefit and ease of access, like that of *Constantinople*, than which nothing could be imagined more noble. What fractions and confusions our ugly stairs, bridges and causeways, make, and how dirty, and nasty it is at every ebb, we are sufficiently sensible of; so as next to the hellish smoke of the town, there is nothing doubtless, which does more impair the health of its inhabitants.

In the disposure of the streets due consideration should be had, what are competent breadths for commerce and intercourse, cheerfulness and state; and therefore not to pass through the city all in one tenor without varieties, useful breakings, and enlargements into piazzas at competent distances, which ought to be built exactly uniform, strong, and with beautiful fronts.

Nor should these be all of them square, but some of them oblong, circular, and oval figures, for their better grace and capacity. I would allow none of the principal streets less than an hundred foot in breadth, nor any of the narrowest than thirty, their openings, and heights proportionable. And of these I suppose there may be three, if not four, between the *Thames* and *London Wall*, reckoning that of *Cheapside* for the chief; which being likewise the largest may extend itself from *Temple* bar to the very upper part of *Tower Hill*, or *Crutched Friars*, and bear the Cathedral of St. *Pauls* upon such an eminence of ground, as would hardly be paralleled in any city of the world. Amongst the streets should be the parochial churches (which may well be reduced to a moiety, for 'tis prodigiously true, that there are some parishes no less than two hundred times larger than others) so placed and interspersed, as may have some reference to the adornment of the profile of the city upon all its avenues, and therefore at studied intervals, and so built after the modern architecture without, and contrivance within, as may best answer their pious designation; for which Mr. Grant has judiciously perstringged[20] our old ones, in that ingenious piece of his upon the bills of Mortality. Most of these I could wish might be founded in the centres of spacious areas, piazzas, &c. so as to be conspicuous to several streets, crossing upon them, as some of the Roman obelisks are; and other at the abutments and extremities of them, which might also be observed for the raising of public fountains. It is about these church piazzas that the Stationers should have their shops, and the Ministers their houses; as about that of St. *Paul* might again be re-established the episcopal palace, the Dean and Prebends' houses; the grammar school, a public library; the prerogative and first fruits office &c. All which would be built at ample distance from the cathedral, and with more stately fronts, in honour of that august pile. As for the church-yards, I would have them universally proscribed to the very utmost wall of the city northwards, upon which inscriptions and monuments might be aptly inserted, and the dead interred, either in vaults, or the open ground, affording a useful diversion to the contemplative passenger of his mortality, and human frailty; for as to that super-stitious custom of burying in churches, or having their dormitories in the very heart of cities, where frequently churches are built, I think it neither decent, nor sufferable.

In the piazzas should be kept the several markets, in others the coaches may wait &c. and in some should be public fountains placed; not as formerly immured with blind and melancholy walls, but left free to play, and show their crystal waters, as in most of the best cities of Europe they do, save this of ours, where an officer for a small stipend, might protect them from injury and pollution, till custom has civilised us.

Between piazzas, market places, and churches, might be the halls for the ancient companies. These if fronted at least with stone, adorned with statues, and other ornaments, would infinitely enrich the streets, and render this city as famous for architecture of the most refined Gusto, and as worthy to be considered of Travellers, as any city in Europe. But especially, should the Guild, or Magistratical Hall of assembly have something of more pompous and great, after the example of the State House at *Amsterdam*;[21] at least to some proportion: and this likewise ought to be built in one of the most eminent parts of the city. Near unto this might be designed a magnificent house for the Lord Mayor and others for the two sheriffs of *London*; which being erected at the public charge, ought to be the constant residence of the Gentlemen, who bear that office *pro tempore*, and would therefore be contrived accordingly. I should think the Royal Exchange might front the quay betwixt *Queenhithe* and the Bridge, about the Steel-yard I conceive were a proper place, respecting the goodliest river in the world, where the traffic, and business is most vigorous (but for this I submit to better judgements) wherover it be built, it will be necessary to amplify the old design, which was much too narrow for the assemblies. If it should be erected near the *Thames*, let there be spacious piazzas about it, either for dwellings, or public warehouses; which yet I should rather advise might be contrived in the vaults under those edifices; because a sad experience has taught us, how secure they are there, being prudently governed. And for such other stores as will not be well preserved under-ground, there would by any means some expedient be found out, that they might not front the Thames on London side, at least very sparingly; not only for that they may yet become obnoxious to the like accidents (being built contiguous to the rest) but because, if there be not ample separations and distances (which would infinitely disfigure and interrupt the face of that quay) they will no where stand commodiously. How greatly therefore were it to be wished, that such a depth of those wretched houses on the opposite side of the water were purchased, and demolished, to make room for those stores? The wharfs before, and yards behind made large enough for the placing and working of cranes, the laying of deal, timber, clap-board, pipestaves, millstones, faggots, wood and coals, and other gross commodities; whilst the goodly quay overagainst it might be built for the owners, and dwellings of the principal merchants. Or if needs the warehouses must be on this side, yet that they were made rather to front *Thames* street than the river, because of the dull and heavy aspect of those kind of erections.

That little bay at Queenhithe would have the quay contrived about it, of a good breadth from the houses, which may be cloistered about for the market-men and fruiterers. And then, where now that wharf is, a stately avenue from the water side up to St. *Pauls*, which might extend itself into an semi-circle upon the quay becoming that lovely market. This I should conceive might be one of the five principal traverse streets of the whole city, and to reach as far as Aldersgate, or, if you will, further along the wall, as it might be carried: that from *Queenhithe* to *Cripplegate*, that from the *Exchange* to *Moorgate*, that opposite to the bridge to *Bishopsgate*, that from *Billingsgate* near as far; that from the Custom-house to *Aldgate*, as that from *Black-friars* stairs as far as into West *Smithfield*: thus decussating and crossing the four longer streets, passing from East to West, whereof one might extend from the channel, which intercepts it at *St. Brides* to the very *Tower*. This is what I call *Thames* street, and would destine for storehouses, in case of necessity. The second is (as has been said) from the *Strand* to the utmost Eastern point of the whole city; where I would have erected a noble gate, in manner of a triumphal arch, in honour of our illustrious Monarch. This street from St. *Pauls* may be divaricated like a Pythagorean Y, as the most accurately ingenious Dr. *Wren* has designed it, and I willingly follow in my second thoughts, because of its handsome addresses to the bridge and to the opposite parts of the town. The third from *Newgate* to *Aldgate*, and with a little assistance butting into *Holborn*. The fourth and last from *Aldersgate* to *Bishopsgate*, which will be the shortest. The wall betwixt *Cripplegate* and *Aldgate* to be employed, as I said, for the church-yards of the several parishes; and the houses opposite to them, with a large street, for the common Inns, receptacle and station of Carriers &c. which being on the North part of the city, and nearest the confines of the fields, and roads, would least cumber and infest the town, and yet have a far more commodious and easy access to them, by reason of their immediate approaches through the traverse streets, than now they are scattered up and down without distinction. For the rest of the necessary evils, the Browhouses, Bakehouses, Dyers, Salt, Soap, and Sugar-boilers, Chandlers, Hat-makers, Slaughter-houses, some sort of Fish-mongers &c. whose neighbourhood cannot be safe (as I have elsewhere showed, and a sad experience has confirmed) I hope his Majesty will now dispose to some other parts about the river, towards Bow and Wandsworth on the water; *Islington*, and about *Spitalfields* &c. The charge of bringing all their commodities into the city would be very inconsiderable, opposed to the peril of their being continued amongst the inhabitants; and the benefit of the carriage, which would employ a world of people both by land and water, without the least prejudice.

I suppose the Custom-house cannot be better situated than where it was; and as it may hold communication with the Tower, here might be the Admiralty, and Navy-office be fitly placed.

I have not forgotten the Hospitals, public Work-houses to employ the poor in, and Prisons; which being built, and re-endowed at the common charge, should be disposed of in convenient quarters of the city. The Hospitals would become one of the principal streets, but the prisons, and Tribunal for trial of criminal offenders, might be built (as of old) near some entrance of the city: about Newgate were a fitting place, as my plot represents it.

The College of physicians would be in one of the best parts of the town, encircled with a handsome piazza for the dwelling of those learned persons, with the Chirurgeons, Apothecaries and Druggists in the streets about them; for I am greatly inclined to wish, that all of a mystery should be destined to their several quarters. Those of the better sort of shopkeepers, who sell by retail, might be allotted to the sweetest, and most eminent streets and piazzas. The Artificers to the more ordinary houses, intermedial and narrower passages (for such will hardly be avoided) that the noise and tintamarre of their instruments may be less importunate. The Taverns and Victualling houses sprinkled amongst them, and built accordingly. But even all these too, even the very meanest, should exactly respect uniformity, and be more substantially built than those in *Covent Garden*, and other places, where once in twenty or thirty years they had need be built again, and therefore to be indulged a longer term.

Spaces for ample Courts, Yards, and Gardens, even in the heart of the city there may be some to the principal houses, for state and refreshment; but with great reservation, because of the fractions they will make, and therefore rarely towards any principal street. And I hope it will please his Majesty to proscribe by a public and irreversible Edict, that no houses whatsoever may for the future presume to be erected, not only about this city, but all the Nation besides, within such a distance from Magazines, Places of public Records, and Churches, which should be preserved as Sanctuaries.

The Gates and Entries of the city, which are to be rebuilt, might be the subjects of handsome architecture, in form of triumphal arches, adorned with Statues, Relievos, and apposite Inscriptions, as Prefaces to the rest within, and should therefore by no means be obstructed by shods, and ugly shops, or houses adhering to them. And I wish this reformation, and the infinite danger of their being continued, might extend to the demolishing those deformed buildings on London bridge; which not only endanger all the rest, but takes away from the beauty of it, and indeed of the whole city near the Thames. Instead of them, if there went a substantial Baluster of iron, decorated with Statues upon their pedestals, at convenient distances, and the foot way elevated on each side, it would be exceedingly convenient; whilst to secure the passengers by night, it might be guarded by responsible house keepers in their turns. Or if they will needs have shops, let them be built of solid stone, made narrow and very low, like to those upon the Rialto at Venice; but it were far better without them.

One of the last, not least Considerations, will be that of a Paving, for which we have a laudable example in those streets of my Lord Treasurers, and *Hatton Gardens*, which may be imitated. And why may not some of the distorted bricks, to be found amongst the rubbish, be reserved for these purposes; especially the elevations destined for the foot causeways before the fronts of the houses? Unless they will be at charge to lay it with Purbeck and flat stones, which indeed were to be preferred. Yet their clinkers in *Holland* do very well; and, as I remember, the *Roman* streets are so paved. I have now no more to add, for the case, and preservation of the streets, than to wish, that the use of sleds were introduced, and as few heavy carts as might be countenanced. And that for the universal benefit (especially of those who are not born to ride in coaches) that intolerable nuisance of spouts and gutters might be strictly reformed, and the waters so conveyed by close and perpendicular pipes (where they cannot be avoided) or to drop only from above the Modillions, as from *Italian* roofs. That no pipes for conveyance of waters for domestic uses be derived from the Heads through church-yards, or like unclean places, without being well immured in plaster of Paris. That plain tile may be only employed instead of pan tile; unless we could be persuaded into the use of slate, which is both beautiful and light. That no Bay windows and uncomely jettings, nor even Balconies (unless made of iron) be for future permitted. And that for the better expediting of this great design (worthy indeed of the greatest and best of Princes) store of all materials may be provided betimes (bricks and tiles especially) because all seasons are not fit for it; and that there be a diligent inspection to examine their goodness: but the greatest and almost only desiderate will be that of Timber, which peace and industry will quickly furnish. And when all these were prepared, and the Undertakers too as ready, if they be permitted to gratify their own fancies, without religiously intending to pursue the Plan; and that his Majesty (who is best able to judge of it) overrule in this; it may possibly become a new indeed, but a very ugly city, when all is done. Whereas, if they permit themselves to be governed in this, we are not yet to despair of seeing (after a few years) such a city to emerge out of these sad and ruinous heaps, as may dispute it with all the cities of the World; fitter for commerce, apter for government, sweeter for health, more glorious for beauty; and in sum for whatsoever indeed could be desired to render it consummately perfect. Facile est Inventis addere.[22] J. EVELYN

Stephen Primatt, from *The City & Country Purchaser & Builder* (1667)

The author, who was a lawyer, may have been involved with the 'Determination of Differences touching houses burnt down, or demolished by reason of the late Fire in London' (the official estimation of the value of burnt houses). His book is dedicated to a number of legal officials who were also involved, including the Lord Chief Justice, Sir Orlando Bridgman, and the Baron of the Exchequer, Sir Matthew Hales. Its intended audience is not artisans, but gentlemen who wished to build. It was the first book in English on building valuation, measurement and prices. It opens with a

'General Treatise on how to compute the value of Lands in England, and what makes them of that value with advise to a Purchaser and Rules prescribed to purchase'; the second part offers patrons practical advice drawn from Sir Henry Wotton, Sir Francis Bacon's essay 'Of Building' (published in 1625 in his *Essays or Counsels Civil and Moral, Newly Produced and Enlarged*) and Gerbier's *Counsel and Advise* (Harris, 1990).

Further reading: Harris (1990).

The Preface to the Reader

Having had some spare time in a long Vacation, I thought I could not employ it better in doing something which might tend to the forwarding the City Building, (being the Metropolitan of this Nation, and so reputed before *Julius Caesar's* time; the Glory of the major part of which is now, Phoenix-like, buried in its own ashes) to do which, I first consulted the Inclination of my Countrey-men, the Noble suffering Citizens and Bees of this Nation, who I found (as they were ever famous for promoting such things which were for the publique Honor and Good) very willing and desirous to build: but some of them were impeded by certain Differences arising amongst them, as to their respective Interests in the Ground, and late Houses; others through their unskilfulness in building were not less indisposed to it, for that many of them are compelled to trust to the Conscience and Fidelity of Workmen and Surveyors, who have been observed to make Harvest in the City Ruines, and combine together to take excessive Rates for their works, which hath dis-encouraged many of them. As to the former of these, there is prescribed certain Rules and Tables, whereby the Proprietors may decide their Differences, as to point of interest, by themselves, without troubling the most Honorable Court of Judicature, and Directions shewed how to Value any Ground in the City. As to the other, there is an Inspection made into the Artificers Trades employed in Building, therein unfolding the several Rates and Prises of several sorts of Work, and after what manner they make their Bargains, and agree for performing the same; then have computed the Charge of several Houses, for several Dimensions, Materials being at certain Rates there proposed. In the first Part, there is a Treatise of Purchasing Lands and Houses, and other things in England, which I thought necessary, for that some men sell their Lands and other things, to the intent to bestow their Money in Building. And that nothing might be wanting wherein my small time and experience could inform you, I have concluded with Surveying and Measuring Superfices and Solids, as a necessary thing to be known to the Builder. If the Non-Confident Author hath been any ways defective in attaining the end proposed by him, he hopes at least it may give occasion to those who are more Learned, to attempt something in this kinde, which may encourage the Re-building this Famous City, wherein any Ingenious Undertaker shall not onely be accompanied with my well-wishes, but shall be assisted by whatsoever is in the power of S. P.

From my Chamber at Cliffords-Inn this 14th of October, 1667.

Advice to the City Builder. The Second Book.
[p. 50] First, let him get his foundation cleared, and his Bricks and Bats laid up against there be use for the same, of else let them be wrought up in the Foundation; let him likewise get all his Rubbish sifted up and cleansed, and to take notice what quantity there be of the same, and so value the same according as direction is hereafter given; let him observe that he doth deal with honest workmen, as near as he can, and such as are able and willing to perform what they shall undertake, whether the same be by the great or otherwise: And let him make choice of such a Master Workman as will set his helping hand to set the work forward; such a Workman will afford to do his work cheaper, than others who walk with their Rules by their sides, and it doth very much discourage those from idleness who work under him. In case where Carpenters, Bricklayers, Labourers, or other Artificers, having undertaken work by the Great, Month, Weck, or otherwise, do depart their work without just cause, as the not payment of wages, or the like, that party grieved may have such Offender before two Justices of the Peace, who have power by virtue of the Statute of Labourers, made 5 Eliz 4. To Imprison such Offender for the space of one Month without bail, and such Offender, the person grieved having notwithstanding such punishment, his losses and dammages to be recovered at the Common Law for his loss sustained. The builder hath likewise a provision made against such Offenders by the late Act for Rebuilding the City.

Let him observe that his materials be good, so as to make substantial work, and that his bricks be well burnt, which he may know by their colour: bricks well burnt looking on a deeper red than those which are not, and if you strike them with any thing, they will make a brisk sound, and not be subject to moulder and break to dirt as others will. Let the builder make election of bricks that are made of a mould that was digged up in the winter, and laid a frosting, it being very advantageous to the substance of the brick. Let him take such lyke observation as to Tyles, as to their colour, and as to their tinckling, when struck so, that he may find whether they are made of a good mould, and whether well burnt or not; let him take care that his Lymne[23] be well burnt, and not by halves; so that the same be half Chalk in stead of Lyme, which is very disadvantageous to the strength of the building, and is dearer to the builder; let the Sand he mixes with his Lyme be as fine as he can conveniently get. [...]

Joseph Moxon, from *Mechanick Exercises* (1678)

The first instalment of Moxon's *Mechanick Exercises, or the Doctrine of Handy-Works Applied to the Arts of Smithing, Joinery* ... was published on 1 January 1678 (in current reckoning) at the price of one sixpence. Not only was it one of the first books published in serial form – thereby coming within the financial means of a new class of readers – but it also set out in an easily comprehensible form the knowledge of crafts such as carpentry, joinery, bricklaying and wood-turning, which until then had been the jealously guarded monopolistic knowledge of the guilds, passed down orally from master to pupil in a very slow process. Scientific theory was the basis for a practical handbook, originally consisting of 238 octavo pages and 18 copperplate engravings. Together these offered explanations of unprecedented clarity. Joseph Moxon (1627–91) was a printer, publisher, translator, author, mapmaker and mathematician, involved in the publication of more than 80 volumes, hydrographer to Charles II and a Fellow of the Royal Society. He was fluent in Dutch, Latin, French and German. Although the aims of the two books are quite different, much material in the *Mechanick Exercises*, in particular in the plates illustrating the joiner's tools, was derived from André Félibien's *Des Principes de l'Architecture et de la Sculpture*, which was published in Paris in 1676 (Harris, 1990).

Further reading: Moxon, *Mechanick Exercises*, 1962 and 1970 editions.

Preface

I see no more reason, why the Sordidness of some Workmen, should be the cause of contempt upon Manual Operations, than that the excellent Invention of a Mill should be dispis'd, because a blind Horse draws in it. And tho' the Mechanicks be, by some, accounted Ignoble and Scandalous? yet it is very well known, that many Gentlemen in this Nation, of good Rank and high Quality, are conversant in Handy-Works: And other Nations exceed us in numbers of such. How pleasant and healthey this their Diversion is, their Minds and Bodies find; and how Harmless and Honest, all sober men may judge?

That Geometry, Astronomy, Perspective, Musick, Navigation, Architecture, &c. are excellent Sciences, all that know but their very Names will confess: Yet to what purpose would Geometry serve, were it not to contrive Rules for Handy-Works? Or how could Astronomy be known to any perfection, but by Instruments made by Hand? What Perspective should we have to delight our Sight? What Musick ravish our Ears? What Navigation to Guard and Enrich our Country? Or what Architecture to defend us from the Inconveniencies of different Weather, without Manual Operations? Or how wasted and useless would many of the Productions of this and other Counties be, were it not for Manufactures. [...]

I thought to have given these Exercises, the Title of The Doctrine of Handy-Crafts; but when I better considered the true meaning of the Word Handy-Crafts, I found the Doctrine would not bear it; because Hand-Craft signifies Cunning, or Sleight, or Craft of the Hand, which cannot be taught by Words, or gained by Practice and Exercise; therefore I shall not undertake, that with the bare reading of these Exercises, any shall be able to perform these Handy-Works; but I may safely tell you, that these are the Rules that every one that will endeavour to perform them must follow; and that by the true observing them, he may, according to his stock of Ingenuity and Diligence, sooner or later, inure his hand to the Cunning or Craft of working like a Handy-Craft, and consequently be able to perform them in time. [...]

Book III. The Art of House-Carpentry

§13. Of the Ten-foot Rod, *and thereby to measure and describe the* Ground-plot

We shall begin therefore to measure the *Ground-plot*, to which Carpenters use a *Ten-foot Rod* for expedition, which is a Rod about an Inch square, and ten foot long; being divided into ten equal parts, each part containing one foot, and is divided into 24 equal parts, and their Sub-divisions.

With this *Rod* they measure the length and breadth of the *Ground-plot* into Feet, and if there be odd Inches, they measure them with the *Two-foot Rules*. Their measure they note down upon a piece of paper, and having considered the situation of the Sides, *East, West, North* and *South*, they draw on paper their several Sides accordingly, by a small Scale, either elected, or else made for that purpose. They may elect their *Two-foot Rule* for some plots; for an Inch and a half commodiously serve to set off one Foot on some small *Ground-plots*, and then you have the Inches to that Foot actually divided by the Marks for the half quarters on the *Two-foot Rule*. But this large Scale will scarce serve to describe a *Ground-plot* above ten Foot in length, because a small sheet of Paper is not above 15 or 16 Inches long, and therefore one sheet of Paper will not contain it, if the *Ground-plot* be longer: Therefore if you make every half quarter of an Inch to be a Scale for two Inches, a sheet of Paper will contain 20 Foot in length: And if you make every half quarter of an Inch to be a Scale for four Inches, a sheet of Paper will contain 40 Foot. And thus by diminishing the Scale, the sheet of Paper will contain a greater number of Feet.

But having either elected, or else made your Scale, you are to open your Compasses to the numbers of Feet on your Scale your *Ground-plot* hath in length, and then transfer that Distance to your paper, and to draw a straight Line between the two points, and mark that straight Line with *East, West, North*, or *South*, according to the situation of that side of the *Ground-plot* it represents. Then again open your Compass to the number of Feet on your Scale one of the adjoining Sides contains, and transfer that Distance also to your paper, and draw a Line between the two points, and note its situation of *East, West, North*, or *South*, as before. Do the like by the other Sides; and if either a Quirk, or any Addition, be added to the Building, on any side of your *Ground-plot*, you must describe it also proportionably.

Then you are to consider what Apartments, or Partitions, to make on your *Ground-plot*, or second, or third Story, and to set them off from your Scale, beginning at your intended Front. As for Example, Suppose your *Ground-plot* be a Long-square, 50 Foot in length, and 20 Foot wide: This *Ground-plot* will contain in its length two good Rooms, and a Yard behind it 10 Foot long. If you will, you may divide the 40 Foot into two equal parts, so will each Room be 20 Foot square. Or you may make the Rooms next the Front deeper, or shallower, and leave the remainder for the Back-Room: As here the Front-Room is 25 Foot, and the Back-Room 15 Foot deep, and a setting off of 8 Foot broad and 10 Foot long taking out of the Yard, for a Buttery below Stairs (if you will) and Closets above Stairs over it. But what width and depth soever you intend your Rooms shall have, you must open your Compasses to that number of Feet on your Scale, and set off that Distance on the *East*, *West*, *North*, or *South* Line, according to the Situation of that side it represents on your *Ground-plot*. If you set it off the *East* Line, you must also set it off on the *West*; if on the *North* Line, you must also set it off on the *South* Line: Because between the two Settings off on the *East* and *West* Lines, or *North* or *South* Lines, you must draw a straight Line of the length of your intended Partition. And in this manner you must from every Direction draw a line in its proper place on the Paper, by measuring the Distances each Partition must have from the outside of the *Ground-plot*.

And thus you are also to describe by your Scale your Front, and several sides of the Carcase; allowing the *Principal Posts*, *Enterduces*, *Quarterings*, *Braces*, *Gables*, *Doors*, *Windows*, and *Ornaments*, their several Sizes, and true Positions by the Scale: Each side upon a Paper by itself: Unless we shall suppose our Master-Workman to understand *Perspective*; for then he may, on a single Piece of paper, describe the whole Building, as it shall appear to the Eye at any assigned Station.

Sir H. Shere, 'Some Directions for my Lord Nottingham's Building' (1695)

It has not been possible to obtain any information on the author of this hitherto unpublished manuscript, 'Sir H. Shere'. Daniel Finch, 2nd Earl of Nottingham and 6th Earl of Winchilsea (1647–1730), was a Tory statesman, member of the Privy Council and First Lord of the Admiralty.

S[r]

You commended me to give you my Opinions touching some general Rules for Building, which if you had digested into Queries on that Subject I should have better known how to obey you. I therefore shortly observe to you.

That the bottom on which your Foundation is to rest ought to be uniform, viz. all Rock, all Gravellground for wherever any part of the Bottom is defective or unequall it will be soon seen in the Building, and tis hardly in the power of art to mend the defect. For which Reason the Italians who give us the best Examples in this Science go any depth and Scruple no expense to obtain an equal uniform Seat for their Buildings. We here in England often build on Clay which is the worst Bottom of all others, which when necessity urges and you cannot avoid it, the safest course is to lay your foundation on a good thickness of Timber in good loughs laid (not cross) but alongst and according to the Range of your Work. The use of this Timber under your foundation I approve almost in all Buildings that have weight except Rock, Chalk, or gravell, but principally on a Clay bottom which being always moist and apt to yield and sink under the Burthen that is laid on it. This defect becomes often very mischievous in great Buildings where you are under a necessity of charging the Foundation with different Weights of matter, as namely in great Stacks of Chimney Pieces where you have great opening Towers, Pavilions and the like. I say those differing Weights pressing and Treading-heavier and lighter on the Foundation while your Masonry is green makes different impressions on the yielding Bottom, which breaks the Bondage, Cracks your Walls, brings your Work out of Square, and becomes a great cause of the decay of most of our great Buildings here in England Where we have over and above the worst Materials and Workmen for the Masonry part in the whole World. Now laying of Timber in the manner I have proposed for your foundation becomes a means of giving those burthensome parts of your Building an ample footing by which means it trades lighter on the bottom by transferring the weight beyond its perpendicular gravitation, and so gives a proportionable share of the Burthen to those parts of the Foundation which without such preventive applications would produce those ill effects I have noted where your Bottom is unsound.

Burying of Timber likewise in the Walls under the Jambs of your Windows and all openings saves the Burthen, and sustains the weight better by carrying a share of the pressure into the void, which often prevents Cracks and Flawes in your Walls which we see about everywhere in ill performed structures, when the openings are wide and the Doors are little. Now tis to be noted that this use of Timber in your foundation and elsewhere is only a Temporary Service, and does its officewhile the work is green and without Strength and Bondage to unite & sustain the parts, which by that time the Timber is decay'd on which it rests, becomes set and cemented and of strength sufficient to bear its own Burthen without any foreign aids as Timber or any matter whatsoever that is substituted (as I may say) to supply and prevent weakness, and is not of a piece and of like duration with the rest of the matter whereof your Masonry is compos'd.

You tell me my Lords purpose to build his House entirely of stone, which I am sorry for having I think very good reason to prefer Brick to any other materiall whatsoever; I mean for the case or carcass of the Building not refusing any Ornement or Cloathing of Stone you may be disposed to give it. My Grounds for this Opinions are first, from Observation; all Works wrought in Brick being more Durable than in Stone. The greatest Pieces and Movements of Antiquity now in the world being of that material, and not to multiply instants of the truth of this Remark I take notice that the Pantheon at Rome built by Agrippa in the time of Augustus continues to this Day perfect in all its Strength and beauty without the least appearance of Defect or Decay. The Walls of which structure are twenty foot thick. The Coar and Solid part whereof is Brick and covered only with Shell of Mortar whereof the Ornaments are composed. Now if I am after a reason for this Superior Strength and surableness of work in Brick, I answer first. The Mortar of Cement which is the Vinculum[24] that binds and holds the parts together is observed to be harder and more Petrified in works of Brick than of any other Materiall, and for as much as the decay of all Buildings takes Beginning at the Mortar or Cement which is the least durable Part, it follows that where that is hardest and most durable the Building must be most lasting and longer endures the Weather and assault of time. Now I say that as the Cement in Brick Work is better and is harder than in stone being found in part to be true, the reason of which I will endeavour to give you, which I take to be this, namely that Brick as everything that is made by fire acquires a warmth by that Element that does not presently forsake it, which adventitious heat cooperating with the Petrifying Quality of the Mortar bakes and hardens it to a greater perfection than in Stone, and so begets a firmer and more durable consistence of the mass. Furthermore Brick hath the advantage of Stone in point of figure being Cast and form'd in such a fashion by Art both for length Breadth and thickness as best consists with that Bondage and Union which is necessary to all Works that are to be made into a Mass and compiled out of divers and lesser parts whereof the whole is to be composed. Bricks are likewise form'd straight flat and with Right angles which gives those an easy and firm seat one upon another, by which means they will rest and stand firm on their Basis without the help of Cement.

This advantage is not to be had in stone work where the irregular figure of the stones and suppleness by the addition of Mortar wherein they are bedded piec'd and sustained without any Principle of Stability but from the Mortar that upholds it, and without which it would fall and forsake its place to which it is assign'd in the Building. Now if the Cement whereof there is a much greater proportion us'd in Stone than in brickwork be the weakest and least desirable Material in the Mass, the more there is used thereof in composing your work, the weaker it will prove proportionably. Whence likewise Brick work becomes more durable than Stone, and this not only from the necessity you are under of using more of the weaker Material, but in regard of the figure, Brick standing on a firm Basis of its own without help, but stone when the Mortar decays having nothing but that for the most part to sustain it, necessarily falls of itself and drops out of the Building, which Birds will not do, and thus a Stone-Wall drops, mouldens and decays by faster degrees than Brick. 'Tis remarkable that Brick being lighter than Stone by 20 percent and will bear to be wrought thinner and with less Dimensions, the Pile when finished contains a lighter burthen to the foundation which is another help towards the strength and permanence of the structure.

This may suffice touching the Reasons of the preference of Brick to stone-work with a respect to the Strength and Duration of the Structure. Let us see now what further motives there are for the choice of Brick rather than Stone in Buildings that are Design'd especially for Habitations, and I hold the argument to be much stronger here in England in favour of Brick then in France, Spain or Italy or any of those warm Climates where the purity of the air and vicinity of the Sun brings all Sorts of Masonry to a quicker perfection than in our Northern moist Country.

Now if a healthy Situation be essential in the choice of a Seat whereon you would build a House, The next best choice you can make is to build a healthy House in a healthy place, which I undertake to say cannot be obtain'd here in England, especially if your Structure be compos'd entirely of Stone, where in great Buildings that requires proportionable thicknesse in the Walls, tis a doubt whether the Morter towards the Center becomes thoroughly set and cemented. – This at least we are sure of that Stone work ripens by so slow degrees in comparison of Brick, that the one in a year or two may afford a tolerable habitation, while the other in thrice the time will continue green, moist cold and unfit to dwell in, greatly poisonous to the health of the Inhabitants and prejudicial and destructive to all sorts of furniture whatsoever that shall be lodged therein, for as your walls must be thicker in stone than Brickwork, which exerts a longer space for the setting of the Work, so the stone itself being a materiell Chyle[25] moist and ministring nothing to the hardening of the Cement, the work will I say for ought I know never be thoroughly set towards the Center by which means in all hot Seasons especially unwholesome Vapours will break out and perpetually affect the health of the Inhabitants etc.

And this is among my reasons why in point of health and for the preservation of the ornaments Goods and Household Stuff that go to the Establishment of great Buildings, which for the most part are very changable, I would give the preference to brick Building.

I am not against carrying up a great Building with stone to the top of the Grounds, but from these upwards I would by any means build with Brick.

All great Openings and little Pieces are to be avoided for Arches or Lintels, do not suffice to prevent the Damage that attends such Errors for whenever a great weight rests upon a little foot it will be hardly possible to prevent the parting and cracking of the Walls for when a great weight rests upon a little foot, the Materialls under it cripple and yield to the Burthen.

For Roofing I prefer Oak everywhere because it is stiff and a Timber of long Duration, and you are at liberty in the framing to design your work by all the strength of art you please, but in flooring where your timber bears its own burthen and you have no help in Principle to sustain it I prefer Fir, as being lighter and will sink less by its own weight in great length than Oak.

In all doorways or openings that adjoyn to chimneys Towers or any other Burthensome part of the Building. Remember to let your Lintels lye higher toward that part than elsewhere because in a short space all openings will otherwise become out of square by reason of the settlement of those weighty parts of the Building more than the rest which this will obviate.

Let no light or openings be higher than 3 diameters nor lower than one.

Avoid as much as may be all sorts of Burthens to your Building that have not a Principle to sustain them as Turrets and Lucorne [lantern] lights fram'd in the Roofe, Stair Cases and the Like, for such weights as are not sustained from the Bottom and hang as I may say by the Nail, will at a long run sink, settle and prove prejudicial to the Roof shaking and disordering the covering begetting leakage and decay in the Structure.

The best way of preparing Morter in the World is what I have already imported to you, but tis very hard to put workmen out of their Road.

All Doorways, Windows and Openings on the Outside of your Buildings ought to be of Stone and not of Timber not only because there is no Society or Union to be made betwixt Timber and Masonry, and therefore in time these two Materials will part and have an Opening where they were joyn'd together, and so let in the air and the weather, but for as much also as the Jambs and Head Pieces being put in when the work is green do very often share a part of the Burthen, and therefore ought to be of a like durable matter with the rest of the Building, least by being of Timber which in time must decay, the taking down the same to repair them may be of ill consequence to the work which it may chance to sustain.

Chimneys void smoak better by a flank then a back Drought by which means a good deal of weight may be avoided, which in these burthensome parts of the Building cannot be too carefully shunned.

All Plastering upon Beams in the Ceiling begets Cracks which is an Eye sore, especially when there is painting or any cost bestowed, I propose therefore to avoid those cracks that your Gipse should drop an Inch and a half or thereabouts below the bottom of your Girders, and then Joyn the ends of your Gipse with a piece nailed up to the Girders of the same thickness with your Gipse on which to tack your Laths. By which means the Plastering not touching the solid Timber of the Girder those Cracks will be avoided.

The Italians Work their Bricks always wet their Morter being much more liquid than ours which makes much better work they having smaller Joints driving down every Brick with the handle of their Trowell, till in some part or other it touches the Brick under it. Their Mortar is always prepared in the manner I have already informed you, whereof you can give my Lords the best instructions.

It is not safe to build too fast, many Inconveniences happening by overcharging a green foundation.

In Terrace walks that are design'd to be cover'd with Flat stone, the Earth is to be made everywhere equal, and there to be very well ramm'd, and to stand a Winter, then let it be levell'd for your Purpose, and pich't with good Pebbles or Flints, very well ramm'd, this done lay your flat Stones bedded in good Mortar and well jointed; no other way will prevent it being perpetually out of Repair, Caution must be had that your Stone be of a Quarry that frost will not touch, otherwise that will likewise put your Terrace continually out of Repair.

All access to your Building by steps or other wise out of Doors exposed to the Rain and Winter weather ought to have a sound Basis upon Brick or other Masonry otherwise the wet gets in and by Degrees carries away the Earth and Matter on which the work rests and brings it quickly to decay.

The Italians are not to be our Example for the height of our Floors here in England where I think 18 foot for the most part enough.

Drains to carry the water quickly off the grounds from about your Buildings ought to be well contrived and as well perform'd – many a Noble Structure having miscarryed through want of due Caution in that particular.

All great Projections are carefully to be avoided as yielding no Ornament and being always a weakening of the Building.

A Line is not a Guide entirely to be rely'd on. Consult therefore your Eye both at hand and at a distance, for an Overseer that hath not a good Eye wants one very necessary Quality.

I think S^{r} by this time I have tired you with my general Notions in Architecture namely that part of it which concerns substantialls and Fundamentals in that Science as they have occurr'd to me without Order or any great Connection.

The ornamental and Embellishing part is contained in Rules published and established into Custom by the Learned in that Profession, to which any man but of slender Capacity may have resource and practice from with ease.

[...] Your most humble and faithfull Servant
H. Shere.

Andrea Pozzo, from *Rules and Examples of Perspective proper for Painters and Architects*, trans. John James (1707)

Andrea Pozzo (1642–1709) was a Jesuit priest, painter and mathematician whose *Prospettiva dei pittori ed architetti* was published in 1693. It was extensively used in Catholic circles both in Europe and in the Spanish colonies as a design manual. It was also the first systematic account of perspective in architectural decoration published in English. John James (*c.* 1672–1746) was an important translator of French and Italian books on architecture, including this edition of Pozzo and a 1708 translation of Claude Perrault's *Ordonnance des cinq espèces de colonnes.*

Further reading: Harris (1990); Kemp (1990), pp. 137–9 and 264–72; de Fea and Martinelli (1996); Battisti (1996); Palmer (2000).

Preface to this Translation

[a] Notwitstanding the Art of Perspective must be acknowledged so highly and indispensably requisite in the Practice of Painting, Architecture and Sculpture, that with the first of these especially, nothing commendable can be perform'd without its Assistance: Yet such have been the Difficulties and Obscurities met with in the first Attempts, and so great the Perplexity and Confusion of Lines in the Practice thereof; that the best Instruction, hitherto made English, have invited very few to such a Prosecution of this Study, as might render their Perfection of this kind, truly valuable. [...]

The Author, in both his Explanations of the ist Plate, has given some Account of what he would have his Reader understand, by Designing in Perspective, such a right Conception of this Print being of Great Use and facilitate the Work, we thought it most improper, to describe something more particularly what is meant by the Art of Perspective: but shall at present speak only of that, which, whether Vertically or Horizontally, is receiv'd on a Flat and Even Superficies: This being of much the same general Use; and, when rightly understood, renders the Difficulty of the Circular and Irregular Surfaces, easy and familiar.

Perspective is the Art of Delineating, on a flat Superficies, as a Wall, Ceiling, Canvas, Paper or the Like, the Appearance of Objects, as seen from one determinate Point: For this in Works of great Length, Two, Three, or more Points of Sight are sometimes made use of; yet such may more properly be said to be Several Views conjoin'd, then one Piece of Perspective.

Advice to Beginners

[c] The Perspective of Structures here treated of, can have no Grace or Propriety, without the help of Architecture. 'Tis therefore absolutely necessary, that you employ yourself for sometime in Drawing, and the Study of that

Art, till you can readily describe the Plan of any Upright, and from thence project the Section or Profile [...]. For as much as the proper Depth of each Part of the Perspective, is determined by the Plan and Profile thereof.

To the Lovers of Perspective
The Art of Perspective does, with wonderful Pleasure, deceive the Eye, the most subtle of all our Outward Senses;[26] and is very essential to be known of all, who in Painting would give a due Place and Propriety to their Figures, and more or less Strength required to the Lights and Shades of the Picture. This might be insensibly attain'd, if Persons, not content with the Study of Drawing Only, would accustom themselves exactly to delineate the several Orders of Architecture [...] Therefore, Reader, my Advice is, that you chearfully begin your Work, with a Resolution to draw all the Points thereof to that true Point, the Glory of God [...].[27]

The Approbation of this Edition
At the Request of the Engraver, We have perus'd this Volume of Perspective and judge it a Work that deserves Encouragement, and very proper for Instruction in that Art.
Christopher Wren, John Vanbrugh, Nicholas Hawksmoor.

John Webb, from 'Memoirs Relating to the Life and Writings of Inigo Jones, Esq.' (1725)

Inigo Jones (1573–1652) was an architect, designer and painter, and Surveyor of the King's Works from 1615 onwards. He was one of the first English artists to travel abroad to study the art and architecture of Roman Antiquity and the Italian Renaissance. This biography of Jones was added to the second edition of *The most notable antiquity of Great Britain, vulgarly called Stone-Heng*, which was originally published by John Webb, Jones's assistant, after the latter's death in 1652; it was based on notes left by Jones (see Chapter 4, below). The anonymous biography was closely connected with the forthcoming *Designs of Inigo Jones* (1727), and states that 'noble persons [e.g. Lord Burlington] have been at the Labour and Expence of producing the Plans' of Jones's buildings. Thus his merits both as a designer and as a historian of architecture would be preserved and made accessible to a larger public.

John Webb (1611–72) was the son of a gentleman and educated at Merchant Taylors' school in the City. He became Jones's pupil in his teens. He gained a wide experience in architecture and the arts by assisting with Jones's masques and the rebuilding of Saint Paul's Cathedral. His career, like that of Jones, was badly disrupted by the Civil War. He built for Royalists and supporters of Parliament alike, which may have contributed to his being passed over for the Surveyorship after the Restoration. Many of his most important buildings have been destroyed, such as Gunnersbury House and the building for the Royal College of Physicians in the City, both of the 1650s. However, Webb's efforts to preserve Jones's drawings and writings helped to preserve his own, as there was no clear distinction made between his papers and those of Jones until the twentieth century (Harris, 1990, entry on Inigo Jones; Turner, 1996, entry on John Webb).

Further reading: Gordon (1975); Bold (1989); Peacock (1996); Summerson (2000).

Mr. Inigo Jones was the Son of Mr. Ignatius Jones, Citizen and Clothworker of London. He was born about the Year 1572, in the Neighbourhood of St. Paul's Cathedral. 'Tis observable, his Christian Name is in Spanish, and his Father's in Latin; for which some have assign'd this Reason, that as his Father was a considerable Dealer in the Woollen Manufactury, 'tis probable, some Spanish Merchant might have assisted at his Baptism. There is no certain Account in what Manner he pass'd his younger Years, or where, or by whom he was brought up. It has however been suggested, that his Education was liberal, and that he laid the first foundations in the University of Cambridge. But there seems to be no other Ground for this Supposition, than a bare conjecture. This indeed we know, that he was early distinguish'd by his Inclination to Drawing or Designing, and was particularly taken notice of for his Skill in the Practice of Landskip-Painting. 'Twas his Progress in these more curious Arts, that recommended him to the Favour of that great Patron of all liberal Sciences. William Earl of Pembroke.[28] At his expence he travell'd over Italy, and the politer Parts of Europe; saw whatever stood recommended by its Antiquity or Value, and from these Plans form'd his own Observations, which upon his Return Home he perfected by Study and Application: And by these Degrees he rose to such an Eminence in the Knowledge of Architecture, that he was deservedly esteemed the Vitruvius of his Age and Countrey. We have a fine Intermixture of Fancy and Judgment, in his Decorations of Dramatick Entertainments, and the Pompous Machinery of Masques and Interludes. These were then the fashionable Diversions of the Court, and were drawn up by the greatest Masters. Several Representations of this nature are still extant by Ben. Johnson, Sir William Davenant, and the most eminent Poetick Writers of that Age.[29] The Subject was set down by the Poet, but the Invention, Ornament, Scenes, &c. were the Contrivance of Mr. Inigo Jones; for these he received a very considerable Encouragement from the Court.

His Capacity and Exactness soon rais'd him to the good Esteem of King James I. Who promoted him to be Surveyor General of His Majesty's Works. He was honoured with the same Employment by the Queen, Prince Henry, Christianus IV, King of Denmark, and upon King James's Demise, by his Successor King Charles I. 'Twas during this Interval, he form'd that most noble Structure, call'd the Banqueting-House, at White-Hall, which was at first design'd for the Reception of foreign Embassadors. The Ceiling was some Years after adorn'd by the Pencil of Sir Peter-Paul Rubens, with the Felicities of King James's Reign; and Draughts of these have been since taken, and lately publish'd by Sim. Gribelin, the Engraver. To him we owe the re-building of Somerset-House in the Strand, and the stately Piazza of Covent-Garden. In this last Performance, our Architect had in View the Piaza of Leghorn, but has vastly surpass'd the Original, by the Beauty and Largeness of his Pillars. But 'tis not in our Power to describe the Number or form a Judgment upon the Excellence of his Designs. This is an Employment deserving the Care of those noble Persons, who have been at the Labour and Expence of procuring the Plans of 'em. And as the Publick is now to be obliged with a View of 'em in Sculpture, the Reader may expect a finish'd Discourse upon their Nature and Value.

And thus there will be rais'd a Monument to our Author's Memory, even more lasting than his own great Performances. Brick and Stone will decay, and Time destroy the Labours of the ablest Architect; but the Works of the Learned will endure, so long as Reason and good Sense shall have any Being in the World.

Mr. Jones was no less distinguish'd by his Knowledge in the Theory or History of Architecture, than he was eminent in the Practice. In Proof of this, we need only refer the Reader to this valuable Discourse of Stone-Heng Restor'd, which we here present him.[30] 'Twas drawn up by Direction of King James I. in the year 1620, tho' not publish'd till after the Author's Death, and is wrote with so much Accuracy and Skill, that 'tis uncertain which most deserves our Commendation, his Industry, or his Sagacity. After much Reasoning, and a long Series of Authorities, he concludes at last, that this antient and stupendous Pile must have been originally a Roman Temple, inscrib'd to Coelus, the Senior of the Heathen Gods, and built after the Tuscan Order.

The dreadful Inundation of Civil War, which soon after follow'd, involv'd Mr. Jones in the common Calamity. His Integrity and Gratitude were strong Motives for adhering to the Royal Family in its Misfortunes, and bearing a Part in its Ruins. 'Twas this his Loyalty, which made him the early Object of Spoil and Robbery, in those licentious Times of Violence and Rapine. We learn from Mr. Lloyd, that it cost him four hundred Pounds by Way of Composition; a large Sum to be paid at such a Time, and upon such an Occasion! See his Memoirs and Martyrology of the Royalists. Had our Author liv'd till the Return of the Monarchy, his Losses would have doubtless been made up to him; but alas! he dy'd eight or nine Years before the Restoration. Antony Wood informs us, upon the Authority of Mr. James, the Son of John Webb, Esq; a near Relation to Mr. Jones, that he dy'd on the 21st of July, 1651. at the Age of about seventy nine Years. And yet the same Mr. Wood tells us, in another Part of the very same Book, that Mr. Jones dy'd about Midsummer-day in the Year following. And this last Account seems the more authentick, as it refers to a very circumstantial Note at the Bottom of the Page, which specifies the particular Time and Place of his interment. 'Tis there said that he was buried in the Chancel of St. Bennet's Church, near St. Paul's Wharf, in London, on the 26th of June, 1652. His Monument was placed on the North Wall, at some distance from his Grave, and was much defac'd by the great Fire of London, which broke out in the Year 1666.

We have already observ'd, that Mr. Jones's Book was not publish'd in his Lifetime. This office was left to the care of Mr. John Webb of Butleigh in Somersetshire, who in the Year 1655, sent it Abroad in a small Folio, under the Title of, The Antiquities of Stone-Heng on Salisbury-Plain Restored; and prefix'd to it Mr. Jones's Effigies, etched by Hollar,[31] after a Painting of Vandyke's. As there were but few Copies originally printed, and these not much dispers'd during the severe Affliction of the great Plague, the most part of the impression was consum'd in the Fire of London the Year following. And by this means being become extremely scarce, and at the same time much sought after by the Curious, as well for the Singularity of the Subject, as the Reputation of the Author, the copies have rose in their Value to an immense Degree, and were still not easy to be procured at any Expense.

Richard Holt, from *A Short Treatise of Artificial Stone* (1730)

In 1722 Richard Holt, who was a gentleman (fl. 1722–30), and the architect Thomas Ripley were granted a patent for 'artificial stone', that is, burnt clay. *A Short Treatise* was published in reaction to Batty Langley's attempt to set up a rival factory also in Lambeth. Holt dedicated it to Lord Burlington, to whom he had supplied his wares for finishing the villa and gardens at Twickenham. The aim of this text was to convince prospective buyers of the superiority and cheapness of his artificial stone; not a word was said about its composition. According to the artificial stone maker Daniel Pincot, writing in 1770, Holt's stone had 'neither taste in the design, nor neatness in the execution'. But it was durable, and the adventure was met with some encouragement until the death of its inventor (Harris, 1990).

[p. 1] Architecture, and the Ornaments of this Science, was justly held in the highest Esteen by the Ancients; by the Goths, as well as by the Romans; and by the Saxons, as well as by the Greeks: as is manifest from the respective Orders of most magnificent Bulldings still extant in this, as well as in the other Parts of the World, to the immortal Glory of their Memories. [...]

Now, among the many great and useful Arts encouraged and improved in our happy Island, none seems to thrive better, nor to raise its Head higher than Architecture; which, it is observable, the general spirit of the Nation runs daily more and more upon. Nor indeed can it make any more generous an Attempt; nor attempt any thing more commendable in itself, more pleasing to private Life, or more engaging to publick Sight. There are not many so lost to common Sensibility, as not to conceive Delight, and take pleasure, in viewing a well-finish'd and embellish'd Structure, belong to who it will.

How great then must needs the Satisfaction of such Proprietors be, especially when their Work is so accomplish'd and done at a small Expence. And here, I think, I may venture to say, our Countrymen can never more be suppos'd to fail in these laudable Attempts; considering that we are now enabled by this new Invention, which I'm just about to lay open to the World, to build, at least to beautify and adorn, full as cheap as ever our Ancestors did, even at their Penny a Day; and that too, with all the Elegance of Greece and the Magnificence of Rome itself. For, to the immortal Honour of our Patrons of Architecture be it said, the present Taste is the most refined, and of the most perfect Kind; free from all Gothick Rudeness and Monkish Foppery: just in its Proportions, and neat in its Embellishments: form'd in short upon the Noble Ancient Plan; which, however may admit of infinite Variety, on account of Singularity in Fancy, or Conveniency in Building, can never, in the Main, be either extoll'd, or alter'd to advantage; because it is founded upon the clearest Demonstration of Truth itself. [...]

The Reader must indulge me in giving previously some short natural Account of Stone in general; next in particular, of the two sorts most in use here in Building, and the Decorations of Buildings. And in doing of this, tho' I'm far from finding fault with the Produce of Nature, yet (I hope) I may freely advert on what's obvious to an ever discerning eye; namely, that there are common Defects in the best Natural Stone, and extraordinary Faults in all the inferior Kinds. [...]

[pp. 10–11] For these Reasons and other Defects in this *Material*, The Ancients did not trust their grand *Buildings*, at least not the *Decorations* and *Capital Ornaments*, to the Work of *Natural Stone* of any kind; but being well acquainted with the other *Products* of Nature, were at no Loss to find out *an extraordinary Tye, a peculiar Cement*, for binding of Clay together, so as to make an Artificial Stone far superior, both in Strength and Beauty, to the best and hardest Natural Stone. [...]

[p. 12] These serious Considerations put me, prompted as I was by a warm Inclination upon the most laborious Search, upon the tedious Tryal of many Experiments, and upon the reiterated Experiments of many odd things, many various Preparations and different Compositions, in order to find out the Old Tye, the Fixt Cement of the *Ancients*. [...]

[p. 13] And when I found, that this part of Natural Knowledge was not to be met with among the *Learned*, the *Virtuoso's*, and great of *Arts* in *Europe*, I quickly resolved and went into *Asia* and *African Turkey*, to see what I could learn from, and pick up among, the *Turks*, and the Race of the *Old Egyptians*, relating to the same affair; and this I was the more readily induced to do, considering the Fame of this most *Ancient People* for the *Invention* of all Arts *and* Sciences. [...]

Now as to the Nature and Quality of what I shall call my Secret Composition; it, briefly then, consists of such Ingredients, as are, by a strong Heat of Fire, reduc'd to a state of Fluidity; melted and run down into a most compact and Solid Mass, according to the Shape and Dimensions of the given Model. I say, my Composition consists of such Ingredients, as (when hot) have a Natural Tendency to Fluidity and Vitrification; and (when cold) consolidate into the hardest Stone, and turn into one absolute and perfect vitreous Substance. Thus, by the means of a few Simple Ingredients, I am able to run down my Clays, or even the hardest Rock in England, and Cast them in the assign'd Moulds, as fast as the Lead-Men do their most Fluid Metal. For, so long as the Particles of my Materials are in a disposition to Motion, gliding over one another's Surfaces, all manner of ways, from the Sphericity of their own Figures; they'll take the Impression, and assume the Form, of any thing propos'd, in the same easy and expeditious Manner, as Lead is known to do. [...]

Upon the whole, in short, if *Sir Isaac Newton* and others were right in pronouncing, all Effects to be proportionable to their adequate Causes, Then, I'm sure, I cannot be wrong, in what I've here Laid down and undertaken to maintain; namely, in a word, that my Artificial Stone is more strong and durable than the best Natural Stone. My Composition, in fine, ties down, binds together, and unites the Parts of any given Body, much more closely and strictly, than Nature does those of Common Stone; and consequently renders whatever is made of its Produce, infinitely more compact, firm and solid, than any thing made of Natural Stone can possibly be or come up to. [...]

Now at last, it may be proper to enter upon Particulars, and the Publick may desire to know the particular Applications of this Artificial Stone: I mean, to what Uses and Purposes it is, or may be, particularly converted? But, on this Head, I find, I've no Occasion to enlarge. A good round Catalogue of these has been already publish'd for me, by the great Industry of another,[33] and runs as follows, viz. Columns' Pedestals, Entablatures, Cornices, Pediments, Ballustrades, Statues, Rusticks, Fascias, Coppings of Walls and Chimneys, Chimney-Pieces, Hearth-Stones, Architraves, Frontispieces of Doors, Windows, Alcoves and Grotto's, Cascades, Obelisques, Arches, Piazza's, Key-Stones, Steps, Pavements, Urns, Balls, &c. [...]

In this place, it may be also proper, to acquaint the Reader, that, for the Goods most in use, and for which, the greatest Demands are made, I keep a Book of Draughts; which may be carry'd to Persons of Distinction, upon Occasion, that they may pick and choose, and please themselves, as to the Models of what they want; in case the Goods made should not hit their Taste. But if any Gentleman has a peculiar Fancy, or Device of his own, I'll undertake to fit him to his Mind; and upon leaving his Draughts, and giving his Commission, the goods so bespoke, shall be faithfully prepar'd, and as exactly made and modell'd after the Designs given, as the Picture (by the best Limner) shall be like the Man.

3

Architecture and Religion

Introduction

Church architecture was one of the most frequently discussed issues in British architectural writing of the seventeenth century. Not much church building actually took place until the last decades of the century, but because of the religious and political turmoil that characterized most of the century it was a very fraught subject, and much in the public's mind, as the variety and quantity of writing on this topic shows. The use of the classical style with its pagan associations had been a sensitive issue in Renaissance architecture on the Continent. A number of strategies were used to purify ancient architecture from these associations, such as replacing the pagan gods traditionally associated with the orders by Christian saints; thus the Doric order with its connotations of strength and masculinity, which had been used in temples devoted to Hercules and Mars, was used in churches dedicated to saints such as Saint Paul; the Corinthian order, used for temples devoted to female deities, was adopted in churches consecrated to the Virgin Mary, or even claimed by Rome in the sixteenth century as the order exclusively to be associated with the Catholic church. Another strategy was to base architectural theory as much on Christian writers as on pagan sources; and to uphold the morally sound character of classical architecture by stressing the importance of concepts such as decorum in church design.

British writing on the subject did not adopt the traditional format of the treatise, and often did not follow the solutions developed in Renaissance Italy. It does not fit into the Vitruvian mould. A variety of genres was used, ranging from the letter of advice to minutes of committee meetings or learned exercises in reconstructing the church buildings of the early Christians. The actual content of British writings is also decidedly unclassical. The authors discuss church design, but they rarely talk about stylistic issues, they hardly consider the use or adaptation of classical forms as was done in Renaissance treatises, and they do not talk about the Orders or proportion. Instead, there are discussions of historical precedent in the native Anglo-Saxon or early Christian traditions; discussions of ritual; of the placement of church furniture such as pews and chancels; of lighting; of burial within or outside the church; of the location of churches within their urban environment; and of issues such as whether women and men should sit next to each other, or whether Dissenters should be welcomed or allowed to leave when they wished to.

Opinions about church design were often expressed indirectly, by means of reconstructions of early Christian churches in the Middle East; sometimes, as in R. T.s *De Templis*, the issue of a specifically Christian version of classical temple architecture was addressed only by allusions in notes and references. When faced with the task of building fifty churches in London in 1712, the Commission appointed to oversee this task chose a resolutely practical approach: the memoranda of advice written by Vanbrugh and Wren concentrate on practical matters, and offer some aesthetic opinions, but ignore all matters of doctrine and its architectonic setting. But within this practical and apparently undoctrinaire approach, some views about the nature of church architecture can be detected. One of the most striking themes is the recurring discussion on whether a church is a theatre of sacrament (as British Protestants perceived Catholic churches to be) or an auditorium for hearing sermons. Sir Christopher Wren is a very clear advocate of the latter view in his *Letter of Recommendation*, but a different view is defended in *De Templis*, where the church is presented as a place in which to stage-direct the religious experience of the faithful. The clergyman Joseph Mede stressed, in a sermon of 1638 not included here, that 'The pulpit is the place where God speaks to us, not we to Him. The Font the place where he reacheth his favour unto us, in accepting us to be his Servants, not where being initiated, we offer our spirituall Service as a Sacrifice unto Him.'[1]

The Bible was a powerful source for thought about architecture, both because of its descriptions of Noah's Ark, the Tower of Babel and the Temple of Solomon and because of the conflicting images it presented about the moral value of building. It was approved as a way of praising God, but it was also rejected as an unjustified indulgence in materialism and luxury, or as an attempt on the builder's part to leave behind some proud material claims to glory instead of trying to save one's soul. Nonetheless Solomon's Temple acted as a powerful inspiration for alternatives to the classical tradition in church building. In the seventeenth century a number of reconstructions were produced, which formed the basis, together with historical enquiries into the architecture of the primitive Christians, for much writing on church architecture.

But architecture was also a widely used metaphor in Christian thought. The community of the faithful, the system of doctrine or the body of the Virgin Mary were all compared to various aspects of building, as is shown by the passages from John Donne, Walter Montague and Henry Hawkins included here. Even though these texts are not strictly speaking architectural theory in the sense that they offer design principles, they give privileged access to the ways in which architecture was perceived, or what meanings it possessed for the beholder. In using the metaphor of the house or the church to describe the structure of Christian doctrine or of the Christian perspective on human life, Donne not only used an evocative metaphor; by using that metaphor while speaking in a church he made his audience look with fresh eyes at the building in which they were gathered. Montague's use of the Court as a figure of for Heaven served as an argument against the traditional criticism of architecture as a vainglorious pursuit. Like Donne's use of architectural metaphor, his defence of the Court as a figure of or type of Heaven made the courtiers he addressed think again about the architectural setting in which they lived their lives.

Further reading:
Primary sources: Joseph Mede, *What is Holinesse* (1638); Peter King, *An Enquiry into the Construction, Discipline, Unity and Worship of the Primitive Church* (1691).

Secondary literature: Addleshaw (1948); Onians (1980); Clark (1982); Onians (1988), pp. 147–57 De la Ruffinière du Prey (2000).

From the Book of Kings, in the Authorized (King James) Version of the Bible (1611)

The Authorized Version of the Bible was a revised version of the Bishops' Bible, a new English translation completed under Archbishop Matthew Parker and first published in 1568. The revisors kept a close eye on the Greek and Hebrew original texts, and tried to steer a middle course between Puritan and Roman Catholic versions. The Authorized Version was commissioned by King James I in 1604.

Further reading: *The Bible: Authorized King James Version* (1997); De la Ruffinière du Prey (2000), pp. 125–33. (The version printed here is from the 1611 Oxford edition.)

Chapter 5

[…]

2 And Solomon sent to Hiram, saying,

3 Thou knowest how that David my father could not build an house unto the name of the LORD his God for the wars which were about him on every side, until the LORD put them under the soles of his feet.

4 But now the LORD my God hath given me rest on every side, so that there is neither adversary nor evil occurrent.

5 And, behold, I purpose to build an house unto the name of the LORD my God, as the LORD spake unto David my father, saying, Thy son, whom I will set upon thy throne in thy room, he shall build an house unto my name.

6 Now therefore command thou that they hew me cedar trees out of Lebanon; […]

8 And Hiram sent to Solomon, saying, I have considered the things which
thou sentest to me for: and I will do all thy desire concerning timber of cedar,
and concerning timber of fir.
9 My servants shall bring them down from Lebanon unto the sea: and I will
convey them by sea in floats unto the place that thou shalt appoint me [...].
10 So Hiram gave Solomon cedar trees and fir trees according to all his
desire.
11 And Solomon gave Hiram twenty thousand measures of wheat for food
to his household, and twenty measures of pure oil; thus gave Solomon to
Hiram year by year.
12 And the LORD gave Solomon wisdom, as he promised him: and there
was peace between Hiram and Solomon; and they made a league together.
13 And king Solomon raised a levy out of all Israel; and the levy was thirty
thousand men.
14 And he sent them to Lebanon, ten thousand a month by courses: a
month they were in Lebanon, and two months at home: and Adoniram was
over the levy.
15 And Solomon had three-score and ten thousand that bare burdens, and
fourscore thousand hewers in the mountains;
16 Beside the chief of Solomon's officers which were over the work, three
thousand and three hundred, which ruled over the people that wrought in
the work.
17 And the king commanded, and they brought great stones, costly stones,
and hewed stones, to lay the foundation of the house.
18 And Solomon's builders and Hiram's builders did hew them, and the
stonesquarers: so they prepared timber and stones to build the houses.

Chapter 6

And it came to pass in the four hundred and eightieth year after the children
of Israel were come out of the land of Egypt, in the fourth year of Solomon's
reign over Israel, in the month Zif, which is the second month, that he began
to build the house of the LORD.
2 And the house which king Solomon built for the LORD, the length thereof
was threescore cubits, and the breadth thereof twenty cubits, and the height
thereof thirty cubits.
3 And the porch, before the temple of the house, twenty cubits was the
length thereof, according to the breadth of the house; and ten cubits was the
breadth thereof before the house.
4 And for the house he made windows of narrow lights.
5 And against the wall of the house he built chambers round about, against
the walls of the house round about, both of the temple and of the oracle: and
he made chambers round about:

6 The nethermost chamber was five cubits broad, and the middle was six
cubits broad, and the third was seven cubits broad: for without in the wall of
the house he made narrowed rests round about, that the beams should not
be fastened in the walls of the house.
7 And the house, when it was in building, was built of stone made ready
before it was brought thither so that there was neither hammer nor axe nor
any tool of iron heard in the house, while it was in building.
8 The door for the middle chamber was in the right side of the house: and
they went up with winding stairs into the middle chamber, and out of the
middle into the third.
9 So he built the house, and finished it; and covered the house with beams
and boards of cedar.
10 And then he built chambers against all the house, five cubits high: and
they rested on the house with timber of cedar.
11 And the word of the LORD came to Solomon, saying,
12 Concerning this house which thou art in building, if thou wilt walk in
my statutes, and execute my judgments, and keep all my commandments to
walk in them: then will I perform my word with thee, which I spake unto
David thy father:
13 And I will dwell among the children of Israel, and will not forsake my
people in Israel.
14 So Solomon built the house, and finished it.
15 And he built the walls of the house within with boards of cedar, both
the floor of the house, and the walls of the ceiling: and he covered them on
the inside with wood, and covered the floor of the house with planks of fir.
16 And he built twenty cubits on the sides of the house, both the floor and
the walls with boards of cedar: he even built them for it within, even for the
oracle, even for the most holy place.
17 And the house, that is, the temple before it, was forty cubits long.
18 And the cedar of the house within was carved with knobs and open
flowers: all was cedar; there was no stone seen.
19 And the oracle he prepared in the house within, to set there the ark of
the covenant of the LORD.
20 And the oracle in the forepart was twenty cubits in length, and twenty
cubits in breadth, and twenty cubits in the height thereof: and he overlaid it
with pure gold; and so covered the altar which was of cedar.
21 So Solomon overlaid the house within with pure gold: and he made a
partition by the chains of gold before the oracle; and he overlaid it with gold.
22 And the whole house he overlaid with gold, until he had finished all the
house: also the whole altar that was by the oracle he overlaid with gold.
23 And within the oracle he made two cherubims of olive tree, each ten
cubits high.

24 And five cubits was the one wing of the cherub, and five cubits the other wing of the cherub: from the uttermost part of the one wing unto the uttermost part of the other were ten cubits.
25 And the other cherub was ten cubits: both the cherubim were of one measure and one size.
26 The height of the one cherub was ten cubits, and so was it of the other cherub.
27 And he set the cherubims within the inner house: and they stretched forth the wings of the cherubims, so that the wings of the one touched the one wall, and the wing of the other cherub touched the other wall; and their wings touched one another in the middle of the house.
28 And he overlaid the cherubims with gold.
29 And he carved all the walls of the house round about with carved figures of cherubims and palm trees and open flowers, within and without.
30 And the floor of the house he overlaid with gold, within and without.
31 And for the entering of the oracle he made doors of olive tree: the lintel and side posts were a fifth part of the wall.
32 The two doors also were of olive tree; and he carved upon them carvings of cherubims and palm trees and open flowers, and overlaid them with gold, and spread gold upon the cherubims, and upon the palm trees.
33 So also made he for the door of the temple posts of olive tree, a fourth part of the wall.
34 And the two doors were of fir tree: the two leaves of the one door were folding, and the two leaves of the other door were folding.
35 And he carved thereon cherubims and palm trees and open flowers: and covered them with gold fitted upon the carved work.
36 And he built the inner court with three rows of hewed stone, and a row of cedar beams.
37 In the fourth year was the foundation of the house of the LORD laid, in the month Zif:
38 And in the eleventh year, in the month Bül, which is the eighth month, was the house finished throughout all the parts thereof, and according to all the fashions of it. So was he seven years in building.

John Donne, from his *Sermons* (1630 and 1625)

John Donne (*c.* 1572–1631) was a metaphysical poet and divine. He was brought up as a Roman Catholic. The early part of his life was spent on the margins of the Court of Queen Elizabeth I. He took part in naval expeditions to Cadiz in 1596 and the Azores in 1597, and travelled on the Continent in 1605–06 and 1611–12. The main part of his poetry was written during his early life. In 1615 he took Anglican holy orders and was appointed chaplain by James I. In 1620 he was appointed Dean of Saint Paul's.

Further reading: Mitchell (1932).

***Deaths Duell, [...] Delivered in a Sermon at White Hall at the Beginning of Lent, 1630* Psa. 68 vers. 20. In fine.** *AND UNTO GOD THE LORD BELONG THE ISSUES OF DEATH.* **i.e.** *FROM DEATH*

Bvildings stand by the benefit of their *foundations* that susteine and *support* them, & of their *butteresses* that comprehend and *embrace* them, and of their *contignations*,[2] that knit and *vnite* them: The *foundations* suffer them not to *sinke*, the *butteresses* suffer them not to *swerve*, and the *contignation* and knitting suffers them not to *cleaue*. The body of our building is in the former part of this verse: It is this, hee that *is our God* is the *God of saluation and salutes*; of salvations in the plurall, so it is in the originall; the *God* that gives us spirituall and temporall salvation too. But of this *building*, the *foundation*, the *butteresses*, the *contignations* are in this part of the *verse*, which constitutes *our text*, and in the three diuers *acceptations* of the words amongst our expositors. *Vnto God the Lord belong the issues from death*. For *first* the *foundation* of this *building* (that our *God* is the *God of all salvations*) is laid in this; That *vnto* this *God the Lord belong the issues of death*, that is, it is in his power to give vs an *issue* and deliuerance, euen then when wee are brought to the iawes and teeth of death, and to the lippes of that whirlepoole, the graue. [...] And then *secondly*, the butteresses that comprehend and settle this building, That hee that is *our God*, is the God of all *saluation*, are thus raised; [...] And so in this *sense* of the *words*, this *exitus mortis*, the *issue of death*, is *liberatio in morte, A deliverance in death*: Not that *God* will *deliver* vs from *dying*, but that hee will *have a care* of vs in the *houre of death*, of what kinde soever our passage be. And this *sense* and acceptation of the *words*, the naturall frame and contexture doth well and pregnantly administer vnto vs. And then *lastly* the *contignation* and knitting of this building, that hee that is *our God* is the *God of all salvations*, consists in this, vnto this *God the Lord belong the issues of death*, that is, that this *God the Lord* having *vnited* and knit *both natures in one*, and being *God*, hauing also *come* into this *world*, in our *flesh*, he could have no other meanes to saue vs, he could haue no other *issue* out of this world, nor *returne* to his former *glory*, but by *death*; [...] And these three considerations, our deliuerance *à morte, in morte, per mortem, from death, in death, & by death*, will abundantly doe all the offices of the *foundations*, of the *butteresses*, of the *contignation* of this our *building*; That he that is our *God*, is the *God of all saluation*, because *vnto* this *God the Lord belong the issues of death*.

***A Sermon Preached at St. Dunstans January 15, 1625 [1625/6]. The First Sermon after Our Dispersion, by the Sickness.* Exod. 12.30: For there was not a house where there was not one dead**

[p. 291] We have (as we proposed to do) surveyed this House in *Egypt*, where the Text lays it, and the House at home where we dwell; there is a third House, which we are, this House of Clay, and of Mud-walls, our selves, these bodies. And is there none dead here? not within us? The House it self is ready to fall as soon as it is set up: The next thing that we are to practise after we are born, is to die. The Timber of this House is but our Bones; and, *My bones are waxen old*, says *David*;[3] and perchance not with age, but as *Job* says, His *bones are full of the sins of his youth*.[4] The lome-walls of this House are but this flesh; and *Our strength is not the strength of stones, neither is our flesh brass*;[5] and therefore, *Cursed is the man that trustheth in man, and maketh flesh his arm*.[6] The windows of this House are but our eyes; and, *the light of mine eyes is gone from me*, says *David*;[7] and we know not how, nor how soon. The foundation is but our feet; and, besides that *Our feet stumble at noon (as the Prophet complains)*[8] *David* found them so cold, as that no art nor diligence could warm them. And the roof and covering of this House, is but this thatch of hair; and it is denounc'd by more then one of the Prophets, *That upon all heads shall fall baldness*: The House it self is always ready to fall [...]

The fourth House falling under this survey, is this House in which we are met now, the house of God; the Church and the ground wrapped up in the same consecration: and in this house you have seen, and seen in a lamentable abundance, and seen with sad eyes, that for many moneths there hath scarce been one day in which there hath not been one dead. [...] And therefore, because these words do not only affect us with that sad consideration, That *there is* none of the houses *in which there is not one dead*; but minister withall that consolation, That there is none so dead, but may have a Resurrection, We shall pass another short survey over all these Houses.

Thus far we have survey'd these four Houses, *Egypt*, our families, our selves, and the Church, as so many places of Infection, so many temporal or spiritual Pesthouses, into which our sins had heaped powder, and Gods indignation had cast a match to kindle it. But now the very phrase of the Text, which is, *That in every house there was one dead, There was*, invites us to a more particular consideration of Gods mercy, in that, howsoever it were, it is not so now; in which we shall look how far this beam of mercy shines out in every of these houses, that it is not so now, There is not one dead in every house now; but the Infection, (Temporal and Spiritual Infection) is so far ceased, as that not only those that are alive, do not die, as before; but those whom we called dead, are not dead; they are alive in their spirits, *in Abrahams bosome*; and they are alive in their very bodies, in their contract and inherence in Christ Jesus in an infallible assurance of a joyful Resurrection. [...]

Lastly, in this fourth House, the House where we stand now, the House of God, and of his Saints, God affords us a fair beam of this consolation, in the phrase of this Text also, *They were dead*. How appliable to you, in this place, is that which God said to *Moses*, *Put off thy shoes, for thou treadest on holy ground*;[9] put off all confidence, all standing, all relying upon worldly assurances, and consider upon what ground you tread; upon ground so holy, as that all the ground is made of the bodies of Christians, and therein hath received a second consecration. Every puff of the wind within these walls, may blow the father into the sons eys, or the wife into her husbands, or his into hers, or both into their childrens, or their childrens into both. Every grain of dust that flies here, is a piece of a Christian; you need not distinguish your Pews by figures; you need not say, I sit within so many of such a neighbour but I sit within so many inches of my husbands, or wives, or childes, or friends grave. Ambitious men never made more shift for places in Court, then dead men for graves in Churches; and as in our later times, we have seen two and two almost in every Place and Office, so almost every Grave is oppressed with twins; and as at Christs resurrection some of the dead arose out of their graves, that were buried again; so in this lamentable calamity, the dead were buried, and thrown up again before they were resolved to dust, to make room for more. But are they all dead? *They were,* says the Text; they were in your eys, and therefore we forbid not that office of the eye, that holy tenderness, to weep for them that are so dead. But there was a part in every one of them, that could not die; which the God of life, who breathed it into them, from his own mouth, hath suck'd into his own bosome. And in that part which could die, *They were dead,* but they are not. The soul of man is not safer wrapt up in the bosome of God, then the body of man is wrapt up in the Contract, and in the eternal Decree of the Resurrection. [...]

No. 12. *The First Sermon Preached to King Charles, at Saint James: 3. April. 1625.* Psalme II: If the foundations be destroyed, what can the righteous doe?

[p. 27] The second is, to Suruay some of such *Foundations,* as fall within the frayltie, and suspition, and possibilitie of this Text, that they may bee destroyed: for when the Prophet sayes, *If they bee,* they may bee. Now *Fundamentum proprie de aedificiis dicitur,* sayes the *Lawe*: when wee speake of *Foundations,* wee intend a *house*: and heere, wee extend this *House* to foure Considerations; for in foure *Houses* haue euery one of vs a dwelling. For, first, *Ecclesia Domus,* the *Church* is a *House,* it is *Gods house;* and in that House, wee are *of the householde of the faithfull,* if (as it is testified of *Moses*) *wee bee faithfull in all his House, as Servants.* You see there is a faithfulnesse required in euery man, *in all the house of God,* not in any roome; a disposition required to doe good to the whole *Churche of God* euery where, and not onely at *home.* Secondly, *Respublica Domus,* The *Commonwealth,* the *State,* the *Kingdome* is a *House;* and this is that which is called so often, *Domus Israel, The House of Israel,* the State, the Gouernment of the *Iewes;* And in this *House, God* dwells, as well as in the other; In the *State,* as well as in the *Church*: For, these words, *The Lord hath chosen Sion, hee hath desired it for a habitation,*[10] are spoken of the whole Bodie, *Church,* and *State.* Thirdly, there is *Domus Habitationis, Domus quae Domicilium*, a House to dwell in, and to dwell with, a *Family*: and in this House *God* dwells too; for, as *David* sayes of the *Building*, wee may say of the *Dwelling*, *Except the Lord build the House, they labour in vaine*:[11] So except the Lord dwell in the House, it is a desolate Habitation. And then lastly, there is *Domus quae Dominus*, a house which is the *Master* of the *House*; for as euery Man is a little World, so every man is his owne House, and dwells in himselfe: And, in this *House God* dwells too; for the *Apostle* seemes so much to delight himselfe in that *Metaphore*, as that hee repeats it almost in all his *Epistles*, *Habitat in nobis*, That the Holy Ghost dwells in vs. Now, of all these foure *Houses*, that *house* which hath no walles, but is spread over the face of the whole Earth, the *Church*, And that *House*, which with vs, hath no other walls, but the *Sea*, the *State*, the *Kingdome*, And that *house* which is walled with *drie Earth*, our dwelling house, our family, and this *house* which is wall'd with *wet Earth*, this loame[12] of flesh, our selfe, Of all these foure houses, those three, of which, and in which we are, and this fourth, which wee our selfe are, *God* is the *Foundation*, and so *foundations* cannot bee destroyed; But, as though the common foundation of all buildings bee the *Earth*, yet wee make particular foundations for particular buildings, of Stone, or Brick, or Piles, as the Soyle requires; so shall wee also heere consider such particular Foundations of these foure houses, as may fall within the frailtie, and suspition, within the possibilitie, and danger of the Text, of being *destroyed*. [...]

[p. 42] There remains yet another *House*, a fourth House, a poore and wretched *Cottage*; worse then our *Statute Cottages*; for to them the *Statute* layes out certaine *Acres*; but for these *Cottages*, wee measure not by *Acres*, but by *Feete*; and fiue or sixe foote serues any *Cottager*: so much as makes a *Graue*, makes up the best of our *Glebe*,[13] that are of the *Inferiour*, and the best of their *Temporalties*,[14] that are of the *Superiour Cleargie*, and the best of their *Demeanes* that are in the greatest *Souueraigntie* in this world: for this *house* is but *our selfe*, and the *foundation* of this *House* is *Conscience*.

Henry Hawkins, from 'The House', in *Partheneia Sacra* (1633)

Henry Hawkins (1577–1646) was a Jesuit and emblematist, the author of two Recusant emblem books, *Partheneia Sacra* of 1633 and *The Devout Hart* of 1634. Because of the penal laws against Recusant Catholics which prohibited Catholic publications, these books were published either abroad or secretly in England. *Partheneia Sacra* (or *Sacred Virginity*) was published in Rouen and then smuggled into England by the Jesuits at the St Omer Press. The frontispiece was executed by the Dutch engraver P. van Langeren, though it is not clear who made the emblems. It is a devotional work in honour of the Blessed Virgin Mary, who is shown in the frontispiece as the woman of the Apocalypse and the Immaculate Conception, framed by a Baroque Corinthian pediment (see Figure 3.1). Each of the 22 chapters

3.1 Frontispiece to Henry Hawkins, *Partheneia Sacra, or The Mysterious and Delicious Garden of the Sacred Parthenes* ... (Rouen, 1633), engraved by P. van Langeren

172 PARTHENEIA SACRA.

THE EMBLEME.

THE POESIE.

The Pause.

HAn, Who dwels heer? A Virgin. What are you?
A Paranymph sent far, am come to sue
For one that pilgrime-like would lodge this night
Vnder your roof, and be a mortal wight,
Comes as a Bride-groome. Heer's no harbouring seat.
But h'is a Monarch. Then for me too great.
H'is GOD. *He now, & euer lodg'd with me.*
Would be a child, your Sonne. How can this be?
By th' Holie-*Ghost you shal be shadow'd ore;*
You let him in by keeping closd your doore.
Then be it donne. *One* Fiat *banisht night,*
And now an other brings from heauen the Light.

THE

3.2 'The Embleme' and 'The Poesie' from 'The House', in Henry Hawkins, *Partheneia Sacra* (p. 172)

163

THE XV. SYMBOL.

THE HOVSE.

THE DEVISE.

THE CHARACTER.

THE *Houſe* is an artificious Plaſme, framed by the hand of man, for his vſe and habitation. It is a creature made in ſpite of Nature, to vye with her: That foraſmuch as Man only is borne naked, and without a houſe to put his head in, afforded him by Nature, Art taking compaſſion on him, abundantly ſupplyes the defect. There is nothing comes ſo ſuddenly to ſo great a growth, as it; for wheras an Elephant being one of the greateſt among beaſts, and yet by manie degrees not ſo big as manie *Houſes* are, he is *The Impreſa*

3.3 'The Device' (or 'impresa') and beginning of 'The Character', from 'The House', in Henry Hawkins, *Partheneia Sacra* (p. 163)

or 'symbols' has a structure of nine sections: two pictures ('Devise' and 'Embleme'), a poem ('Poesie', see Figure 3.2) and six prose passages ('Character', 'Morals', 'Essay', 'Discourse', 'Theories' and 'Apostrophe'). Not all of these sections have been included here. Each chapter begins with a 'Devise', which is a picture of the symbol together with a motto; then follows 'The Character', an introductory passage which offers definitions and impressions (see Figure 3.3). Next come 'The Morals', a discussion of some of the ethical aspects of the device (*res picta*). 'The Essay' is based on Etienne Binet's *Essay des Merveilles de la Nature et des plus nobles artifices* of 1621, an encyclopaedia on the marvels of nature and art intended for orators and preachers, and an exercise in the vivid description of natural phenomena which can be traced back to the rhetorical stylistic strategy of *enargeia* (vividness, making the public see while listening). After the 'Essay' begin the 'Discourse', 'Theories' and 'Apostrophe', offering theological applications of the natural symbol to the Virgin. Taken together, these sections of 'The House' offer a catalogue of the religious meanings associated at the time with architecture (see the discussion in the 1993 edition). It has often been cited as a model for Andrew Marvell's country-house poem 'Upon Appleton House'.

Further reading: Fumaroli (1980); Hawkins, *Partheneia Sacra* (1993 edn); Bath (1994), Chapter 9; Gent (1995a).

[p. 163] *The Character.*

The *House* is an artificious Plasme, framed by the hand of man, for his vse and habitation.[15] It is a creature made in spite of Nature, to vye with her: That forasmuch as Man only is borne naked, and without a house to put his head in, afforded him by Nature, Art taking compassion on him, abundantly supplyes the defect. There is nothing comes so suddenly to so great a growth, as it; for whereas an Elephant being one of the greatest among beasts, and yet by manie degrees not so big as manie *Houses* are, he is twentie yeares ere he comes to his ful growth: a goodlie *house* will be reared, and brought to perfection in lesse then a yeare. Plants will not grow without rayne, or waters cast vpon them, where this plantation hath no need of waters, but rather al industries are vsed to keep them out. The Tortoyes in this respect, is better housed, not charged with reparations as long as his Lease lasts, for terme of his life: but yet hauing none else to trust, to looke vnto it, he is faine to carrie it about him. The Cockle hath his house, tiled with slate; which *hauing* no lock and key too, he is forced to keep at home for feare of theeues. And not so much as the poor Snayle but hath a *house* of his owne, which in his pace, like a Pedler with his pack, will he carrie about him throughout the world, and do that with time, which the Sunne can no more then do, with al his swiftness. Nay you can eate not an Oyster, but you *vn-house* him and put him out of his tenement. The Sun is the house of light, that needs no windowes, being nothing els but light. And for the 12. Principal houses and Pallaces in the Heavens, they are but weakely built without foundation, more then the Astronomers working braines. The Moone is the *house* of the Flux and Reflux of the Seas, who thence go in and out by turnes at their pleasures. The Almond is a *house* of the kernels within, which neuer comes forth til the roof comes fluttering downe her eares, that costs her life. The Hiue, is a house and Colledge of Bees, where they liue Collegially togeather; the Combs are their Refectorie. The Birds, for proper houses, haue their neasts; whose children are yong ones, and she the good huswif that keeps at home.

The Morals
Sedes Sapientiae [The seat of wisdom]
[In the margin: The Motto.] Looke where the Prince is, there is the Court; and where the Court, there his Seate. Wisedome is the Prince of the whole Microcosme of man: His Court then, and seate must needs be in the Power of the Vnderstanding, where he chiefly resides, and not where soeuer his dominion stretcheth; for so should he be in euerie place in person, which stands not with the Maiestie of so great a Prince.[16] Wel may his Ministers, like Purseuants and Heralds, performe and execute the Royal commands: as the hands, to make prouisions to maintaine the State; the feet, to trauel for that purpose; the eyes, to keep Centenel in the turrets of his pallace, and that neer his person, against forren inuasions, and the like: but yet the Prince himself in his Royal person departs not a whit from his proper Chamber of presence, the Intellect. And God himself, the Monarck of the whole Vnivers, is seen to be eueriewhere within his Dominions, through his essence, power, and presence, but not in that particular manner, as he is in heauen, in his proper seat; or as he was in earth, in his humanitie, or in the Sacrament itself most mysteriously, and Diuinely. For to speake in general, his seat is euerie where: The Heavens, are the roof; the Starres, the Seelings; the earth al diaperd and diuersifyed with infinit colours, his footstool and pauements; and the maruels of Nature, his shop of wonders, but his proper and peculiar seat, where he resides in, as in his Court, is either in the Empyreal Heaven (as I sayd) or in Christ's excellent Humanitie, or in the most Venerable and dreadful Sacrament of the Aultar; nor hath he made choice of anie other feats to dwel in, as not worthie or able to comprehend him. Where then had Wisedom properly set vp his seat, but in that pallace he had built for himself, founded in so great an humilitie, and so wel sustained with the seauen-gold pillars of the *Holie-Ghost*, I meane, in the Virgin-Womb of the Incomparable Ladie? Who receauing, and so long entertaining the *Wisedome* Increated, in her virginal Lap, as the true *Salomon* indeed, reposing sweetly in his Iuorie Throne, may wel be stiled: SEDES SAPIENTIAE.

The Essay.
[In the margin: The Review.] A House being a meer artificial, and no natural thing, hath its first subsistence in the Idea of Man's brayne; according to whose model, good or il, the house so built, proues good or il. We recurre then to the Architect, for direction in al. This Architecture is a soueraigne

Mistris of building, which giues the addresses, for disposing all the parts of a house, with relations in themselues, in comlines,[17] proportion, ornaments, situation, distances, eleuations, and a thousand of the like; of al which yealds it a pertinent and satisfactorie reason to the curious examiners, why euerie thing is so done, this and not that. Some are Architects by hand only, and no more, who frame their buildings by roat, taking forth copyes heer and there, but can afford no reason at al for what they do, nor inuent ought that is worth a rush; and for a final reason say nothing but, such is the custome so to do. Others are Architects by booke only, and by discourses which they have read; but they haue no hands to put in practise, and know but the Theorie only; such as they, are good for nothing, but to build a house for Plato, of Ideas, al suspending in the ayre. The good Architect should linck his spirit with his hand, and the compas with his reason, setting his hand to work, as wel as the brayne. The first do frame but bodies without a soule; the second, soules without a bodie; the third do build the whole, and are men of note and reputation indeed. The perfect Architect indeed should be ignorant in no science; otherwise, if he do wel, it is by chance, or els by nature, as beasts do, which do manier goodlie things, and know not why, nor wherefore. He had need be a Painter, to make his plaines, eleuations, designes, & to copie-out his plaines, eleuations, designes, & to copie-out a thousand rarities to please the phantasie withal; a Geometrician, to handle the compas, for the vse of Circles, rulers, squares, plummets, and the like; To haue the Perspectiue, to let-in lights into his house, to steale-in the day in certain corners, to content the eye with diuers aspects; and if not directly to introduce the Sunnie rayes, at least obliquikly through reflexions; The Arithmetick, to cast vp and calculate the charges he is at, to number the materials and degrees that belong thereto; The Historie: for al the enrichments of buildings, Armes, statues, and other ornaments, are nothing but Historie, true and fayned, which if he knowes not, he shal commit a thousand errours; To have Philosophie, to know the nature of beasts, the seas, the elements, flowers, fruits, and al whatsoeuer in nature; Astrologie and Phisick, in planting his house in a holsome and sound climat, in choosing the best Sun, a good wind, the purest ayre, holseome waters, a faire and free prospect, a good situation for pleasure and profit. This is certain, that al art is then truest perfection, when it may be reduced to some natural Principle of other. For what are the most iudicious Artizans, but the Mimiks of Nature? This same in our House is seen, comparing it with the fabrick of our natural bodies, wherein the high *Architect* of the world hath displayd such skil as euen stupifyes the human reason to enter into it: Where the Hart, as the Fountain of life, is placed in the midle, for the more equal communication of the vital spirits; the Eyes seated aloft, to comprehend the greater circuit in their view; the armes, proiected on each side for the vse and commoditie of reaching;

Briefly, the place of euerie part, is determined by the vse. Wherefore, the principal chambers of delight (as Studies and Libraries) should be towards the East: for the Morning is a friend to the Muses;[18] All offices requiring heat, as Kitchins, Stil-houses, stoues, and roomes for baking, brewing, washing, or the like, would be Meridional; Al that needs a coole & fresh temper, as Cellars, Pantries, Butteries granaryes, to the North; and so likewise al Galleryes appointed for gentle motion, especially in warm climes, to the West.

The Discovrse.
[In the margin: The Survey.] The Chiefest grace, splendour, and glorie of a house, is, that the Maister therof, who dwelles therin, be markable & illustrious for single & eminent vertues; since the chiefest ornament of a house is, the vertue of the Lord therof. Now then the blessed *Virgin*, being eternally ordayned to be a House and habitation of the Diuine *Word* Incarnate, and wherin the *Holie* of *holies* for nine months, and the endless Fountaine of all sanctitie was corporally to inhabite, this sacred House must borrow needs so great a splendour & dignitie, as no other, nor the Empyreal heauen itself, might anie wayes compare with it. What more? How beit the glorie of that ancient house and Temple of *Salomon* were great, yet can none deny this defect in it, for being incapable to hold the greatnes of God in its ample galleries & spaces, euen by the genuin confession of *Salomon* himself: *If the Heaven and the Heaven of heavens can not containe thee, how much lesse this house which I haue built?*[19] [...]

Besides that, which highly aduanceth & sets forth the glorie of a house, this same prerogatiue is of no smal moment, to haue been deciphered, delineated, plotted, and contriued, & euen raysed and built from the first foundation by a skilful & exquisit Architect. Behold God himself, the Supreme Architect, not only designed this House, but euen finished it himself, & brought the same to that eminent perfection, it is of: *I have been eternally ordayned.* Behold the plotting, contriving, & designing of our House; *The Highest himself hath founded her,* where note the foundation.[20]

I know, how *Ouid* in his *Metamorphosis* describes the house of the Sun very elegantly in this manner:

The Pallace of the Sun, on pillars highly placed,
With burnisht gold did shine, and Pyropsstone,
And seeling roofs with purest Iu'rie graced.[21]

But who sees not, how this House heer, wherin the *Sun* of *Iustice* dwelt, did farre exceed the same, whose ornaments surpasseth those, by infinit degrees? For whose golden pillars, where the Guifts of the Holie-Ghost erected in her; for whose Pyropus or Carbuncle, which euen glows like a burning cole, her most ardent Charitie abundantly supplyed; & for the white &

purest iuorie, her inuiolable & immaculate Virginitie. Whence, while the most blessed *Virgin Marie* more plentifully abounded with the guifts of the *Holuie-Ghost*, she burned more ardently with Charitie; and in virginal puritie was more neat, then the heauenlie Spirits themselues; surely more strong and statelie Pillars sustained this house, more precious Carbuncles enriched it, & purer Iuorie adorned it, then those others did the *Ouidian* Pallace of the Sun. [...]

The Theories

[p. 173. In the margin: The Contemplation.] Contemplate first, that as in euerie House wel built, and orderly disposed, there is a Dining-romme at least; and a handsome chamber for some principal guest to lodge in; so this *golden House*, the *Mother* of God, which he had so eternally prepared for himself, was not contriued without them both. And first for the Dining-roome, King *Salomon* made him a Throne of the wood of Libanus; which wooden Throne was the blessed *Virgin*, because the heauenlie Prince and bride-groome sate and lay sweetly reposed in her armes and wombe delightful vnto him, while he took flesh of her. She was a Bride-chamber, because a *golden couch*. For as gold is beautiful, incorruptible, and refulgent: So was her vertue *golden*, because beautiful for sinceritie of manners; *incorruptible*, through priuiliedge of Virginitie; and *refulgent*, for her luster of Vertues. [...]

Consider then, that as a *House* hath also Galleries for recreation and delight, so had our Mystical House heer, delicious galleries to walke in, and, for varieitie, three: to wit, the lower, the middle, and the vpper gallerie. The lower was susteained with siluer pillars; and therefore it is sayd, *that wisedome erected siluer pillars*. The middle was paued with precious stones, according to that: *The middle was strewed with charitie*. The highest was hangd with silks and purples; and therefore is added *a purple ascent*. The lower gallerie of this virginal house, was the precious bodie of the Virgin; the middle, her purest soule; and the highest, her sublime and Angelical spirit. Her bodie was the lower gallerie, because hersensualitie was neuer prone to euil, but alwayes conformable to reason. Her soule, the second; because strewed with precious stones, that is, Diuine vertues. Her Spirit was the vpper gallerie, & adorned with purple hangings, for being so enflamed with charitie, or wounded with the sorrow of her *Sonne's* passion, or sprinckled with his bloud.

Ponder lastly, as a house, especially the Pallace of Kings, requires to be spacious and ample; so was this House, our Ladie, being the House of God, most spacious & wide; according to that which the Church sings of her: *Whom the Heavens can not containe, hast thou held in thy Lap*. Secondly, wide and ample in compassion, while she receaves al, and refuseth none, in protecting them from the snares of the Diuel; Sinners, in obtaining mercie and grave for them; the Iust, in conseruing them in grace obtained; and lastly the Dying, in receaving their soules into her protection: and therefore sayd to be *Mother of grace, and mother of mercie.*

R. T., from *De Templis* (1638)

R. T. has not been identified, but he probably adhered to the views of Archbishop Laud, who was in favour of sumptuous religious ceremonial as a way of putting the Anglican truth across to the masses. *De Templis* is a very learned enquiry into the nature of church architecture and early Christian sources. It is also an exposition of the ways in which church building could be used to direct the church-goer's religious experience by architectural means.

Further reading: Newman (1993); de la Ruffinière du Prey (2000).

Chapter V. The Definition of a Temple
A Temple is by some thus defined, *Templum est aedificium Deo consecratum*, it is an edifice consecrated to God. And in this definition is conteined the whole nature of any Temple. [...]
[p. 36] When wee say, it is consecrated to God, we not only distinguish it from all profane buildings, but also teach the end, for which it was built. And if by God, we will understand the feigned deities, in this definition may also bee comprehended, the *Fana* and *Delubra* [sanctuaries and shrines], of the Heathens, as well as the Temples of the Jewes, and Christians, or any other, who ignorantly worship the true God [...].

Chapter VI. Of the Forme or Figure of Temples
The Forme of a Temple is twofold, either the externall forme, which is obvious to every beholder, or the internall forme, which bodily eyes, cannot see. That consists in the figure, and outward workmanship; This in the dedication. The external forme [...] depending almost wholly on the fancie of the Architect, has ever been various, and uncertaine. The Gentiles, commonly fitted their buildings to the nature of their Gods. *Iupiter Olympius*'s Temple, was built after the Dorique order, with columnes round about the outsides of it and by *Iupiter was signified the fire, as by* Iuno the ayre, whose Temple they builded after the self-same order, and manner, intending doubtlesse thereby, to signify, the great strength of the two elements, of fire, and ayre; as also, the vicinity of the nature of ayre, in its supreme region to the fire.[22] [...]

Saint Gregory in an Epistle to *Melitus an Abbot*, gives command, that *Augustine* the Bishop [...] of *Canterbury*, and he to whom England owes much for her conversion, should destroy the Idols in England, but suffer their Temples still to stand: *Nam gens illa verum Deum cognoscens* (saith hee) *ad loca quae consuevit familiarius concurret.*[23] [...] And by this, we may guess at the figure of the Churches, which the primitive Christians first used. The figure most affected by the ancient heathen, was the round, imitating (as it were) thereby the Heavens. Of this figure was *Vesta's* Temple [...], of this figure was also the famous *Pantheon*. Indeed the Temples which the Christians erected from the very foundation, were of other figure, yet some of them were of the round; such was that stately Temple of *Sancta Sophia* builded by the Emperor Constantine [...]

Pet: Gregorius Tolozanus saith, that the Apostles themselves gave order, that the body of the Church should be built long, after the figure of a ship, in which the Bishop should sit as a Pilot, the Deacons as Mariners; the Bishop's seat should be placed in the middle; on the side, should sit the Priests and Deacons; on the other Side the Lay men; and the women should bee separated from the men, in a place by themselves.[24] [...]

Divers Churches have many Isles, joyned to the body of the Church, like so many boats, or ships, compacted and tyed together; and some think that by this figure, the Christian builders did desire to expresse Saint *Peter's* boat, warning us, that saile here in this world, amongst so many rocks, and dangers, to be sure wee commit ourselves, to a safe bottom, by whose help, we may at last arrive at our blessed haven, for want of which care, many dayly make shipwrack of their salvation.

We see many Churches built after the figures of a Crosse, and without doubt, the pious builders, did by that figure desire to resemble the Crosse on which CHRIST was crucified.

Chapter VII. Of the Parts of Christian Temples

Bellarmine observes, that Christian Temples are built with three parts, after the Fashion of Salomons Temple.[25] First there is the porch [...]. Secondly, there is the ship or body of the Church. Thirdly [...] the quire or chancell, divided from the body of the Church by an ascent of steps and certaine *cancelli*, latices, bars, or hangings, which part belongs to the Priests only.

Chapter XIII. Of the ends, for which Temples were built

It is most certaine, that some Temples were built only to flatter great Kings, with the vaine conceit of a Deity. [...] Other Temples were built to the Honour of some famous men, zealous error mistaking them to be Gods. The ends for which they were erected to the true God, may be foure.

First, To offer Sacrifice in them.

Secondly, to bee Sepulchers, and Repositories of the corps of his blessed Martyrs, untill the generall Resurrection.

Thirdly, To offer and present in them Prayers unto Almighty God.

Fourthly, that Christian people might meet together in one place, to heare the Word of God and receive the Sacraments. Some adde to these a fifth, viz., that the Divine Majesty might vouchsafe still to continue with us, and to dwell amongst us. [...] God, we piously believe, to bee in every place, but we cannot say, that he dwells in any place, but in his Temple. There, as in his Court and Palace, he distributes his divine gifts and graces, to the hearts of his faithfull servants: there we more plainely behold in his glory and majesty, in the statelinesse, and beautie of the building, in the richnesse of the several vessells and ornaments, the numerous multitudes of his Servants, the various fruits of the blessed Sacraments, the dignity, holinesse, and sacred pompe of his Ministers.

Chapter XIV. How the whole world may bee said to bee a Temple

Hitherto of Temples built by men, as well Jewes, and Gentiles, as Christians, all which proclaime the Art, Magnificence, or Pietie of the burdens. There are also Temples built by the powerfull hand of the Almighty Creator, as the vast and the great Universe what is it but a Temple, according to which patterne, mortall men have corrected theirs, imitating its figure in their rotundaes, before spoken of. *Diogenes* saies plainly, *Mundum esse Dei Templum sanctissimum*: the World is the sacred Temple of God [...].[26]

The primitive Christians, indeed called the Universe the Temple of God because the tyrannies of the Gentiles, would not permit them to enjoy any other. [...] The whole Universe were they wont to say is our Temple, or rather the soule of every Christian, is the Temple of his God, which is of larger capacity than the whole world: and more glorious Temples than these can no where bee builded, to our great and good God.

And well may the Universe be called a Temple, there has been nothing said of Temples, but may very well bee said of it; If they be called Temples, because they bee vast, and great structures, is any thing greater than the Universe, which conteines all things in its vast capacity. If *Basilicae*, from their state and majesty, how much better does that name fit the Universe, than which nothing more royall. It has the Firmament for its roof, the Starres for tapers, the Heavens, for its Altar, Woods and Groves instead of Tapestry and Hangings, and the Earth for its pavement, which God himselfe besprinckles with the dew of heaven.

Chapter XX. Of Adorning Christian Temples

And surely if Wrestlers and Gladiators have their Amphitheaters, and Palesters [wrestling-places], if the Senators have their Courts and Capitolls, if the Philosophers their *Lycea*, if mortall Princes have their Palaces, nay if every private man, hath his dwelling house dressed and adorned, with all the sweetnesse and beauty he can devise, what reason has any man to thinke, that the Temples of the Eternall God, should be base and sordid, or why should any man (like that traitor *Judas*) thinke all lost that is bestowed on him.

Chapter XXI. A decent form of building and adorning a Church
For the situation Eastward, I shall need say no more [...] that it were very gracefull, that there should bee an ascent of steps up to the church.

The best and most received figure is the long, and though some may think the broad square, the ovall, or round more convenient (as being of more capacity) to heare Sermons, and Lectures, yet surely the Majesty and reverence of the place appears not so much in them. And the man who enters the West door from farre beholding the Altar, where he seriously intends to offer his devotions to his God and Saviour, shall find his devout Soule, more rapt with divine awe and reverence, more inflamed with pure and holy zeale, in the delay and late approach unto it, than if at first he had entered upon it.

Pillars in all other buildings, are very inconvenient; in Churches, gracefull, stately and necessary, as well for supporting the roof, distinguishing of the Iles from the body of the Church, and different from profane buildings; besides it has beene so received a manner of building, that to leave them out, savours too much of noveltie.

The Chancell or Quire must bee higher than the body of the Church. [...]

The Chancell being divided from the Church by grates of wood, curiously carved, or of iron, or brasse cast into comly works, is not only very gracefull, but according to the lawes and orders of building observed by the primitive Christians. [...]

When there are no Iles adjoyning to the body of the Church, Pilasters wrought into the wall, with well framed capitals, would adde much beauty to the fabrique, and much strength to the wals, between which could bee convenient spaces to beautifie the Church, with some excellent paintings of Sacred stories, which may strike into the beholder, religious and devout meditations.

Over the Capitals according to the common rules of Architecture must run an Architrave freeze, and Coronis [...] according to the order of building. Over these, let the windoores be placed, which because they stand high differ more from profane buildings, keep our thoughts from wandring abroad, whilst our eyes have nothing but Heaven, and heavenly objects to behold, and besides cast an excellent light for the paintings on the wals. The number of windoores ought to observe the grace of the whole structure, which if they cannot be of common glazie, but painted, adorne the Church with a glorious light, and moderate that bright light, which is a hinderness to devotion. The Utopian Temples, saith St *T:More*, were *subobscura*, somewhat dark: Nec id aedificandi inscitia factum sed consilio Sacerdotum, quod immodica lux cogitationes dispersit.[27] For devotion requires collected Spirits, as Sir H: *Wotton* seems to interpret him in his Elements of Architecture.[28] And we find it by experience, that in our light Churches did wee close our eyes, wee could hardly keepe our thoughts from distractions till the end of a short collect.

[...] I verily believe that the holy fervour of devotion was more intense in the primitive Christians' dark obscure vaults, then hath ever beene in our lightsome churches.

The roof if it be vaulted, is more agreeable to antiquitie, than if flat, it makes the voyce more audible; you may adorn it with an azure colour, and gilded stars, and then as in figure, so in colour it resembles the Hemisphear of the Heavens [...].

[...] Of all parts of the Chancell, that where the Communion Table stands, has ever beene accounted most sacred. In adorning that, no cost ought to be thought too much. There we behold the mystery of our Redemption lively expressed [...]. Hither bring your stateliest hangings, and adorn the wals; hither your richest carpets; hither the most glorious silks, and finest linen, to cover the holy Table [...]. And truly if Ladies and Gentlewomen, were studious in working holy vestments [...] how much more acceptable would it bee to God, than in wearing those curious needle works, on their own backs?

Walter Montague, from *Miscellanea Spiritualia* (1648)

Walter Montague (1603?–77) was the second son of Sir Henry Montague, the 1st Earl of Manchester. He was educated at Sidney Sussex College in Cambridge. After leaving university he went abroad. On his return he was well received at the Court of Charles I, in particular by the Duke of Buckingham, and became a friend of Queen Henrietta Maria, to whom he dedicated the *Miscellanea Spiritualia*. He repeatedly returned to France and Italy on secret diplomatic missions. In 1635 he abjured the Anglican faith at the hands of the Pope after having witnessed the exorcism of the Ursuline nuns at Loudun. In spite of this highly publicized conversion he was allowed to return to England. During the Civil War he was imprisoned in the Tower of London, but in 1649 he was released and forced into exile in France, where he became Abbot of St Martin's near Pontoise and a great help to many Royalist exiles. He died in Paris in 1677 (*DNB*).

Montague presents the Court and its actual architectural setting as a symbol of divine mysteries, and in doing so offers an apology for its display of wealth and opulent ceremonies. It is a typical case of figural analysis, a technique of interpretation originating in Bible exegesis, but whose range extended to everything created by God or Man, in which objects, events or persons in the Old Testament are seen as foreshadowings (or *figurae*) of objects, events or persons in the New Testament. For example the Tree of Jesse is seen as a prefiguration of the Cross on which Christ died.

Further reading: Auerbach (1967), pp. 55–93; Korshin (1982); Smuts (1987), pp. 217–45.

[p. 86] *The ninth Treatise. Of the Condition of Courts, Princes and Courtiers. Divided into three Sections Section I. The best Notion of Courts proposed.*

In the Law of Moses, all the Rites and Ceremonies were not only declaratory formes of the present Religion, but significative figures of a future state; and howsoever, most of the vulgar looked no farther then the glosse and lustre of the exterior vaile, which was the beauty and decency of the forme, and order that affected them; yet the nobler sort passed their sight through their vaile, and fixed it upon the signification, and mysterie itselfe, and thereby, had not only their eye of sense delighted, but that of their understanding enlightened by these objects.

In reference whereof I may hope not improperly to apply these considerations to the Courts of Princes, since all the exteriour state and Ceremony and Reverence (being truly conceived) is significative as referr'd to the images of God, and thus all the distinguished ranks of honour, which compose the formall order of Courts, are figures of those different degrees of Ministers, which attend their Originall, the King of Kings: and in this order, the Glory and Majesty which exteriorly in all sorts, resideth about the persons of Princes, may be fitly understood to represent (in such shaddowes as these materialities can make) the celestiall magnificence of the King of Heaven: so that one who will interpret religiously the Ceremonies of Princes Courts, may say, *all things befall them in figures*.

But certaine it is, that many in Courts, who determine and center their thoughts upon the fronts and out-sides of these mansions, which are honour, riches, & pleasure, and raise all their Devotions to the place upon those objects (and such are truly the meaner sort of Courtiers, though they be greatest in the measure of the world) and there are some of the other party, who penetrate into the religious sense of these exteriour figures, and derive from them, sprituall conceptions and appetites; concluding by these Glories, (which are but the shaddowes that signifie) that the substance it self must needs be *above what eye hath seene, or eare heard, or hath entred into the heart of Man*; and so by this view are quickned in their ambition, towards those originall endeavours; and these are the nobility of Courts, though they be never so interiour in office.

Of these two kinds of Courtiers is verified, *The first shall be the Last, and the Last first*. And likewise of the first sort we may say, as the *Apostles* saith of the Law, *The Letter kills*. If the litterall sense of the faire text of this worlds glories take up and fix their mindes; and of the latter sort *the spirit quickens*, when out of these specious objects they extract a spirituall sense, which excites in them a celestiall aspiring and emulation.

Such a figurative conception Saint Fulgentius framed out of these images, when he was asked, whether the beauty and Majesty of Rome did not worke upon his affections. He answered, If terrestiall Rome be so beautifull, how glorious must be celestiall Jerusalem? His minde was so little taken or retarded on her way, as she stayed not at all in the outward Court of the Gentiles, but passed on, as in her way through it, to the Holy of Holies; and by this method, who attend the offices of their mindes upon earth, and waite not upon the places of their bodies, concluding that they are but strangers and passengers through these courts, and Fellow-Citizens of the Saints and Domestikes of God; make excellent use of all the lustrous, and polished glories of the place; for instead of looking on them as flattering glasses, and mirrours which reflect only the materiall beauty of the earth, they make opticke glasses of them, through which they do the easier take the height of the celestiall glories: and surely, the sight of our minde is much helped by such materiall instruments, in the speculation of spiritualities, by reason that in this her prison, all the intelligence of our minde with immaterialities, passeth as I may say, through her keepers hands, which are her senses, that can carry nothing but corporeall images to her; and therefore we see the Apostle Saint John draws the image of the court of heaven, in such colours as are most visible and affecting in the Courts of the earth; whereby to raise our imaginations upon these steps, which they can tread upon to some proportionate conception of such fruitions, as are truly spirituall, and Intellectuall.

Sir George Wheler, from *An Account of the Churches* (1698)

George Wheler (1650–1723) was a traveller and divine. He was born in exile in the Netherlands, educated at Oxford and started travelling on the Continent in 1673. He accompanied the physician James Spon to Greece and the Levant in 1675–76. Spon published a separate account of this journey in 1678 in Lyon under the title *Voyage d'Italie, de Dalmatie, de Grèce*. Wheler's *Journey into Greece* was not published until 1682. He returned to England in 1676, bringing an extensive collection of marbles, coins and botanical specimens which he bequeathed to Oxford University. He took holy orders *c*. 1683 (*DNB*). In presenting his reconstruction of a primitive Christian church (see Figure 3.4) Wheler stressed that 'What Form or Figure this was built of, Eusebius gives no account'; the visual reconstruction Wheler offered is remarkably eclectic, combining Corinthian columns with Byzantine domes. Eusebius (*c*. AD 260–*c*. 340) was one of the first historians of the Church; he delivered the inaugural sermon, which embodied a description of the building, at the consecration of the church at Tyre in 314.

Further reading: Smith (1989); Knight (2000).

Chapter X. The Application to the Church of England

It would not be a matter of any great difficulty, or charge, to Accomodate our Churches according to the Manner of the Primitive Church: Especially the Cathedrals, where they have space enough to do this in many ways. They being neither Encumbered with Pues, nor otherwise straitened. It is but Removing their Shrines, or rather Screens in most of them, And the Holy Table stands where it Anciently did; and setting a Reverend Pulpit, Adorned with the Commandments, in the place of the Throne.

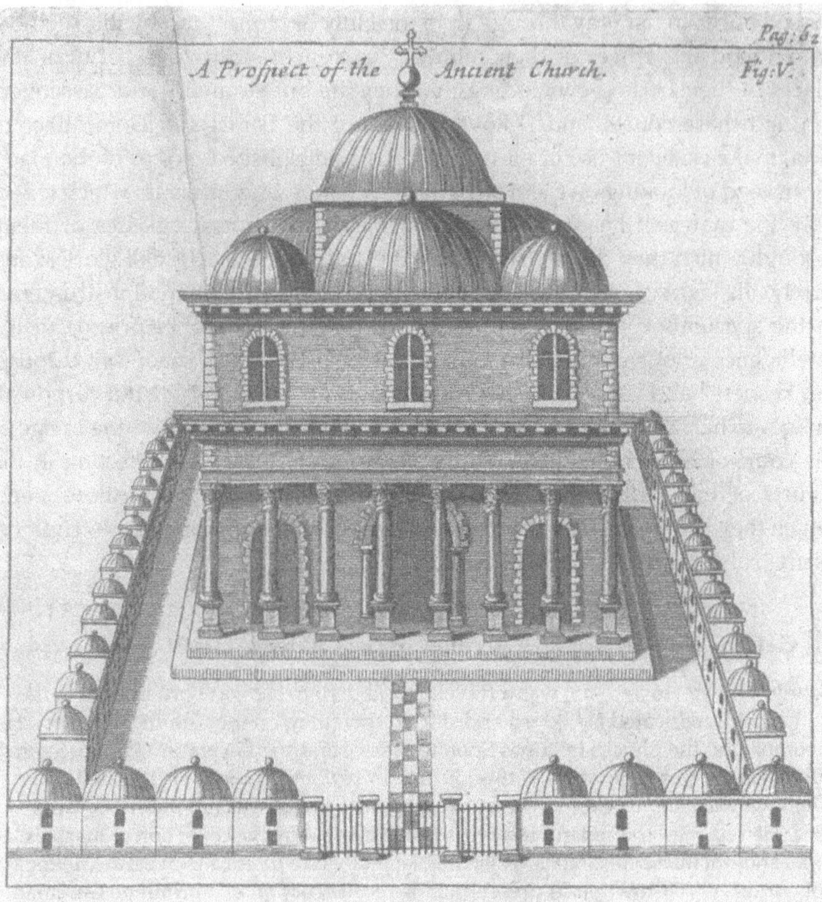

3.4 George Wheler, *An Account of the Churches, or Places of Assembly, of the Ancient Christians from the Churches of Tyre, Jerusalem and Constantinople* … (London, 1698), plate 5, showing Wheler's reconstruction of a primitive Christian church

Thus within the Choirs would be sufficient Capacious for the Faithful, and within the Rails for the Clergy and other Ministers: And then there would be sufficient Place for Dissenters of All Sorts in the Iles, with liberty to come and go when they think fit; or rather by the admonition of the Minister.

Sir Christopher Wren, 'Letter of Recommendation to a Friend on the Commission for Building Fifty New Churches' (1711)

This letter was addressed to a fellow member of the Commission for Building Fifty New City Churches, which had been established by Act of Parliament in 1711. The Act imposed a new duty on coal, the proceeds of which were to be used for 'Building [...] fifty new churches of Stone and other proper Materials, with Towers or Steeples to each of them; and for purchasing of Sites of Churches and Church-Yards, and Burying-places, in or near the Cities of London and Westminster, or the suburbs thereof'. The Tories, who in 1710 had defeated the Whigs to obtain control of the House of Commons for the first time in 22 years, saw the Act as a way of leaving a monument to their recent political victory and High Church principles. The committee included a few architects: Sir Christopher Wren and his son Christopher, Sir John Vanbrugh (for whose views see below) and Thomas Archer. A working committee included Wren senior, together with Nicholas Hawksmoor and William Dickinson, who were appointed as Surveyors (Soo, 1998, pp. 107–9).

Further reading: Summerson (1983), pp. 187–203; de la Ruffinière du Prey (2000), pp. 3–47.

Since PROVIDENCE, in great Mercy, has protracted my Age, to the finishing the cathedral church of *St. Paul*, and the parochial churches of *London*, in lieu of those demolished *by the fire*; (all which were executed during the Fatigues of my Employment in the Service of the Crown, from that Time to the present happy Reign;) and being now constituted one of the Commissioners for Building, pursuant to the late *Act*, *Fifty* more Churches in *London* and *Westminster*; I shall presume to communicate briefly my Sentiments, after long Experience; and without further ceremony exhibit to better Judgment, what at present occurs to me, in a transient View of this whole Affair; not doubting but that the Debates of the worthy Commissioners may hereafter give me occasion to change, or add to these Speculations.

1. First, I conceive the churches should be Built, not where vacant Ground may be cheapest purchased in the Extremities of the Suburbs, but among the thicker Inhabitants, for Convenience of the better sort, although the Site of them should cost more; the better Inhabitants contributing most to the future Repairs, and the Ministers and Officers of the Church, and Charges of the Parish.

2. I could wish that all Burials in Churches might be disallowed, which is not only unwholesome, but the Pavements can never be kept even, nor Pews upright: And if the Churchyard be close about the Church, this also is inconvenient, because the Ground being continually raised by the Graves, occasions, in Time, a Descent by Steps into the Church, which renders it damp, and the Walls green, as appears evidently in old Churches.

3. It will be inquired, where then shall be the Burials? I answer, in Cemeteries seated in the out-skirts of the Town; and since it is become the Fashion of the age to solemnize Funerals by Train of Coaches, (even where

the Deceased are of moderate Condition) though the Cemeteries should be half a Mile, or more, distant from the Church, the Charge need be little or no more than usual; the Service may be first performed in the Church: but for the Poor, and such as must be interred at the Parish Charge, a publick Hearse of two Wheels and one Horse may be kept at small Expense, the usual Bearers to lead the Horse, and take out the Corpse at the Grave. A Piece of Ground of two Acres in the Fields will be purchased for much less than two Roods among the Buildings: This being inclosed with a strong Brick Wall, and having a Walk round, and two cross Walks, decently planted with yew-trees, the four quarters may serve four Parishes, where the Dead need not be disturbed at the Pleasure of the Sexton, or piled four or five upon one another, or Bones thrown out to gain room. In these Places beautiful Monuments may be erected; but yet the Dimensions should be regulated by an Architect, and not left to the Fancy of every Mason; for thus the Rich, with large Marble Tombs, would shoulder out the Poor; when a Pyramid, a good Bust, or Statue on a proper Pedestal, will take up little Room in the Quarters, and be properer than Figures lying on Marble Beds: The Walls will contain Escutchions and Memorials for the Dead, and the Area good Air and Walks for the Living. It may be considered further, that if the Cemeteries be thus thrown into the Fields, they will bound the excessive Growth of the City with a graceful Border, which is now encircled with Scavengers dung-stalls.

4. As to the Situation of the Churches, I should propose they be brought as forward into the larger and more open Streets, not in obscure Lanes, nor where Coaches will be much obstructed in the Passage. Nor are we, I think, too nicely to observe East or West in the Position, unless it falls out properly: such Fronts as shall happen to lie most open in View should be adorned with Porticoes, both for Beauty and Convenience, which, together with handsome Spires, or Lanterns, rising in good Proportion above the neighboring Houses, (of which I have given several Examples in the City of different Forms) may be of sufficient Ornament to the Town, without a great Expense for inriching the outward Walls of the Churches, in which Plainness and Duration ought principally, if not wholly, to be studied. When a Parish is divided, I suppose it may be thought sufficient, if the Mother-church has a Tower large enough for a good Ring of Bells, and the other Churches smaller Towers for two or three Bells, because great Towers, and lofty Steeples, are sometimes more than half the Charge of the Church.

5. I shall mention something of the Materials for publick fabrics. It is true, the mighty Demand for the hasty Works of thousands of Houses at once, after the Fire of *London*, and the Frauds of those who built by the great, have so debased the Value of Materials, that good Bricks are not to be now had, without greater Prices than formerly, and indeed, if rightly made, will deserve

them; but Brick-makers spoil the Earth in the mixing and hasty burning, till the Bricks will hardly bear Weight; though the Earth about *London*, rightly managed, will yield as good Bricks as were the *Roman Bricks*, (which I have often found in the old ruins of the City) and will endure, in our air, beyond any Stone our Island affords; which, unless the Quarries lie near the Sea, are too dear for general Use: the best is *Portland*, or *Roche-Abbey* stone; but these are not without their Faults. The next Material is the Lime; Chalk-lime is the constant Practice, which, well mixed with good Sand, is not amiss, though much worse than hard Stone-lime. The Vaulting of St. Paul's is a Rendering as hard as Stone; it is composed of Cockle-shell-lime well-beaten with Sand; the more Labour in the beating, the better and stronger the Mortar. I shall say nothing of Marble, (though *England*, *Scotland*, and *Ireland*, afford good, and of beautiful Colours) but this will prove too costly for our Purpose, unless for Altar-pieces. In Windows and Doors *Portland* Stone may be used, with good Bricks, and stone Quoyns. As to Roofs, good Oak is certainly the best; because it will bear some Negligence: the Church-wardens' Care may be defective in speedy mending Drips; they usually whitewash the Church, and set up their Names, but neglect to preserve the Roof over their Heads; it must be allowed, that the Roof being more out of Sight, is still more unminded. Next to Oak is good yellow Deal, which is a Timber of length, and light, and makes excellent Work at first, but if neglected will speedily perish, especially if Gutters (which is a general Fault in Builders) be made to run upon principal Rafters, the ruin may be sudden. Our Sea-service for Oak, and the Wars in the North Sea, make Timber at present of excessive Price. I suppose 'ere long we must have recourse to the *West-Indies*, where most excellent Timber may be had for cutting and fetching. Our Tiles are ill made, and our Slate not good; Lead is certainly the best and lightest covering, and being of our own Growth and Manufacture, and lasting, if properly laid, for many hundred years, is, without question, the most preferable; though I will not deny but an excellent Tile may be made to be very durable; our Artisans are not yet instructed in it, and it is not soon done to inform them.

6. The Capacity and Dimensions of the new Churches may be determined by a Calculation. It is, as I take it, pretty certain, that the Number of Inhabitants, for whom these Churches are provided, are five times as many as those in the City, who were burnt out, and probably more than 400,000 grown Persons that should come to Church, for whom these fifty Churches are to be provided, (besides some Chapels already built, though too small to be made parochial.) Now, if the Churches could hold each 2000, it would yet be very short of the necessary Supply. The Churches therefore must be large; but still, in our reformed Religion, it should seem vain to make a parish Church larger, than that all who are present can both hear and see. The *Romanists*, indeed, may build larger Churches, it is enough if they hear the

Murmur of the Mass, and see the Elevation of the Host, but ours are to be fitted for Auditories. I can hardly think it practicable to make a single Room so capacious, with Pews and Galleries, as to hold above 2000 Persons, and all to hear the Service, and both to hear distinctly; and see the Preacher. I endeavored to effect this, in building the Parish Church of *St. James's, Westminster*, which, I presume, is the most capacious, with these qualifications, that hath yet been built; and yet at a solemn Time, when the Church was much crowded, I could not discern from a Gallery that 2000 were present. In this Church I mention, though very broad, and the middle Nave arched up, yet as there are no Walls of a second Order, nor Lanterns, nor Buttresses, but the whole Roof rests upon the Pillars, as do also the Galleries, I think it may be found beautiful and convenient, and as such, the cheapest of any Form I could invent.

7. Concerning the placing of the Pulpit, I shall observe – a moderate Voice may be heard 30 Feet distant before the Preacher, 30 feet on each Side, and 20 behind the Pulpit, and not this, unless the Pronunciation be distinct and equal, without losing the Voice at the last Word of the Sentence, which is commonly emphatical, and if obscured spoils the whole Sense. A French man is heard further than an *English* Preacher, because he raises his Voice, and not sinks his last Words: I mention this as an insufferable Fault in the Pronunciation of some of our otherwise excellent Preachers, which School-Masters might correct in the young, as a vicious Pronunciation, and not as the *Roman* Orators spoke: for the principal Verb is in Latin usually the last Word; and if that be lost, what becomes of the Sentence?

8. By what I have said, it may be thought reasonable, that the new Church should be at least 60 Feet abroad, and 90 Feet long, besides a Chancel at one end, and the Belfry and Portico at the other. These Proportions may be varied; but to build more Room, than that every Person may conveniently hear and see, is to create Noise and Confusion. A Church should not be so filled with Pews, but that the Poor may have Room enough to stand and sit in the Alleys, for to them equally is the Gospel preach'd. It were to be wish'd there were to be no Pews, but Benches; but there is no stemming the tide of Profit, and the Advantage of Pew-keepers, especially too since by Pews, in the Chapels of Ease, the Minister is chiefly supported. It is evident that these fifty Churches are not enough, for the present Inhabitants, and the Town will continually grow; but it is to be hoped, that hereafter more may be added, as the Wisdom of the Government shall think fit; and therefore the Parishes should be so divided, as to leave Room for Subdivisions, or at least for Chapels of Ease.

I cannot pass over mentioning the Difficulties that may be found, in obtaining the Ground proper for the Sites of the Churches among the Buildings, and the Cemeteries in the Borders without the Town; and therefore I shall recite the method that was taken for purchasing in ground at the North-side of *St. Paul*'s Cathedral, where in some Places the Houses were but 11 Feet distant from the Fabric, exposing it to the continual Danger of Fires. The houses were seventeen, and contiguous, all in lease-hold of the Bishops or Dean alone, or the Dean and Chapter, or the petty-canons, with divers Undertenants. First we treated with the superior landlords, who being perpetual Bodies were to be recompensed in Kind, with Rents of the like Value for them and their Successors; but the Tenants in Possession for a valuable Consideration; which to find what it amounted to, we learned by diligent Inquiry, what the Inheritance of Houses in that Quarter were usually held at: this we found was fifteen Years Purchase at the most, and proportionably to this the Value of each Lease was easily determined in a Scheme, referring to a Map. These Rates, which we resolved not to stir from, were offered to each; and, to cut off much Debate, which may be imagined every one would abound in, they were assur'd that we went by one uniform Method, which could not be receded from. We found two or three reasonable Men, who agreed to these Terms: Immediately we paid them, and took down their Houses. Others who stood out at first, finding themselves in Dust and Rubbish, and that ready Money was better, as the case stood, than to continue to pay Rent, Repairs, and Parish Duties, easily came in. The whole ground at last was clear'd, and all concern'd were satisfied, and their Writings given up. The greatest Debate was about their Charges for fitting up their new Houses to their particular Trades: for this we allowed one Year's Purchase, and gave leave to remove all their Wainscote, reserving the Materials of the Fabric only. This was happily finished without a Judicatory or Jury; although in our present Case, we may find it perhaps sometimes necessary to have recourse to Parliament.

Commission for Building Fifty New City Churches, from 'Rules for the Fifty New Churches' (1712)

(See the note on the letter written by Sir Christopher Wren, above, this chapter.)

Further reading: de la Ruffinière du Prey (2000), pp. 52–9.

[...] *The committee further came to the Several Resolutions following, viz.:*

That one Generall Modell be made and Agreed upon for all the fifty New intended Churches.[29]

That the Situation of all the said Churches be Insular where the Sites will admit thereof.

That the Ministers Houses be as near the said Churches as conveniently may be.

That there be at the East end of Each Church two small Roomes, One for the Vestments, another for the Vessells & other Consecrated things.

That there be at the West end of each Church, a convenient Large Room for Parish business.
That, the Fonts be so large as to be capable to have Baptism administered in them by dipping, when desir'd.
That, the Churches be all built with Stone on the Outside, and Lined with Brick on the Inside thereof.
That, the pews be all of Equal height,[30] so low that every person in them may be seen, either Kneeling or Sitting, and so contrived that all persons may Stand and kneel towards the Communion Table.
That, Moveable Forms be so contrived as to run under the Seats of the Pewes, and draw out into the Isles upon occasion.
That, the Chancels be raised three Steps above the Nave or Body of the Churches.
That, there be handsome Porticoes at the West end of each Church where the Site will admit of the same.
That, no Person shall be admitted a General Undertaker to build any of the said New intended Churches, but that every Artificer be separately agreed with, to perform the Work belonging to his particular Trade or business.

Sir John Vanbrugh, 'Mr Van-Brugg's Proposals about Building ye New Churches' (1712)

Sir John Vanbrugh (1664–1726) was a soldier and dramatist as well as an architect. He started his professional life in the wine trade, tried soldiering, travelled to France and was arrested in September 1688 for speaking in favour of King William III. He spent four years in prisons at Calais, Vincennes and Paris. After his release he returned to soldiering, but resigned his commission on becoming Comptroller of the Works in 1702. By then he had started to write successful plays such as *The Relapse* (1696) and *The Provok'd Wife* (1697). He also turned to architecture. It is not clear where or in what manner he obtained his knowledge of architecture. In 1699 he made designs for Castle Howard in Yorkshire, which were to be executed in 1700 in collaboration with Nicholas Hawksmoor. In 1704–05 he was commissioned to design Blenheim Palace near Woodstock in Oxfordshire. He became a member of the Commission for Building Fifty New City Churches in 1711 (see above, this chapter). His designs were not executed, but his memorandum had some influence.

Further reading: Downes (1977); Beard (1986); McCormick (1991).

Since it will perhaps be thought reasonable, that the fifty new Churches the Queen has gloriously promoted the Building of, in London and Westminster; should not only serve for the Accomodation of the Inhabitants, in the Performance of their Publick Religious Dutys; but at the same time, remain Monuments to Posterity of Her Piety & Grandure And by consequence become Ornaments to the Towne, and a Credit to the Nation; the following

Considerations are humbly offer'd, to the Commissioners who are Instructed with the direction of them.

That amongst the several kinds of Buildings by which Great Citys are Adorn'd; Churches, have in all Ages, and with all Religions have been placed in the first Rank. No Expence has ever been thought too much for them; Their Magnificence has been esteem'd a pious expression of the Peoples great and profound Veneration towards their Deitys, And the contemplation of that Magnificence has at the same time augmented that Veneration.

If therefore on the one hand it be reasonable to design Churches in such Manner, that the People may both hear what is utter'd by the Minister, and at the same time be so accomodated, as not to be disturb'd in their devotions by one an Other, or by the Inconveniencys of too much heat or cold; So on the other, these necessary dispositions in the usefull part of the Fabrick, shou'd be made consistent with the utmost Grace that Architecture can produce, for the Beauty of it: which Grace shou'd generally be express'd in a plain but Just and Noble Stile, without running into those many Divisions and Breaks which other buildings for Variety of uses may require; or such Gayety of Ornaments as may be proper to a luxurious Palace.

To form the Churches now to be built, to these two general Propositions, it will be necessary to observe these following Rules.

First. That their Situations may ever be Insulate.[31] This do's not only give them that Respectfull Distinction & Dignity which Churches Always ought to have; but it makes the Access to them easy, and is a great Security from Fire.

2dly. That they may be so plac'd, to be fairly View'd at such proper distance, as is necessary to shew their Exterior Form, to the best Advantage, as at the ends of Large and Strait Streets, or on the Sides of Squares and Other open Places.

3dly. That they may be all Accomodated and Adorn'd with Portico's;[32] no part in Publick Edifices being of greater use, nor no production in Architecture so solemnly Magnificent.

4ly. That they may be form'd for the utmost duration both in respect of the material, the Solidity of their Walls, and the Manner of their Construction: The extraordinary Expence of which is so small, That in a Church of Ten thousand pounds cost, it turns upon five hundred, whether it shall be crippled in a hundred Years, or stand like a Rock a Thousand.

5ly. That for the Ornament of the Towne, and to shew at a distance what regard there is in it to Religious Worship; every Church (as the Act of Parliament has provided) may have a Tower, but to Answer these endes, they shou'd be all of Stone or Brick; High and Bold Structures; and so form'd as not to be subject to Ruin by fire, but of such Solidity and Strength, that nothing but Time, and scarce that, shou'd destroy them.

6ly. That as to the Insides, both for the Accomodation of the Ordinary People, and the Beauty of the Place, they may not be too much crowded with Pews; but that a considerable Space may be left in the Middle Line with decent Forms regularly plac'd for People to repose themselves by Turns.

7ly. That for the Lights, there may be no more than what are necessary for meer use; many Windows making a Church cold in Winter, hot in Summer, and being very disagreeable and hurtfull to the sight. They likewise take off very much, both from the Appearance & reality of srength in the Fabrick; giving it more the Air of a Gay Lanthorn to be set on the Top of a Temple, than the Reverend look of a Temple it self; which shou'd ever have the most Solemn and Awfull Appearance both without and within, that is possible.

8ly. That they may be free'd from that Inhumane custome of being made Burial Places for the Dead. a Custome in which there is something so very barbarous in itself besides the many ill consequences that attend it; that one cannot enough wonder how it ever has prevail'd amongst the civiliz'd part of mankind. But there is now a sort of happy necessity on this Occasion of breaking through it: Since there can be no thought of purchasing ground for Church Yards, where the Churches will probably be plac'd. And since there must therefore be Caemitarys provided in the Skirts of the Towne, if they are ordered with that decency they ought to be, there can be no doubt but the Rich as well as the Poor, will be content to ly there.

If these Caemitarys be consecrated, Handsomely and regularly wall'd in, and planted with Trees in such form as to make a Solemn Distinction between one Part and another; there is no doubt, but the Richer sort of People, will think their Friends and Relations more decently inter'd in those distinguish'd Places, than they commonly are in the Ailes and under Pews in Churches; And will think them more honourably remember'd by Lofty and Noble Mausoleums, erected over them in Freestone (which no doubt will soon come into practice,) than by little Tawdry Monuments of Marble, stuck up against Walls and Pillars. This manner of Interment has been practic'd by the English at Suratt and it come at last to have this kind of effect.[33]

Upon the whole it may be worth considering, that since Christianity began, there is but one instance, where the Inhabitants of a City have had so Glorious an Occasion as this, to Adorn both their Religion and their Towne at once. A Resolution taken, and money provided to raise fifty New Churches in so short a time shews so glowing a Zeal, and so Noble a Generosity, that 'twere pitty Posterity shou'd not have an equal opinion of the Politeness of the Age, by finding the Edifices Suitable to what produc'd them.

Charles Wheatly, from *The Church of England Man's Companion; or a Rational Illustration of the Book of Common Prayer* (1710)

Charles Wheatly (1686–1742) was a divine with interests in liturgy and the occult. He was educated at St John's College, Oxford, and had various appointments as lecturer and curate. His chief work is the *Rational Illustration*, based on much existing scholarship on the liturgy, its history and meaning. First published in 1710, it received its last edition in Cambridge in 1858 (*DNB*).

Further reading: Besençon (2000)

[p. 88] §2. It cannot be thought that in the first Ages, while the flames of persecution rag'd, the Christian Churches should be very *stately* and *magnificent*: It was sufficient if they were such as the condition of those times would bear: their splendor increasing according to the entertainment Christianity met withal in the world; till, the Empire becoming Christian, their Temples rose up into grandeur and stateliness: as, amongst others, may appear by the particular description which *Eusebius* gives of the Church of *Tyre*, and of that which *Constantine* built at *Constantinople* in honour of the Apostles; both which, the Historian tells us, were incomparably sumptuous and magnificent.

§3. I shall not undertake to describe at large the several parts and dimensions of their Churches (which varied according to the different times and ages) but only briefly reflect upon such as were most common and remarkable, and are still retain'd amongst us. For the *form* and *fashion* of their Churches, it was for the most part *oblong*, to keep the better correspondence with the fashion of a *ship*; the common notion and metaphor by which the Church was wont to be represented, to remind us that we are toss'd up and down in the world, as upon a stormy and tempestuous sea, and that out of the Church there is no safe passage to heaven, the country we all hope to arrive at. It was always divided into two principal parts, viz. the *Nave* or *Body* of the Church, and the *Sacrarium*, since call'd *Chancel*, from its being divided from the body of the Church by neat rails, call'd in Latin *Cancelli*. The *Nave* was common to all the people, and represented the visible world; the *Chancel* was peculiar to the Priests and sacred Persons, and typify'd heaven: For which reason they always stood at the *East* end of the Church, towards which part of the world they paid a more than ordinary reverence in their worship; wherein *Clemens Alexandrinus* tells us, they had respect to Christ: for as the East is the birth and womb of the natural day, from whence the sun (the fountain of all sensible light) does arise and spring; so Christ, the true Sun of righteousness, who arose upon the world with the light of truth, when it sat in the darkness of error and ignorance, is in Scripture stil'd the EAST: and therefore since we must in our prayer turn our faces towards some quarter, 'tis fittest it should be towards the *East*; especially since it is possible even from Scripture it self, that the Majesty and Glory of God is in a peculiar manner in that part of the Heavens, and that the Throne of Christ and the Splendor of his Humanity has its residence there. In this Chancel always stood the *Altar* or *Communion-table*; which none were allow'd to approach, but such as were in holy Orders, unless it were the Greek Emperors at *Constantinople*, who were allow'd to go up to the table to make their offerings, but were immediately to return back again.

§4. But tho' the Christians of those times spar'd no convenient cost in founding and adorning publick places for the worship of God; yet they were careful not to run into a too curious and over-nice superstition. No *Images* were worship'd, or so much as us'd in Churches for at least four hundred years after Christ: and therefore certainly, might things be carry'd by a fair and impartial trial of antiquity, the dispute about this point would soon be at an end. Nothing can be more clear than that the Christians were frequently challeng'd by the Heathens for having no images nor statues in their Churches, and that the Christian apologists never deny'd it; but industriously defended themselves against the charge, and rejected the very thoughts of any such thing with contempt and scorn: as might be abundantly shewn from *Tertullian, Clemens Alexandrinus, Origen, Minutius Felix, Arnobius*, and *Lactantius*.[34] But I shall only cite one of them, and that is Origen, who, amongst other things, plainly tells his adversary (who had objected this to the Christians) that the Images, that were to be dedicated to God, were not to be carv'd by the hands of artists, but to be form'd and fashion'd in us by the word of God; viz. the virtues of justice and temperance, of wisdom and piety, &c. that conform us to the image of his only Son. 'These (says he) are the only statues form'd in our minds; and by which alone we are persuaded 'tis fit to do honour to him, who is the *Image of the invisible God*, the prototype and archetypal pattern of all such images.' Had Christians then given adoration to them, or but set them up in their places of worship; with what face can we suppose they could have told the World, that they so much abhorr'd them? But more than this the Council of *Illiberis*, that was held in Spain some time before Constantine, expresly provides against them; decreeing, That 'no pictures ought to be in the Church, nor that any thing that is worship'd and ador'd should be painted upon the walls:' Words too clear to be evaded by the little shifts and glosses which the expositors of that Canon would put upon it. The first use of statues and pictures in the Churches was merely historical, or to add some beauty and ornament to the place, which after-ages improv'd into superstition and idolatry. The first we meet with upon good authority, is no older than the times of *Epiphanius*, and then too met with no very welcome entertainment; as may appear from *Epiphanius's'* own epistle to *John* then Bishop of *Jerusalem*: Where he says, that coming to *Anablatha*, a village in *Palestine*, and going into a Church to pray, he espy'd a curtain hanging over de door, whereupon was painted the image of Christ, or of some Saint; which then he had look'd upon, and saw the image of a man hanging up in the Church, contrary to the authority of the holy Scriptures, he presently rent it, and order'd the Church-wardens to make use of it as a winding-sheet for some poor man's burying. This instance is so close to home, that the patrons of image-worship are at a loss what to say to it, and after all are forc'd to cry out against it as suppositious: tho' the famous *Du Pin*, who is himself of the Romish Communion, and Doctor of the *Sorbon*, allows it to be genuine, and owns that one reason of its being call'd in question, is because it makes so much against that doctrine. More might be produc'd to this purpose: but by his, I hope, 'tis clear enough, that the primitive Christians, as they thought it sufficient to pray to God, without making their addresses to Saints and Angels; so they accounted their Churches fine enough without Pictures and Images to adorn them.

4

The Sense of the Past

Introduction

At first sight, British writings on architectural history may seem to be atheoretical. They give an account of buildings from the past and hardly ever openly address issues that are usually associated with architectural theory, such as matters of design or style. The choice of subject matter and the method of history writing, however, often point to implicit theoretical or political issues which are relevant for architecture as well. A characteristic example of very widespread views about the nature of history is that of the clergyman George Hakewill, who opposed the commonly held view that the world was irredeemably decaying with a cyclical view of history, and argued for the superiority of the modern Christian world over pagan Antiquity. To support this view he also discussed architecture, comparing the splendours of None-Such Palace to those of the Pantheon and finding them not at all inferior. Political issues also influenced King James I's decision to send Inigo Jones to Stonehenge to prove that it had been built by the Romans: it was part of his campaign to create a classical past for Britain. Jones's *Stone-Heng Restored*, published posthumously by John Webb on the basis of the notes Jones had left, is not an essay in historical enquiry, although it was presented as such, but an exercise in cultural assimilation. The argument presented by the text for the Roman origins of Stonehenge is based on a careful listing of statements of Roman authorities such as Vitruvius and Tacitus. The plates argue for the same thesis using different means. They show the groundplan, façade, section and orthogonal and perspectival projections, all carefully drawn to scale. By giving the same representational treatment to Stonehenge as the Roman antiquities received in the treatises of Serlio or Palladio, the monument was assimilated into the Vitruvian tradition.

Antiquarian writing also had important theoretical implications, because antiquarians were interested not only in the remains of classical 'high culture' but in all material remains of the British past, including humble objects such as bones, pot shards or fragments of pavement. By means of this inclusive approach they questioned classical historiography, which concentrated on political and military history, and the Academic theory of art, with its narrow definition of what was acceptable as art and worthy of historical enquiry.

Whereas antiquarianism was a European movement, the appreciation of the mediaeval architectural heritage in the late seventeenth and early eighteenth centuries was very much a British phenomenon. In Britain, the Gothic continued in use in collegiate and church architecture. Both Nicholas Hawksmoor and Sir Christopher Wren adapted their designs for All Souls' and Christ Church Colleges in Oxford to their Gothic environment. Wren also showed interest in documenting the history of two Gothic monuments, Westminster Abbey and Old Saint Paul's Cathedral. For the latter, he made use of the work of the antiquary Sir William Dugdale. John Wood took a much more radical approach in his attempt to rewrite the history of European architecture by presenting the Bible and sacred history as historical sources that possessed the same or greater value than Vitruvius.

Sir John Vanbrugh's plea for the preservation of the ruins of Woodstock Manor is one of the earliest documents articulating the Associationist view of the meaning and impact of works of art on the beholder. In this approach their beauty does not reside in some intrinsic, objective property such as proportion or symmetry, but in their power to evoke trains of associations, memories and emotions. It was to be the basis of the aesthetics of the Picturesque movement in landscape gardening and architecture. Claude Perrault had already argued in his *Ordonnance des cinq espèces de colonnes selon la méthode des anciens* of 1683 (of which an English translation by John James was published in London in 1708 under the title *A Treatise of the Five Orders of Columns in Architecture*) that we associate beauty with proportion in architecture out of custom and convention, not because of some inherent and objective aesthetic quality of these proportions, but Vanbrugh and his Picturesque successors took this relativism much further by allowing a much greater role for the personal, subjective or national feelings and memories of the spectator.

Further reading: Momigliano (1950); Eastlake (1970); Germann (1972); Aston (1973); Myrone and Peltz (1999).

George Hakewill, from *Apologie or Declaration of the Power and Providence of God* (1627)

George Hakewill (1578–1649) was educated at Exeter College, Oxford, where he read philosophy and theology. He travelled on the Continent from 1604to 1608, spending one year in Calvinist circles in Heidelberg. After his return he was appointed chaplain to Prince Charles, to protect him from Catholic influences. He had to resign from the Court because of his opposition to Prince Charles's intended marriage to the Spanish Infanta, and spent the rest of his life mainly as a writer on theological subjects. The *Apologie* sets out to refute the generally held view that the world was in a process of progressive decay. Instead, he defended a cyclical view of world history, which had been a commonplace for ancient historians, and had been applied to the arts by Vasari: 'There is (it seemes) both in *wits* and *Arts*, as in all things besides, a kinde of *circular progresse*: they haue their *birth*, their *growth*, their *flourishing*, their *fayling*, their *fading*, and within a while after their *resurrection*, and *reflourishinge* againe' (p. 230). The modern world therefore does not represent a stage of decay. It is also an improvement because Christianity made the modern world morally superior to that of the Ancients.

Further reading: Levine (1991); Gent (1995); Lecocq, *La Querelle des Anciens et des Modernes*.

Liber III. Of the pretended decay of mankinde in regard of age and duration, of strength and stature, of art and wits.
Section 3. Of the Arts of Painting and Architecture revived in this latter age.
[p. 265] Herevnto may be added the *Arts* of *Horsemanship*, and *Heraldry*, *Agriculture*, and *Architecture*, *Painting* and *Navigation*, all which haue beene not a little both *inlarged* and *perfected* in these latter ages: yet with this difference, that some of them together with the other *Arts* decayed, and againe reuiued with greater perfection: Others were neuer in their perfection till now: I will instance onely in the three latter. [...]

Such is the *affinitie* betwixt the *arts* of *painting & building*, by reason they both stand chiefely vpon *proportion* & *just dimensions*, that *Vassari*, who was both himselfe, hath likewise written the liues of the most famous & best skilled in both. [...]

The publique buildings of the *Graecians* and *Romans* were doubtles very artificiall and magnificent, and so were likewise many of those of the ancient *Christians*, I meane their *Churches*, *Monasteries*, *Castles*, *bridges*, and the like: But the houses of private men were in the memorie of our *Fathers*, for the most part very homely, till the Princes of *Italy* began to bestow more art and cost vpon them. *Cosmo Medices* Duke of *Florence* being one of the first who set vpon this worke; the *Italians* were soone followed by the *French* after the victorious returne of *Charles* the eight from *Naples*, and they againe by vs euer since the vniting of the *two roses* in King *Henry* the seaventh, who at his comming to the Crowne, had spent the greatest part of his time in *France*: Before his entrance we had indeede some huge vast buildings, but his house at *Richmond* & his *Chappell* at *Westminster* (except perchance some would preferre *Kings* Colledge Chappell in *Cambridge* begun by *Henry* the sixth) were the two first neate curious peeces that this Kingdome had seene: The latter of which may enough compare, not only with any peece this day in *Christendome*, but for the bignes of it, with any thing in *antiquity* of that kinde. But for a stately dainty house, that of *None-Such* excells, which King *Henry* the eight, saith our great *Antiquarie* [in margin: Camden in *Surrey*], built with so great sumptuousness, and rare workmanshippe, that it aspireth to the very top of ostentation for shew: So as a man may thinke, that all the skill of *Architecture* is in this peece bestowed and heaped vp together. So many statues and liuely images there are in euery place: so many wonders of absolute workemanshippe & workes seeming to contend with *Romane Antiquities*, that most worthily it may haue and maintaine still this name it hath of *None-Such*, according as *Leland*[1] hath written of it.

> *Huic quia non habeant similem laudare Brittani*
> *Saepe solent, nullique parem cognomine dicunt.*
> The Brittains oft were wont to praise this place for that through all
> The Realme they cannot shew the like, and *None-Such* they it call.

So as what *Sebastianus Serlius* a skilfull Architect spake of the *Pantheon* at *Rome*, may not vnfitly be applied to this pile of building, that it is *vnicum exemplar consummatae Architecturae*, the only patterne we haue of perfect Architecture, whether we cast our eyes abroad in the country vpon the houses of Noble-men & Gentle-men, or vpon the Colledges & Schooles in the Vniversities, or vpon the dwellings of the Merchant & Artificer in the towne & city, specially in the *Metropolis*; wee shall generally finde a wonderfull great change in building within these last hundred yeares, this latter as much exceeding the former, as *Augustus* his *marble Rome* did that of *bricke*. And if we looke into forraine parts, the *Escuriall* in *Spaine*, and the *Gallery* in *France*, will yeeld to nothing, *Antiquity* can boast of in that kinde: Yet if wee may beleeue reports, the King of *Chinaes* pallaces, at least-wise for riches & state, put downe any thing which is to be seene in *Europe* at this day.

Inigo Jones, from *Stone-Heng Restored*, and dedication 'To the Favourers of Antiquity' by John Webb (first published 1655)

Like *The Designs of Inigo Jones* (1727), *Stone-Heng Restored* appeared posthumously, in 1655, edited by Jones's pupil John Webb. In 1620, when James I was at Wilton House near Salisbury Plain visiting the 3rd Earl of Pembroke, Stonehenge was discussed and the King ordered Jones to investigate it. Jones continued to work on this project until his death in 1652. Because the original notes are lost, there is no way to distinguish Webb's contributions from Jones's notes. According to Jones, Stonehenge was originally a Roman temple. A refutation was published in 1663 by Walter Charleton, physician to Charles II. John Webb then came to the defence of his master. In 1725 Jones's *Stone-Heng Restored*, Charleton's *Chorea Gigantum* and Webb's 'Vindication' were reprinted in one volume, prefaced by the anonymous biography of Jones included in this volume (Harris, 1990). (See also the notes on Inigo Jones in Chapter 1, above, and on John Webb in Chapter 2, as well as the note on Jones in Chapter 5, and the relevant extracts.)

Further reading: Orgel (1971); Tait (1978).

To the Favourers of Antiquity.

This Discourse of *Stone-heng* is moulded off, and cast into a rude Form, from some few indigested notes of the late judicious *Architect*, the *Vitruvius* of his age *Inigo Jones*. That so venerable an *Antiquity* might not perish, but the world made beholding to him for restoring it to light, the desires of severall his learned *Friends* have encouraged me to compose this Treatise. Had he survived to have done it with his own hand, there had needed no Apology. Such as it is, I make now yours. Accept in *his* name, from

J.W.

STONE-HENG RESTORED by *Inigo Jones* Esquire.
Being naturally inclined in my younger years to study the *Arts of Designe*, I passed into forrain parts to converse with the great Masters thereof in *Italy*; where I applied myself to search out the ruins of those ancient *Buildings*, which in despight of *Time* itself, and violence of the *Barbarians* are yet remaining. Having satisfied my self in these, and returning to my native *Countrey*, I applied my minde more particularly to the study of *Architecture*. Among the ancient monuments whereof, found here, I deemed none more worthy of the searching after, then this of *Stoneheng*; not only in regard of the *Founders* thereof, the *Time* when built, the Work itself, but also for the rarity of its *Invention*, being different in *Forme* from all I had seen before: likewise, of as beautifull *Proportions*, as elegant in *Order*, and as stately in *Aspect*, as any.

King *James*, in his progresse, the year one thousand six hundred and twenty, being at *Wilton*, and discoursing of this *Antiquity*, I was sent for by the right Honourable *William* then *Earl of Pembrook*, and received there his Majesties commands to produce out of mine own practice in *Architecture*, and experience in *Antiquities* abroad, what possibly I could discover concerning this of *Stoneheng*. What mine opinion was then, and what I have since collected in relation thereunto; I intend to make the subject of this present Treatise. And certainly, in the intricate, and obscure study of *Antiquity* it is far easier (as *Camden* very well observes) to refute and contradict a false, then to set down a true and certain resolution. For mine own part, in what I shall here deliver, I intend not to struggle against any opinion commonly, and long since received. Let every man judge as it pleaseth him. What opinion soever the Reader inclines to, I shall not make much materiall, my aime being, a desire only to vindicate, as much as in me lies, the *Founders* of this venerable *Antiquity* from oblivion, and to make the truth, as far forth as possibly I may, appeare to all men.

[…] [p. 3] But, whatsoever these, or other Historians have written of the *Druides*, certainly, *Stoneheng* could not be builded by them, in regard I find no mention, they were at any time either studious in *Architecture*, (which in this subject is chiefly to be respected) or skillful in any thing else conducing thereunto. For, *Academies* of *Designe* were unknown unto them: publique Lectures in the *Mathematiques* not read amongst them: nothing of their

Painting, not one word of their *Sculpture* is to be found, or scarce of any Science (*Philosophy* and *Astronomy* excepted) proper to informe the judgment of an *Architect*; who, (as *Vitruvius* saith) should be *peritus graphidos, eruditus Geometria, & Optices non ignarus &c. perfect in Design, expert in Geometry, well seen in the Opticks, skilfull in Arithmetick, a good Historian, a diligent hearer of Philosphers, well experience'd in Physick, Musick, Law and Astrologie.*[2]

[...] [p. 11] Touching the manner of the buildings of the ancient *Britans*, and of what materialls they consisted, I find them so far short of the magnificence of this Antiquity, that they were not stately, nor sumptuous; neither had they any thing of *Order*, or *Symmetry*, much lesse, of gracefulnesse, and *Decorum* in them, being only such as *Ovid* (relating to the first Age of the world) makes mention of.

> *— domus antra fuerant*
> *Et densi frutices, & junctae cortice virgae.*

Thus Englished by *Arthur Golding*.

> *— their houses were the thicks,*
> *And bushy queaches, hollow caves, and hardles made of sticks.*

[...] [p. 55] This *Antiquity* [...] because the *Architraves* are set upon the heads of the upright stones, and hang (as it were) in the air, is generally known by the name of *Stoneheng*. It is sited upon the Plain in the Country of *Wiltshire* in *England*, not far from *Ambresbury* (the foundations of whose ancient buildings, frequently digged up, render it to have been in times past a *Town* of no small fame) six miles at least from new *Salisbury* northwards.

The whole work, in generall, being of a circular form, is one hundred and ten foot diameter, double winged about without a roof, anciently environed with a deep Trench, still appearing about thirty foot broad. So that, betwixt it, and the work itself, a large and void space of ground being left, it had, from the Plain, three open entrances, the most conspicuous thereof lying North-east. At each of which, was raised, on the outside of the Trench aforesaid, two huge stones gate-wise, parallel whereunto, on the inside two others of lesse proportion. The inner part of the work, consisting of an *Exagonall* figure, was raised, by due symmetry, upon the bases of four equilaterall triangles (which formed the whole structure) this inner part likewise was double, having, within it also, another *Exagon* raised, and all that part within the Trench sited upon a commanding ground, eminent, and higher by much, then any of the Plain lying without, and, in the midst thereof, upon a foundation of hard chalk, the work it self was placed. Insomuch, from what part soever they came unto it, they rose by an easie ascending hill.

Which, that it may be the more clearly demonstrated, (being by me, with no little pains, and charge measured, and the foundations thereof diligently

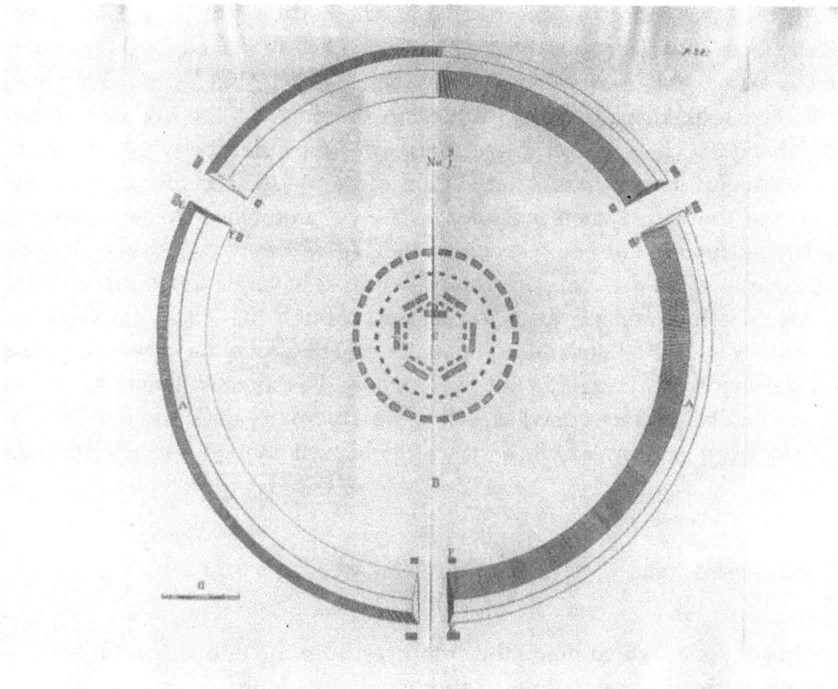

4.1 Inigo Jones, *The most notable antiquity of Great Britain, vulgarly called Stone-Heng, on Salisbury plain, restored* (London, 1725), plate 1: 'the Plant of the whole work in generall, with the Trench round about it, drawn by a small scale, that it may be seen all at one view', engraving by Wenceslas Hollar and E. Kirkall (after A. Van Dyke and J. Hassell)

searched) I have reduced into *Design*, not onely as the ruine thereof now appears, but as (in my judgement) it was in its pristine perfection. And that the groundplot, with the uprights, and profyle of the whole work may be the more distinctly be understood, I have purposely countersigned each *Design* of them with *Numbers*, and the particular thereof with *Letters*. [See Figure 4.1.]

A

The Trench.

B

The Intervall betwixt the Trench and Work.

C

The work it self; in the inmost part whereof, there is a stone appearing not much above the surface of the earth, (and lying towards the East) four foot broad, and sixteen foot in length. Which, whether it might be an *Altar* or no, I leave to the judgement of others, because so overwhelmed with the ruines of the Work, that I could make no search after it, but even with much difficulty, took the aforesaid proportion thereof. Yet for my part, I can apprehend no valid reason to the contrary, except that the whole structure being circular in form, the Altar should rather have been placed upon the Center of the Circle, then inclining to the circumference. Neverthelesse it cannot be denied, but being so sited, the *Cell* (as I may call it) was thereby left more free, for the due performance of those severall superstitious rites, which their Idolatry led them to. Besides, though the *Altare* amongst the *Ancients* was exalted and raised somewhat high above the earth; yet, their *Ara* was made quadrangular, not very high, and as some will have it close to the ground, being consecrated as well to the supernaturall as infernall Deities: and therefore in respect of form, it may hold well enough it as anciently an Altar.

D

The supposed Altar.

E

The great stones which made the entrances from the outside of the Trench, seven foot broad, three foot thick, and twenty foot high.

F

The parallel stones, on the inside of the Trench, four feet broad, and three foot thick; but they lie so broken, and ruined by time, that proportion in height cannot be distinguisht, much lesse be exactly measured.

G

The scale of fifty foot.

N

[p. 61, see Figure 4.2] The *Architrave* lying on the top of the great stones of the *Hexagon*, and mortaised also in them, sixteen foot long, three foot nine inches broad, and three foot four inches high. This *Architrave* continuing only from stone to stone, left bettwixt every two and two, a void space free to the Air uncovered. For, if they had been continued throughout the whole *Hexagon* then necessarily there must have been two tenons upon each of the said stones, as those of the outward circle had, but being disposed as aforesaid, that one, which was in the middle, and yet remains apparent, was sufficient for the thing intended.

The *Designs* follow [see Figures 4.3 and 4.4 and their captions.]

[see Figure 4.5.]

4.2 Inigo Jones, *The most notable antiquity of Great Britain, vulgarly called Stone-Heng, on Salisbury plain, restored* (London, 1725), plate 3: 'The upright of the work, as when entire, in which the perpendicular stones of the outward Circle, are countersigned with the Letter I, as in the groundplot', engraving by Wenceslas Hollar and E. Kirkall (after A. Van Dyke and J. Hassell)

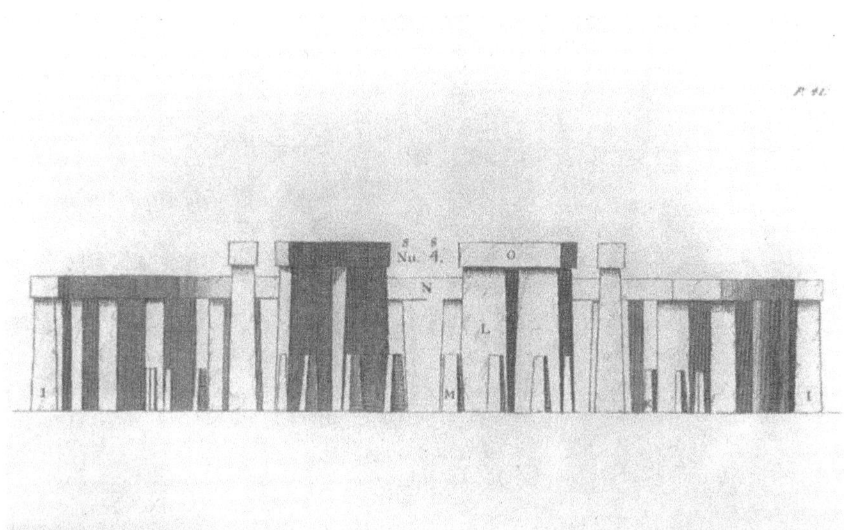

4.3 Inigo Jones, *The most notable antiquity of Great Britain, vulgarly called Stone-Heng, on Salisbury plain, restored* (London, 1725), plate 4: 'the Profile, or cut, through the middle of the work, as entire, countersigned with the Letters of the Ground-plot', engraving by Wenceslas Hollar and E. Kirkall (after A. Van Dyke and J. Hassell)

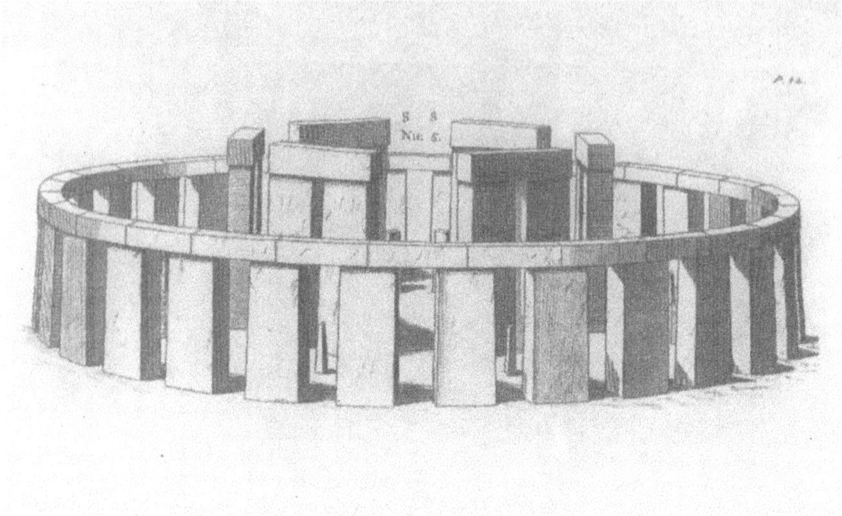

4.4 Inigo Jones, *The most notable antiquity of Great Britain, vulgarly called Stone-Heng, on Salisbury plain, restored* (London, 1725), plate 5: 'The whole work in *Prospective*, as when entire, whereby the general composure of the particular Parts of the uprights, are all together all seen; and by which also, the stately Aspect, and magnificent greatness thereof, are fully, and more apparently conspicuous', engraving by Wenceslaus Hollar and E. Kirkall (after A. Van Dyke and J. Hassell)

4.5 Inigo Jones, *The most notable antiquity of Great Britain, vulgarly called Stone-Heng, : on Salisbury plain, restored* (London, 1725), plate 7: 'The Ruin yet remaining drawn in *Prospective*', engraving by Wenceslaus Hollar and E. Kirkall (after A. Van Dyke and J. Hassell)

P

The manner of the tenons, of a round form, mortaised into the *Architrave* of the outward Circle.

Q

The tenons of like form in the middle of the stones of the greater *Hexagon*.

R

The English foot (by which the work itself was measured) divided into twelve inches, and each inch subdivided into four parts.

[...] [p. 65] It restes now to endeavour the discovering by whom *Stoneheng* was built; in what time, and, for what use anciently erected [...].

Touching the *Founders* of *Stoneheng*. Among the *Aegyptian Antiquities*, or those *Eastern* Nations from whom the *Grecians* deducted their learning, I find not any such composure ever used: or with the *Greeks* themselves, mention made of any work conformable to this, in point of *Order*. [...]

Howsoever, considering what magnificence the *Romans* in prosperous times anciently used in all works, both publick and private: their knowledge and experience in all *Arts* and *Sciences*; their powerfull means for effecting great works: together with their *Order* in building, and manner of workmanship accustomed amongst them: *Stoneheng* in my judgment was a work, built by the *Romans* and they the sole *Founders* thereof. For, if look upon this Antiquity, as an admired and magnificent building, who more magnificent than the *Romans*? (...) If take notice of their power and ways by which they effected such goodly structures, their means were not ordinary according to the common costume of other *People*; and why? Because, besides being particular *Artisans* practiced in severall *Arts*, they employed in their works whole bodies of their *Armies*, and whatever *Nations* subdued by them. [...]

If observe *their Order* in building; the only *Order* of *Architecture*, which Italy may truly glory in the invention of, is the *Tuscane Order*, so called, because first found out by the *Tuscans*, that in a more than ordinary manner they might reverence their *Deities* in *Temples* composed thereof. [...] Which *Order*, though first used by the *Tuscans*, certain it is, the *Romans* took from them, and brought it in use with other *Arts*, in severall parts of the world, as their conquests led them on. Now of this *Tuscan Order*, a plain, grave, and humble manner of *Building*, very strong and solid *Stoneheng* principally consists. So that, observing the *Order* whereof *Stoneheng* built, there being no such Elements known in this Island as distinct *Orders* of *Architecture*, until the *Romans* introduced them, the very work it self, of so great *Antiquity*, declares the *Romans Founders* thereof. [...]

[p. 75] These pressing occurrences therefore, to wit, civill broyls among the *Romans* themselves, frequent insurrections of the *Britans*, daily inrodes by the *Picts* and *Scots*, together with the *Downfall* of *Paganism*, *decay* of *Arts*, and fatall *ruine* of the whole *Empire*, making the times both long before and after *Constantine* incompatible for undertaking such works as this *Antiquity*, it may safely enough be concluded, if *Stoneheng* not founded by *Agricola*, yet erected it might be about fifteen hundred and fifty years ago, in the time somewhat after his government, *the* Province *being formerly left by him in good order and passeable state*, the *Britans* reduced from *Barbarity* to order and civill conversation, and the *Romans* flourishing in all manner of *Arts* and *Sciences*.

[…] [p. 101] *Stoneheng* was dedicated, as I conceive, to the God *Coelus*, by some Authors called *Coelum*, by others *Uranus*, from whom the Ancients imagined all things took their beginnings. My reasons are, First in respect of the *situation* thereof; for it stands in a Plain, remote from any *Town* or *Village*, in a free and open air, without any groves or woods about it.

Secondly, in regard of the *Aspect*; for *Stoneheng* was never covered, but built without a roof. Wich *Decorum*[3] the *Romans* ever observed, both in the *Situation* and *Aspect* of the *Temples* dedicated to this their God, and to *Jove* the *Lightner*, the *Sun*, and the *Moon*. […] *Jovi fulgatori, & Coelo, & Soli, & Lunae, aedificia sub divo Hypaethraque constituuntur. To* Jove *the Lightner, and to Coleus, and to the Sun, and to the Moon, they erected buildings in the open air and uncovered*, saith *Vitruvius* in the second Chapter of his first Book. Take with you also this reason. *Horum enim Deorum & species & effectus in aperto mundo atque lucenti [raesented videmus, because both the forms and the effects of these Deities, we behold present before our eyes, in a clear and open view.*[4] Another reason I find why they built their Temples to *Coelus*, and those other Deities uncovered as *Stoneheng*: because they counted it an hainous matter to see those Gods confined under a roof, whose doing good consisted in being abroad.

[…] Fourthly, in respect of the *Order* whereof *Stoneheng* built. The severity of this *Tuscane* work, retaining in it a shew (as it were) of that first face of *Antiquity* (as *A. Palladio* terms it) being most agreeable to the nature of this their God, reputed the ancientest of all their *Deities*, and Father of *Saturn*. For, it was the custome of the Ancients (as in part I remembred before) to appropriate the severall *Orders* of *Architecture*, according to the particular qualifications of those they deified. […]

[p. 105] Sixthly, all the upright stones in this *Antiquity* are *Pyramidall* like flames, in imitation of those *Aetheriall* fires, wherewith the *Heaven* is adorned. […]

[p. 106] Lastly, that *Stoneheng* was anciently dedicated to *Coelus* I collect from the *Conformations* of the work. For the *Conformation* of the *Cell* and *Porticus* in the Plant, was designed with four equilaterall *Triangles*, inscribed in a *Circle*, such as the *Astrologers* use in describing the twelve *celestiall* signs in musicall proportions. [...]

[p. 108] History affords only *Contemplation*, whereby their great Actions are made conceivable alone to reasoning: but the ruines of [the secular and sacred structures of the Romans] are *Demonstration*, which obvious to sense, are even yet so many eye-witnesses of their admir'd achievements.

> *Roma quanta fuit, ipsa ruina docet,*
> *How great* Rome *was, her ruins yet declare.*[5]

Opinions fancied to the contrary, I have rendred improbable, the Authors of them in respect of this *Antiquity* being not only modern; but also, what is said by them *Romance-Romans* of old.[6] Men possest neverthelesse, with a former conceit of things, endure not by any means new opinions, having not commonly patience to search after the truth thereof. To them, ever the more generally received, the truer things seem, accounting all of their own time despicable; insomuch, as some are so far in love with vulgarly receiv'd reports, that it must be taken for truth, whatsoever related by them, through nor head, nor tail, nor foot nor footstep in it oftentimes of reason or common sense. They that beleeve *Geffrey Monmouth ipse dixit*, may make themselves merry therewith; in pleasing their own fancy, they displease not mine. As I have delivered my own judgement freely, all reason they should enjoy theirs. But such as sail in the vast Ocean of time, amongst the craggy rocks of *Antiquity*, steering their course, betwixt anciently approved customs, and convincing arguments, guided by good Authority, and sound judgement, arrive much safer, and with better repute, in the secure Haven of undoubted *Truth*. For mine own part, I had rather erre happily with venerable *Antiquity*, than so much as trouble my thoughts with modern conceits. (...)

Sir Christopher Wren, from 'Of the Surveyor's Design for repairing the old ruinous structure [of Saint Paul's]' (1666)

(See the notes on Wren and extracts in Chapter 3, above, earlier in this chapter and in Chapter 5.)

Further reading: Summerson (1983), pp. 122–4 and 203–21; Sool (1990), p. 34–6; Szambien (1995). See Figures 4.6 and 4.7 for Wenceslas Hollar's views of Saint Paul's before the Great Fire of London.

Amongst the many Propositions, that may be made to your Lordships, concerning the Repair of St. *Paul's*, some may possibly aim at too great a Magnificence, which neither the Disposition, nor Extent of this Age will probably bring to a Period. Others again may fall so low as to think of piecing up the old Fabrick, here with Stone, there with Brick, and cover all Faults with a Coat of Plaister, leaving it still to Posterity, as a further Object of Charity.

4.6 Wenceslas Hollar, engraving of Old Saint Paul's seen from the west, from William Dugdale, *History of Saint Paul's Cathedral* (London, 1658)

I suppose your Lordships may think proper to take a middle Way, and to neglect nothing that may conduce to a decent uniform Beauty, or durable Firmness in the Fabrick, or Suitableness to the Expence already laid out on the Outside: especially since it is a Pile both for Ornament and Use. For, all the Occasions either of a Quire, Consistory, Chapter-House, Library, Court of Arches, Preaching-auditory, might have been supplied in less Room, with less Expence, and yet more Beauty; but then it had wanted of the Grandeur, which exceeds all little Curiosity; this being the Effect of Wit only, the other a Monument of Power, and mighty Zeal in our Ancestors to publick Works in those Times, when the City had neither a fifth Part of the People, not a tenth Part of the Wealth it now boasts off.

I shall presume therefore to enumerate as well the Defects of Comeliness as Firmness, that the one may be reconcil'd with the other in the Restitution. And yet I should not propose any Thing of meer Beauty to be added, but where there is a Necessity of rebuilding, and where it will be near the same Thing to perform it well as ill.

First, it is evident by the Ruin of the Roof, that the Work was both ill design'd, and ill built from the Beginning: ill design'd, because the Architect

4.7 Wenceslas Hollar, engraving of Old Saint Paul's, interior of the nave, from William Dugdale, *History of Saint Paul's Cathedral* (London, 1658)

gave not the Butment enough to counterpoise, and resist the Weight of the Roof from spreading the Walls; for, the Eye alone will discover to any Man, that those Pillars as vast as they are, even eleven Foot diameter, are bent outward at least six Inches from their first Position; which being done on both Sides, it necessarily follows, that the whole Roof must first open in large and wide Cracks along by the Walls and Windows, and lastly drop down between the yielding Pillars.

This bending of the Pillars was facilitated by their ill Building; for, they are only cased without, and that with small Stones, not one greater than a Man's Burden; but within is nothing but a Core of small Rubbish-stone, and much Mortar, which easily crushes and yields to the Weight: and this outward Coat of Free-stone is so much torn with Age, and the Neglect of the Roof, that there are few Stones to be found that are not moulder'd, and flaw'd away with the Salt-peter that is in them; an incurable Disease, which perpetually throws off whatever Coat of Plaister is laid on it, and therefore not to be palliated.

From hence I infer, that as the Outside of the Church was new flagg'd with Stone of larger Size than before, so ought the Inside also: And in doing this, it will be as easy to perform it, after a good *Roman* Manner, as to follow the *Gothick* Rudeness of the old Design; and that, without placing the Face of the new Work in any Part many Inches farther out or in, than the Superficies of the old Work; or adding to the Expence that would arise were it perform'd the worse Way.

This also may be safely affirm'd, not only by an Architect, taking his Measures from the Precepts and Examples of the Antients, but by a Geometrician, (this Part being liable to Demonstrate) that the Roof is, and ever was, too heavy for its Butment; and therefore any Part of the old Roof new pieced, will still but occasion further Ruin, and the second Ruin will much sooner follow than the first, since 'tis easier to force a Thing already declining. It must therefore be either a timber Roof plaister'd, (which, in such Buildings where a little Soke of Weather is not presently discover'd or remedied, will soon decay) or else, a thinner and lighter Shell of Stone, very geometrically proportion'd to the Strength of the Butment. The Roof may be Brick, if it be plaister'd with *Stucco*, which is a harder Plaister, that will not fall off with the Drip of a few Winters, and which to this Day remains firm in many ancient *Roman* Buildings.

The middle Part is most defective both in Beauty and Firmness, without and within; for, the Tower leans manifestly by the settling of one of the ancient Pillars that supported it. Four new Arches were, therefore, of later Years, incorporated within the old ones, which hath straighten'd and hinder'd both the Room, and the clear thorough View of the Nave, in that Part, where it had been more graceful to have been rather wider than the rest.

The excessive Length of Buildings is no otherwise commendable, but because it yields a pleasing Perspective by the continu'd optical Diminution of the Columns; and if this be cut off by Columns ranging within their Fellows, the Grace that would be acquir'd by the Length is totally lost.

Besides this Deformity of the Tower itself within, there are others near it; as, the next Intercolumniation in the *Navis* or Body of the Church, is much less than all the rest. Also the North and South-wings have Aisles only on the West-Side, the others being originally shut up for the Consistory. Lastly, the Intercolumniations or Spaces between the Pillars of the Quire next adjoining to the Tower are very unequal. Again, on the Outside of the Tower, the Buttresses that have been erected one upon the Back of another to secure three Corners on the inclining Sides, (for the fourth wants a Buttress) are so irregular, that upon the whole Matter, it must be concluded, that the Tower from Top to Bottom, and the next adjacent Parts, are such a Heap of Deformities, that no judicious Architect will think it corrigible, by any Expence that can be laid out upon new dressing it, but that it will remain unworthy the rest of the Work, infirm and tottering; and for these Reasons, as I conjecture, was formerly resolv'd to be taken down.

I cannot propose a better Remedy, than by cutting off the inner Corners of the Cross, to reduce this middle Part into a spacious *Dome* or *Rotundo*, with a *Cupola*, or hemispherical Roof, and upon the *Cupola*, (for the outward Ornament) a *Lantern* with a spiring Top, to rise proportionably, tho' not to that unneccessary Height of the former Spire of Timber and Lead burnt by Lightning.

By this Means the Deformities of the unequal Intercolumniations will be taken away; the Church, which is much too narrow for the Heighth, render'd spacious in the Middle, which may be a very proper Place for a vast Auditory: the outward Appearance of the Church will seem to swell in the Middle by Degrees, from a large Basis rising into a *Rotundo* bearing a *Cupola*, and then ending in a *Lantern*: and this with incomparable more Grace in the remoter Aspect, than it is possible for the lean Shaft of a Steeple to afford. Nor if it be rightly order'd, will the Expence be much more than that of investing the Tower and Corners yet unfinish'd, with new Stone, and adding the old Steeple anew; the Lead of which will be sufficient for a *Cupola*; and the same Quantity of Ashler makes the Corners outward, that would make them inward as they now are: And the Materials of the old Corners of the Ailes will be filling Stone for the new Work: for I should not persuade the Tower to be pull'd down at first, but the new Work to be Built round it, partly because the Expectations of Persons are to be kept up; for, many Unbelievers would bewail the Loss of old *Paul's* Steeple, and despond if they did not see a hopeful Successor rise in its stead; and chiefly because it will save a great Quantity of scaffolding Poles; the Scafforls which are needful being fix'd from the old to the new Work; and when the *Tholus* or inward Vault is to be laid, the Tower taken down to that Height will rest the enters of the Vault with great Convenience, and facilitate the planting of Engines for raising the Stones; and after all is finish'd and settl'd, the Tower that is left may be taken clear away from within. All which can only from the *Designs* be perfectly understood.

And for the Encouragement and Satisfaction of Benefactors that comprehend not readily Designs and Draughts on Paper, as well as for the inferior Artificers clearer Intelligence of their Business, it will be requisite that a large and exact Model be made; which will also have this Use, that if the Work should happen to be interrupted, or retarded, Posterity may proceed where the Work was left off, pursuing still the same Design.

And as the *Portico*, built by *Inigo Jones*, being an intire and excellent Piece, gave great Reputation to the Work in the first Repairs, and occasion'd fair Contributions; so to begin now with the *Dome* may probably prove the best Advice, being an absolute Piece of itself, and what will most likely be finished in our Time; will make by far the most splendid Appearance; may be of present Use for the Auditory, will make up all the outward Repars perfect; and become an Ornament to his Majesty's most excellent Reign, to the Church of *England*, and to this Great City, which it is pity, in the Opinion of our *Neighbours*, should longer continue the most unadorn'd of her Bigness in the World.

In the mean Time, till a good Quantity of Stone be provided, Things of less Expence, but no less Consequence, ought to be regarded; such as fixing all Cramps that the Roof hath been spoil'd of; covering all Timber from Weather; taking down the falling Roofs; searching the Vaults beneath, and securing them. And before the Foundation be digg'd for the *Dome*, the Arches on which the Tower stands must be secur'd after a peculiar Manner represented in the Designs.

P.S. I shall crave leave to subjoin, that if there be Use of *Stucco*, I have great Hopes, from some Experience already had, that there are *English* Materials to be brought by Sea at an easy Rate, that will afford as good Plaister as is any where to be found in the World; and that with the Mixture of cheaper Ingredients than Marble-meal, which was the old, and is now the modern Way of *Italy*.

The Proposer also, (considering that high Buildings grow more and more expensive as they rise, by reason of the Time and Labour spent in raising the Materials), take this Occasion to acquaint your Lordships, that having had the Opportunity of seeing several Structures of greater Expence than this, while they were in raising, constructed by the best Artists, *Italian* and *French*; and having had daily Conference with them, and observing their Engines and Methods, he hath promoted this *geometrical* Part of *Architecture* yet farther, and thinks the raising of Materials may yet be more facilitated, so as to save in lofty Fabricks, a very considerable Part of the Time, and Labourers Hire.

Roger North, from 'On Gothic Architecture' (*c.* 1696)

North did not publish this essay during his lifetime. Because of its unbiased consideration of the remains of Gothic architecture in England, and its investigation of the tectonic principles at work in the arch and vault system, North's essay on Gothic architecture can be compared with other writings on architecture produced by members and associates of the Royal Society, such as John Ansrey's 'Chronologia Architecturae' (an unpublished manuscript now in the Bodleian Library in Oxford) or Sir Christopher Wren's analysis of Gothic buildings in his 'Report on Old St. Paul's before the Fire' (see above, this chapter). But in spite of the empiricist set of mind revealed here, North preferred the classical style to the Gothic for aesthetic reasons. (See also the entries on North in Chapters 1 and 5 in this volume.)

[BLMS 32540 fol. 316] It is usuall for dablers in this art (as I am,) as well as the adept, to pretend to skill in all sorts of fabricks, publik as well as private; therefore wrighters will run thro all branches of the art, tho their skill ly's but in some, the rest, as rime, for forme sake. And if I have any knowledge of building, I must owne it to ly in the reforming part. I doe not pretend either to great publick designes, nor new models of great howses. It requires an extraordinary genius, to exceed what is now common in the world; and builders, as poets, should blush at mediocrity as well as faults. But notwithstanding this, like my fellow dablers, I will venture my bolt, in somewhat more intire, and new than what I have profest; and first of publick buildings.

The distinction now of building in the world, is reducible to Gothick and Regular. The former was a mode introduc't by a barbarous sort of people, that first distres't, then dissolved the Roman Empire.[7] These fell into a new way of great buildings, which was mixt of their owne invention, and what they found, and had for the most part destroyed among the Greekes and Romans. And this manner is most eminent in our cathedrall churches. But Westminster Hall, one of the best fabricks not dedicated to sacred uses of the time in the world, is purely Gothick.

It is no unpleasant thing to observe the cours of proceeding, in that sort of building, which prevailed in our nation, till almost King James the first. For the elder are more rude, heavy and speak the clumsyness of their contrivers, and came finer, and I think ceast, in Henry VII's Chappell at Westminster, which was all that Gothick witt could doe. Now I give three periods, exemplified in the building of the respective times. The first is the antidiluvian of the Danes, who to England were worse than the deluge to the world, which sent all to peace, they held the nation in dismall torment severall ages. This I suppose to be seen in the church of Durham, and is the most antique of any. The order is round upright lumps for columnes, with perfect semi-circular arches, as rudely expres't in the margin. This church hath had the fortune not to be much ruined, as the more southerne were by the frequent inundations of the infamous Danes, so remaines more intire in its old order, than others are, tho first built neer the same time, which was, I take it, when the Saxon kings took to an humour of cloystering themselves, and thought there was no composition with heaven, for their infinite wickedness, but at the price of a church or monastery.

There are severall other cathedrall churches, which have some foot steps of this antiquity, as Glouster, and at Norwich. And indeed most have some, many are composed of divers sorts according to the severall ages wherein they happned to be repaired, which I have bin much enterteined to observe, as I allwais concluded this order of round and compass to be the oldest. And one would wonder what should guide the fancys of me to a different order of pillar, and arching more remote from naturall beauty, which may consist in easy and reasonable composition, rather than in regulating this, which would have at last brought it to the condition of that what is called regular, which consists in adjusting the proportions of weight and support, agreeing with the previous opinions of the spectators, who are apt to pronounce what is enough, and what too much or too litle, and so determine naturall beauty. Which method, with much study, art, canvassing and experience in Greece, produc't the laws of the 5 orders, and the (now) knowne method of regular building, which I shall consider in another place.

But to proceed in the consideration of the Gothick, (which now is apply'd to all that is not Regular). The next step was to make the arches angular or as half a birds eye and the supports quadrat diagonall and thredded, as Westminster Abbey [...]. And this manner hath come downe to our time, when first the regular way hath bin used in publick buildings, being introduc't by Inigo Jones in repairing St Pauls London. And most of our parochiall churches are of this order, but some more fine than others, as the ages, or persons happened to affect.

I must owne to prefer much the former, being the round way, which I conceive was derived from the Greek and Roman regular columned, but for want of art, and learning in the reason of it, so rudely executed as wee see. But devious from the right as it is, none can deny but, it bears not onely an air of grandure, but hath a strength and reasonableness beyond the other; and is such as an extraordinary high spirited judicious barbarian might be supposed originally to invent, and leave to his posterity to refine upon as a subject capable of being improved to the greatest perfection. And I must needs excuse their grossness of support, as also in latter times, from the want of materialls. It may be they had not the art, nor had found quarrys for raising and leading massy stones such as are necessary to strengthen finer works, for wee observe all is put together of small stones, and so small as makes it strange how they could make the work hang with them, having not the aid of iron cramps, which are now used in the best works.

Then considering that it is seldome, that men vary for the better, tho often in degrees of greater nicety, and seeming fineness, whatever the true reason and judgment happens to be, not often better, but worse than those who went before; so here to be finer, they fell into the birdsey way of arching; and at length, so great a rarity was art, that shewing that, or rather an empty shadow of it, was allow'd to be the best ornament a magnifick structure was capable of. And this brought in that way of thredding the inward work, as I noted, to make the art wondred at, as if all that weight of roof stood on these thredds. If one may guess what ledd to this, I may set out these conjectures.

First the old way seemed clumsey, and dark, because the supports were great and the apertures small. Therefore they might pretend to correct those excesses, and in so doing fall into a worse; as, if they judg'd the lights too small, this carry'd on a conceipt that light was good, and consequently that there could not be enough of it. So whole sides of churches, all that was possible to be gained by pinching the support, was turned into a windoe, according to the rule, stulti dum vitant vitia in contraria currunt.[8] For the same reason, when they observed the supports or pillars took up too much room, they would mend the fault, by making them so small, that one could not imagine them capable to sustein the rooffe. And being sensible, that their light was too much, and offensive, as really it is, they came to darken the windoes with painted glass, which could not be so studiously, and generally used, if reason had not ledd to it. And without they were driven to strange deformity of propps (as I observed) to make good the support, at the same time conceling it within; as if the same persons were never to see both sides. And as to the windoes, they were driven to a great puzle to hang their glass in such vast breadths, which brought in that variety of frame, and rose work in the windoes, as wee see in Westminster Abbey, and King's Colledge chappell in Cambridge, which I propose as the 2 best peices of the Gothick work in England.

But to proceed, this round work lasted to the inroads of the Danes, the next order was the birdsey arch and diagonall collumne, which I propose lated to the Edwards time, and then a still finer sort of building came in, which is exemplified in the Cathedrall of New Sarum, which church, for the area of it, I beleeve stands upon the least support of any in the world. It is all of one order, and in stead of the diagonall thredded columne, it is composed of rounds, whereof one is in the midle, and four about it much smaller, upon which the thredds of the arches fall, and are therefore diagonall to the range. This conceipt is taken from the Temple Church in London, which is more ancient, but its columne are four rounds consolidated [...]. It hath bin thought, both these and Salsbury were made and not quarr-stones, but it is not clear, nor whence they had them. These are the 3 periods of the Gothic building, which is now expired in the world, and the Regular taken from old ruins and books succeeds it.[9]

But before I take leave of the subject, I will observe 2 manners, which are inviolably observed, 1. The single range, which is for chappells, and the treble range, which wee call the nave and two iles, or the shipp, as the words import, and two wings, but more properly the body. This hath bin affirmed by the cheif architect of this age,[10] to have bin the manner of the Greek and Roman courts of justice, used in latter time, those fabricks were most cultivated, and was coevall with the Christians beginning to build churches; whether there [are] any basilike yet remaining I know not, scarce thinck any; if att all, they must be converted to churches. All other fabricks [by] one rage or other, of warr or frenzie, hath demolisht, and allmost all monuments of antiquity about Greece are lost; even the people, however of old brave learned and free, now are like as abject and illiterate slaves. It was peculiar to these basilike to have 2 iles or wings, devided from the main fabrick by columnes, because they were to conteine and keep dry as well as cool vast multitudes of people; and it was hard to cover such a breadth any other way, which should contein such numbers. Therefore the columnes are in the place of upright supports to the maine weight of the roof, and the wings as abuttments to the outward thrust of it, so as the whole stands firme, and founded on the likeness of a man, and his two armes, or any thing reasonably attended, as a great person leaning on 2 pages: one great pile with smaller neer, which with regard to uniformity and strength, are the best and most universally approved order of things, and may be introduc't in all sorts of finishing work, as well as fabrick, which lay'd out thus in almost any proportion will be well. If this were so used for courts of justice, as the word basiliche imports, it was onely strait ranges, with the justice seat at the upper end. But that which wee call the cuppolo, dome or tower in the midle, with the cross iles, and east end, those were introduc't in the forme of a cross by the Christians and are peculiar to their churches, which, from the manner whence they were derived, are still in the antique languages called basiliche, and with us means a capitall or cathedrall church. There has bin much alteration in the middle part, which generally was a Gothick tower square upon 4 uprights, and abbutted upon the 8 walls centring in it. But the elder times, I mean not with respect to the primitive, but our owne, when building in Grece and Itally began to draw towards Regular, and the Goths themselves to be reformed, there was a way of volting this midle introduc't whereof the Santa Sofia in Contantinople is a glorious example. And these were the use if not the invention of that time, for I doe not find in the wrighters of Antiquitys any arches made like half sphears or half ovalls, as the use then, and since has bin. And because in Itally the great churches were called Il domo, and were of this manner, the manner itself is now called a dome, and is in my judgment a greater perfection in architecture than the ancients knew or made use of, for they ordinarly covered with timber, and seldome made arches, but architraves, unless in latter times the triumphall arches for spear men to pass throo. But volts of this magnitude, as in those Greek fabriks, and Roman now, particularly St. Peter's at Rome, and as I hope to see in St. Paul's London, are types of art, never enough to be admired and encouraged. And even the barbarous Turks are in this glorious, who cover stupendious fabricks with hemisphere volts and open the four sides, as well abutt the whole with 4 quarter spheres, which is a figure of so great perfection, I wonder it is not introduc't with us, who so much love room, and lofty coverings. [...]

And in this state wee must leave the Gothick, which being arrived to its ultimate refinement must submitt to the course of changing the world was allwais given to, and lett in the old formes apply'd to our fancys; and that will be in perpetuall change, and new modes come in fashion, but probably will not so easily truckle to mutability, as the Gothick hath done, which goes off all at once.

Sir John Vanbrugh, 'Reasons Offer'd for Preserving some Part of the Old Manor [at Woodstock]' (11 June 1709)

This text – originally a memorandum by Vanbrugh to Lady Churchill, for whom he was building Blenheim Palace – is one of the earliest documents of the Associationist view of the meaning and impact of works of art on the beholder: their beauty does not reside in some intrinsic, objective property such as proportion or symmetry, but in their power to evoke trains of associations, memories and emotions. It was to become the basis of Picturesque aesthetics in landscape gardening and architecture. (See also the note on Vanbrugh and extract in Chapter 3, above.)

Further reading: van Eck (2000); Ridgway (2000), pp. 172–92.

There is perhaps no one thing, which the most Polite part of Mankind have more universally agreed in; than the Vallue they have ever set upon the Remains of distant Times Nor amongst the Severall kinds of those Antiquitys, are there any so much regarded, as those of Buildings; Some for their Magnificence, or Curious Workmanship; And others; as they move more lively and pleasing Reflections (than History without their Aid can do) On the Persons who have Inhabited them; On the Remarkable things which have been transacted in them, Or the extraordinary Occasions of Erecting them. As I believe it cannot be doubted, but if Travellers many Ages hence, shall be shewn The Very House in which so great a Man Dwelt, as they will then read the Duke of Marlborough in Story;[11] And that they Shall be told, it was not only his Favourite Habitation, but was Erected for him by the Bounty of the Queen And with the Approbation of the People, As a Monument of the Greatest Services and Honours, that any Subject had ever done this Country: I believe, tho' they may not find Art enough in the Builder, to make them Admire the Beauty of the Fabrick they will find Wonder enough in the Story, to make 'em pleas'd with the Sight of it.

I hope I may be forgiven, if I make some faint Application of what I say of Blenheim, to the Small Remains of ancient Woodstock Manour.

It can't indeed be said, it was Erected on so Noble nor on So justifiable an Occasion, But it was rais'd by One of the Bravest and most Warlike of the English Kings; And tho' it has not been Fam'd, as a Monument of his Arms, it has been tenderly regarded as the Scene of his Affections. Nor amongst the Multitude of People who come daily to View what is raising to the Memory of the Great Battle of Blenheim; Are there any that do not run eagerly to See what Ancient Remains are to be found of Rosamonds Bower. It may perhaps be worth some Little Reflection Upon what may be said, if the Very footsteps of it Are no more to be found.

But if the Historicall Argument Stands in need of Assistance; there is Still much to be said on Other Considerations.

That Part of the Park which is Seen from the North Front of the New Building, has Little Variety of Objects Nor dos the Country beyond it Afford any of Vallue, It therefore Stands in Need of all the helps that can be given, which are only Five; Buildings, And Plantations. These rightly dispos'd will indeed Supply all the wants of Nature in that Place. And the Most Agreable Disposition is to Mix them: in which this Old Manour gives so happy an Occasion for; that were the inclosure filld with Trees (principally Fine Yews and Hollys) Promuscuously Set to grow up in a Wild Thicket. So that all the Building left, (which is only the Habitable Part and the Chappel) might Appear in Two Risings amongst 'em, it wou'd make One of the Most Agreable Objects that the best of Landskip Painters can invent. And if on the Contrary this Building is taken away; there then remains nothing but an Irregular, Ragged Ungovernable Hill, the deformity of which are not to be cured but by a Vast Expence; And that at last will only remove an Ill Object but not produce a good One, whereas to finish the present Wall for the Inclosures, to forme the Sloops and make the Plantation (which is all that is now wanting to Compleat the Whole Designe) wou'd not Cost Two Hundred pounds.

I take the Liberty to offer this Paper with a Picture to Explain what I endeavour to Describe, That if the Present Direction for destroying the Building, shou'd happen hereafter to be Repented of, I may not be blam'd for Neglecting to set in the truest Light I cou'd, a Thing that Seem'd at least to me so very Matteriall.

J VANBRUGH

Robert Castell, from *The Villas of the Ancients Illustrated* (1729)

Robert Castell (?–1728) appears to have been a gentleman of scholarly inclination rather than a practising architect. Nothing is known about his life before 1728, when an advertisement was published for his translation of Vitruvius. He had been encouraged by Lord Burlington to produce an English translation of Vitruvius, and became convinced that it would make more sense to publish his own books on Roman villas, a subject not covered by Vitruvius, after his translation would have appeared. *Villas of the Ancients* was published posthumously in 1729 and was dedicated to Burlington. The translation of Vitruvius was never published and has not survived. When *Villas of the Ancients* appeared it did not have the impact on practising architects Castell hoped it would have; in fact, its greatest influence was on the layout of gardens. It is a typical case of the humanist approach to architectural history, based on careful of classical sources combined with techniques of virtual reconstruction as developed by Serlio, Palladio and Desgodets. Well into the twentieth century Castell's reconstructions were considered by archaeologists to be highly reliable. (See Harris, 1990; Colvin, 1995; see also Figure 4.8–10.)

4.8 Frontispiece to Robert Castell, *The Villas of the Ancients Illustrated* (London, 1729), T. Wilson, artist, and P. Fourdrinier (attr.), engraver

The Preface

A Desire I have long entertain'd of translating and explaining *Vitruvius*, determin'd me first to set about some inferior Performance in Architecture, as a necessary Preparation to my entering on a Work of so much Labour and Difficulty: And as I thought nothing would be more proper for my Choice than such a Branch of the Art as that great Master had been least Curious to explain, I resolved to take for my subject the Rules that were observed in the situating and disposing of the *Roman Villas* which he speaks of only in a cursory Way lib. 6 cap. 10, and to this End I have been at the Pains to peruse many ancient Authors, who have treated more at large of that Part, not the meanest of the Architect's Business.

Most of the Roman Writers upon Agriculture that are remaining have thought fit at the Beginning of their Works, to tell what were to be consider'd

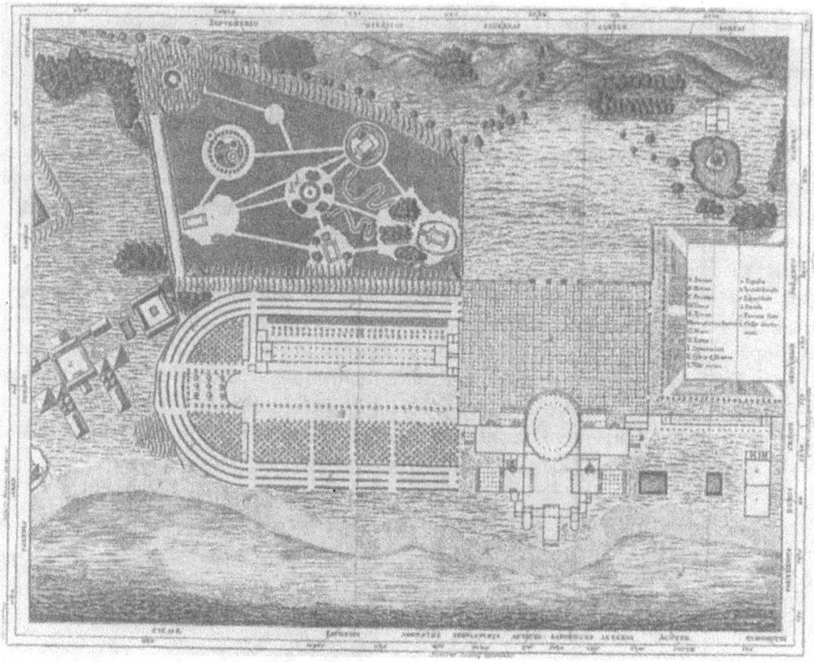

4.9 Robert Castell, *The Villas of the Ancients Illustrated* (London, 1729), plan of Laurentinum, T. Wilson, artist, and P. Fourdrinier (attr.), engraver

in the Situation and Disposition of *Villas. Cato*, the eldest of these left the fewest Rules on that Head, and of the least Consequence; but *Varro* that was the next after him, has been more ample and judicious in his observations, and seems to have laid the Foundation for what *Columella, Palladius*, and those several *Greek* Authors mention'd by *Constantine*, have since wrote on that Subject.[12] He has discours'd more fully than any of them on those Parts of the Villa that were design'd as well for the Pleasure of a retir'd Life as the Convenience and Profit of Agriculture. *Pliny* the Younger alone has exceeded *Varro* in this Particular; he has left us two Epistles containing an exact Description, of his *Villas* of *Laurentinum* [see Figure 4.9] and *Tuscum*, and tho' we find not in him any direct Rules for the Disposition of the *Villa Urbana* or Country House of Pleasure, yet he gives us to understand, that those buildings were contriv'd according to the strictest Rules of Art, and points out what were principally regarded in the placing and ordering of them, and how they were at once accomodated by the Architect for enjoying the Benefits, and for avoiding the Inconveniencies of the several Seasons.[13] He speaks of the Situation and Disposition of those Buildings, knowing his Friends, to whom he wrote, could not but be sensible that the Rules laid down by

Vitruvius with respect to Building and Proportion were equally to take Place in the City and Country.

I thought it proper to quote my Authorities at large, and especially the Epistles of *Pliny*, which the Reader hath here both in *Latin* and in *English*. And as I attempt only to shew the Distribution and Disposition of such Buildings, I have omitted to draw any Elevations and Sections but what are taken from the express Words of the Ancients or are evidently necessary to illustrate the Meaning of some difficult Passages. The Whole work consists of three Parts. The first contains the Description of a *Villa Urbana*, a Country House of Retirement near the City, that was supplied with most of the Necessities of Life from a neighbouring Market-Town. The second sets forth the rules that were necessary to be observed by an Architect, who had the Liberty to chose a Situation, and to make a proper Distribution of all Things in and about the Villa; but particularly with Relation to the Farm-House, which in this Sort of Buildings, according to the more ancient *Roman* Manner, was always join'd to the Master's House and but very little removed from it. In the third Part is shewn the Description of another *Villa Urbana*, on a Situation very different from the former, with the Farm-House and its Appurtenances so far remov'd as to be no Annoyance to it, and at the same time so near as to furnish it conveniently with all necessities.

[From Castell's translation of Pliny's Book II, Epistle XVII]
[p. 11] From hence a[14] *Cryptoporticus* extends itself, for Largeness comparable to publick Buildings; on both sides are Windows, on that next the Sea the greater Number, on the Garden Site they are single, and in the higher Row they are not so many. These, when the Day is serene and calm, are all open'd; but when the Wind is troublesome on either side, those on the Opposite side are open'd without any Inconveniency.

[From Castell's text]
[p. 44] *Hinc Cryptoporticus*, &tc. [See Figure 4.10.] The Room he is now about to describe and which was the greatest Part of this Building, seems to have been an Invention since *Vitruvius*, who makes one mention of no such Part in his Account of the *Roman* Houses, tho' by the following Description of it, and the Uses, it appears to have been very necessary in a Country House, where the Person inhabiting went through such a daily course of Exercise, as our Author did. The Form of it or in what manner it was built, does not appear by his Account. But without Doubt it was a long Room, and there was one manner common to all of them, which, as its Name implies, was that of a *Porticus*, enclos'd by a Wall on all sides, differring no otherwise from our present Galleries, than that they had Pillars in them. This Room *Pliny* has here considered under three Heads: First, its Size; secondly, its Contrivance to admit or exclude the Wind and light at Pleasure; and, lastly,

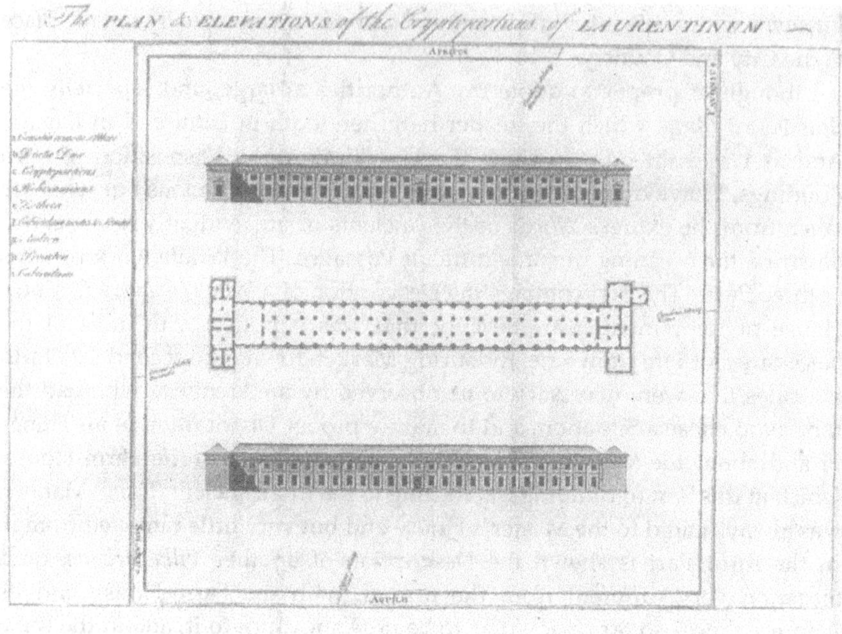

4.10 Robert Castell, *The Villas of the Ancients Illustrated* (London, 1729), the Cryptoporticus of Laurentinum, plan and elevation, T. Wilson, artist, and P. Fourdrinier (attr.), engraver

with Respect to the Heat of the Sun both in Winter and in Summer. In this Place he seems to follow the Rule of Conveniency rather than of proportioning Rooms to the main Building, as appears by the Character he gives to this of its being equal in Size to Publick Buildings, and to which no other Room in or about this Villa has any Equality. The Reason of this extraordinary Grandeur must have been in consequence of the Use for which it was designed, which was that of walking: Besides, as this appears to have been a Room in which he proposed to enjoy the Pleasures of Summer as well as Winter, it must at that Season, by its Capaciousness have been cooler, and the Sun, by means of the Breadth of the Room, always avoided; at the same time one side of it was shady though all the Windows were open, and the Air had a thorough Passage, as the Prospect of this Room itself was more agreeable to those that walked in it. The Method taken in this Room to receive the Benefit and avoid the Inconvenience of the Wind at all times, was nothing more than two Ranges of Windows on each side; and though this Room had conveniencies for Summer, yet as if he was desirous to have more for Winters, those that were on the *South-West* side were large, and in two Ranges compleat, and those on the *North-East* were less, with the upper Range not equal in

Number to those on the lower. The principal Convenience of those Windows on both sides he tells us himself, was, that as *Vitruvius* required those Winds that were agreeable might be admitted, and the others excluded [...].

John Wood, from *The Origin of Building* (1741)

John Wood the Elder (1704–54) was born in Bath. In his early years he was one of the most important builders on the Cavendish–Harley Estate in London. Lord Bingley employed him to lay out the grounds of his estate in Yorkshire. While he was in the north in 1725 he started to plan the improvement of Bath for which he is now chiefly famous. He published *The Origin of Building* in 1741, and *An Essay towards a Description of Bath* in 1742. Wood's views (which included Freemasonry) were in part derived from Sir Isaac Newton's *Chronology of Ancient Kingdoms Amended* of 1728. For Wood, the Tabernacle of Moses, the Temple of Jerusalem, Stonehenge and Gothic churches were all examples of a divinely ordained system of architecture independent of classical architecture and unknown to Vitruvius (Harris, 1990).

Further reading: Mowl and Earnshaw (1988).

Book the First. Containing an Account of the Rise and Progress of Building, from the Creation of the World, to the Time in which Moses finished his Tabernacle in the Wilderness.

Chapter I. The Introduction

As Riches and Captives in the early Ages of the World were the natural Effects of Conquest; so it soon became a Rule among the People in most Nations to employ them upon Works of Building; sometimes in Honour of their Gods; sometimes in Honour of their Kings and Heroes; and therefore Architecture was held in such high Veneration and Esteem by the Antients, that the greatest Monarchs of the East made it their chief Study, in order to transmit, by some Noble Work, their Names, their Riches, and their great Atchievements to Posterity. [...]

Architecture thus becoming the chief Study and Delight of Princes, the most renowned in History, we need not wonder that the People of every Nation shou'd endeavour to be thought the Inventors of the Rules for building such Structures as, by their Beauty, attracted the Admiration of the intelligent World; and herein the *Grecians* bore away the Palm from all the others; for being a People naturally inclined to Fiction, they dressed up their Story of the Origin of the *Orders*, that the *Romans* very readily have given the Invention of those beautiful Parts to them, as appears by the Writings of *Vitruvius*, who thus accounts for the *Rise of Building* in general, and of *Order* and *Proportion* in particular. [...]

The Chance or Fortune which superintended the Rise of every Thing curious in *Architecture*, as above, was, under all its Appellations, esteemed by the Antients as a Divine Power, and no less than God alone. And indeed if we examine into the Writings of the most eminent Authors of antient History, as well Sacred as Profane, we shall find them all confess, that the *Knowledge* our Ancestors first had in Arts and Sciences, *was given them immediately by God.* And therefore tho' *Vitruvius* lays it down as a Principle, that *Mankind are by Nature teachable, and inclined to Imitation,* he has nevertheless declared, they were above Three Thousand Years before they, even by Chance, did any thing worthy to be recorded, and that many Centuries pass'd before another Step was taken towards Perfection in their Works of *Architecture* [...].

This Account, which *Vitruvius* has collected, however specious it may appear from its remaining still, in a great measure, uncontroverted, has its Foundation in the Holy Scripture, for therein we shall find it most expressly declared, that Mankind at first dwelt in a Garden of Trees, quited the Place of their original Abode thro' an impetuous Wind, was kept out of it by the Fire that ensued that Wind, in the third Generation began to build Huts to dwell in, and that it was above two thousand five hundred Years before they had any Idea of *Order* in Building, the first Structure that is mentioned by the Sacred Writers to be erected with Pillars being the *Tabernacle* built by *Moses* in the Wilderness by the Directions of GOD; after which the Heathens began to erect *Temples* to their Idols; for we read of divers of them subsequent to the *Tabernacle,* but not of one before it; and tho' by this Structure the Form of *Order* was introduced into the World, yet we don't find that the Pillars in it were made according to any of those *Proportions* which were afterwards established for these essential Parts of a beautiful Building. [...]

Now since *Vitruvius* attributes the Rise of Building to Chance, which under all its Appellations was esteemed by the Antients to be no less than God alone; and since his Account, from whatever Authors collected, agrees with what is contained in the Writings of *Moses,* and the succeeding Penmen of Holy Scriptures; and since the most eminent Authors of Antient History, in many Instances, own, that the *Knowledge* our Ancestors first had in Arts and Sciences, *was given them immediately by* God; we purpose, in the following Sheets, not only to weigh and consider, the Origin, Progress, and Perfection of Building, so as to make an Account thereof consistent with Sacred History, with the Confession of the Antients, with the Course of great Events in all Parts of the World, and with itself; but, from Time to Time, to point out the *Plagiarism of the Heathens;* and then, to shew, that the *Dignity* to which *Architecture* was rais'd by the Grandeur of the *Egyptian,* the *Assyrian,* the *Median,* the *Babylonian,* the *Persian,* the *Grecian,* and the *Roman Empires,* was not comparable to the *Lustre* with which it first shined in the Sacred Works of the *Jews.*

Book the Fourth. Containing an Account of the Progress of Building From the Completion of Solomon's Temple, 'till it arriv'd to its highest Perfection in Asia, Egypt, Greece and Italy.

Chapter XIII.
[…] [p. 180] Herod's Buildings were antecedent to those of *Augustus*; the *Jewish* Monarch, full of Gratitude to the *Roman* Emperor, dedicated most of his Works to him; and the *Jewish* Buildings furnished the *Romans* with Examples, as their History did with Precepts, to bring *Architecture* to its highest Perfection in *Italy*. Examples and Precepts were accordingly, in this glorious Age, collected by *Vitruvius*, for *Caesar's* Instruction; but whether from the *Grecian* Works and Writers, or from the *Jewish*, let the Description of the *Orders* of Columns, as well as the *Forms* and *Proportions* of *Temples* declare. […]

Book the Fifth. Containing a Description of the Orders of Columns; of the Forms and Proportions of Temples, Basilica's, and other celebrated Edifices of Antiquity […].

Chapter II.
[…] [p. 186] The first Building mention'd in sacred History, in which Pillars were made use of, was the *Tabernacle*; and those of the Veil were the first directed by GOD, who did not give any Proportion for them, as he did for most other Things in the same Edifice: But when *Solomon* erected his *Temple*, he made the Porch six Times its Length, in Height, and he caused two brazen Pillars to be cast, and set up in the same Porch, each of which, including the Capital, was 23 Cubits high, and 12 Cubits in Circumference; by which the Diameter of those Pillars was very near the 1–6th Part of their Height: So that by comparing this with what *Vitruvius* relates, it appears to be the very same; and therefore the Truth of the original Proportion of Columns comes from the *Temple* of *Solomon*, and not from that of *Apollo Panionius*, which the *Ionians* built in *Caria*, supposing Sir *Isaac Newton's* Chronology to be right.

But if we follow the other Accounts, and place the Death of *Erectheus* 264 Years after the *Israelites* left *Egypt*, then we must have Recourse to the *Tabernacle*, and prior Works of GOD, to see whether the same Proportion *Vitruvius* gives to the *Columns* of *the Dorick Order*, is not to be found in them. The first Proportion revealed by the Almighty Architect of the World to Man, was that of the Length and Breadth of *Noah's Ark*, the latter being 1–6th of the former; and the first Dimension given for the Tabernacle was for the Curtains that were to cover it, which had for their Length seven Times their Breadth; exactly corresponding with the Text of *Vitruvius*, who most expressly tells us, That the *Columns* at first were six Diameters high; then the *Ionians* encreased them to seven; of which Lengths he himself makes them:[15] And supposing them to have Bases, it will answer the very next Dimension given by GOD, for the Curtains that made the second Covering for the *Tabernacle*, which had for their Length just seven Times and one half their Breadth.

There is no doubt but *Vitruvius* well consider'd that notable Action of *Sampson*'s raising the Pillars themselves, with all the Burthen they bore, when he made Choice of a strong Man to found the Proportions of the *Dorick Column* upon; and indeed, if we consider that noble Figure as the Principal of GOD's Creation, we can't doubt of the excellent Proportions by which it is framed. *Alberti* tells us, the Antients found the Breadth of a Man to be the 1–6th, and the Thickness, from the Navel to the Reins, to be the 1–10th of his Height;[16] of which Proportion *Nebuchadnezzar* made his golden Image, which he set up in the plain of *Dura*, by *Babylon*; but the *Hercules* of *Farnese* is about 1–8th of his Height in Thickness; which is also the Proportion of his medium Breadth, when viewed in Front, and measured at both Ancles, both Knees, at the Waist, and at the Head: However, disregarding this Example of executive Strength, this certain Proportion there is in the whole Man, when we compare his solid Content either to a square, or to a round Pillar, of equal Altitude with himself; for the first will produce for the Length of its Side the 1–9th, and the second will also produce for its Diameter the 1–8th of the Length of such Pillars, as we have often experimentally proved, by filling a Vessel with Water, immersing a strong and well-grown Man therein, then by measuring the Water forced away, and reducing it to a square and round Pillar, of equal Altitude with the Man, as above.

Notwithstanding what *Vitruvius* hath written of this *Order*, it is nevertheless true, that before and after the Time in which he lived, the Antients had this determinate Rule for the *Columns*, to wit, their Shafts were seven Diameters in Length, to which they added Base and Capital, each half a Diameter high; thus the whole *Column* was eight Diameters of its Body in Altitude, and six Times the Length of its Base, grounding these Proportions on the Figure of a Man, as above; the Length of whose Foot was 1–6th of his Height, and the Diameter of his solid Content the 1–8th of the same Height.

Chapter XII. The Summary, and Conclusion.

[...] [p. 231] The Debate is between sacred and profane History; and they are both unanimous in this, that Mankind had no such Thing as Houses to dwell in for some Generations after the Creation; But *Shame* for the Forfeiture of PARADISE, and *Fear* for the horrid Act of *Murder*, having suggested to Man a Place for the *Shelter*, as well as *Security* of his Person, he very ingeniously imitated the Birds, and so began to build Huts to dwell in; After which, Mankind, by dwelling together, began to invent many Arts, and such Things as were further useful and beneficial to them.

However, these Arts were only a Prelude to that Mark of GOD's Displeasure, which he executed in Destroying the World; and those Men, whose utmost Skill in Building amounted to no more than erecting Tents, were enabled by those Arts, to perform a Timber Structure, surpassing the Art of all succeeding Generations; for that Structure was not only built, but it performed the Office it was intended for; and, for near four Months Time, surmounted both Earth and Sea. [...]

[p. 235] To the Supreme Power and collected Riches of the Earth, *Architecture* became a sure Accessory; for every Monarch employ'd his Captives, consisting chiefly of the best Artificers of every vanquish'd Country, upon some stupendious Buildings, as the principal Object of his Ambition, to perpetuate his Name, the Power of his People, and the Wealth of his Kingdom. But this Monument of Pride, instead of answering its desir'd End, became the Destruction of him for whom it was erected; for the Riches exhibited in it, animated the People of other Nations to endeavour for them, who soon obtained their Prey; because *those inured to Fatigues and Poverty* could not fail of being too powerful for *those that wantoned in Ease and Wealth*. And thus, in a continual Succession, *Architecture* has been the chief Cause of the Glory and Envy, as well as the Ruin of Kings and Kingdoms, Emperors and Empires, each Potentate endeavouring to outdo in Works that wou'd render him most remarkable to Posterity.

OUR CONCLUSION THEREFORE IS:

That the *Pagans*, finding how the Parts of the *Jewish* Structure coincided with the Matters contained in the History of the *Israelites*, they soon copied those very Parts, and applied them to their own Idols in the *Temples* they erected to them; which, on this Account, they held so sacred, *that a Profanation of them was punish'd with present Death*: That those *Pagans*, not satisfied with this Application, in Process of Time, ASSUMED THESE THINGS TO THEIR OWN INVENTION, and then Traduced the *Jews* with being Blasphemers and Deriders of the DIVINITY; those People, by neglecting the Real Part of the Law, having also forgot the *Symbolical*, nor could they tell to what divine Matters the various Parts of their Sacred Edifices referr'd!

5

Following the Example of Antiquity

Introduction

Although the classical vocabulary was used in British architecture from the sixteenth century onwards, the term 'classicism' was not used in architectural theory until the end of the nineteenth century.[1] Instead, architects and theorists spoke of building after the Antique, in the manner of the Ancients, architecture *all'antica* or even 'regular architecture'. 'Classicism' is now used to refer to a major current in Western architectural history, characterized by the use of modular proportion a formal vocabulary based on the five Orders, derived from the architecture of ancient Greece and Rome, and by the development of a body of theoretical literature based on Vitruvius' *Ten Books on Architecture*, the only surviving architectural treatise from Antiquity. For British architects and theorists of the period 1540–1750, however, matters were not so clear. Architecture *all'antica* was not an indigenous style. As the poet Samuel Daniel wrote in his *Defence of Rhyme* (1603):

> All our understandings are not to be built by the square of Greece and Italy. [...] Let us go no further but look upon the wonderful architecture of this state of England and see whether they were deformed times that could give it such a form.[2]

Classical architecture had been used by the Romans during their occupation of England, and it had been introduced in England and Scotland in the sixteenth century, but the indigenous style was the Gothic, and this continued to be used in collegiate and church architecture after the end of the Middle Ages. Britain followed the general European cultural trend of the Renaissance, but architects and patrons who wanted to build in the classical way had to turn to sources abroad, both built and written, to learn how to do so. John Shute and Inigo Jones were among the first English architects to travel to the Continent to see the remains of Antiquity and Renaissance architecture with their own eyes. But this was not enough for understanding classical architecture and being able to design according to its rules. An arduous learning process of analysis and assimilation was needed. The intense annotation in Jones's copies of the treatises of Alberti, Palladio and Scamozzi shows how he struggled to grasp the principles of classical architecture.

The origins of classical architecture in the pagan culture of Greece and Rome, and its use in the Catholic culture of contemporary Italy, also made the acceptance of classical architecture in Britain problematic, particularly in the early seventeenth century. Classical architecture was made acceptable by cleansing it of its Catholic and pagan associations and stressing the moral authority of its decorous use. Thus Inigo Jones did not select the Corinthian order for Saint Paul's Covent Garden, because that order had very much come to be regarded as the order of Papal church architecture. Instead he used the sober and masculine Doric order, which according to Vitruvius should be used in temples devoted to male deities. An appreciation of Renaissance art and architecture came to be recognized as an attribute of the gentleman.[3] By the beginning of the eighteenth century Colen Campbell presented *Vitruvius Britannicus* as the British answer to classical architecture on the Continent, celebrating the good taste of the British nation against of the Baroque excesses of architects such as Bernini and Fontana.

Books and prints were the main vehicles for the introduction of classical architecture. Relatively few architects travelled abroad before the 1750s. The major treatises – those by Vitruvius, Alberti, Serlio and Palladio – did not receive complete translations until the early decades of the eighteenth century. Before that time, the large majority of translations consisted of the most practical parts: Serlio's Books I and II or Book VI of Scamozzi on the orders. An important exception to this trend is John James's complete and very faithful translation of Claude Perrault's *Ordonnance des cinque espèces de colonnes* of 1683, which was published in 1708 and numbered Lord Burlington, Henry Aldrich, Lord Bathurst, John Tallman, James Thornhill, Nicholas Hawksmoor and John Vanbrugh among its subscribers. These translations offer very revealing glimpses of the process of assimilation of Vitruvian theory through the selection of what was translated. The versions of Palladio's chapter on errors and abuses in architecture show how this passage gradually became the statement of a rigid aesthetic doctrine. John Evelyn's *Parallel* of 1664 is unique because it does not offer a translation from one of the treatises, but a concordance of what the major authors had written on the orders.

British writing on classical architecture sometimes has a political dimension. Classical architecture was also an important element in the representation of the English and Scottish monarchy, as is shown for instance by the famous engraving of Queen Elizabeth flanked by Corinthian columns of 1596, made by Crispin de Passe, and by the expedition Inigo Jones made to Stonehenge to create a classical tradition for Britain (see Chapter 4). Architecture was also a powerful metaphor for political views. Colen Campbell's Introduction to his *Vitruvius Britannicus* presents a British equivalent to Roman and French classicism as an important part of national identity. It is also distinguished by a tectonic approach to the origins of both the Orders and the architrave, as witnessed by the passage from Roger North's unfinished treatise included here. But above all, the British approach is characterized by a great interest in the visual and emotional effect of a building on its beholder, as is shown by Sir Christopher Wren's analysis of the design of the architrave of the Temple of Peace in Rome (now identified as the Basilica of Maxentius or Constantine), and by the passage from Sir Henry Wotton's *Elements* included above in Chapter 1, on the nature of architecture. In the case of Wotton, this fits in with his rhetorical view of architecture as the visual expression of power.

Further reading: Evelyn, *A Character of England*; Pope, 'Epistle to Richard Boyle.'; Sprague (1937); Summerson (1980); Friedman (1989); Gent (1995); Worsley (1995).

John Shute, from *The First and Chiefe Groundes of Architecture* (1563)

(See the note on Shute and extract in Chapter 2, above.)

John Shute Painter and Architecte unto the Loving and Freindly Readers
[...] Notwithstanding I know well there hath bene a multitude and at this time be very many lerned men who hath (throughe travaile received) the ful perfection of the prudent ladye Scientia, of whom so depely learned I crave pardon for my rude rashnes that I having but tasted a certaine swetenes of her excellencie and liberalitie, wherefore naturall love hath drawne me to advaunce her reputation and honour, according to my poore abilitie and good wil, the thinge nothing garnished as it ought to be, but most briefly and playnelye with suche demonstrations that it might edifie them which of a long time have desired and reached at it to attaine Also for the encoraging of those which ernestly studied and favored it. [...] I thought it best neither with the lightest or least profitable parte to beginne, nor altogether after the moste slender sorte to handell that which I purposed to intreate upon. I have therefore taken my first enteraunce into the writing of this arte, at the five antique pillers or Columnes, comonly named of the places and persones partely where and of whom they were invented, and partely of their virtues and properties of those that they wer likned unto, which pillers names are these as followeth. Tuscana, Dorica, Ionica, Corinthia & Composita. The treatise of these pillers, as it hath in its most delectation and pleasure in the beawtie and comlines of the workmanship appertayning unto them. So though at the beginning, it be mingled with a littell asperitie and as it were bitternes (for the dificultie and hardnes wherwith as both principalles and also other thinges of any excollencye at the first are coustomed to be, it is somewhat Comberous) yet it is both so necessary and profitable, that neither without it any man may attaine to any estimable part of the reste of this science, and with it as by a klew of thred or plaine path way a man may

most eassely pearse and lightely pass over the most darke & unknowen corners of the whole processe therof. [...] Now for examples which are necessarily required to the opening of such darke matters, I have every where through the whole procese of this present treatise after the preceptes to the lightning of them sette both demonstration and figure, and as for practice and experience of those thinges which I teache, I assure the moste gentle reader and all other that shalbe readers so this my little worke that I have put no title in any part thereof concerning the proportion & simetry to use the accustomed terme of the arte of the fornamed columbes which I have not as well seene and measured in Italie, from whence they cam first unto us amongest the Antique woorkes as read and studied in England in the Antique writers, that I might with so muche more perfection write of them as both the reading of the thinge and seinge it in dede is more then onely bare reding of it.

The chiefe Groundes. Here followveth the maner and forme of the secound pillor called Dorica, being ascribed to Hercules and Mars, for his strength, according to the rule aforesayde. [See Figure 5.1.]

This pillor called Dorica, shalbe. 7 Diameters in height, with the Base, and Capitall Now if ye will set Stylobata, or Pedestal, vnder your pillor, thus ye shal begin. First you shall make a foure square, which shalbe your ground, the which is in my figure marked with A and then draw a lyne ouerthwart from the one corner to the other, which line is called Dyagonalis, and is marked with B. and that lyne being directly vpright set, one ende shalbe the height of the square or body of the Pedestall marked with C. measure and deuide that height into the. 5. partes whiche is marked with D. and admitte also as muche, as one of the. 5. partes which is marked with E so that the Pedestale is. 7 suche partes in height like vnto the pillor, which is 7. Dyameters, in height. The height of the Basis of the Pedestale which is marked with D. shalbe deuide into 5. partes. Three of those partes geue vnto Torus, marked with G. the other. 2. partes shalbe deuided into. 3. partes, geue. 2. partes vnto Astragalus, marked with H. the third parte is lefte for the edge which Vitruuius calleth Regula, the Proiecture, of eche side of the Base, of the Pedestall as Vitruuius saieth shalbe halfe a Modulus, but the antiques haue made their Proiectures like vnto their heightes. Then deuide the height of the Coronix marked with E into. 3. partes geue one vnto Astragalus, with his Regula, marked with I. the other. 2. partes deuide into. 3. partes admiting. 2. of those partes to Cymatium, marked with K. and the thirde parte thereof is lefte for Regula, whose marke is L. the Proiectures of the same is like vnto their heightes. Thus endeth the Pedestale or Stylobata.

5.1 John Shute, *The First and Chiefe Groundes of Architecture used in all the auncient and famous monymentes* (London, 1563), illustration of the Doric order, drawn and engraved by Shute (fol. iii verso)

From Sebastiano Serlio, *The first Booke of Architecture* (1611), dedication and 'To the Lovers of Architecture' by Robert Peake

Sebastiano Serlio (1475–?1553–55) was an Italian architect, theorist and painter. Initially trained as a painter, he was the author of one of the most influential architectural treatises of the Renaissance. Its chapters or Books were published separately: Books I and II (on geometry and perspective) were published in Paris in 1545, after Book IV (*Regole generale*, 1537, the first Renaissance codification of the Orders) and Book III (*Delle antichità*, on the ancient buildings of Rome, published in 1540). This edition of Book I was published in English in London in 1611, from the Dutch edition by Pieter Coecke van Aelst (published in Antwerp in 1549), at the charge of Robert Peake (*c.* 1551–1619), who had been Serjeant-Painter to the King since 1607 (together with John de Critz). It is unclear who made the English translation. The publication, with its dedication to Henry, Prince of Wales, was probably connected to the extensive programme of rebuilding and improvement of the Prince's palace and gardens at Richmond. From the 1570s Serlio's treatise was widely circulated in various foreign editions; at the time there was a great need for a practical, well-illustrated manual in English offering instruction in geometry and particularly perspective (Harris, 1990).

Further reading: Harris, Orgel and Strong (1973); Gent (1995a), pp. 383–4; Serlio (1996).

To the High and Mightie Prince, Henry, Prince of Wales.
Sir,
No vaine ambition of mine owne Desire, much lesse presumption of my none Desert, incited me to present this Volume to your Princely view; but rather, the gracious Countenance, which (euen from your Childehood) you haue euer daigned to all good endeauours, invited Mee also (after so many others) to offer at the high-Altar of your Highnesse fauour, this New-Naturalized Worke of a learned Stranger: Not with pretence of Profit to your Highnesse (who want not more exquisite Tutors in all excellent Sciences), but, vnder the Patronage of your powerfull Name, to benefite the Publicke; and conuay vnto my Countrymen (especially Architects and Artificers of all sorts) these Necessary, Certaine, and most ready Helps of *Geometrie*: The ignorance and want whereof, in times past (in most parts of this Kingdome) hath left vs many lame Workes, with shame of many Workemen; which, for the future, the Knowledge and vse of these Instructions shall happily preuent, if the euent but answere (in any measure) to that Hope of mine, which alone both induced this Desire and produced this Designe: Wherein I must confesse my part but small, sauing my great aduenture in the Charge, and my great Good-will to doe Good. All which, together with my best Services, I humbly prostrate at your Princely feete, as beseemes

Your Highnesse
most humble Servant
Robert Peake

To the Lovers of Architecture.
Our learned Author *Sebastian Serly*, having great foresight to shew and explaine the common rules of Architecture, did first publish his Fourth Booke, entreating of Architecture, and after his Third Booke, declaring excellent Antiquities. Fearing that if hee had begunne with *Geometrie* and Perspective, common workmen would have thought (that the two former although small) had not beene so needefull to studie and practice as the other: Which friendly Reader, considered, hindered mee long either from Translating or Publishing the two former, being perswaded by sundry friends and workemen, to have desisted my purpose, both from translating or publishing. The which I had surely effected, if I had beene over-ruled by their requests and perswasions; alleadging strong reasons, that the common Workemen of our time little regarded or esteemed to Worke with right Simmetrie: the which is confused and erronious, in the iudgement of the Learned Architect, if they will follow the Order of Antiquities hereafter ensuing. Wherefore least my good meaning, together with my Labour in Translating and Publishing, should not be regarded and esteemed (as worthie) considering it not onely tendeth to the great profit of the Architect or Workeman, but also generally to all other Artificers of our Nation: I aduise all generally, not to deceive themselves, nor to be selfe-conceited in their owne workes, but well understand this my labour (tending to common good) and be perswaded that who shall follow these rules hereafter set downe, shall not onely have his Worke well esteemed of the common people, but also generally commended and applauded of all workemen, and men of iudgment. *Vale.*

Inigo Jones, from his notes written in his copy of Andrea Palladio, *I quattro libri dell'architettura* (1613–18)

(See the notes on Jones and extracts in Chapters 1 and 4, above, and Wren's observations on the Temple of Peace below.)

Further reading: *Inigo Jones on Palladio*, ed. Allsopp; Marini (1980); Newman (1980, 1988); Anderson (1997).

Book I.xv [on the Doric Order]
[p. 26] Line 9. ye architrave is a module in heygh and is deuided into 7 Partes of on is maad ye Tenia or Bend marked I and give yt as much sayle Then deuide all agayne into 6 partes and give on to ye drops [guttae] wch ar 6 and fillet wch is under ye Bende and is ye 3 part of ye Dropes From ye Bend downewards devide the rest into 7 partes, give 3 to ye first faccia and 4 to ye seconde

Line 13. The freese is a module and a halfe in heyght, ye Triglifio is a module in Bredth the capitell the 6 part of ye module, devide ye Triglifio into

6 partes 2 goes to ye too flutes in ye middell on to ye half flutes on ye sides and ye other 3 make ye Spaces betwene ye sayde flutes.

Line 15. the metopa is as Brode as heygh.

Line 16. ye Cornish is heygh a module and a 6 parte and is deuided in to 5 partes and a halfe 2 gose to ye Casement and ovols of ye Casement is less then ye Ovole by his fillett The other 3 and a half is giuen to the Corrona and to the strayte Gollett [cyma recta] and Gollett reuerset [cyma reversa] The Corrona must have of ayle of 6 partes of ye modules ye 4 and underneath ye sayle of the Corrona ouer ye Triglifies six Drops in length and 3 in bredth wth his filletes

Ouer ye mettopa Roses

Ye Drops ar rownd and answer wth ye drops under ye Bende the whch ar in fourme of a Bell. ye Gullett is Thikeer then the Corrona ye eyght Partte and is deuided into 8 Partes too is giuen to ye Orlo [ovolo], and 6 remayne to ye Gollett, yt hath his Sayle 7 Parts and a halfe So that ye Archittrave freese and Cornish is ye fourth part of ye heigh of the Pillor Palladio somwhat varries from Vittuuius allowing ye members and making them a litell bigger:

[p. 27, in upper margin] This Corrona is taken from the Theater of Marcellus, but the members both aboue and beelow are varied. (The freese is wholy taken from the said Theater of Marcellus The Architraue is taken from the tempell in Foro Boario. So Anto: Abacco fo. 16 and Sorlio li. 4 fo. 20 in folio. The wave [ovolo] and corrona is taken from the tempell Foro Boarjio so is the Ouolo and Casement but thear the ouolo is carued. See Abbaco

[In left-hand margin] o underye corrona is carued a casment a fillett a quadrette and 3 drops pendent in breadth and 6 in length but this Pendency is made to the members under the corrona in thear proportion and if ye corrona not to narrow the same discression is yoused in the fassions of architraues not too take away ye breadth of ye bottons of the architraue thus [...].

Book I.ib [On the Ionic Order]

[p. 34, in left-hand margin] To make this Capitell deuide ye foote of ye Pillor into 18 partes and 19 of these partes is ye length and Breadth of ye abacco. And ye halfe of yt is ye heygh of ye Cappitell wth his vollutte so yt is hygh 9 partes and a half

On part and a half is guien to ye abacco wth his Simmato [cymatium].

The other 8 Remayne for ye vollutte:

To make ye vollut, from ye extremitie of ye Cimatio inwards noot on part of ye 19 and lett falle a Perpendicular line Caled Catheto and wheare in that lyne is the Poyntt that separates the 4 partes and a half aboufe from ye 3 partes and a half beneath make ye Center of ye eye of ye vollutte, the diamiter of wch is on

of the 8 partes, and from the sayd point Draw a Crose lyne Rectangled wth ye other Deuiding ye vollutte into 4 partes. The rest is Playne. ye astragolo or Boultell of ye Pillor is eune [even] wth ye eye of the vollutte
The vollutte is so thicke in ye middle as ye sayle of the Ouolo wch is beyound ye abacco as much as the eye of the vollutte.
of the diametre
The Canale of ye vollutte is iust as much as yt of ie Pillor
The Astragola or Boultell of the Pillor goeth round vnderneath ye vollutte and ys still seene fo yt is naturall that a soft thinge shuld giue waye to a hard and ye vollutte doth sticke from yt equally.
[...]

Book II.i [On the decoration of private buildings]
[p. 3, in right-hand margin] Loges and large halles in great me(n)s houses.
for meaner Jentleme(N) lesser houses
Auocates must haue faire places for their clientes to walk in
Marchantes must hauve Places to put their merchandise in
diccorum in makynd the Roomes bigg or lyttell according to ye bignes of the house

Book II.ii [On the division of rooms]
not only the principl partes, but ye menist accommodated for yous of the Best Comparason to a mans boddi
the most butiful partes of mans boddy most exposed to sight so in building in the Partes vnderground Sellors woodhouses kicchens and all such Places of dayly youse of this Commes 2 commodities first the Part aboufe is free secondly by reason of fiers underneath yt is more holsum

Book III
[p. 32, in left-hand margin] Note That ye Greeke architecture is fytter for ous then Romain is for the building wear for youse and not so profuse [...]

Book IV.vi [On the Temple of Peace, see Figures 5.11 and 12]
[p. 13, in upper margin] The Templle of Peace 2
[In right-hand margin] these be round collomes within to beare vp the volt a crochara [cross vault] and the great lightes aboue them in ye wale weare immitated in ye thearmi Dioclesiani see ye dessigne of.
Wils I was in Roome on of thes great Pillors was pulled doune to sett a figure on before St Marie ma. Jan. anno 1614. yt was erecting
[Against lower design, see Figure 5.11] A this corrnish is 1/8 part from the Tarrese [terrace] vnto the topp of itt and the moulding vnder ye cartouses is euene with the great cornish with in marked B.
an inclosed walke, 3 arches open ouer ye Portico and statues ouer the hedes of the Pillors The modales of Vespasian and Titus in Choulego are with a

portico of high collomes as thus within the tempell and I do thinke that it was so for this porti[c]o of Paladio is not like the Romain greatnes but it may bee as Palladio saith that this temple being burnt or ruined by an earthquake was restored in a time when architecture was not so well vnderstoode and then this littell portico may haue binn made of which ye foundationes being discouered by digging Paladio and Gamuzzi [scamozzi] made by coniecture this facciata, for I haue trydeyt and yt may haue had 10 collombs in the front as bigg as thos within and I thinke ye spases will bee near to eustilos, and ye portico in length on third of ye breadth of the temple
[p. 14, in upper margin] The templl of Peace 3
[In left-hand margin] E the scale of feete euary starr is a foote deuided in to 4 partes making 3 yn [inches]: to eueri parte
H The middle of the spase beetwen the cartousses do answer with the middell of ye floure [flower] in the cappitell
Thees Cartouses ar insted of the Corrona [the part of the cornice normally between the cyma reversa and the modallion]
I thinke that ye members myght bee the greater and loose none of ye Aspecte of ye Cornish being farr from ye eye & the two oulos [ovolos] in the cornish without any variation of caruing is odd [...]

Sir Henry Wotton, from *The Elements of Architecture* (1624)

(See the note on Wotton and extract in Chapter 1, above.)

[p. 29] The intermissions [...] are either by *Pillars*, or *Pylasters*.

Pillers [*sic*] which we may likewise call *Columnes* (for the word among Artificers is almost naturallized) I could distinguish into *Simple* & *Compounded*. But (to tread the beaten and plainest way) there are fiue Orders of Pillers, according to their dignity and perfection, thus marshalled:[4]

The *Tuscan*.
The *Dorique*.
The *Ionique*.
The *Corinthian*.

And the *Compound Order* [...] In which fiue *Orders* I will first consider their *Communities*, and then their *Proprieties*. Their Communities (as farre as I obcerue) are principally three. First, they are all Round; for though some concciue *Columna Atticurges* mentioned by Vitruuius, lib 3 cap. 3. to haue beene a squared Pillar yet wee must passe it ouer as irregular, neuer receiued among these *Orders*, no more then certaine other licentious inuentions, of *Wreathed*, and *Vined*, and *Figured Columnes*, which our Author himselfe condemneth, being in his whole Booke a professed enemy to *Fancies*.

Secondly, they are all Diminished, or Contracted insensibly, more or lesse, according to the proportion of their heights, from one third part of the whole *Shaft* vpwards, which *Philander*[5] doth prescribe by his owne precise measuring of the Ancient remainders, as the most gracefull *Diminution*. And here I must take leaue to blame a practice growne (I know not how) in certain places too familiar, or making Pillars swell in the middle, as if they were sick of some *Tympany*, or *Dropsie*, without any Authentique Paterne or Rule, to my knowledge, and vnseemely to the very iudgement of sight. True it is that in Vitruuius, lib. 3.cap.2. wee finde these words, *De adiectione, quae adijcitur in medijs Columnis, quae apus Grecos entasis apellatur, in extremo* libro erit formatio eius; which passage, seemeth to haue giuen some conntenance to this error.[6] But of the promise there made, as of diuerse other elsewhere, our Master has fayled us, either by slip of memory, or iniury of time, and so wee are left in the darke. Alwayes sure I am, that besides the authority of example which it wanteth, It is likewise contrary to the Originall and Naturall *Type*, in *Trees*, which at first was imitated in *Pillars*, as Vitruuius himselte obserueth, *lib.5.cap.1*. For who euer saw any *Cypresse*, or *Pine*, (which are there alledged) small below and above, and tumerous in the middle, vnlesse it were diseased Plant, as Nature (though other wise the comliest Mistresse) hath now and then her deformities and Irregularities.

Thirdly, they haue all their *Vndersettings*, or *Pedistals*, in height a third part of the whole *Columne*, comprehending the *Base* and *Capitall*; and their vpper Adiuncts, as *Architraue*, *Frize*, and *Cornice*, a fourth part of the sayd Pillar [...].

These are their most considerable Communities and agreements.

Their *Proprieties* or *Distinctions* will best appeare by some reasonable description of them all, together with their *Architraves*, *Frizes*, and *Cornices*, as they are vsually handled.

First therefore the *Tuscan* is a plain, massie, rurall Pillar, resembling some sturdy well-limmed Labourer, homely clad, in which kinde of comparisons *Vitruuius* himselfe seemeth to take pleasure, *lib.* 4 *cap.* 1. The length thereof shall be six *Diameters*, of the grossest of the Pillar below. Of all proportions, in truth, the most naturall; For our Author tells vs, *lib.* 3 *cap.* 1. that the foote of a man is the sixt part of his bodie in ordinary measure, and *Man* himselfe, according to the saying of *Protagoras*[7] [...] as it were the *Prototype* of all exact *Symmetrie* [...]: This *Columne* I haue by good warrant called *Rurall*, *Vitru. cap.* 2. *lib.*3. And therefore we need not consider his rank among the rest. The distance or *Intercolumniation* (which word Artificers doe vsually borrow) may bee neere foure of his owne *Diameters*, because the *Materials* commonly layd ouer this Pillar, were rather of wood then Stone; through the lightnesse whereof the *Architraue* could not suffer, though thinnely supported, nor the *Columne* it selfe being so substantiall. The *Contraction* aloft shall be (according to the most receiued practice) one fourth of his thicknesse below. To conclude, (for I intend only as much as shall serue for a due Distinguishment, and not to delineate every pretty member) the *Tuscan* is of all the rudest Pillar, and his Character *Simplicity*.

The *Dorique Order* is the grauest that hath beene receiued into ciuill vse, preserving, in comparison of those that follow, a more *Masculine Aspect*, and little trimmer then the *Tuscan* that went before, saue a sober garnishment now and then of *Lions heads* in the *Cornice*, and of *Triglyphs* and *Metopes* alwayes in the *Frize*. Sometimes likewise, but rarely, chaneled, and a little slight sculpture about the *Hypotrachelion*, or *Necke* under the *Capitall*. The length, seuen *Diameters*. His ranke or degree, is the lowest by all *Congruity*, as being more massie then the other three, and consequently abler to support. The *Intercolumniation*, thrice as much as his thicknesse below. The *Contraction* aloft, one fift of the same measure. To discerne him, will bee a peece rather of good *Heraldry*, then of *Architecture:* For he is best knowne by his place, when he is in company, and by the peculiar ornament of his *Frize* (before mentioned) when he is alone.

The *Ionique Order* doth represent a kinde of Feminine slendernesse, yet saith *Vitruvius*, not like a light Housewife, but in a decent dressing, hath much of the *Matrone*. The length eight *Diameters*. In degree as in substantialnesse, next aboue the *Dorique*, sustayning the third, and adorning the second Story. The *Intercolumniation* two of his owne *Diameters*. The *Contraction* one sixt part. Best knowne by his trimmings, for the bodie of this *Columne* is perpetually chaneled, like a thicke plighted Gowne. The *Capitall* dressed on each side, not much vnlike womens Wires, in a spirall wreathing, which they call the *Ionian Voluta*. The *Cornice* indented. The *Frize* swelling like a pillow; And therefore by *Vitruvius*, not vnelegantly tearmed *Pulvinata*.[8] These are his best *Characters*.

The *Corinthian*, is a *Columne*, laciuiously decked out like a Curtezane, and therein much participating (as all Inuentions doe) of the place where they were first borne: *Corinthe* hauing been without controuersie one of the wantonest Townes in the World.[9] This *Order* is of nine *Diameters*. His degree, one Stage aboue the *Ionique*, and alwaies the highest of the simple *Orders*. The *Intercolumniation* two of his *Diameters*, and a fourth part more, which is of all the comeliest distance. The *Contraction* one seuenth Part. In the *Cornice* both *Dentelli* and *Modiglioni*. The *Frize*, adorned with all kinds of *Figures* and various Compartments at Pleasure. The *Capitall*, cut into the beautifullest leafe, that Nature doth yeeld, which surely next the *Aconitum Pardalianches* (reiected perchance as an ominous Plant) is the *Acanthus or Branca Vrsina* though *Vitruvius* doe impute the choice thereof vnto Chance, and wee must be contented to beleeue him: In short, As *Plainenesse* did charactarize the *Tuscan*, so must *Delicacie* and *Varietie* the *Corinthian* Pillar, besides the height of his Ranke.

The last is the *Compounded Order*: His *name* being a briefe of his *Nature*. For this Pillar is nothing in effect, but a *Medlie*, or an *Amasse* of all the precedent *Ornaments*, making a new kinde, by stealth, and though the most richly tricked, yet the poorest in this, that he is a borrower of all his Beautie. His length, (that he may haue somewhat of his owne) shalbe of ten *Diameters*. His degree should, no doubt, bee the highest before yeelded. But few *Palaces* Auncient or Moderne exceede the third of the Ciuill *Orders*. The *Intercolumniation*, but a *Diameter* and an halfe, or alwayes somewhat lesse than two. The *Contraction* of this Pillar must be one eight Part lesse aboue than belowe. To know him will be easie by the verie mixture of his *Ornaments*, and *Cloathing*. [...]
[p. 43] [...] yet let me before I passe to other matter, preuent a familiar Obiection; It will perchance bee said, that all this Doctrine touching the fiue *Orders*, were fitter for the *Quarries* of *Asia* which yeelded 127 *Columnes* of 60 *Foote* high, to the *Ephesian Temple*,[10] or for *Numidia* where *Marbles* abound; than for the spirits of *England*, who must be contented with more ignoble *Materials*: To which I answere, that this neede not discourage vs: For I haue often at *Venice* viewed with much pleasure, an *Atrium Graecum* (we may translate it an *Anti porch*, after the Greeke Manner) raised by *Andrea Palladio* vpon eight *Columnes* of the *Compounded Order*; the *Bases* of Stone, without *Pedistals*, The *shafts* or Bodies, of meere Brick; three foote and an halfe thicke in the *Diameter* below, and consequently thirty fiue foote high, as himselfe hath described them in his second Booke;[11] Then which, mine Eye, hath neuer yet beheld any *Columnes*, more stately of Stone or Marble; For the Bricks, hauing first beene formed in a *Circular Mould*, and then cut before their burning into foure quarters or more, the sides afterwards ioyne so closely, and the points concenter so exactly, that the *Pillars* appeare one *entire Peece*; which short description, I could not omit, that thereby may appeare, how in truth wee want rather *Art* then stuffe, to satisfie our greatest *Fancies*.

From VIGNOLA: *or, the Compleat Architect* (1655), dedication 'To the Ingenious Artists' by Joseph Moxon

This English edition is based on the Dutch version, published in 1650 by Cornelius Danckerts, of the French abridgement by Le Muet. Le Muet's version had appeared in at least seven editions in French, Dutch and German. Moxon had visited the Netherlands in 1649 and may have acquired Danckerts's version there when it appeared. Moxon's English edition omits the preface by Vignola, but has an alphabetical glossary of difficult terms with references to the illustrations, five plates of capitals from Wendel Dietterlin's *Architecturae*, and alterations to Vignola's designs for arches, Michelangelo's 'Porte' and five of Le Muet's portals. It has a portrait of Moxon as frontispiece [first edition, 1655]. The fourth edition (1694) was published by James Moxon, the son of Joseph (who had died in 1691), and he added a dedication to Sir Christopher Wren. Moxon's VIGNOLA served for almost fifty years,

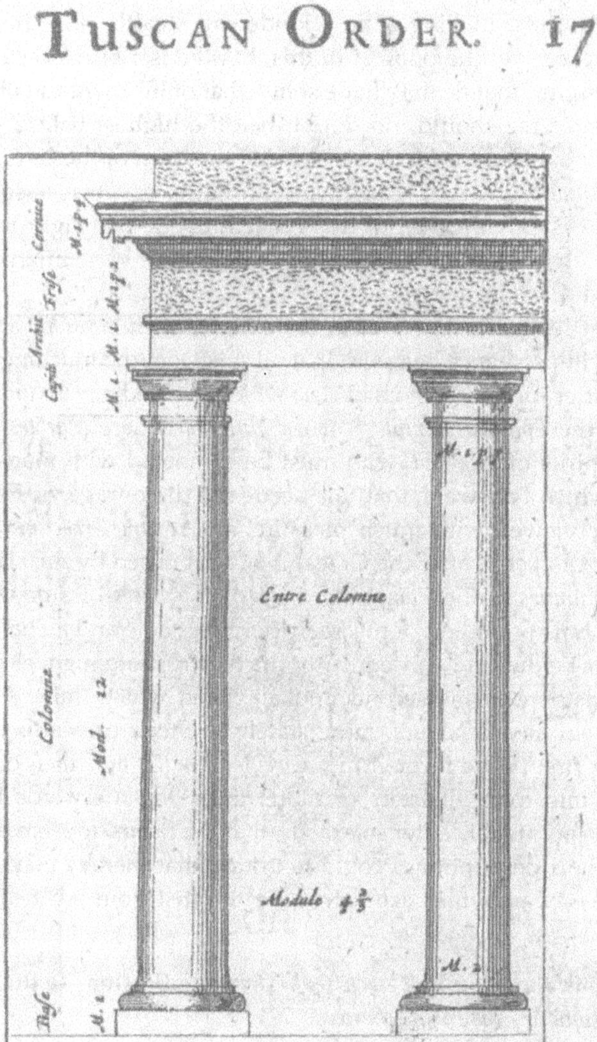

5.2 VIGNOLA: *or, the Compleat Architect*, translated into English by Joseph Moxon (London, 1694; 4th edn), illustration of the Tuscan order (p. 17)

before it became superseded by Palladio's even more simple modular system, as a practical manual for craftsmen and artisans (see Figure 5.2; Harris, 1990). (See also the note on Joseph Moxon and extract in Chapter 2, above.)

[A2] To the Ingenious ARTISTS

I have here presented you with the Works of Mr. *James Barozzio* of *Vignola* in English, who for his great Skill and Knowledge in the *Art* of *Architecture*, is much respected, and highly applauded among all Artificers throughout *Christendom*, there being few Nations of any note, that have not his Works translated into their own Language: Only we here in *England* (I know not whether it be through carelessness of *Artists*, or else Covetousness) mind not those things which make other Countries (that have nothing else to boast of) so famous among their Neightbours: Certain I am, that *England* breeds as good Wits as other Lands do, and would they but shew themselves more forward in commendable Studies, would doubtless share with them in their Praises.

Our Author first Collected those things together for his own private use: And by the Solicitations of many Persons of Worth and Honour, did at last (though unwillingly) consent to make the World for a small price, partakers of that which cost him so much labour, study, and travel.

And whereas former Authors left their Works uncertain, or at least doubtful to all but their own Nations, in respect of the several measures they used; as some the Fathom, some the Foot, some the Span, some the Inch of their own particular Country, which seldom agrees with the Fathom, Foot, or Inch of any other Land; our Author to avoid that great Inconvenience, and certain uncertainty hath reduced all his measure, to a convenient and universal measure, which is called by the name of a Model [i.e. module]: The Invention whereof hath made the whole Art of Architecture very easie to all Students therein: For it is nothing else but the half Diameter of the Collumn at the lower end thereof: as if the whole Diameter should be *10, 12, 14*, or *16* inches, then will the half Diameter be *5, 6, 7*, or *8* inches, and that is called the Model: which Model he divided into *12* equal parts, when he Frames the Tuscan and Dorick Order: and into 18 for the Ionick, Corinthian and Composite.

In the Translation of this Book, I have followed (so near as I could) the words of our Author, unless here and there I have been a little more large, thereby endeavouring the better to express his meaning, and instruct the Young Practitioner. I confess the Book was formerly translated by another hand, but it was so generally disliked (indeed not without cause) that I chose rather to take the pains to translate it a-new, than run the hazzard of discouraging Young Artists with those dark and unproper directions. […]

I know some that are already sufficient Artists, may think the sleighter of this Book, meerly because I have made it plain to common Capacities: But if such will but look back upon their own younger endeavours, they may perhaps remember the time when themselves would have been glad of any help that might have furthered them in their then-thought tedious and difficult Studues. Besides they may already know, that it is easier for themselves to know the meaning of plain and easie expressions, than for young Students to understand the directions of hard and difficult Instructions.

Joseph Moxon.

Sir Balthazar Gerbier, from *A Brief Discourse Concerning the Three Chief Principles of Magnificent Building* (1662)

Gerbier claimed that Charles I had promised him the reversion of Inigo Jones's post as Surveyor-General of the King's Works some time in 1638–41, when he was serving the King as diplomatic and artistic agent in Brussels. During the Civil War he had dedicated his treatise on military architecture to Lord Fairfax, the Commander of Parliament's Army (see the first note on Gerbier above, Chapter 2). When he returned to London in 1660 to claim the reversion, he was suspended from office. Excluded from the Court after the Restoration, Gerbier advertised his talents as an architect by publishing in 1662 this *Brief Discourse*, and in 1663 a *Counsel and Advise to All Builders*. He died in 1663 leaving unfinished a large house at Hampstead Marshall in Berkshire for Lord Craven, in whose regiment Gerbier's son was serving (Colvin, 1995).

To the Kings most Excellent Majesty.
May it please your Sacred Majesty:
[…] And in regard the Place of Surveyor Generall was also intended to me (after late *Inigo Jones*) I doe make bold to introduce the three Capitall Principles of good Building to your Sacred Majesty, who hath seen more stately Palaces and Buildings, than all your Ancestors, and may be a Pattern to all future Posterity, by Building of your own Palace worthy your Self, and placeing it as the *Italians* for their health, delight, and convenience (as well as Solidity and Ornament,) *La Matina alli Monti, la Sera alli Fonti,*[12] according to which the main body of your Royal Palace may be set on the side of Saint *James*'s Park, and the Gardens along the River. […]

A Brief Discourse Concerning the Three Chief Principles of Magnificent Building, viz. Solidity, Conveniency, and Ornament
Whereas Building is much minded in these times, I thought fit to publish some Principles thereon, which may stand the lovers of it instead. Yet without spending time and Paper to Note how a Point, Line, Angle, Demi-circle, Cube, Plint, Baze, Pedestal, Colombe, Head, Architrave, Frize, Cornice, or Frontispice must be made, and what Dimensions all those several Parts (a Point excepted) must have, since all Master-Workmen ought to remember (as Schollars their Grammar, and Arithmaticians their Table) how every Particle must have its just Proportion; and that the height of Windowes and

Doores must be double their breadth; and also to be carefull to maintain the due esteem of their Art, since its Dimensions and Rules came directly from Heaven, when the great Architect and Surveyor of Heaven and Earth, prescribed the Rules and particular Orders for the Building of a floating-Pallace, (*Noahs* Ark) and the glorious matchlesse Temple of *Solomon*, the perfect House of Prayer.

And therefore such Precedents may serve to convince those who say, That a wise-man never ought to put his finger into Morter, since there is a necessity for Building, especially among Nations who do not, or cannot live in Caves and hollow Trees, or as the Wilde *Indians*, who have no other Roofs, but of Palmito-Leaves, nor Wainscot, but Bambouses, as they call the Poles to which they tye a Woollen Hammac to lye in.

There are three Capital Points to be observed by men, who intend to build well:
VIZ,

Solidity
Conveniency
Ornament

Those who have Marshald the Orders of Colombs (to make good the first Point) have ranged the Toscan to be the Supporter of a Building, but such an Atlas must stand on a firm Ground, not as ill Builders place Colombs (either of Brick or Stone) like things Patcht or glewed against a Wall, and for the most part against the second Story of a Building, (contrary to the very *Gothish* Custome, who at least did begin their Buttrises from the Ground) as if their intent were, that the weight of the Colombs should draw down the Wall, on the heads of those that passe by.

Such Builders confound the first and essential point of Building, (to wit, *Solidity*, with *Ornament* and *Conveniency*).

They will make a shew of some thing, but misse thereby (as ill Bow-men) the Mark: They may perchance have heard of rare Buildings, nay seen the Books of the *Italian* Architects, have the Traditions of *Vignola* in their Pockets, and have heard lectures on the Art of Architecture, which have laid before them the most necessary Rules, as also the Origine of the several Orders of Colombs, and Discourses made thereon [...].

The *Barbarians* and naked *Tapoyers, Caripowis, Alibis* and several *Charibdiens*[13] do place pendants in their Nostrils, which are proper for the Eares; and these hinder not the use of the Lips, which ought to be observed by all Builders.

And as for the inside of Fabricks, Builders should in the first place set the Doores, Chimnies, and Windows, as may be most convenient for use.

Builders ought to be not onely experimented in House-keeping, but also good Naturalists, to know (before they spend Time and Materials) the required Property to every part of a building. A Doore to be so set as it may not convey the Wind toward the Chimney or Bedstead, though opened never so little.

The Windows to be so placed, as that the Fire made in the Chimney, may not attract the Aire and Moysture, and so prove the unwholesomest part of the Room for those that are near the Fire [...].

And though it be not my design in this small Discourse to Treate of Dimensions (which are fit for a Primar to Apprentices,) Yet I cannot desist (by reason of the West-*Indian* Herican-like-windes) which happened *February* last, to perswade all Builders to forbear the Building any more those exorbitant Chimney-Shafts, which when they fall, break both Roofs and Sealing of Roomes, and kill good People in their Beds: since a Chimney some two Foote higher than the Ridges of the Roof of a Building, (which is not overtopt by a Church or Steeple, or some other eminency,) is as good a conveyance for the smoak, as any of a greater height. Neither are those high Shafts of Chimnies real Ornaments to a Building, much lesse to a Palace of a Soveraign: nor do the *Germane* Travellers of this Age any more fill (as formerly) their Table-Books with the number of them. [...] And as the best Ornaments of a Face appears [*sic*] at the first sight by the Eyes, Mouth, and Nose; so doth the best qualities of a perfect Building, by Windowes, and Doores well placed, as also by a large, magnificent, commodious, and well-set Staircase.

Noble, magnificent, and commodious Staircases, must in the first place participate of a Noblemans manner of Pace and Attendance. [...]

And [...] as *Solidity* must be the first Principle in all good Building; so much more ought it to be observed in that of Sovereigns, unto whom the whole world hath access.

And as there must be specious Ground before their Palaces, their Inner-Court ample, the Offices for their Retinue large and commodious, and so placed as they may neither be an annoyance nor of ill-aspect. [...]

And as there is a necessary Magnificence to be exprest on the Front and inside of Princely Buildings, answerable to their greatness; so is it absolutely necessary, that the Architect be possest with a Soul as great as the Player in the French Play, called the *Visionaries*,[14] where he perswades himself to be *Alexander*, and governs his Motions accordingly. And the Lines and Strokes of the Architect must be *Alexander*-like: his Figures and Statues *Colosses*, his *Pyramidis* like those of *Aegypt* [...].

Since the greatness of a Nation consists not in a Husk, but in itself, and in its Sovereign, nothing should be suffered to diminish the appearance of that greatness within or without Doores. A Sovereign and his Retinue, in a too vast Roome in height, width and length, doth appear like a company in a Valley near high Mountains. Whenas a body standing on the brow of a Hill, and seen from below, seems to be a kind of *Colosse*, which argueth that there must be a great discretion used in the making them fit and pleasing. [...]

May therefore the oldest and most tottering House in the Land, breath forth of its Windows what may answer that true love, and in point of good Building, wherewith this Discourse is begun, (next to this giving such a new Form to the Streets of *London* and the Suburbs, as may in a manner equalize those in *Holland* in neatnesse if the Inhabitants will but take the right and onely course therein). May his Sacred Majesty during his long prayed for and wished Raign, see St. *Paul's* Church in that magnificency, as the Metropolitan of the Houses of God, in the chief City of *Albion*[15] justly requires. [...].

From Andrea Palladio, *The first Book of Architecture* (1663) (based on the French translation and abridgement by Pierre Le Muet), Preface and Book I, Chapter XX from the translation by Geoffrey Richards

This was the earliest English edition of any part of Palladio's *Quattro libri*. Like Moxon's edition of Vignola (see above), it was based on the vulgarized abridgement by Pierre le Muet, but it is a much freer adaptation to English requirements than the Moxon *VIGNOLA*. It was 'intended for an assistance to our Ingenious Workmen, and Improvement of English *Architecture* [...]'. The book is dedicated to Daniel Colwal, one of the original Fellows of the Royal Society; this circumstance, together with Evelyn's 'commendation and encouragement', the frequent mention of Geoffrey Richards in the diary of Robert Hooke and the references here to the Louvre and the early 'model' for Saint Paul's all suggest that Richards was a member of the circle of the learned Fellows of the Royal Society (see Figures 5.3–5; Harris, 1990).

The versions of Palladio's Book I, Chapter XX ('Dico adunque, che essendo l'Architettura (come ancho sono tutte le altre arti) imitatrice della Natura; niuna cosa patisce, che aliena e lontana sia da quella, che esse Natura comporta') included here show how the translations of these aesthetic principles could vary: whereas Richards speaks of 'that which is natural' (p. 197), Nicholas Du Bois has 'that order which Nature has prescrib'd to all things' (p. 202), and Edward Hoppus refers to 'that Order and Harmony which Nature observes in all her Works' (p. 203). From being considered as an imitation of what is there for everyone to see, architecture becomes an embodiment of the hidden laws of the universe.

The Preface to the Reader.

The Subject of this Translation, being *Architecture*, doth, in the opinion of Sr *Henry Wotton*, need no Commendation, where there are Noble Men or Noble Minds; Therefore I shall only give you an accompt of the Authors, and my own concernment herein; He was *Andrea Palladio*, a famous Architect of *Italy*, where taking notice of the Irregularities and Deformities in Building, introduced by invasions of the *Gothes*, and other *Barbarians*, to prevent those inconveniences for the future, he thought fit to instruct the world in the Rules and Practices of the Learned Ancients; having opportunity to observe the foot-steps of their labours even at *Rome* itself, where being the greatest Concourse of Noble men and Noble Minds, they spared neither

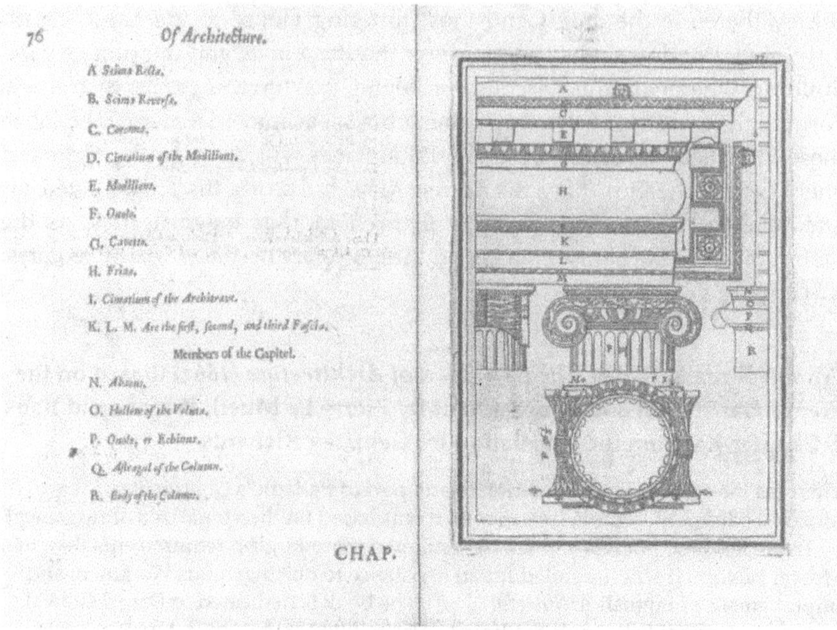

5.3 *The first Book of Architecture, by Andrea Palladio. Translated out of Italian … by P[R] le Muet Translated out of French. By G. R. [Geoffrey Richards]* (London, 1663), illustration of the Ionic order (p. 77)

Care nor Cost in Building; And in Imitation of them, our Author is exact in his directions touching every material, as in the choice of *Stone, Timber, Lime, Brick,* &c what good, and what not, how to be prepared and put in use; 'tis observed how careful they were in the making of their *Brick* and *Lime;* not forbearing the hardest *Stone;* for, as *S[r] Henry Wotton* observeth, that the *Italians* to this day, and much more the Ancients, did burn their firmest *Stone,* and even *Marble* it self, where it was plentiful, which in time became *Marble* again, or at least of Indissoluble Durity, as appeareth in the Standing Theatres. And other learned Men have required that all the Timber be cut out of the same Forest, all the *Stone* out of the same Quarry, and the *Lime* to be made of the same *Stone* of which the Building is intended, imagining that they will sympathize and joyn better by a kind of Original Kindred. But instead of this Curiosity, we too often make *Lime* without any great Choice, and of Refuse-Stuff, which is an English Errour, of no small moment in our Buildings. After these Particulars, our Author proceeds to treat of the Five Orders of *Columnes,* whose Members and Proportions, as he hath laid them down, are by the Judicious esteemed the most excellent in their kind; and for some of their termes, which I have changed, it was

72 *Of Architecture.*

A. *Abacus,*

B. *Hollowes of the Voluta.*

C. *Ouolo, or Echinus,*

D. *Astragal under the Echinus,*

E. *Ceincture, or Annulet.*

F. *Body of the Column,*

G. *Line called Cathetus,*

On the Plat-form of the Capitel of the Column, the said Members are marked with the same Letters.

S. *The eye of the Voluta in a large form.*

Members of the Base, according to Vitruvius.

K. *Body of the Column*

L. *Ceincture, or Annulet.*

M. *Torus.*

N. *Scotia prima.*

O. *Tondino, or Astragal.*

P. *Scotia secunda.*

Q. *Orlo, or Plinth,*

R. *Projecture.*

The

5.4 *The first Book of Architecture, by Andrea Palladio. Translated out of Italian ... by P*[R] *le Muet Translated out of French. By G. R. [Geoffrey Richards]* (London, 1663), illustration of Ionic column (p. 72)

not without the Advice of Skilful Artists, thereby to conform to our Workmen. [...]

The Scarcity of Books of *Architecture* in *English*, and the zeal which I find our Ingenious Artists have to entertaine any thing of that Subject, incouraged me to this *Essay*; wherein, I hope, I have rendred the Authors sence, without disadvantage; and for the Designes, they will speak for themselves.

G. R.

Book I. Chap. XX. Of errours.

[p. 122] Having set down the Ornaments of Architecture, that is to say, the Five Orders, and shewed how they are made and laid down, the Profiles of each of their parts, which I found that the Ancients did observe; It seemes to me not unfit here to acquaint the Reader of many abuses, which being brought in by the Barbarous are yet observed, to the end that the studious in this art may avoid them in their own Workes, and understand them in others.

I say then, that Architecture (as all other arts) being Imitatrix of Nature, accounts nothing tollerable which is estranged, and differs from that which is natural; Wherefore we see that those Ancient Architects who built with

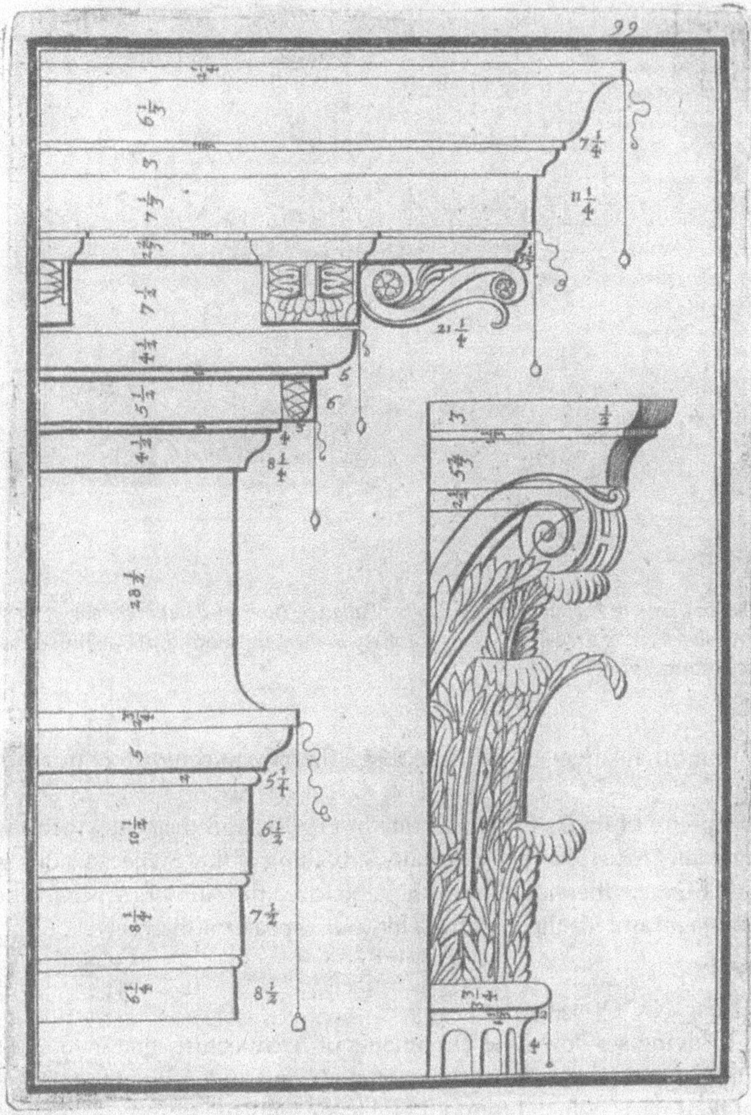

5.5 *The first Book of Architecture, by Andrea Palladio. Translated out of Italian ... by P*[R] *le Muet Translated out of French. By G. R. [Geoffrey Richards]* (London, 1663), illustration of the Corinthian order (p. 99)

Timber, when they began to build with stone, directed that the Columnes might be lesse at the top than at the foot, taking example from Trees, which are all lesse at the top, than in the trunk and near the root. Likewise because it is very convenient that those things upon which any great weight is put should be pressed, under the Column they put a *Base*, which with their *Torus* and *Scotia*, seem by the burthen over the top be swelled; so also in the *Cornice*, they bring in the *Triglifes, Modiglions*, and the *Dentills*, which should represent the heads of the Joices, which in the sealing are placed to bear up the Roof. The same may be observed in all other parts, if you are curious: And being so you cannot but blame that form of building which deviates from that which Nature instructeth, and from that simplicity which is directed in things by her produced, framing (as it were) another nature, and departs from the true good and handsome manner of building; For which reason you ought not (instead of Columnes or *Pillasters*, which are to bear up some great weight) to place *Cartouches*, which are certain Scroles, which to the intelligent seem deformed, and to the ignorant rather confusion than pleasure, nor do they produce other effects, than increase the charge of the Builders. Likewise you must not make any of those *Cartouches* come out of the *Cornice*; for it is requisite that all the parts of the *Cornice* be made to some end, and to make appear what it would be if the work were framed of Timber. And besides, being it is convenient that to uphold a great weight something solid and fit to support that weight to be required, questionlesse those *Cartouches* are altogether superfluous, because it is impossibe that any Timber what ever could really perform what these seem; for feigning it self to be soft and gentle, I know not by what rule they put them under any thing heavy and hard. [...] And although Variety and Novelty should please all, yet we are not to go against the precepts of Art, and that which Reason demonstrates; Whence we see that although the Ancients did vary, they never departed from the general and necessary Rules of Art, as may be seen in my Books of Antiquities.

From *The Architecture of Palladio; in Four Books* (1715) (a translation by Nicholas Du Bois, published by Giacomo Leoni after the French version of Roland Fréart de Chambray), 'Preface' by Nicholas Du Bois and extract from Book I, Chapter XX

Giacomo Leoni's interest in Palladio probably began when he worked on Schloss Bensberg at Düsseldorf, which had been designed by his fellow Venetian, Count Matteo d'Alberti. The latter had closely studied Palladio and travelled to England in 1682–83 to study the work of Inigo Jones and Wren. The *Four Books* were advertised by Leoni in 1715, describing himself as 'author and undertaker'. Subscribers had to commit themselves to all four volumes, which may explain why initial sales were low. Among early subscribers were Thomas Archer, Hawksmoor, Vanbrugh and the mother of Lord Burlington. Leoni's edition was the only complete English version until Benjamin Cole's appeared in 1734. The translation is not based on Palladio's original Italian, but on the French edition by Roland Fréart de Chambray, published in 1650. The copperplates were Leoni's, and replaced the original sixteenth-century woodcuts; but they are not always reliable because they are reworkings of the original wood-blocks, not based on the actual buildings (Harris, 1990).

[p. 1] *The Translator's Preface*
One of the most judicious Remarks that have been made upon the Variety of Opinions, which prevail among those Authors, who have written concerning *Architecture*, and given us the proportions of its Orders, is in my judgment, that of *Mons. Le Clerc* in a new Treatise lately publish'd by him on that Subject.[16] *If the orders of Columns* (says he), *had real and undisputable beauties, the* Architects, *both Ancient and Modern, would have agreed among themselves about their rules and proportions: but those beauties, being only arbitrary, as not being grounded upon demonstrations, the Authors, who have treated of them, have given us different rules, according to their Taste and Genius.* And indeed, so great is this Variety, that it may be perceiv'd, even in those stately remains of ancient Buildings, which are recommended to us, to this very day, by the greatest Masters, as so many Models. However, if it be true, as *Mons. Le Clerc* adds, that *among those several beauties, s[o]me are certainly more pleasi[n]g and more universally approv'd*; till somebody is so happy, asto be able to demonstrate that such, or such a rule, or proportion, ought to be preferr'd to another, no reasonable Man will scruple to follow those great and noble Ideas, those magnificent Ordinances, those learned and judicious Observations, those just and exact proportions which the most famous *Architects* have left us, and which have gain'd a general applause. Among those great Masters of Civil *Architecture, Palladio*, whose Work I have undertaken to translate, is doubtless the most eminent. If therefore the Book of that Learned Man has been admir'd all over *Europe*, tho his *Designs* have only been coursly engrav'd in *Wooden Cuts*; will any one deny that the generous Foreigner, who has spent several Years in preparing the *Designs*, from which the following *Cuts* have been engrav'd, make a very considerable Present to the Publick? [...]

[p. 2] Every one may rest satisfy'd that the two new Translations publish'd in this Volume, and join'd to the *Italian* Original, are very faithful, and that I have left nothing unattempted to make them as perfect as could be wish'd, and answerable to the Beauty of the *Cuts*, with which they are attended, and which have been engrav'd by the best Masters. But I leave this to the judgment of the Publick. All good Judges must needs own that we wanted a Work of this Nature; and there is no doubt, but it will prove very useful, as much to Architects and Workmen, as to those who design to build for themselves; since it contains the necessary Rules for raising the plainest Buildings, as well as the most adorn'd. Every body cannot build Palaces, nor enrich their

Houses with Columns, Pilasters, and so many other Ornaments of Architecture, which require great charges. But since there are no Houses, tho never so small, without doors and windows, and some of the other parts, first invented by necessity, and then adorn'd that they might be more graceful, it is not more chargeable to make them according to their just proportions, by following the directions of some intelligent Person, than to leave them to the management and discretion of the workmen, who generally mind nothing but what is profitable to them. But as most of those who undertake to build, neglect to make use of any Architect, in order to raise a House, in which they will have none of those Ornaments, as being, in their judgment, either needless, or too expensive; they also neglect the other parts, which are the most material in a building. And because they don't understand the Rules of Art, that affords those beautiful proportions, which, even in the plainest buildings, do often raise the admiration of the most unskilful, without their knowing the reason of it; they look upon them as the most learned and experience'd Architects: or, at most, they rely upon Workmen, who are often very ignorant, or dare not find fault with any plan, tho never so bad, for fear of displeasure, and so losing their Work. Hence it is that we see so many bungled Houses and so oddly contriv'd, that they seem to have been made only to be admir'd by ignorant Men, and to raise the laughter of those who are sensible of such imperfection. Most [p. 3] of them are like Bird-cages, by reason of the largeness and too great number of windows, or like prisons, because of the Darkness of the rooms, passages and stairs. Some want the most essential part, I mean the *Entablature,* or Cornice; and tho it be the best sence against the injuries of the Weather, it is left out to save charges. In some other Houses, the rooms are so small and strait, that one knows not where to place the most necessary furniture. Others, through the oddness of some new and insignificant ornaments, seem to exceed the *wildest Gothick*. It were an endless thing to enumerate all the absurdities, which many of our Builders introduce every day into their way of building. I shall be contented to apply to them what the ingenious Mr. *Campbell* says of the Architecture of *Boronimi*[17] [*sic*], in his *Vitruvius Britannicus*, the first part whereof he has newly published with a labour and exactness equal to his skill in Architecture. *They are,* says he, *chimerical beauties, where the Parts are without proportions, solids without their true bearing, heaps of materials without strength, excessive ornaments without grace.* I add, and a ridiculous mixture of *Gothick* and *Roman,* without Judgment, Taste, or *Symmetry*.

I confess that the imperfections observable in our buildings, are often to be ascrib'd to the Caprice and Infatuation of those for whom they are made: but I think it cannot be denied that they do also proceed, in a great measure, from the ignorance and ill taste of the *Designers,* Undertakers, or Builders. Nevertheless, we have good reason to hope, more than ever, that those absurdities will be laid aside, and that the noble and majestic simplicity of the Ancients will prevail again. Many Persons, even among the most illustrious Nobility, begin to relish Architecture. They take delight in learning its most beautiful proportions; and by comparing the buildings of eminent and experience'd Architects with those that have been rais'd by unskilful Men, they easily perceive what a vast difference there is between the noble productions of the former, and the extravagant performances of the latter. And indeed, they are most concern'd in it: there is hardly any body else that can bear the Charges of a beautiful and perfect Architecture, and undertake those great and stately buildings, wherein the *Work* and the *Matter* seem to contend about the preference, and strive to immortalize the memory of their Masters. Tis therefore very proper for them to be able to judge of the Plans that are propos'd to them.

I hope this Work will meet with a general approbation: if those, who have no skill in Architecture, read it, their curiosity will perhaps move them to learn an Art, which several great Princes did not think unworthy of their application. Those who begin to study Architecture, and whose taste is not come yet to its perfection, will be cur'd of their wrong notions; and finding in this Work a method no less experience'd than beautiful and safe, they will learn by it to work with good success, and without any fear of being mistaken. As for those Learned Architects, who are better known by the reputation of their works, than by any thing I could say of them, tis not doubted but they will be glad to see *Palladio* come out under a form more suitable to the nobleness of his *Designs*, and the great Esteem the Publick has always had for him.

NICHOLAS DU BOIS, *Architect, and one of his Majesty's Engineers.*

Book I. Chap. XX. Of the Errors and Abuses introduc'd into Architecture.

[p. 35] Having set down all those Ornaments of *Architecture* which consist in the right use of the five Orders, and having shewn how they ought to be made by drawing the *Profils* of each of their parts, according as I found that the Ancients did practice; it seems to me not unfit here, to inform the Reader of many abuses, which having been formerly introduc'd by *Barbarians*, are observ'd even to this day; and this I do to the end, that the Studious in this Art may avoid them in their own works, and be able to take notice of them in those of others. I say then, that *Architecture* (as all the other Arts) being grounded upon Rules taken from the imitation of Nature, admits of nothing that is contrary, or foreign to that Order which Nature has prescrib'd to all things. [...] And this being so, what shall we say of that form of Building? Which is so contrary to what Nature has taught us, that it deviates from that Simplicity which is visible in things by her produc'd, and departs from all that is good, or true, or agreeable, in the way of Building: for which reason, instead of Columns, or Pilasters, which are contriv'd to bear great Weight, one ought not to place those Modern Ornaments call'd *Cartooshes*, which are certain *Scroles* that are but an eye-sore to the Artists, and give others only a confused Idea of *Architecture*, without any pleasure or satisfaction, nor indeed do they produce any other effect than to increase the expences of the Builder. [...] and altho variety and novelty should please all, yet we are not to go against the precepts of Art, and that which Reason demonstrates; whence we see that the Ancients in their several contrivances have never departed from the general and necessary Rules of Art and Nature, as may be seen in my Book of *Antiquities*.

From *Andrea Palladio's Architecture in Four Books*, translated and edited by Edward Hoppus (1735)

This was the second complete edition of Palladio published in English, a conflation of Colen Campbell's painstaking edition of the first Book and Du Bois's more free version of the other three Books in the Leoni edition. It was originally published in weekly parts by the engraver, Benjamin Cole, from 1732 to 1734. Its aim was to make Palladio in English affordable to 'Journeymen, Apprentices, &c', who could not afford Leoni's or Campbell's editions. Despite these laudable intentions, the main effect was to demonstrate the urgent need for a reliable, correct and complete edition (see Figure 5.6; Harris, 1990).

Book I, Chap. XX: Concerning the Errors and Abuses in Architecture

[p. 49] [...] Architecture therefore being, as all the other Arts are, an Imitation of Nature, will never admit of any thing either repugnant to, or inconsistent with that Order and Harmony which Nature observes in all her Works [...]. If we duly examine we shall find that the same was observed in all the other Parts; upon which Account one cannot but dislike those Forms of Building, which swerving from those Rules that Nature herself dictates, and that Simplicity which is conspicuous in all her Productions, form to themselves another kind of Nature, by deviating from whatever is good, just and beautiful in Architecture. [...] And though Variety and Novelty naturally please all Mankind, yet they are not to be introduced in direct Opposition to the Rules of Art, and the Dictates of Reason; and it must be acknowledg'd, that the Antients never departed from any general and necessary Precepts of Art in their various Inventions, as I shall shew in my Book of *Antiquities*.

Sir John Evelyn, from *A Parallel of the Antient Architecture with the Modern* (1664)

As early as 1664 Evelyn advocated the foundation of an English university of civil and military architecture. He urged Charles II to follow the example of Louis XIV and to set aside some apartments in his palace at Whitehall in which architects,

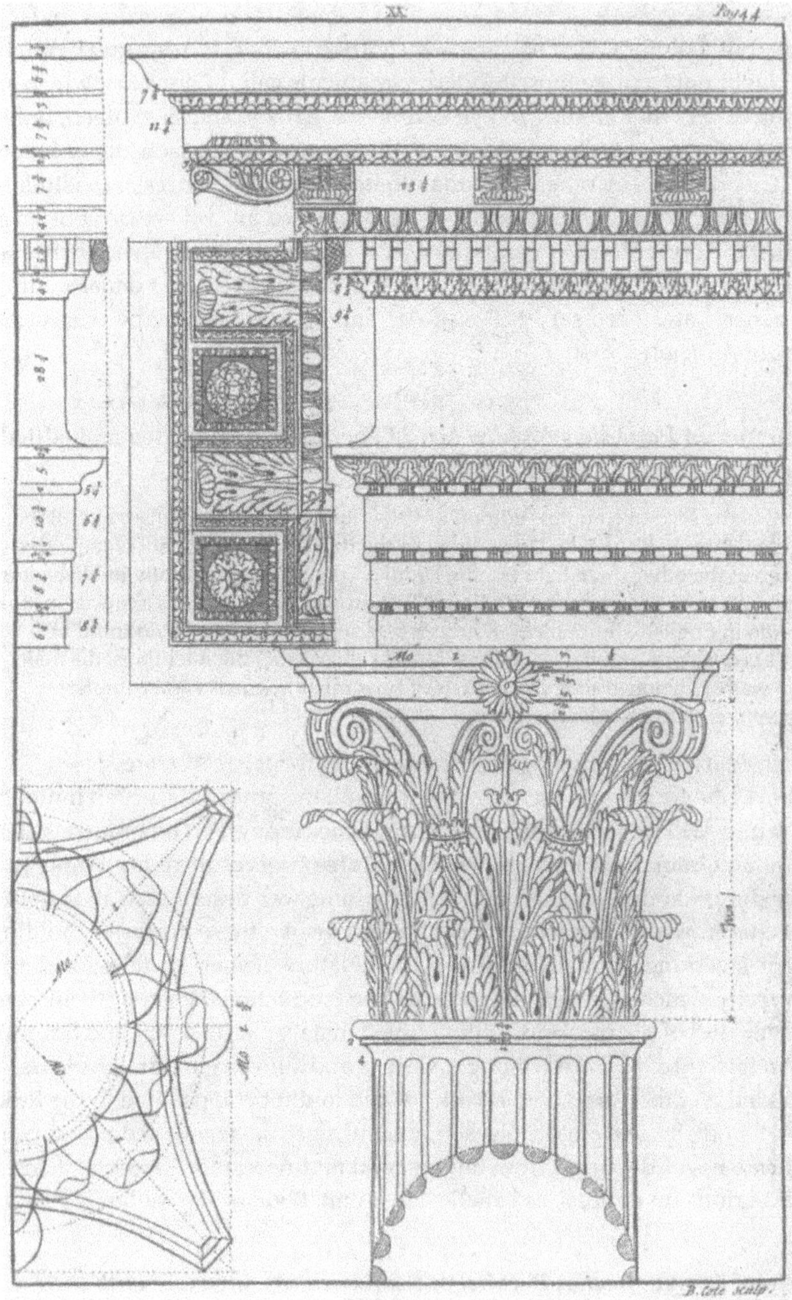

5.6 *Andrea Palladio's Architecture in Four Books ... Carefully Revis'd and Redelineated by Edw.[d] Hoppus, Surveyor* (London, 1735), illustration of the Corinthian order (p. 44), engraved by Benjamin Cole from a plate in Colen Campbell's edition of Palladio's first book (London, 1726); the plates in Campbell's edition were copied from the first Italian edition of Palladio's *I quattro libri* of 1570

painters and sculptors could work; Evelyn's interest in the arts also led him to participate in the foundation of the Royal Society in 1661. Subsequently, Evelyn translated Leon Battista Alberti's *De Statua* (first published in Venice in 1568, although written more than a century earlier) in *Sculptura, or the History and Art of Chalcography and Engraving in Copper* of 1662, which is the first book in English on sculpture, and Fréart's *Idea of Perfection in Painting* (1668). The *Parallel* also included an 'Account of Architects and Architecture', which was originally intended to be an extension of the brief list of technical terms provided by Fréart, and the first of its kind to be published in English. In the second edition of the *Parallel* of 1707 this was considerably enlarged. Although in 1664 there were no complete English translations available of the treatises of Palladio, Serlio, Scamozzi or Alberti, the *Parallel* met with little success, unlike Evelyn's *Sylva*, a treatise on tree-growing written at the instigation of the Royal Navy (Harris, 1990).

To Sir John Denham, Knight of the Honourable Order of the Bath, Superintendent and Surveyor of His Majestie's Buildings and Works[18]

Sir, It is now some *ten* years since, that to gratifie a *friend* of mine in the *Country*, I began to interpret this *Parallel;* but other things intervening, it was lay'd aside, and had so continu'd without thoughts of resumption, had not the passion of my worthy Friend Mr. *Hugh May*[19] to oblige the *Publick*, and in commiseration of the few assistances which our *Workmen* have of this nature (compar'd to what are extant, in other Countries) found out an expedient, and by procuring a most accurate *Edition* of the *Plates*, encourag'd me to finish what I had begun; and to make a willing *Present* of my *labour* and of whatever else I was able to contribute to so generous a designe.

Sir, I am not to instruct *you* in the merits and use of this excellent *Piece;* but it is from your approbation and particular influence, that our *Workmen* ought to esteem it, and believe me too when I affirme it: That the Ten *Authors* in this *Assembly*, which compose both so many, and (for not being vulgar) unintelligible *Volumes*, will neither afford them so full instructions in the *Art*, nor so well inable them to judge, and pronounce concerning the true *Rules* and *Maximes* of it as this one *little*, but incomparable, *Collection*. You well know, that all the mischiefs and absurdities in our modern *Structures* proceed chiefly from our busie and *Gotic* triflings in the *Compositions* of the *Five Orders;* and that an able *Workman*, who is *Master* of his *Art*, and has a true relish indeed, carries on all his undertakings with applause and satisfaction: That there is not in the whole *Catalogue* of *Authors* who have written on this Subject, a more safe, expedite, and perfect guide than this *Parallel;* where, from the noblest *Remaines* of *Antiquity* accurately *Measur'd*, and perspicuously *Demonstrated*, the *Rules* are lay'd down; and from a solid, judicious, and mature comparison of *modern Examples*, their *Errours* are detected; so that were but a little more pains taken by our young *Architects* and their *Subsidiairies*, about the easier *Principles of Geometrie*, the *Rudiments of Perspective*, and a ready address of well *Designing*, we might by the conversation of this *Author* alone, promise our *Country*, and the *Age* to come, a miraculous improvement of their *Building* in a short time. Nor would this be in the least, to the augmentation of their *expenses;* since there is nothing costs dearer, and displeases more, than our undigested contrivances, and those intolerable defects which we have enumerated. It is from the *asymmetrie* of our *Buildings*, want of *decorum* and proportion in our *Houses*, that the irregularity of our *humors* and *affections* may be shrewdly discrn'd: But it is from His Majesties great *Genius*, and the choice he has made of such an *Instrument*, that we may hope to see it all reform'd; it being in so worthy an imitation of that magnificent *Emperour*, that touch'd with the like indignation at the *Encroachments* and *Deformities* of the publick *Edifices* and *Waies*, caused a like *reformation* also; so as we may now affirme of *London*, as the *Poet* once of Rome,

Nunc Roma *est, nuper magna taberna fuit* [Mart. Lib. 7 Epig. 60] [...][20]

The Preface.
Reader,
[...] There are others to be found (though truely very rarely) that having their first studies well founded on the *Principles of Geometry* before they adventur'd to work, do afterwards easily, and with assurance arrive to the knowledge of the perfection of the *Art*: It is to such onely that I address my self, and to whom I willingly communicate the thoughts which I have had of separating in two branches the *five Orders of Architecture*, and forming a *body* a part of the *Three* which are deriv'd to us from the *Greeks*; to wit, the *Dorique, Ionique*, and the *Corinthian*, which one may with reason call the very flower and perfection of the *Orders;* since they not onely contain whatsoever is excellent, but likewise all that is necessary of *Architecture;* there being but three manners of *Building*, the *Solid*, the *Mean*, and the *Delicate;* all of them accurately express'd in these three *Orders* here, that have therefore no need of the other two (*Tuscan*, and *Composita*), which being purely of *Latine* extraction, and but forrainers in respect to *them*, seem as it were of another *species;* so as being mingl'd, they do never well together, as those to whom I discourse will soon perceive, when they shall have once put off a certain blind respect and reverence, which *Antiquity*, and a long custome (even of the greatest abuses) does commonly imprint in the most part of men, whose judgements they so pre-occupate, that they find it afterwards a difficult matter to undeceive themselves; because they deferr too much, and hardly dare to examine what has been receiv'd by the vulgar approbation for so long a time [...]. It is the very least of my thoughts to broach *Novelties;* on the contrary, I would (were it possible) ascend even to the very source of the *Orders* themselves, and derive from thence the *Images*, and pure *Ideas* of these incomparable *Masters*, who were indeed their first *Inventors*, and be

instructed from their own mouths; since doubtless the farther men have wander'd from their *Principles*, transplanting them as it were into a strange soile, the more they become degenerate, and scarce cognoscible to their very *Authors*. For to say truth, have we at this present any reason in the World to call those *three* by the name of *Orders*, viz. *Dorique, Ionique*, and the *Corinthian*, which we daily behold so disfigur'd, and ill treated by the *Workmen* of this age? to speak seriously, remains there so much as a simple *Member*, which has not receiv'd some strange and monstrous alteration? Nay, things are arriv'd to that pass, that a man shall hardly find an *Architect* who disdains not to follow the best and most approved *examples* of *Antiquity*: Every man will now forsooth compose after his own fansie, and conceives, that to imitate *Them*, were to become an *Apprentice* again; and that to be *Masters* indeed, they must of necessity produce something of new: Poor men that they are, to believe, that in fantastically designing some one kind of particular *Cornice*, or like *Member*, they are presently the *Inventors* of a new *Order*, as if in that onely consisted, what is call'd *Invention*; as if the *Pantheon*, that same stupendious and incomparable *Structure* (which is yet to be seen at *Rome*) were not the *Invention* of the *Architect* who built it, because he has vary'd nothing from the *Corinthian* Ordinance of which it is intirely compos'd? 'Tis not in the *retail* of the *minuter portions*, that the talent of an *Architect* appears; *this* is to be judg'd from the general distribution of the *Whole* Work. [...] As for those others to whom Nature has been more propitious, and are indu'd with a clearer imagination, they very well perceive that the true and essential beauty of *Architecture* consists not simply in the minute separation of every member *apart*; but does rather principally result from the *Symmetry* and *Oeconomy* of the *whole*, which is the union and concourse of them all together, producing as 'twere a visible harmony and consent, which those eyes that are not clear'd and enlightned by the real Intelligence of *Art*, contemplate and behold with excess and delectation. [...]

For my part, I find so excellent, and particular a beauty in the three *Greek Orders*, that I am hardly at all concern'd with the other *two* of the *Latine* in comparison; and the Station which has been assign'd them, sufficiently demonstrates that there was no place for them, but after all the rest, as if indeed they had been refus'd by them both: The rusticity and meanness of the *Tuscan* having exil'd it from the *Cities*, has sent it to the *Country Cottages*; and as unworthy of entering into *Temples* and *Palaces*, 'tis become the very last, as even destitute of employment: For the *other*, which would pretend to exceed, and refine upon the *Corintian*, and what they name the *Composita*, tis in my apprehension yet more irrational, and truely methinks altogether unworthy to be call'd an *Order*, as having been the source of all that confusion which has been brought into *Architecture*, since *Workmen* have taken the liberty to dispense with *those* which the *Antients* had prescrib'd us, to

Engotish[21] (as one may say) after their own capricious humour an infinite many which do all pass under this appellation. Honest *Vitruvius* in his time well foresaw the ill consequence which those of the *Profession* would introduce out of their love of *Novelty*, which already began it seems to incline them to *Libertinism*, and the disdain of the *Rules* of that *Art*, which ought to remain most sacred and inviolable; so that we must look on this as on a grey-headed evil which grows worse and worse daily, and is become now almost incurable: Notwithstanding, would our Modern *Architects* but yet fix any limits to the freedom they have taken, and keep themselves within the precincts of the *Roman Order*, which is the legitimate and true *Composita*, and which has likewise its *Canons* and *Rules* as well as the rest, I should find no cause of complaint, since we see instances of it among the *Vestigia*'s [*sic*] and footsteps of the most flourishing ages; as in particular, that of *Titus Vespasianus* [...]:[22] But then it should never be employ'd without mature advice, and always alone by itself; for so we find the *Inventors* of this *Order* us'd it, who well knowing its defects (compar'd with the rest) did ever forbear to paragon[23] them together: But our *Architects* never entring into this consideration, have faln into an *Errour* which admits of no excuse, by forcing the weaker to support the stronger. [...] Let it suffice to have given you this *Caution*: Those who shall be so curious as to try, and which will (I assure them) be no fruitless attempt, shall soon find difficulty enough in the extraordinary confusion of the different manners of those *Architects*, who instead of working upon the accompt of the *Models* [i.e. modules] of *Columns* (which is the most natural *Method*, and particularly affected to the *Proportions* of *Architecture*) amuse us with *Palms*, *Feet*, and other general *Measures* (as meer *Masons* would do) which so confounds the Imagination, that 'tis extream difficult to dis-intangle ones self out of them, and costs a world of time ere one comes at last to reduce and apply them to the *Scale* of the *Model*, without which, all their industry becomes fruitless, and to no purpose. To this it is I have principally endeavour'd to apply a timely remedy, reducing all the *designs* of this *Treatise* to one *Common Model*, namely, to the *Semidiameter* of the *Column* divided into thirty *Minutes*, that so I may approach the *precise* measures as near as is possible [...] But to the end we may proceed solidly [...] it will first be requisite to be thoroughly instructed in the *Principles of Architecture*, and to have apply'd our studies to *Antiquities*, which are the very *Maxims* and *Rules* of this Art: not as if generally the *Antients* were to be imitated indifferently; on the Contrary, there are but few of *them* good, and an infinite number of them bad, which is *that* has produced this confus'd variety amongst our *Authors*, who treating of the *Orders*, and their *Measures*, have differ'd so strangely from one another. It is therefore undoubtedly the safest way to have access to the *Sources* themselves, and to follow precisely the *Models* and *Proportions* of such ancient *Structures* as have the universal consent, and approbation of those of the *Profession*. Such *Examples* we have at *Rome* in the *Theatre* of *Marcellus*, the Temple of the *Rotunda*, the three *Columns* near the *Capitol* [...] whose several *Profiles* I shall produce on every of the *Orders*, and after them, those of our more Modern *Architects*, that so in confronting them to these glorious *Examples* which are the *Originals* of the *Art*, they may as to an impartial *Touchstone* have recourse to *them*, for the tryal and examination of their *Works* [...].

Chap. I. Of the Orders *in General.*
It is sufficiently difficult to determine precisely, what the name of *Order* may signifie amongst our *Architects*, though it be indeed very necessary to understand it well. [...] to get out of this *Labyrinth* we must even take it in pieces, and consider the things apart, that so it may, as it were, touch our imagination, and distinctly form its *Idea's* in us, which is the business we are to enquire after: For the *Art* of *Architecture* does not consist in *Words*; the *Demonstration* ought to be sensible, and ocular. It is very perspicuous to all those of this *Mystery*, that the principal Piece of an *Order* is the *Columne*, and that its *Entablature* being once placed on the *Capital* produces the entire *Composition*. If therefore we will define it exactly, and give the most express meaning of it, we must, as it were, make a very *Anatomy* of the parts, and say, that the *Column*, with its *Base* and *Chapiter*, crown'd with an *Architrave*, *Frieze*, and *Cornice*, formes that kind of *Building* which Men call an *Order*; seeing all these individual parts do generally encounter, and are found through all the *Orders*; the difference amongst them consisting in no other particular, then in the proportion of those *parts*, and the figure of their *Capitals*. [...] the excellency and perfection of an *Art*, consists not in the multiplicity of her *principles*; but contrarily, the more simple they are, and few in number, the more worthy they are of our admiration: This we see manifested in those of *Geometry*, which is in truth the very foundation, and universal magazine of all those *Arts*, from whence *This* has been extracted, and without whose aid it were impossible it should subsist. Well therefore may we conclude, That the *Orders* being no other then the very *Elements* of *Architecture*, and these *Three first* which we have deduc'd from the *Greeks*, comprehending all the *Species* of Building; it were but a superfluous thing we should pretend to augment their number.

Chap. II. Of the Dorique *Order.*
It is no small advantage for the *Dorique Order*, to demonstrate that it has been the very first regular *Idea* of *Architecture*; and that, as the first-born and heir of this *Queen* of *Arts*, it has had the honour also to have been the first builder both of *Temples* and *Palaces*. [...] Having then propos'd for a foundation, that this *Order* represents *Solidity* to us, as its *Specifique* and principal quality, we ought not to employ it but in great massive Buildings and Edifices of the like

nature; as for *Ports* of *Citadels*, and *Fortresses* of *Towns*, the outside of *Churches* or *Publique places*, and the like, where the delicateness of the Ornament is neither convenient, nor profitable; for as much as the heroick and gigantine manner of this *Order* does excellently well in those places, discovering a certain *masculine* and natural beauty, which is properly that the *French* call *la grand Maniere* [*sic*].

[...] to introduce into *Architecture* this *grandure* of *Manner* of which we speak, we ought so to proceed, that the division of the principal Members of the *Orders* consist but of few parts, that they be all *great* and of a bold and ample *Rilievo* and Swelling; that the *Eye* beholding nothing which is little and mean, the *Imagination* may be the more vigorously touch'd and concern'd with it.

Chap. V. Another very antient Profile *after the* Grand Maniere *elevated in* Perspective, *and now extant at* Albano *near* Rome [see Figure 5.7].
I conceiv'd it very advantegeous, and indeed in some sort necessary the better to represent the beauty and goodly effect of this *Profile*, to give you *one* elevated in *Perspective*; because I would gratifie the eye with as much as *Art* is capable to add to the real and natural *Relievo*, and show how it ought to succeed in the execution.

This incomparable *Dorique* Master-piece was discovered at *Albano*, joyning to the Church of St. *Mary*, amongst divers other odd fragments of *Architecture* very curious, and of which I have a good number design'd, and with great diligence examin'd as to their measures, though drawn something in haste and as it were in passing, by the hand of the famous *Pyrrho Ligorio*.[24]

Chap. VI. A Judgment in general upon all the Authors summon'd together in this Collection. That the Reader may now come with some kind of preparation to the particular Examen of the *Designes* which follow, I shall here endeavour to give him a general hint of the severall talents and abilities which I have remark'd in every one of those *Masters* we are taking a survey of in paragon one with the other.

The first of all is without any contest the famous *Andrea Palladio*, to whom we are oblig'd for a very rare Collection of antique *Plans* and *Profiles* of all sorts of Buildings, design'd after a most excellent manner, and measur'd with a diligence so exact, that there is nothing more in that particular left us to desire: Besides the very advantageous opportunities which he has had at *Venice*, and in all the *Vicentine* his native Country do leave us such markes as clearly shew'd him not onely to have been a Spectator of these great *Masters* of *Antiquity*; but even a Competitor with them, and emulous of their glory.

The Man who nearest approaches to him is also another *Vicentine*, *Vincent Scamozzi*[25] by name, a far greater talker (as well appears in his Books) but a much inferiour workman, and less delicate in point of design: A man may

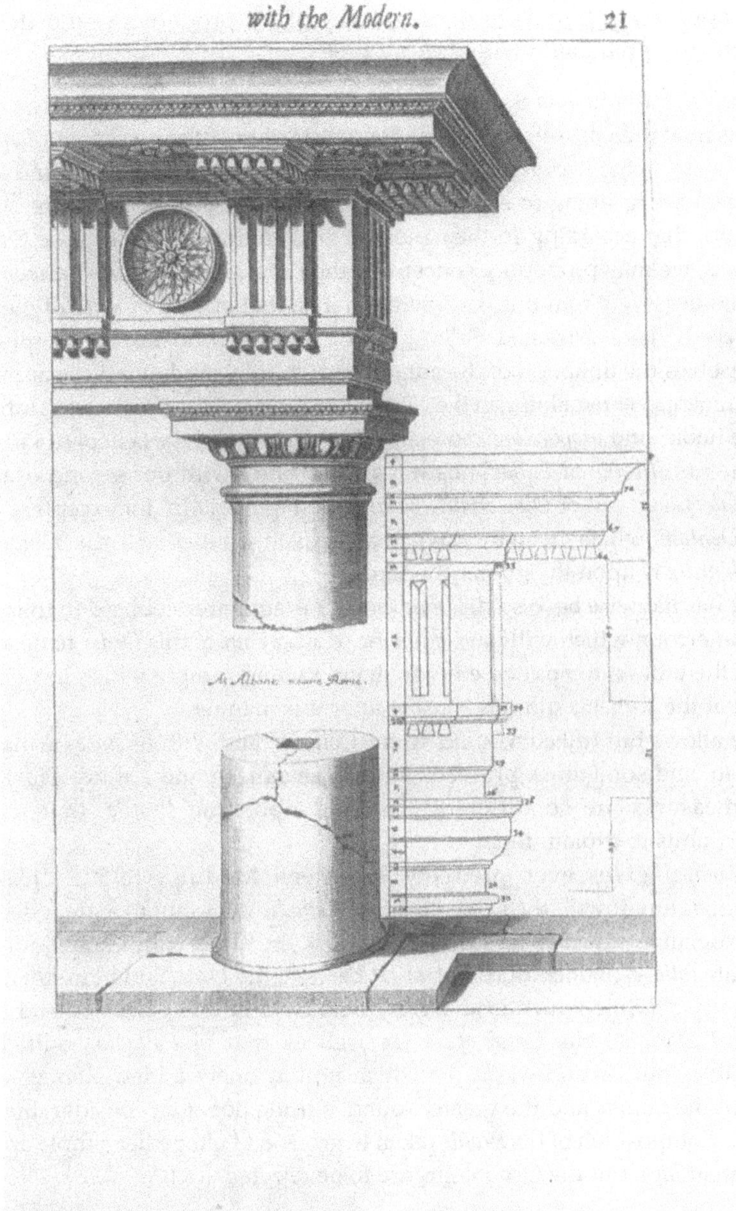

5.7 John Evelyn, *A Parallel of the Antient Architecture with the Modern* (London, 1664), Doric profile at Albano (p. 21), artist and engraver Charles Errard

easily perceive it by the *Profiles* which he has left us of the five *Orders*, the manner whereof is a little dry; besides that, he is very poor and trite in his Ornaments, and but of an ill *gusto*: He is notwithstanding *this* the nearest that approaches him as to the regularity of his proportions, and the most worthy to be parallel'd with *Palladio*. [...]

Chap. VII. Palladio *and* Scamozzi *upon the* Dorique Order [see Figure 5.8].
Let us now then pass to the Ocular Demonstration of the precedent *Chapter* by the *Parallel* of the *Architects* which I have there assembled together, and whose *designs* I am hastning to examine by comparing them with our three *Antique Designs*, that according to their more or less conformity with these Original Models, we may pronounce concerning their merit, and see what esteem they indeed deserve. From this consideration it is, that of all the *choice* of the other *Masters*, I have extracted *Palladio* and *Scamozzi*, who having propos'd to themselves the imitation of the antient *Architects* by studying those admirable Monuments yet remaining in the City of *Rome*, have follow'd a *manner* infinitely more noble, and *proportions* more elegant then those of the School of *Vitruvius*.

The first *Profile* of *Palladio* hath a great affinity with our second example, *Antique*, taken out of *Diocletian's Bathes* [see Figure 5.9];[26] for excepting onely the *Dentelli* which he may have with reason omitted, all the rest of the *Entablature* is upon the matter the same.

He has likewise been so discreet (being peradventure oblig'd to follow the vulgar errour, which will have the *Base* of a *Column* of this *Order* to be all one with the others) to advertise before hand by an example which has none at all, that the *Antients* did never use it after this manner.

He allows but fifteen *Modules* to the *Column*, and with its *Base* he makes it sixteen, and sometimes proceeds even to seventeen and a third. The rest of the measures are so differently mark'd upon the *Profile*, that it were superfluous to explain them.

Scamozzi gives ever precisely seventeen Modules to his *Columnes*, accomodating it with the same *Base* that *Palladio* does; but to a great deal less purpose, in as much as he thinks fit to deck the *Tore's* with I know not what delicate *foliages*, which does not at all become the *Order*; no more then does the *Ionique fluting* which is abusively employ'd in this place in stead of the natural *Dorique*. His *Entablature* (as well as that of *Palladio*), sufficiently resembles our second *Model*, to which he has onely added a small cavity bewixt the *Corona* and the greater round, a thing not at all considerable.

The Composition of his *Profile* taken in gross, and altogether simple appears of a great *Idea*, but the Ornaments are to be rejected. [...]

Chap. XIII. Of the Ionique Order
[...] This is the Example which *Vitruvius* has made use of to prove how necessary it is that an *Architect* should be knowing in *History*, to the end he

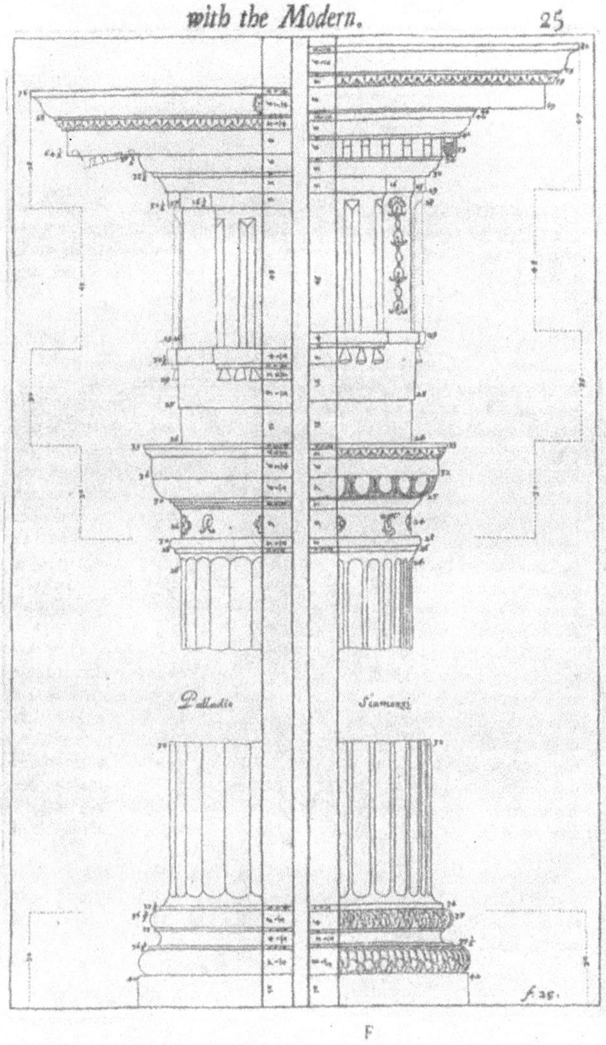

5.8 John Evelyn, *A Parallel of the Antient Architecture with the Modern* (London, 1664), illustration of the Doric order according to Palladio and Scamozzi (p. 25), artist and engraver Charles Errard

5.9 John Evelyn, *A Parallel of the Antient Architecture with the Modern* (London, 1664), Doric profile at the Baths of Diocletian (p. 19), artist and engraver Charles Errard

introduce nothing impertinently in his works, and without good reason. The *Gotique Order*, which is the folly and very *Ape* of *Architecture*, in imitation of the *Caryatides* has compos'd certain lame figur'd *Mutils* or *Corbells* in stead of *Cartouzes* sustained by I know not what *Chimera's* and ridiculous *Monkeys*, to be met with in every corner of our old *Churches*; but some of the *Modern* having (with very good reason) found fault that such extravagances should be seen in holy Places where reverence and modesty are so essential, and considering how much more decent it were to fit those places with some devout Representations, without any respect at all to their Profession, or for want rather of understanding the propriety of the *Orders* of *Architecture*, have amused themselves to place the figure of *Angels* and other *Saints* in stead of the *Caryatides*; making them like so many *Slaves* to carry huge *Cornices*, and even entire *Altars* upon their shoulders, testifying thereby how preposterously and without judgment they consulted *Vitruvius* upon the occasion of the Original of the *Caryatides*; For they would otherwise have understood that this Order cannot be employed or indifferently enter into all sorts of Buildings, and that it requires no small discretion to be aptly and discreetly placed: Above all, that it should never be used in *Churches*, which are the Houses of *God*, and *Asylum's* of Mercy, where servitude and revenge ought never to appear. [...]

Chap. XVI. The Perspective *Elevation of a* Profile *drawn from the* Baths *of* Dioclesian *at* Rome [see Figure 5.10].
I would needs make an Elevation in *Perspective* of this *Profile*, that so I might add some variety to my designs, and for that likewise it is an advantageous means to represent the *Idea* of an *Order*, and the effect which it produces being put in *Work*, for their sakes who are not much practis'd in the Mystery. This piece stood in the *Baths* of *Dioclesian* at the *angle* or *coinage* of a return of a Wall, as I have found out by a *Design* of mine very antient and of a good hand, where the Proportions as well of the *Plan* as of the *Profile* are exactly noted, even to the least particulars. I have reduced and accomodated them to the division of my ordinary *Model*, as you may perceive them on the *Profile* which is under the *Perspective Entablature*. [...]

From Vincenzo Scamozzi, *The Mirror of Architecture* (1676) (based on Joachim Schuym's Dutch edition), 'To the Lovers of Architecture' by William Fisher

This address to the reader appears at the beginning of a translation by the publisher William Fisher, based on Joachim Schuym's reduction of Scamozzi's Book VI on the Orders to a few pages and a number of plates, the *Grondt-Regulen der Bouw-Konst* or fundamental rules of the art of architecture. It resulted in a manual that could vie with Vignola's *Regole* (Harris, 1990).

5.10 John Evelyn, *A Parallel of the Antient Architecture with the Modern* (London, 1664), perspective elevation of an Ionic profile at the Baths of Diocletian (p. 43), artist and engraver Charles Errard

To the Lovers of Architecture.
Reader,
As in all things Order is to be observed that we may avoid Confusion, or else they will be a Chaos, as the Poets fancy; So especially in this excellent Art of Architecture it is requisite that every part and member have its right Order and due Proportion: And there having been many Masters who have with great Care and Industry brought this Art to a great Perfection, among whom this famous Master *Vincent Scamozzi*, Chief Builder of the Magnificent City of *Venice*, deserves to be placed in the first and chiefest rank by the consent of all Judicious Artists. Therefore for the benefit of our own Nation, and that it may be made most useful for all Artificers in Building, and Lovers and Practitioners in this most useful Art; who are or may be employed in Royal and Magnificent Structures. The larger Book is here reduced into a smaller Volume, and the Author his given Parts divided into Minutes; whereby the Principal Rules of Architecture are made plain to ordinary Capacities by *Joachim Schuym*, an Ingenious Artist. And for your better understanding, take notice, that by Models [modules] are signified the Measure of the Column: as for example: Let the Diameter be 18, 16, or 12 Inches, which shall be the Model divided into 60 Equal Parts or Minutes [...] by using which Measure all the Parts of the said Column shall be proportionable [...].

Accept favourably, and judge impartially.

Farewel

Sir Christopher Wren, 'Tract I' and extract from 'Tract IV: Observations on the Temple of Peace, built by the Emperor Vespasian' (both written after 1680)

The majority of Sir Christopher Wren's undated writings on architecture were probably written after 1680, because they show a familiarity with Desgodets's *Edifices antiques de Rome* (1682) and Claude Perrault's *Ordonnance des cinq espèces de colonnes* (1683) and with the second, enlarged edition of Perrault's translation of Vitruvius (1684).[27] Stephen Wren, the grandson of the architect, published these writings, with those on scientific subjects, in a volume called *Parentalia* (1750). Together with an unpublished 'Discourse on Architecture' which was transcribed by Christopher Wren, Jr and inserted in the Heirloom copy of *Parentalia* at the Royal Institute of British Architects in London, they are the only surviving theoretical writings on architecture by Wren. *Parentalia* is the second biography of a British architect (the first being the 'Memoirs Relating to the Life and Writings of Inigo Jones', see above, 'Chapter 2, pp. 98–101); (See also the notes on Wren and extracts in Chapters 3 and 4, above.)

Further reading: on 'Tract 1': Bennett (1972); Soo (1998); on seventeenth-century French theory see Herrmann (1973); Wilton-Ely (1993).

On 'Tract IV': For light and shadow in classical architecture see Evans (1995), pp. 107–23; on the role of the corona and other parts of the entablature see Payne (1999), pp. 230–35.

'Tract 1'

Architecture has its political Use; publick Buildings being the Ornament of a Country; it establishes a Nation, draws People and Commerce; makes the People love their native Country, which Passion is the Original of all great Actions in a Common-wealth. The Emulation of the Cities of *Greece* was the true Cause of their Greatness. The obstinate Valour of the *Jews*, occasioned by the Love of their Temple, was a Cement that held together that People, for many Ages, through infinite Changes. The Care of publick Decency and Convenience was a great Cause of the Establishment of the *Low countries*, and of many Cities in the World. Modern *Rome* subsists still, by the Ruins and Imitation of the *old*; as does *Jerusalem*, by the Temple of the Sepulchre, and other Remains of *Helena's* Zeal.[28]

Architecture aims at Eternity; and therefore the only Thing uncapable of Modes and Fashions in its Principals, the *Orders*.

The *Orders* are not only *Roman* and *Greek*, but *Phoenician*, *Hebrew*, and *Assyrian*; therefore being founded upon the Experience of all Ages, promoted by the vast Treasures of all great Monarchs, and Skill of the greatest Artists and Geometricians, everyone emulating each other; and Experiments in this kind being greatly expenceful, and Errors incorrigible, is the Reason that the Principles of Architecture are now rather the Study of Antiquity than Fancy.

Beauty, Firmness, and Convenience, are the Principles;[29] the two first depend upon the geometrical Reasons of *Opticks* and *Staticks*; the third only makes the Variety.

There are natural Causes of Beauty. Beauty is a Harmony of Objects, begetting Pleasure by the Eye. There are two Causes of Beauty, natural and customary. Natural is from *Geometry*, consisting in Uniformity (that is Equality) and Proportion. Customary Beauty is begotten by the Use of our Senses to those Objects which are usually pleasing to us for other Causes, as Familiarity or particular Inclination breed a Love to Things not in themselves lovely. Here lies the great Occasion of Errors; here is tried the Architect's Judgment: but always the true Test is natural or geometrical Beauty.

Geometrical Figures are naturally more beautiful than other irregular; in this all consent as to a Law of Nature. Of geometrical Figures, the Square and the Circle are most beautiful; next, the Parallelogram and the Oval. Strait Lines are more beautiful than curve; next to strait Lines, equal and geometrical Flexures; an Object elevated in the Middle is more beautiful than depressed.

Position is necessary for perfecting Beauty. There are only two beautiful Positions of strait Lines, perpendicular and horizontal: this is from Nature, and consequently Necessity, no other than upright being firm. Oblique Positions are Discord to the Eye, unless answered in Pairs, as in the Sides of an equicrural Triangle:[30] therefore *Gothick* Buttresses are ill-favoured, and were avoided by the Ancients, and no Roofs almost but spherick raised to be visible, escept in the Front, where the Lines answer; in spherick, in all Positions, the Ribs answer. Cones and multangular Prisms want neither Beauty nor Firmness, but are not ancient.

Views contrary to Beauty are Deformity, or a Defect of Uniformity, and Plainness, which is the Excess of Uniformity; Variety makes the Mean.

Variety of Uniformities makes compleat Beauty: Uniformities are best tempered, as Rhimes in Poetry, alternately, or sometimes with more Variety, as in Stanza's.

In Things to be seen at once, much Variety makes Confusion, another Vice of Beauty. In Things that are not seen at once, and have no Respect one to another, great Variety is commendable, provided this Variety transgress not the Rules of *Opticks* and *Geometry*.

An Architect ought not be jealous of Novelties, in which Fancy blinds the Judgment:[31] and to think his Judges, as well as those that are to live five Centuries after him, as those of his own Time. That which is commendable now for Novelty, will not be a new Invention to Posterity, when his Works are often imitated, and when it is unknown which was the Original; but the Glory of that which is good of itself is eternal.

The Architect ought, above all Things, to be well skilled in Perspective; for every thing that appears well in the Orthography, may not be good in the Model, especially where there are many Angles and Projectures; and every thing that is good in Model, may not be so when built; because a Model is seen from other Stations and Distances than the Eye sees the Building: but this will hold universally true, that whatsoever is good in Perspective, and will hold so in all the principal Views, whether direct or oblique, will be as good in great, if this only Caution be observed, that Regard be had to the Distance of the Eye in the principal Stations.

Things seen near at hand may have small and many Members, be well furnished with Ornaments, and may lie flatter; on the contrary, all this Care is ridiculous at great Distances; there bulky Members, and full Projectures casting quick Shadows, are commendable: small Ornaments at too great Distance, serve only to confound the Symmetry, and to take away the Lustre of the Object, by darkening it with little Shadows.

There are different Reasons for Objects, whose chief View is in Front, and for those whose chief View is sideways.

Fronts ought to be elevated in the Middle, not the Corners; because the Middle is the Place of greatest Dignity, and first arrests the Eye; and rather projecting forward in the Middle, than hollow. For these Reasons, Pavilions at the Corners are naught; because they make both Faults, a hollow and depressed Front. Where Hollows and Solids are mixed, the Hollow is to be in the Middle; for, Hollows are neither Niches, Windows, or Doors: The first require the Middle to give the Statue Dignity; the second, that the View from within may be direct; the third, that the Visto may be strait. The Ancients elevated the Middle with a Tympan, and Statue, or a Dome. The triumphant Arches, which now seem flat, were elevated by the magnificent Figure of the Victor in his Chariot with four Horses abreast, and other Statues accompanying it. No sort of Pinnacle is worthy enough to appear in the Air, but Statue. Pyramids are *Gothick*; Pots are modern *French*. Chimnies ought to be hid, if not, to be well adorned. No Roof can have Dignity enough to appear above a Cornice, but the circular; in private Buildings it is excusable. The ancients affected Flatness. In Buildings where the View is sideways, as in Streets, it is absolutely required, that the Composition be square, Intercolumnations equal, Projectures not great, the Cornices unbroken, and every thing strait, equal, and uniform. Breaks in the Cornice, Projectures of the upright Members, Variety, Inequality in the Parts, various Heights of the Roof, serve only to confound the Perspective, and make it deformed, while the Breaches and Projectures are cast one upon another, and obscure all Symmetry. In this Sort of Building there seems no Proportion of Length to the Heighth; for, a Portico the longer the more beautiful in *infinitum*: on the contrary, Fronts require a Proportion of the Breadth to the Heighth; higher than three times the Breadth is indecent, and as ill to be above three times as broad as high. From this Rule I except Obelisks, Pyramids, Columns, such as *Trajan*'s, *&c.*[32] which seem rather single Things than Compositions: I except also long Porticoes, though seen direct, where the Eye wandering over the same Members infinitely repeated, and not easily finding the Bounds, make no Comparison of them with the Heighth.

Vitruvius hath led us the true Way to find out the Originals of the Orders. When Men first cohabited in Civil Commerce, there was Necessity of Forums and publick Places of Meeting. In cold Countries, People were obliged to shut out the Air, the Cold, and the Rain; but in the hot Countries, where Civility first began, they desired to exclude the Sun only, and admit all possible Air for Coolness and Health: this brought in naturally the Use of Porticoes, or Roofs for Shade, set upon Pillars. A Walk of Trees is more beautiful than the most artificial Portico; but these not being easily preserved in Market-places, they made the more durable Shades of Porticoes; in which we see they imitated Nature, most Trees in their Prime, that are not Sapplings, or Dotards,[33] observe near the Proportion of *Dorick* Pillars in the Length of their Bole,[34] before they part into Branches. This I think the more natural Comparison, than that to the Body of a Man, in which there is little Resemblance of a cylindrical Body. The first Pillars were the very Boles of

Trees turned, or cut in Prisms of many Sides. A little Curiosity would induce to lay the *Torus* at the Top; and the Conjecture is not amiss, to say it was first a Band of Iron, to keep the Clefts, occasioned by the Sun, from opening with the Weight above; and to keep the Weather from piercing those Clefts, it was necessary to cover it with the Plinth, or square Board. The Architrave conjoined all the Pillars in Length, the Couples joined them cross-ways. I suppose now, that the Ends of the Couples might be hollowed away, as in this Scheme.**** [*The rest is wanting*.][35]

From 'Tract IV: Observations on the Temple of *Peace*, built by the Emperor *Vespasian*' [See Figures 5.11 and 5.12.]

[…] 6. But shall I accuse Antiquity for want of Skill in Opticks, of which every where it shews such admirable Proofs? since particularly here the Architect hath given great Testimony of it in the Contrivance of his Cornice, wherein he hath left out the *Corona*, or Hanging-square, by an unusual Example. The *Corona* seems an essential Part in all Cornices, as that which gives Denomination to the whole, and is necessary to the Beauty of a Cornice; because, by its Projecture, it shadows all the lower Members, receiving upon its plane Surface a terse Light from above; this gives the Eminence and distinct Appearance which we see in the Parts of a Cornice at distance; but the Artist here ingeniously apprehending that his Lights in this Fabrick stood level with his Cornice, and therefore it would want the Effect for which it is used, and that the Hanging-face of it would be fore shortened to nothing, to the Eye which beholds it from beneath, wisely left out this Member, which, if these optical Reasons did not prevail, would never have been used, since, of all Members, this is that which most loads the Cornice, and makes us, for want of Stones of such Vastness, and Money to move them, despair, in these Days, of coming near the Greatness of such a Pillar and Entablement as is here used, where the Projecture of the Cornice is near 5 Feet.

7. It was not therefore Unskilfulness in the Architect that made him chuse this flat Kind of Aspect for his Temple, it was his Wit and Judgment. Each Deity had a peculiar Gesture, Face, and Dress hieroglyphically proper to it; as their Stories were but Morals involved: and not only their Altars and Sacrifices were mystical, but the very Forms of their Temples. No language, no Poetry can so describe Peace, and the Effects of it in Men's Minds, as the Design of this Temple naturally paints it, without any Affectation of the Allegory. It is easy of Access, and open, carries an humble Front, but embraces wide, is luminous and pleasant, and content with an internal Greatness, despises an invidious Appearance of all that Heighth it might otherwise justly boast of; but rather fortifying itself on every Side, rests secure on a square and ample Basis.

5.11 *The Architecture of Palladio; in Four Books. Containing a Short Treatise of the Five Orders, and the most necessary Observations concerning all Sorts of Building ... Revis'd, Design'd, and Publish'd by Giacomo Leoni*, (London, 1715) 'Temple of Peace', Rome [now thought rather to be the Basilica of Constantine or Maxentius], sections and façade (plate 13 in vol. 4). Wren had never seen what was then assumed to be the Temple of Peace with his own eyes; the illustration is taken from Andrea Palladio's reconstruction, published in his *I quattro libri* (1570), an important source for Wren

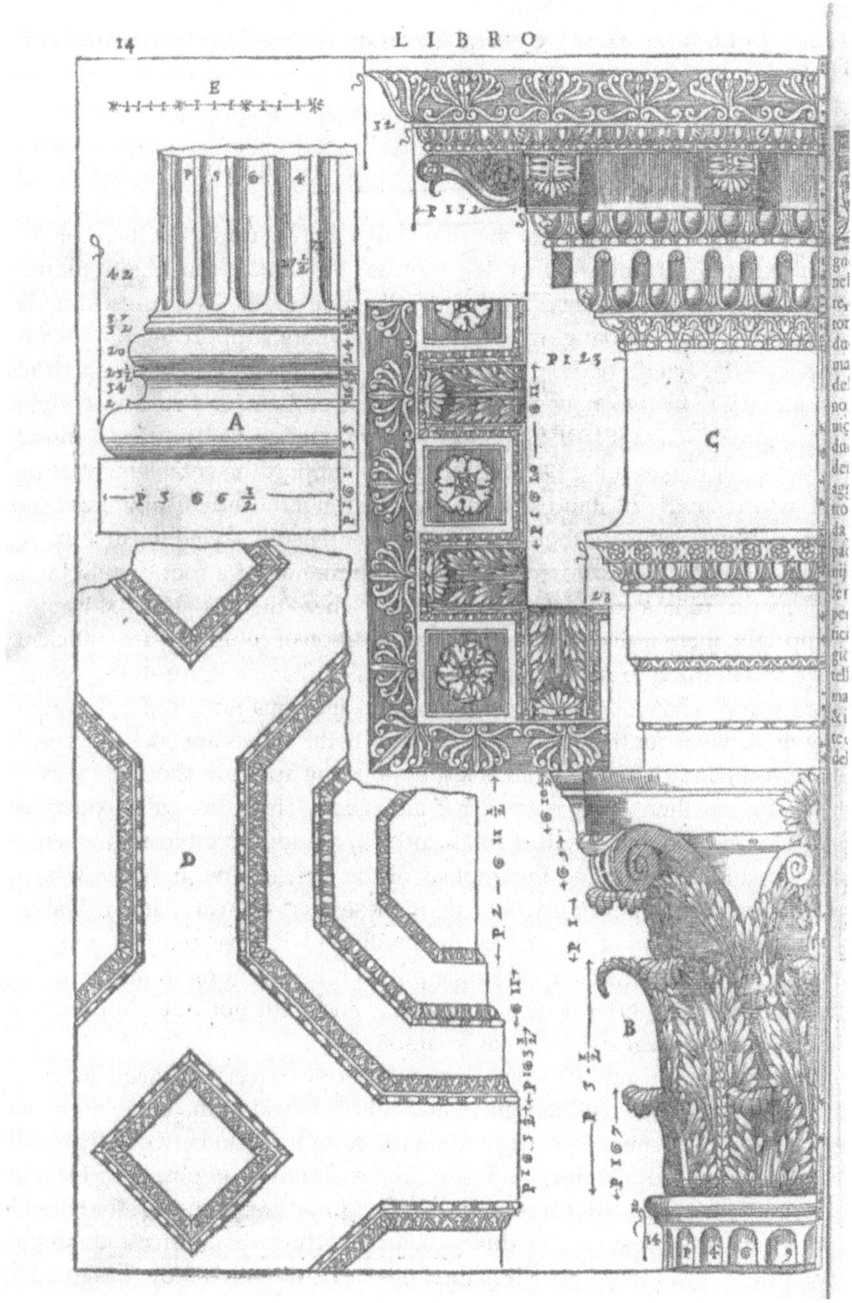

5.12 *The Architecture of Palladio; in Four Books. Containing a Short Treatise of the Five Orders, and the most necessary Observations concerning all Sorts of Building … Revis'd, Design'd, and Publish'd by Giacomo Leoni*, (London, 1715) 'Temple of Peace', Rome [now thought rather to be the Basilica of Constantine or Maxentius], illustration of its Composite order (plate 14 in vol. 4) (See the note to Figure 5.11)

Roger North, from 'The Origin and Development of Regular Architecture' (*c.* 1690)

(See the notes on North and extracts in Chapters 1 and 4, above.)

Let us now venture upon that which is knowne by the name of Regular, in the Italian and Greek manner.

A building hath two uses of the side walls, that is support of the roof and defence from heat, and weather. The roof, as I observ'd before, ought for that end also to overhang, else the wett will come to the apertures and the foundation. The overhanging will need some more support than the walls, otherwise the weight of the roof looks too heavy; this makes pillars needfull, and I take it to be the onely ground for the use of them, and consequently of the ornament. Thus it is that wee see the antique temples portico'd round, and where it makes not a portico, the pillars support the entablement of the roof, which could not stand so foreward had it not the aid of columnes. And in my opinion, pillars without this entablement, usully styled the architrave, freeze and cornish, supposed to be the contignation of a roof, would be as improper as pillars supporting nothing; for where there is no weight but in the upright, there walls, without the superaddition of columnes, are sufficient. It is a usuall thing to turne arches upon single pillars, but, for the foregoing reasons and what follows, in my sence not decorous nor proper. For first, they're too weak for the imployment, secondly the arches are onely apertures in the wall, and therefore what is left besides the aperture shoud be part of the wall, and then all appears firme and good. Those are called peers or pilasters, and are set off with a small cornish, for adorning the arch where it setts on, and that is called the imposts of the arches. Now if you will have pillars, you must superinduce them upon these peers and carry an entablature strait upon the keys of the arches; then will the whole seem firme and fair. Whereas wall and arches upon single pillars is as if it hung in the air, or, as the comon people often say, by geometry, and hath not due support, the pillars seeming weaker than what lys upon them.

This puts me in mind to reproove another error very frequent in great structures otherwise well designed, and that is breaking the entablature, so as it shall project more forewards upon the columns than between them, all which breaks are a defect and should be shunned if possible; for the entablature is supposed a frame of a roof and nothing else, therefore ought to be strait. Much less can I endure when the architrave and freese dy in the upright of the columne, which is the fault of Pauls as it is now designed,[36] wherein the Surveyor hath bin in my opinion most opiniatrely improvident in concealing the designe till it appear'd in the execution, for no eye that hath bin acquainted with good designes but would have relucted at that, and the universall consent would have oblidg'd him to conforme, as now it doth to repent. I must confess in structures so great, where by reason of windoes and doors the intercolumniations are so large that to carry the entableture strait would be difficult, and not practicable without vast stones or massy counterpoises, it may be tollerable to break the tableture, as the case is of the Banqueting house, but to doe it in joynery is nonsense.

It is another error to place the orders of architecture on the inside of rooms. For I thinck they look too gross, and seem useless, because the annoyance of wether, against which they are contrived, comes not there, and whatever is useless is ugly. Sometimes in halls where there are galleries, supporting pillars doe well, the like in churches; but roomes should be uncumber'd and easy distributed onely into decoruous compartiments. Thus much for the use and introduction of collumnes, which, being so proper for the porpose, fall in with every one's fancy, therefore must be agreable and handsome. All the rest is but judgment of too long and too short, which by the critiscisme of ages is setled in the proportions of the knowne orders, upon the foundation I have already layd downe, of strength betwixt the two evils of too much and too litle. The like may be sayd of the entablature upon it, which is adjusted to our hands in the same manner.

As for the bases, capitals and other ornaments of the orders so much pleaded for and so religiously executed, I cannot ascribe such necessity to them; but all the world must agree they are beautyfull, having past censure of times, and nothing since found of equall request. So that I must allow an ingenious architect to vary in those particulars as his judgment prompts; but let him take heed, few in the world have ventured but have succeeded ill, and there is no excuse for going out of the way, when that very thing is a fault in the opinion of most, and to follow the patterne is right, the sence of all; which to mee seems a great consolation to the men of designe, that they are sure to please, if they are not capricious.

In most cases mankind seek beauty as a positive thing, which for the most part rests wholly in opinion without reall ground in nature, and in truth is no more than not deformed. This is much in the business of architecture, wherein fashions change in every country, and all countrys have somewhat distinct that is esteemed good not used by others, which demonstrates the assertion. Therefore a man is weak that in building or finishing doth not follow the fashion of his time and his country. It is most true that things which change seldomest are those that are seldomest renew'd. For cloths that are renew'd quarterly change the fashion almost as often, so beds that are renew'd once in 10 years change in about that period; houses are not renew'd in less than 100 years, therefore the fashion is permanent accordingly; finishing somewhat oftner, but no man need fear outliving his house, at least he will be so old to have outlived his curiosity tho his malice increaseth, which will dispose him to opiniastre upon old fashion against all the world, and thinck to mortifie his enimie, the youth, by dispising their ways.

There is some reason that inclines to affect fashions, and it is that wee are partly acquainted, and not satiated; and as a thing intirely new is not of a suddaine understood, so carrys no enterteinement at first, so a thing that is vulgar is knowne as well without seing, as with it, and there is neither desire nor enterteinment about a thing that wee have had too much of. A mixture of these pleaseth; as when upon an old approv'd ground a new contrivance is superinduc't, and old orders are newly apply'd, and disposed, the mind runs instantly into contemplation of it, and is pleas'd. Besides, that which follows great characters, is thought great and brave, for it is like what such a one hath, for whose greatness and wisdome wee have a reverence and are proud of any thing like him. And after all every particular man hath somewhat singular, and will like this or that by accident or caprice without any account to be given, which leads fashions. These matters occurring my pen drops them, tho they be of a nature too metaphisicall for the instruction of a builder who deals in solids, and also must deal somewhat with humors too or shall have small imployment.

For this reason I will not goe about to give a rationall of all the ornaments, which I hold but a mode or fashion, and are alterable ad libitum without deforming a designe, provided the mode allows it; altho somwhat might be sayd towards it, and yet not upon that excellent basis of man's symmetry, of which I have no sort of opinion. But take the bases, capitalls, ovolys, triglifs, fretts, and other enrichments of the orders, they have bin so much considered, that they are not in any thing absurd, and of all the innovations that I ever saw, they have bin much for the worse. In the transition between the Gothick, and the Regular, which was about King James time or somewhat sooner, they made very bold with the orders, and put stockins[37] on to the pillars, and wringled them, breaking the measures very much in the intableture, making odd crotesque ornaments every where, which are most fulsome; a speciall instance of this is in the Scools at Oxford, where over one of the avenues within are the 5 orders plac't in proper degrees, but so ill handled, that it is a shame;[38] tho I must confess the designe was very suitable for an academy. For these reasons lett an architect have a care of varying, for if he doth it well he is at mercy, and it is great odds but he will doe ill; at most it is his buissness not more to excell, than to avoid blame and the handles to it. [...]

[...] [T]he method and economy of the orders or Regular building are originally derived from wood, which in very truth by reason of the straitness, and shape is most butyfull, by rendring all more polite and fancifull, as the ingenious and ignorant together have bin pleased to vary the methods in their different ways.

That which I had in my thoughts during the insertion of a few of the last lines to reflect upon, is that which wee call a strait arch, much used in Regular building, and absolutely necessary, because the entableture must be strait, but is the great defect of Regular building, especially in great proportions, wherein, by reason that vast materialls cannot be had, and then scarce manageable and at last the weight overcome[s] its owne strength, it is almost impracticable. Therefore architects fall into those mean shifts of breaking the orders or heiths into two or more, whereas in no height ought there to be above one columne. And then also they break the entableture, to rest it upon the wall, because they cannot secure it streight. And yet after all these devices they are forc't to cramp all with lead and iron, so that such works are not so much masonry, as blacksmiths work, and not courses of stone but frames of iron. In short such is the mortality of a flat arch, that I have seen few of any considerable width but have gaped, and for the most part failed. The best in the world I beleeve will be in Pauls, especially over the doors of the north and south iles, in which I very well know, what iron and lead, besides the work of perforating the stones, hath bin employed to the fixing of them.[39]

Yet after all I must needs allow that the flatt arch is the most beautyfull part of the Regular building and cannot but lament the imperfection of it, that as it is derived from the strait lying of wood, which is corruptible, it is not as easily effected in all demensions, in the most durable stone.

Anthony Ashley Cooper, Lord Shaftesbury, from 'A Letter concerning Design' (1714)

Anthony Ashley Cooper, 3rd Lord Shaftesbury (1671–1713), was born in London and educated at Winchester College under the supervision of the Empiricist philosopher John Locke. He travelled in Europe and entered Parliament in 1700, but had to retire from public life because of ill-health. In 1711 he went to live in Naples, where he died. The philosophical and literary heir to the Cambridge Platonists, he devoted himself in his retirement to moral philosophy and aesthetics. His essays were collected in *Characteristicks of Men, Manners, Opinions and Times,* first published in London in 1711 and widely read; the 'Letter concerning Design', however, although finished in 1712, was first published in the second, much revised edition of *Characteristicks* of 1714.

Further reading: Downes (1984).

[...] [p. 400] As for Architecture, 'tis no wonder if so many noble Designs of this kind have miscarry'd amongst us; since the Genius of our Nation has hitherto been so little turn'd this way, that thro' several Reigns we have patiently seen the noblest publick Buildings perish (if I may say so) under the hand of one single Court-Architect;[40] who, if he had been able to profit by Experience, wou'd long since, at our expence, have prov'd the greatest

Master in the World. But I question whether our Patience is like to hold much longer. The Devastation so long committed in this kind, has made us begin to grow rude and clamorous at the hearing of a new Palace spoilt, or a new Design committed to some rash or impotent Pretender.

'Tis the good Fate of our Nation in this particular, that there remain yet two of the noblest Subjects for Architecture; our Prince's *Palace*, and our *House* of *Parliament*. For I can't but fancy that when *Whitehall* is thought of, the neighbouring *Lords* and *Commons* will at the same time be plac'd in better Chambers and Apartments, than at present; were it only for Majesty's sake, and as a Magnificence becoming the Person of the Prince, who here appears in full Solemnity. Nor do I fear that when these new Subjects are attempted, we shou'd miscarry as grosly as we have done in others before. Our *State*, in this respect, may prove perhaps more fortunate than our *Church*, in having waited till a national Taste was form'd, before these Edifices were undertaken. But the Zeal of the Nation cou'd not, it seems, admit so long a Delay in their Ecclesiastical Structures, particularly their *Metropolitan*. And since a Zeal of this sort has been newly kindl'd amongst us, 'tis like we shall see from afar the many Spires arising in our great City, with such hasty and sudden growth, as may be the occasion perhaps that our immediate Relish shall be hereafter censur'd, as retaining much of what Artists call the *Gothick* Kind.

Hardly, indeed, as the Publick now stands, shou'd we bear to see a *Whitehall* treated like a *Hampton-Court*, or even a new Cathedral like St. PAUL'S. Almost every-one now becomes concern'd, and interests himself in such publick Structures. Even those Pieces too are brought under the common Censure, which, tho rais'd by private Men, are of such a Grandure and Magnificence, as to become National Ornaments. The ordinary Man may build his Cottage, or the plain Gentleman his Country-house according as he fansys: but when a great Man builds, he will find little Quarter fom the Publick, if instead of a beautiful Pile, he raises, at a vast expence, such a false and counterfeit Piece of Magnificence, as can be justly arraign'd for its Deformity by so many knowing Men in Art, and by the whole *People*, who, in such a Conjuncture, readily follow their Opinion.

In reality *the People* are no small Partys in this *Cause*. Nothing moves successfully without 'em. There can be no PUBLICK, but where they are included. And without a *Publick Voice*, knowingly guided and directed, there is nothing which can raise a true Ambition in the Artist; nothing which can exalt the Genius of the Workman, or make him emulous of after-Fame, and of the approbation of his *Country*, and of *Posterity*. For with *these* he naturally, as a *Freeman*, must take part: in *these* he has a passionate Concern, and Interest, rais'd in him by the same Genius of *Liberty*, the same *Laws* and *Government*, by which his Property, and the Rewards of his Pains and Industry are secur'd to him, and to his Generation after him.

Every thing co-operates, in such a *State*, towards the Improvement of *Art* and *Science*. And for the *designing Arts* in particular, such as *Architecture, Painting*, and *Statuary*, they are in a manner link'd together. The Taste of one kind brings necessarily that of the others along with it. When the *free* Spirit of a Nation turns it-self this way, Judgments are form'd; Criticks arise; a right Taste prevails, and in a manner forces its way. Nothing is so improving, nothing so natural, so *con-genial* to the liberal Arts, as that reigning Liberty and high Spirit of a People, which from the Habit of judging in the highest Matters for themselves, makes 'em freely judge of other Subjects, and enter thorowly into the Characters as well of *Men* and *Manners*, as of the *Products* or *Works* of Men, in Art and Science. So much, my Lord, do we owe to the Excellence of our National Constitution, and Legal Monarchy; happily fitted for Us, and which alone cou'd hold together so mighty a People; all sharers (tho at so far a distance from each other) in the Government of *themselves*; and meeting under *one* Head in *one* vast *Metropolis*; whose enormous Growth, however censurable in other respects, is actually a Cause that Workmanship and Arts of so many kinds arise to such perfection.

What Encouragement our higher Powers may think fit to give these growing Arts, I will not pretend to guess. This I know, that 'tis so much for their advantage and Interest to make themselves the chief Partys in the Cause, that I wish no Court or Ministry, besides a truly virtuous and wise one, may ever concern themselves in the Affair. For shou'd they do so, they wou'd in reality do more harm than good; since 'tis not the Nature of a Court (such as Courts generally are) to improve, but rather corrupt a *Taste*. And what is in the beginning set wrong by their Example, is hardly ever afterwards recoverable in the Genius of a Nation.

Content therefore I am, my Lord, that BRITAIN stands in this respect as she now does. Nor can one, methinks, with just reason regret her having hitherto made no greater advancement in these affairs of Art. As her *Constitution* has grown, and been establish'd, she has in proportion fitted her-self for other Improvements. There has been no Anticipation in the Case. And in this surely she must be esteem'd wise, as well as happy, that ere she attempted to raise her-self any other Taste or Relish, she secur'd her-self a right one in *Government*. She has now the advantage of beginning in other Matters, on a new foot. She has her *Models* yet to seek, her *Scale* and *Standard* to form, with deliberation and good choice. Able enough she is at present to shift for her-self; however abandon'd or helpless she has been left by those whom it became to assist her. Hardly, indeed, cou'd she procure a single *Academy* for the training of her Youth in Exercises. As good Soldiers as we are, and as good Horses as our Climate affords, our Princes, rather than expend their Treasure this way, have suffer'd our Youth to pass into a foreign Nation, to learn to ride. As for other *Academys*, such as those for Painting, Sculpture, or

Architecture, we have not so much as heard of the Proposal; whilst the Prince of our Rival Nation raises Academys, breeds Youth, and sends Rewards and Pensions into foreign Countrys, to advance the interest and Credit of his own.[41] Now if, notwithstanding the Industry and Pains of this foreign Court, and supine Un-concernedness of our own, the National Taste however rises, and already shews it-self in many respects beyond that of or so highly-assisted Neighbours; what greater Proof can there be of the Superiority of Genius in one of these Nations above the other?

Colen Campbell, from the Introduction to his *Vitruvius Britannicus* (1715)

Colen Campbell (1676–1729) was in his early life a lawyer in Scotland. Very little is known about his education, but he probably visited Italy. It is not clear how he became an architect, but he was associated, perhaps as a pupil, with the Scottish architect James Smith (*c.* 1645–1731), whom he described in *Vitruvius Britannicus* as the most experienced architect in Scotland. He made his name as the chief propagandist of the Neo-Palladian movement in Britain. *Vitruvius Britannicus* was conceived in 1713 as an anonymous printseller's survey, the successor to William Kip's *Britannia Illustrata* of 1707, but with plans and elevations instead of perspective views. By means of his selection of architects and buildings (his rival Thomas Archer, for instance, was not included) Campbell made what was presented as an unbiased representation of modern British architecture into both an advertisement for his own work, and a proclamation of the superiority of Palladianism and Inigo Jones, whose works, both genuine and attributed, took a large place in the three volumes (Harris, 1990). To give some idea of the way the plates in *Vitruvius Britannicus* represented this building in a highly abstract way, his plate of the Banqueting House is reprinted here together with a view by William Marlow showing its actual situation *c.* 1775 (see Figures 5.13 and 5.14).

The Introduction

The general Esteem that Travellers have for Things that are Foreign, is in nothing more conspicuous than with Regard to Building. We travel, for the most part, at an Age more apt to be imposed upon by the Ignorance or Partiality of others, than to judge truly of the Merit of Things by the Strength of Reason. It's owing to this Mistake in Education, that so many of the *British* Quality have so mean an Opinion of what is performed in our own Country; tho', perhaps, in most we equal, and in some Things we surpass, our Neighbours.

I have therefore judged, it would not be improper to publish this Collection, which will admit of a fair Comparison with the best of the Moderns. As to the Antiques, they are out of the Question; and, indeed, the Italians themselves have now no better Claim to them than they have to the Purity of the Latin.

We must, in Justice, acknowledge very great Obligations to those Restorers of *Architecture*, which the Fifteenth and Sixteenth *Centurys* produced in Italy.

5.13 · Colen Campbell, *Vitruvius Britannicus or the British Architect* … (London, 1715), façade of the Banqueting House, Whitehall, drawing by Campbell

Bramante, Barbaro, Sansovino, Sangallo, Michael Angelo, Raphael Urbin, Julio Romano, Serglio [*sic*], *Labaco, Scamozzi,* and many others, who have greatly help'd to raise this Noble Art from the Ruins of Barbarity: But above all, the great *Palladio,* who has exceeded all that were gone before him, and surpas'd his contemporaries, whose ingenious Labours will eclipse many, and rival most of the Ancients. And indeed, this excellent Architect seems to have arrived to a *Ne plus ultra* of his Art. With him the great Manner and exquisite Taste of Building is lost; for the *Italians* can no more now relish the Antique Simplicity, but are entirely employed in capricious Ornament, which must at last end in the *Gothick.*

For Proof of this Assertion, I appeal to the Productions of the *Last Century*: How affected and licentious are the Works of *Bernini* and *Fontana*? How wildly Extravagant are the Designs of *Boromini,* who has endeavoured to debauch Mankind with his odd and chimerical Beauties, where the Parts are without Proportion; Solids without their true Bearing, Heaps of Materials without Strength, excessive Ornament without Grace, and the Whole without Symmetry? And what can be a stronger Argument, that this excellent Art is near lost in that Country, when such Absurdities meet with Applause?

It is then with the renowned *Palladio* that we enter the lists to whom we oppose the famous Inigo Jones: Let the *Banquetting-House,* those excellent

5.14 William Marlow, *Whitehall* (*c.* 1775), oil on canvas, 71.1 × 91.1 cm, Yale Center for British Art, Paul Mellon Collection

pieces at *Greenwich*, with many other Things of this great Master, be carefully examined, and I doubt not but an impartial Judge will find in them all the Regularity of the former, with an addition of Beauty and Majesty, in which our *Architect* is esteemed to have out-done all that went before; and when those Designs he gave for *Whitehall*, are published, which I intend in the second Volume, I believe all Mankind will agree with me, that there is no Palace in the World to rival it.

And here I cannot but reflect on the Happiness of the British Nation, that at present abounds with so many learned and ingenious *Gentlemen*, as Sir *Christopher Wren*, Sir *William Bruce*, Sir *John Vanbrugh*, Mr. *Archer*, Mr. *Wren*, Mr. *Wynne*, Mr. *Talman*, Mr. *Hawksmoor*, Mr. *James* &c. who have all greatly contributed to adorn our Island with their curious Labours, and are daily embellishing it more.

I hope, therefore, the Reader will be agreeably entertained in viewing what I have collected with so much Labour. All the Drawings were either taken from the Buildings themselves, or the original Designs of the Architects, who have very much assisted me in advancing this Work; and I can, with great Sincerity, assure the Publick, That I have used the utmost Care to render it acceptable [...].

James Ralph (attr.), from *A Critical Review of the Publick Buildings, Statues and Ornaments, In and about London and Westminster* (1734)

The *Critical Review of the Publick Buildings ... In and About London* appeared from 20 October 1733 to 6 April 1734 in the *Weekly Register* as essays; they were also issued as a separate pamphlet in 1734, with a dedication to Lord Burlington and a prefatory 'Essay on Taste in General', also originally published in the *Weekly Register*, in 1731. Although Ralph very much admired Palladianism and Lord Burlington, he was not associated with him; instead, his aim was to reform the taste of his age through close criticism of public building and statues. His criticism is based on liberty, not reason. He was a man of the theatre, not a practising architect, and he was much more interested in the impact of a building on the spectator and in grand, uninterrupted vistas than in practicalities or rational design. The *Critical Review* received much attention but little approval, both because of Ralph's lack of architectural expertise (a criticism voiced by Robert Morris) and because of his support for Italian architecture (as in Batty Langley's articles for the *Grub Street Journal*) (Harris, 1990).

(Harris, 1990; see also the note on Ralph in Chapter 1, above.)

[Dedication, to Lord Burlington] At a time, my Lord, when so much money is lavish'd in building, and too often with so little pretence to beauty, or magnificence, it could not be unseasonable to publish some hints on a subject so frequently employ'd, and so seldom understood: I grant, indeed, if buildings could be read as easily as books, there would be no need of any comments of mine, and your Lordship's plans would be of more service to the world, than the most refin'd speculations. But as few have a talent of laying out their fortunes with propriety, or making their own private judgment a publick ornament, I have ventur'd to warn them of the danger of attempting what they are not equal to, or declaring their weakness at their own expence.

Folly in building is one of the most lasting reflections on a man's character, because 'tis not only universally known in his own time, but is often perpetuated thro' many generations.

It is incumbent, therefore, on every man of quality and fortune, to weigh very seriously every undertaking of this nature, and not precipitate himself into an expence, that can neither convenience, or grandeur can justify.

The way to do this most effectually, is to consult the models your Lordship has oblig'd the publick with, and then they will learn that beauty is first founnded in simplicity, and harmony; and magnificence in propriety of ornament, and nobleness of imagination.

Preface. Being An Essay on Taste

[p. i] What we understand by taste, is the peculiar relish that we feel for any agreeable object; and is more or less perfect, according to the degree of judgment we employ in distinguishing its beauties. It ought always to be founded on truth, or veri-similitude at least; but we often find it to be only the child of opinion, or the mere result of accident. [...] Truth, should be considered as the design in painting; and beauty, the colouring and decoration. Falsehood and deformity, are the contrasts of the groupe; and to be able to detect the one, we should be capable of admiring the other.

A Critical Review of the Publick Buildings, Statues and Ornaments of London and Westminster

[p. 5] No nation can reproach us for want of expence in our publick buildings, but all nations may for our want of elegance and discernment in the execution. In the first place, there are very few of our fine pieces of architecture in sight; they are generally hid in holes and corners, as if they had been built by stealth, or the artists were asham'd of their works: or else they are but essays, or trials of skill, and remain unfinished, till time himself lays them in ruins. After this, 'tis unnecessary to mention that our structures are generally heavy, disproportioned, and rather incumbered than adorned: beauty does not consist in expence, or decoration; 'tis possible for a slight building to be very perfect, and a costly one to be very deformed [...].

To begin with the remotest extremity of the town: as there were no attempts, till lately, ever made there, to erect any building which might adorn it all, there was the more necessity to be more particularly careful that the first design of this nature should not miscarry; and yet the four following churches which have been built at *Limehouse*, *Ratcliff*, *Horsley-down*, and *Spittle-fields*, tho' they have all the advantage of ground which can be desired, are not to be looked at without displeasure. They are mere Gothique heaps of stone, without form or order; and meet with contempt from the best and worst tastes alike. The last, especially, deserves the severest condemnation, in that 'tis built at a monstrous expence, and yet is, beyond question, one of the most absurd piles in *Europe*. [...]

[p. 17] The grand cathedral of St. *Paul*'s is undoubtedly one of the most magnificent modern buildings in *Europe*; all the parts of which 'tis compos'd are superlatively beautiful and noble; the north and south fronts in particular are very perfect pieces of architecture, neither ought the east to go without due applause. The two spires at the west end are in a finis'd taste, and the portico with the ascent, and the dome that rises in the centre of the whole, afford a very august and surprizing prospect; but still, with all these beauties, it has certainly yet more defects; and the pleasure we receive from the first is so much qualified and tam'd by the last, that we rather wonder how we can be pleased so much, than why we are so displeased at all. [...]

In the first place therefore, there is a most notorious deficience in point of view; such a huge fabrick as St. *Paul*'s ought at least to be survey'd at the distance of *Temple-Bar*, and the vista ought to be considerably wider than the front of the building. But is so far from the case here, that we can't see it till we are upon it, and this defect is still made worse by turning the edifice from the eye even where it can be view'd, for the sake of that ridiculous superstition of erecting it due east and west. In the next place, the dividing the portico, and indeed the whole structure into two stories on the outside, certainly indicates a like division within: a circumstance abounding with absurdities, and defeating even the very end of erecting it at all. If indeed the architect had been embarrass'd to reconcile the distance and height of his columns, I am humbly of opinion that a light and proper *Attick* story had answer'd all ends both of use and beauty, and left him room to have enlarged his imagination, and have given an air of majesty to the whole: let me add that I apprehend the portico should have been farther projected on the eye, instead of retreating from it, in order to have given a grand contraste to the whole front, and aided the perspective within.

I shall say no more on the outside than this, that according to my best notions of regularity and order, the dome should have been raised exactly in the centre of the whole, and that there should have been two corresponding steeples at the east as well as the west end, with all other suitable decorations: if a view of the whole length of the building too could have been opened to the water-side, it would have added greatly to its grandeur and magnificence, and have afforded a most noble prospect from off the river into the bargain. However odd or new the first of these propositions may seem, let any body take a view of St. *Paul*'s from any of the neighbouring hills, and they will instantly discern that the building is defective, and that the form of a cross is more favourable to superstition than beauty: in a word, they will easily see at least, that the dome, in its present circumstance, is abundantly too big for the rest of the pile, and that the west end has no rational pretence to finer and more splendid decorations than the east. [...]

Whoever understands the nature of publick ornamental buildings critically, always lays it down for a rule, that they cannot be too expensive or magnificent; for which reason St. *Paul*'s is so far from being admir'd for being so grand and august as it is, that nothing is more common than to hear it censur'd for not being more so. Every body knows that the fund which raised it from its ruins to its present glory, was equal to any design of beauty or majesty; and as those who had it in trust went so far towards this necessary end, 'tis a thousand pities they did not carry it on much further, and make this pile not only the ornament of *Britain*, but the admiration and envy of all *Europe*. St. *Peter*'s at *Rome* was already built; a model which the most finish'd architect need not have been ashamed to imitate, and as all its particular beauties have been long publickly known and admir'd, I think it was incumbent on us to have equall'd it at least; and if we had excell'd it too, it would have been reasonably expected from such a nation as ours, and such a genius as *Wren*.

On such principles it is that men of taste and understanding are surpriz'd at entring this church, to see so many faults, and miss so many beauties: they discover at once that it wants elevation to give it a proportionable grandeur, and length to assist the perspective: that the columns are heavy and clumsy to a prodigious degree, and rather incumber the prospect, than enrich it with symmetry and beauty: half the necessary breaks of light and shadow are hereby wanting, and half the perspective in general cut off: at the same time I don't deny but many parts of the decoration are exceedingly grand and noble, and demand very justly a sincere applause. The dome is without question a very stupendous fabrick, and strikes the eye with an astonishing pleasure: 'tis indeed one of those happy kinds of building that please all kinds of people alike, from the most ignorant clown up to the most accomplish'd gentleman: but yet even here the judge cannot help taking notice that it bears no proportion to the rest of the building, and that after you have seen this, you can look at no other part of it; whereas a judicious builder would husband his imagination, and still have something in reserve to delight the mind, tho' nothing perhaps could be contriv'd to surprize after it.

For example, the very nature of a choir would not admit of any thing so marvellous as the dome, yet it might have relieved the eye with something equivalently beautiful; the entrance in front might have been more noble and uniform; either compos'd of wood entirely, or marble; for the present mixture of both makes a disagreeable piece of patch-work, that rather disgusts than entertains: the opening on the inside thro' the present beautiful range of stalls, might have terminated in a much more magnificent alcove than we see there at present, adorn'd with all the elegance and profusion of decoration: the altar should have been rais'd of the richest marble in the most expensive taste; that it might have been of a piece with the rest of the church, and terminated the view of the whole, with all the graces of the most luxuriant imagination. All the intermediate spaces should have been fill'd up with the noblest historical paintings; all the majesty of frize-work, cornices, heighten'd with the most costly gildings, should have been lavish'd to adorn it; and one grand flow of magnificent curtain depended from the windows, to finish and adorn the same.

Notes

Introduction

1. For a recent overview of the Vitruvian tradition see Hart and Hicks (1998), and Kruft (1994); for a long time, the standard interpretation of Renaissance architectural theory has been Rudolf Wittkower's *Architectural Principles in the Age of Humanism*, first published in 1948, with many reprints. This interpretation has been revised by Smith (1992) and Payne (1999).
2. Cf. *Oxford English Dictionary*, s.v. Theory, Pauly (1975), s.v. *Theoria*, and Rutherford (1995), pp. 225–8.

1 The nature of architecture

1. On classical and mediaeval classifications of the arts see Kristeller (1980); for their role in architectural theory, see van Eck (1998).
2. L. B. Alberti, *On Painting*, Book I; *On the Art of Building*, Prologue.
3. Giorgio Vasari, *Lives of the Painters, Sculptors and Architects*, trans. Gaston du C. de Vere, introduction and notes D. Ekserdjian, London: Everyman, 1996 [1st publ. 1927], 'Author's Preface to the Whole Work' (vol. I, pp. 245–57).
4. See for instance the Prologue to Alberti's *On the Art of Building* of 1486, or Daniel Barbaro's series of definitions of architecture in terms of the liberal arts in Book I of his 1567 edition of Vitruvius.
5. See Wittkower (1971) and Barkan (1975).
6. See Lee (1967); on Academic teaching see Pevsner (1940) and Goldstein (1996).
7. See Summers (1977).
8. See Vickers (1988).
9. See Peacock (1990).
10. See below, introduction to Chapter 2, on 'Building'.
11. [Note in margin:] An Obiection.
12. [Note in margin:] An Answer. Principals: the first principles that govern all becoming and passing away on Earth. See Aristotle, *Metaphysics*, Book I.
13. Leo Baptista Albertus: Leon Battista Alberti (1404–72), whose *On the Art of Building* (completed largely in the 1450s and first published in Latin in Florence in 1486), is the first Renaissance treatise on architecture.
14. Vitruvius, *Ten Books on Architecture*, I.i.
15. Ctesibus was an inventor who flourished *c.* 270 BC in Alexandria. He was the first to make pneumatic devices. His work is now lost, but descriptions are preserved among others by Vitruvius. Archimedes was a mathematician and inventor who lived *c.* 287 to 212 or 211 BC. Several of his works survived in Greek or Arabic.
16. Ambries: sounding vessels.
17. For this list of ancient architects see Vitruvius I.i, and the commentary by Ingrid Rowland in her edition of Vitruvius.
18. In the Prologue to his *Art of Building*.
19. [Note in margin:] The immaterialitie of perfect Architecture.

20. Cf. Alberti, *On the Art of Building*, I.i.
21. Plato, *Republic*, 259[c].
22. *Naupegie*: ship building.
23. Bederoll: bead-roll, long list of names or catalogues (*OED*).
24. Grataroli here illustrates how to construct a mental image of a house containing ten mnemonic places.
25. Summerson (1957), p. 219.
26. Vitruvius, *Ten Books on Architecture*, I.1: 'Reasoning, however, is what can demonstrate and explain the proportions of complicated works skillfully and systematically.'
27. Vitruvius, *Ten Books on Architecture*, I.2: 'Shapeliness (*eurythmia*) is an attractive appearance and coherent aspect in the composition of the elements. It is achieved when the elements of the project are proportional in height to width, length to breadth, and every element corresponds in its dimensions to the total measure of the whole.'
28. Civil discipline: corpus of doctrine or branch of learning that has to do with well-bred and educated life, polite society, public utility or the commonwealth.
29. Pheidias (*c.* 490–430 BC) was a Greek sculptor who carved a statue of Zeus commissioned by the great pan-Hellenic sanctuary of Olympia near Elis (470 BC), which is now lost, and only known from coins and a description in Pausanias' *Description of Greece*, V.xi.10.
30. Zeuxis (fl. late 5th century BC – early 4th century) was a Greek painter, working in Athens; none of his paintings survive, but many anecdotes about his work are preserved in Pliny's *Natural History*, XXXV.
31. [Author's note in margin:] vide cap. 18, lib. 2.
32. Vitruvius, *Ten Books on Architecture*, I.2. See also VII.5.
33. Leon Battista Alberti, *On Painting*, p. 90.
34. Vitruvius, *Ten Books on Architecture*, III.1.i. *Commodulatio* is the shared or common adaptation of parts to a standard unit of measurement.
35. Constantine the Great (Flavius Valerius Constantinus, *c.* AD 272/3–337) became Roman Emperor in 312. With his conversion to Christianity that religion became the official religion of the Roman Empire. Giotto (di Bondone, born in Vespignano near Florence *c.* 1267–75, died in Florence in 1337), painter and designer, was presented already during his lifetime not only as the first painter to revive art after the decline that had begun with the reign of Constantine, but also as the first since the Ancients to imitate nature so well that he deceived the viewers of his work. It is not clear who is meant by Andrino di Edesia. It may be a misspelling of a Greek or Roman name mentioned in Pliny's *Natural History* in a mediaeval manuscript. I am very grateful to Sara Blake McHam for this suggestion.
36. Operative arts: Aristotle distinguished between the theoretical, poetical and productive arts. The first (theology, mathematics) are concerned with pure learning, the first principles of everything under the sun; the second, also called operative arts, with producing lasting works, including for instance poetry and architecture; the last with doing things, such as dancing. See Aristotle, *Nicomachean Ethics*, 1140a.
37. Contignation: joining together of beams and bonds; every conjoined structure; a floor, storey or stage (*OED*).
38. Fancy: imagination; the process, and the power, of forming mental representations of things not present to the senses, chiefly applied to the so-called creative or productive imagination (*OED*).
39. Iconography: see Vitruvius I.ii, where the species of design are listed as ichnography (plan), orthography (elevation) and scenography, 'the shaded rendering of the front and receding sides as the latter converge on a point', i.e. perspectival drawing.
40. Rickets: rachitis, a disease caused by Vitamin D deficiency, which can lead to deformations of the body.
41. Zanfoin: i.e. sainfoin, a low-growing perennial herb (*Onobrychis sativa*), much grown as a forage plant (*OED*).
42. Cf. North, *Of Building*, p. 10. On fol. 11 of the British Library manuscript used by Colvin and Harris, this interlocutor is identified as Sir Christopher Wren.
43. North is here referring to the Aristotelian doctrine of the three unities of action which should be

observed in drama (cf. Aristotle's *Poetics*, 5.23–4, and Horace's *Ars Poetica*). In the sixteenth and seventeenth centuries drama critics in Italy, France and England, such as Castelvetro (*Poetica d'Aristotele vulgarizzata e sposta* of 1541) and Dryden (*Essay of Dramatic Poetry* of 1668/1684), added to Aristotle's recommendation of unity of action those of place and time for the sake of verisimilitude. See Weinberg (1961). This is somewhat elaborated in another part of the manuscript BL Add. MS 32540, fols. 43v–44r: 'And first I observe, that there is in the very shape of a fabrick somewhat, which in a person we call an air, and falls under no rule, but is studyed by painters with practise and examples and not precept; this where it happens (for it very often casuall, and seldome produc'd otherwise, than from example or patterne) delights the eye no less at distance, than neer hand, and shall be so conspicuous by the meer tour of the outline, which onely is distinguish't farr off, that however confused, and small it seems, the understanding shall pronounce it great.'

44. Cf. Wittkower (1971), pp. 101–42; on Morris see pp. 145 and 151 in Wittkower.

2 Building

1. See Colvin (1993).
2. Pulchruse: beautiful, fair.
3. Cesarius: Cesare Cesariano (1476/8–1543), the editor of the first published Italian edition of Vitruvius' Latin text (1521), with marginal notes and 119 plates: *Di Lucio Vitruvio Pollione de Architectura*. Shute is here referring to the opening section of Book I of *De Architectura*.
4. Sebastian Serli: Sebastiano Serlio. Shute is referring to the first chapters of the Second Book of his treatise, in which he discusses perspective.
5. Bondage: see Vitruvius, I.iv.
6. Lets: hindrances.
7. Waynie: by the waggon-load.
8. Veriuce: verjuice, the juice of unripe grapes.
9. Latine Georgickes: The *Georgics*, a didactic poem on husbandry by the Latin poet Publius Vergilius Maro, 70–19 BC.
10. Cato: Marcus Porcius Cato (234–149 BC), Roman politician, orator and author of *De Agri Cultura* of *c*. 169 BC.
11. Mounts: elevations on which to place cannon or guns; angles; projections (*OED*).
12. Norwood was a teacher of mathematics and a surveyor, who published *Trigonometrie, or the Doctrine of Triangles* in 1631 and *The Seaman's Practice* in 1637. It is not clear who Ward and Chrisso were.
13. *Enchiridion of Fortification, or a handfull of Knowledge in Martiall Affaires*, by Nicholas Stone, London, 1645.
14. These were all cities or castles besieged during the Civil War. See for instance Kishlansky, 1996, pp. 134–87.
15. Tyre was a famous seaport in ancient Phoenicia (now Lebanon); Rochell is La Rochelle on the French coast.
16. Champion Countrey: campaign country, an expanse of level open country; battlefield (*OED*).
17. A petard was a small bomb made of a metal or wooden box filled with powder, used to blow in a door or make a hole in a wall (*OED*).
18. Rasat: from French *rasant*, a term used in fortification: sweeping, grazing or glancing.
19. Com-case: comb case.
20. Perstringged: from to perstringe, to bind tightly, draw together, constrain.
21. The City Hall on the Dam in Amsterdam (now the Royal Palace), designed by Jacob van Campen, which was begun in 1648.
22. It is easy to add to that which has already been invented.
23. Lymne: lime.

24. Vinculum: bond or binding agent.
25. Chyle: the white milky fluid formed by the action of the pancreatic juice and the bile, and contained in the lymphatics of the intestines; fluid in the intestines just before absorption of food (*OED*).
26. Cf. L. Pascoli's Life of Pozzo in his *Vite de'pittori scultori ed architetti moderni*, vol. II (Rome, 1736), p. 192: 'Piu prodigiosa pero di tutti mi pare la prospettiva, la quale ingannando a suo piacere la vista ci tira a vedere qual che non e, e fa cadere su' nostri sensi cioche poscia veduto, o da piu vicino, o da piu diverso punto non trova' ('But perspective seems to me to be most wonderful, because deceiving vision at its will it draws the eye to see what does not exist, and makes perceptible whatever can be seen, either from very close, or from various points of view'). And cf. Pascoli's remark on rhetoric: ' ... all'energia dell'eloquenza [...] che si gloria di trarre il cuore dell'uome ovunque vole, e di movere lo al suo arbitrio all'ira, al diletto, allo sdegno, e all'amore' (' ... the vividness of eloquence, which prides itself on drawing a man's heart wherever it wants, and on moving his judgement to anger, disdain or love'), quoted by W. Oechslin in Battisti (1996), p. 192. There was a long tradition of rejecting the use of linear perspective in architectural drawing because it is impossible to calculate the exact dimensions of a design from a perspectival drawing; see for instance Alberti, *On the Art of Building*, II.i, pp. 33–4. In this passage, however, the deceit is turned into a rhetorical strategy through which the eye is drawn to the true vanishing point of all creation, God.
27. Cf. the original : ' ... al vero punto dell'occhio che è la Gloria Divina'.
28. William Earl of Pembroke: William Herbert, 3rd Earl of Pembroke (1580–1630); patron of the arts who supported Ben Jonson and who perhaps sent Jones to Italy at his expense.
29. Ben. Johnson: Ben Jonson (*c.* 1572–1637), poet and playwright. He collaborated with Jones in the creation and production of court masques from 1605 to 1631, when the two men fell out. For D'Avenant see Chapter 1, above, on Hobbes, 'Answer to Davenant's Preface to *Gondibert*'.
30. See the extract from Jones's *Stone-Heng Restored* in Chapter 4, below.
31. Wenceslaus Hollar (1607–77) was a Bohemian etcher, illustrator and draughtsman, who spent the major part of his working life in England, where he arrived in 1636 in the company of Lord Arundel, the patron of Inigo Jones.
32. See the entry on Batty Langley in Chapter 1, above.

3 Architecture and religion

1. Joseph Mede, 'What is Holinesse', (1650), p. 63.
2. Contignation: a structure formed by, or joining together, timber, specifically a floor or stage so formed; the joining together of beams or boards (*OED*).
3. Psalms 32.3.
4. Job 20.11.
5. Job 6.12. Loam is a kind of clay, in particular a composition of moisturized clay and sand with an admixture of horse-dung, chopped straw and the like, used in making bricks or plastering walls (*OED*).
6. Jeremiah 17.5.
7. Psalms 38.10.
8. Isaiah 59.10.
9. Exodus 3.5.
10. Hebrews 3.5.
11. Psalms 132.13.
12. Loame of flesh: a plastering or dressing of flesh.
13. A piece of land assigned as part of a parish clergyman's living (*OED*).
14. Secular possessions, especially the property and revenues of a religious foundation or of an ecclesiastic (*OED*).

15. Artificious plasme: from the Greek *plasma*, a thing moulded or formed, here used in the sense of 'a mould or matrix in which something is cast or formed', such as shells. Lucy Gent has argued that Hawkins's use of this term to describe the relation between a house and its inhabitant, which is based on a perfect fit between the actual shape of the body and its dwelling, is fundamentally different from the Vitruvian view of architecture as based on an abstract system of mathematical proportion. See Gent (1995a), p. 387.

16. The same train of thought runs through the fragment from Gerbier's *Counsel and Advise to All Builders* included in Chapter 2, above.

17. Comlines: comeliness or beauty.

18. Cf. Alberti, *On the Art of Building*, V.17 and 18.

19. [Author's note:] 3. Reg. 8.

20. [Author's note:] Prov. 86.

21. Ovid, *Metamorphoses*.

22. That is, the sanctuary of Zeus at Olympia. See Pausanias (1971), pp. 222–34.

23. [Author's note in the margin:] Lib. 9 Epist. 7. Saint Gregory is Gregory the Great (*c.* AD 540–604), who was Pope from 590. He sent Saint Augustine (d. between 604 and 609), subsequently Archbishop of Canterbury, in 596 to England to lead a mission. Saint Mellitus (d. 624) was also an Archbishop of Canterbury. The quotation from Saint Gregory's letter actually reads: 'Aqua benedicta fiat, in eisdem fanis aspergatur, altera construantur, reliquiae ponentur, quia, si fana eadem bene constructa sunt, necesse est ut a cultu daemonum in obsequio veri Dei deberant commutari, ut, dum gens ipsa eadem fana sua non videt destrui, de cordu èrrorem deponat at Deum verum cognoscans ac adorans ad loca quae consuevit familiarius concurrat' (*Sancti Gregorii Magni Registrum Epistolorum Libri VIII–XIV*, Epistle XI.56, in Norberg, 1982). See the translation in Markus (1997): '[...] that by no means the shrines of idols in that nation should be destroyed, but only the idols within. Let holy water be sprinkled on these shrines, altars be constructed, relics be placed, so that the shrines, if they be well built, might be converted from the cult of demons to the worship of the true God. Thus when the people see that their shrines have not been destroyed, they will banish error from their hearts and recognizing and adoring the true God, they will be more inclined to come to the place they are accustomed to [...]' (see Markus, 1997, pp. 180–83).

24. [Author's note in the margin:] Lib. 12 de Rep. Cap. 22. The reference is to Pierre Grégoire (1540–1617), *De republica libri six et viginti*, Francoforti: ex officina Paltermiana, sumptibus Petri Fischeri, 1597.

25. [Author's note in the margin:] Lib. 3 de Cultu Sanctorum cap. 3. Saint Robert Bellarmine (Roberto Francesco Romolo, 1542–1621) was a theologian and controversialist. He spent much of his life in trying to vanquish Protestantism by means of argument instead of dogmatic assertion and abuse. James I engaged in correspondence with him.

26. [Author's note in the margin:] Laert. In Vita eius. Diogenes Laertius was the author of a collection of biographies of philosophers, the *Lives of Eminent Philosophers* (third century AD), which included a life of the Cynic Diogenes, a contemporary of Alexander the Great. A passage in the life of Zeno (VII.148), in which it is asserted that 'the substance of God is declared by Zeno to be the whole world', comes closest.

27. Thomas More, *De Optimo Rei Publicae Statu deque Nova Insula Utopia*, Louvain, 1516, Book II, 'De religionibus Utopiensium': 'Sunt tamen omnia subobscura: nec id aedificandi inscitia factum sed consilio sacerdotum ferunt quod immodicam lucem cogitationes dispensere, partione ac velut dubia colligi animos at intendi religionem putent.' See More, *Utopia*, p. 234.

28. Sir Henry Wotton, *Elements of Architecture*, p. 55.

29. In the amended version of 11 July this was changed to: 'That, one general design or Forme be agreed upon for all of the fifty New intended Churches, where the Sites will admit thereof; the Steeple or Towers excepted.'

30. This was amended to: 'That the pewes be Single and of equal height (...).'

31. Insulate: detached or isolated.

32. This was amended to: 'That there be handsome Porticoes to each Church.'

33. This sentence was added as a note in the margin. 'Suratt' refers to Surat, to the north of Bombay on the west coast of India; on Vanbrugh's possible stay in India see R. Williams, 'Vanbrugh's India and his Mausolea for England', in Ridgway and Williams (2000), pp. 114–31.

34. On these authors see Besançon (2000), Part I, Chapter 2, The passage by Origen is his *Homily* on *Genesis*, XIII.4.

4 The sense of the past

1. This is a quotation from John Leland's *De Rebus Britannia's Collectanea*, which first appeared in print in Oxford in 1715. Leland lived from *c.* 1506 to 1552.
2. Genaeus Julius Agricola (40–93) was the Roman governor of Britannia from 77 to 84 and did much to establish Roman rule in England and Scotland, Jones refers in a marginal note to Tacitus' *Agricola*.
3. Decorum is the sense of that which is fitting, appropriate or apt. It was originally a rhetorical term. In classical oratory, decorum should govern the style of the speech, behaviour, gestures, dress and attitude of the speaker, in accordance with the speech's subject, the audience and the occasion, so that the orator is able to establish a rapport with the audience and manage to move and thereby to persuade. See for instance Cicero, *De Oratore* III.ix.38; Quintilian, *Instituto Oratoria* XII.x.58ff and I.ii.1. On decorum in Inigo Jones's work see Tucker (2000).
4. [Author's note:] Vitr. L1. Cap. 2.
5. This is the motto in the frontispiece of Serlio's Book III, on Roman Antiquities.
6. [Author's note:] Camden fo. 8. This is a reference to William Camden's *Britannia*, first published in 1586. Geoffrey of Monmouth (*c.* 1100–1155) was a medieval chronicler, author of the *Histories of the Kings of Britain*.
7. See Raphael's letter to Pope Leo X of *c.* 1519, modern edition in Di Teodoro (1994), for the first formulation of this view of architectural history.
8. 'Fools in avoiding one fault fall into another' (Horace, *Satires*, I.ii.24).
9. See Eastlake (1970).
10. Sir Christopher Wren.
11. Blenheim Palace was given by Queen Anne and the nation to John Churchill, 1st Duke of Marlborough, in gratitude for his victory in 1704 at Blenheim in Germany over the French during the War of the Spanish Succession.
12. Lucius Junius Moderatus Columella, fl. AD 50. He was the author of *De Re Rustica* (*On Agriculture*), the most systematic surviving Roman manual on agriculture. Book I treats of the layout of villas. Palladius (Rutilius Taurus Aemilianus) was the author of the only surviving treatise on agriculture from late Antiquity (*De Re Rustica*, *c.* AD 450); Constantine: the Byzantine Emperor Constantine VII Porphyrogennetos, who ruled 912–59, ordered various collections of scientific works to be edited to stem the decline of scientific learning and scholars to compose an encyclopaedia of what best deserved to survive. The *Geoponika*, or *On Agriculture*, was excerpted and edited from older works on this subject dating from the fourth and the fifth centuries AD.
13. Pliny the Younger (Gaius Plinius Caecilius Secundus, *c.* AD 61–*c.* 112). The son of a landowner at Comum (now Como in Northern Italy), he was brought up by his uncle Pliny the Elder, the author of the *Naturalis Historia* (*Natural History*), an encyclopaedia of all contemporary knowledge. The younger Pliny studied rhetoric with Quintilian, practised as a lawyer, became a senator and held various imperial appointments. He published nine books of literary letters, the *Epistolae*, which include the two descriptions of his country estates used by Castell. Varro (Marcus Terentius Varro, 116–37 BC) was a polymath. He was asked by Julius Caesar to plan and organize the first public library in Rome, and completed 490 books on every known branch of learning by the end of his life. Only two of them survive: *De Lingua Latina* (*On the Latin Language*) and *De Re Rustica*. Laurentinum: now Tor Paterno on the Tyrrhenian coast to the south of Ostia; Tuscum: Tuscan; Villa urbana: a Roman villa was a rural dwelling associated with a country estate, varying from functional farms to luxurious country estates for the Roman elite. The 'pars urbana' of the estate referred to the residential part, as opposed to the 'pars rustica', the parts that served practical purposes.
14. [Author's note:] This Room, as its Name signifies, was an enclos'd or private Porticus, so call'd to distinguish it from the Porticus whose Roof was only supported by Pillars. The Use of this Room was for the Exercise of Walking, when the Weather would not permit the Use of those Walks they had sub dio [under the open sky]; and the Method they took to make it at all Seasons Convenient, may be seen by the Description Pliny gives us of this.

15. [Author's note:] Vit. I.4.c.3.
16. [Author's note:] Lib. 9 c. 7.

5 Following the example of Antiquity

1. According to the *Oxford English Dictionary*, its first uses in English can be traced back to literary criticism of the 1830s, in which classicism is opposed to romanticism in contemporary French literature; but Sir Edward Sandys used the term 'classical' in the sense of 'canonical' in 1599; 'classic', however, in the sense of belonging to the art and culture of ancient Greece and Rome, became current from the early eighteenth century onwards.
2. Daniel, *Poems* (1965 edn), pp. 139–40 and 145.
3. See Allen (1937); Gent (1995).
4. On the heraldic connotations of this term see Hart (1993).
5. Guillaume Philandrier (1505–65), *In decem libros M. Vitruvii Pollionis De architectura annotationes. Cum indicibus graeco & latino locupletissimis* [...]. Impressum Romae : apud I. Andream Dossena, 1544. For a modern edition see Lemerle (2000).
6. The reference to Vitruvius should be III.iii.13 not, as Wotton wrote, III.ii.
7. Protagoras: Greek Sophist (*c.* 490–420 BC), who said that man is the measure of all things.
8. Pulvinata: cushion-shaped.
9. Corinth was one of the richest cities in ancient Greece and an important harbour commanding the Isthmus, which may help to explain the bad reputation for morals it already enjoyed in Antiquity. It was famous for its cuisine, pottery and prostitutes.
10. Ephesian temple: the great temple of Artemis in Ephesus, built in the fifth century BC.
11. Palladio, *Four Books on Architecture*, II.6. Wotton is refering to the *Consento della Coritò.*
12. 'In the morning at the mountains, in the evening at the fountains.'
13. Indian tribes.
14. French comedy by Desmarets de Saint Sornin, published in 1637.
15. Albion [Celtic, probably cognate with the Latin 'albus']: white. Originally it was the Greek and Roman name for Britain, alluding to its white cliffs (*OED*).
16. [Author's note in the margin:] Pag. 16 Art. 6. Paris edition 1714, 4to.
17. [Author's note in the margin:] An *Italian* Architect of the last century. The reference is to Francesco Borromini (1599–1667).
18. Sir John Denham (1615–69) was Surveyor-General of the King's Works from 1660 to 1669. He was known as a 'celebrated Poet and eminent Royalist', but appears to have been a competent administrator rather than an architect. There is no evidence that he actually designed any buildings (Colvin, 1995).
19. Hugh May (1621–84). Nothing is known of his early life. He was in Royalist service, probably that of the Duke of Buckingham, in his early years, and was made Paymaster of the Works in 1660; his principal task was to preside over the great overhaul of royal palaces immediately after the Restoration. During Sir John Denham's illness he replaced him as Surveyor-General from 1662 to 1669, and he had hopes to succeed him, but in the end he was passed over in favour of Sir Christopher Wren. He did become Inspector of French and English Gardens at Whitehall, St James, Greenwich and Hampton Court, and in 1673 Comptroller of Works at Windsor. He assisted Evelyn in publishing the *Parallel*. After the Great Fire of London he was one of the three surveyors to supervise the rebuilding of the City, but he did not design any of the new churches. Most of his built work was for acquaintances at the Court; he often collaborated with the painter Verrio and the sculptor Grinling Gibbons. Few of his buildings survive, but his work at Windsor is of great interest for an understanding of the development of Baroque architecture in England.
20. 'Now it is Rome, but shortly ago it was a shed.' Evelyn is probably referring to the Emperor Augustus, who claimed that he had found a brick city and left a city built of marble at the end of his life.
21. Engotish: that is, to Gothicize, here used in a pejorative sense.

22. Titus Flavius Vespasianus, Roman Emperor AD 79–81, dedicated in 79 the Colosseum, begun by his father Vespasian.
23. From the Italian *paragone* or comparison.
24. Pirro Ligorio (1513–83), Italian architect, painter, draughtsman and antiquary. He is best known for the Casino he built for Pius V in the gardens of the Vatican and the gardens at the Villa d'Este at Tivoli, but he also published maps of ancient Rome that offered archaeological reconstructions (1553 and 1561), and he wrote extensively on Roman antiquities. *Delle antichità di Roma* was published in Venice in 1533, but he also left a substantial body of unpublished material.
25. Vincenzo Scamozzi (1552–1616), Venetian architect and pupil of Palladio. He published *Discorsi sopra le antichità di Roma* (Venice, 1592) and *L'idea dell'architettura universale* (Venice, 1615).
26. Diocletian (Gaius Aurelius Valerius Diocletianus, AD ?244, ruled 284–305, d. ?). Roman Emperor and patron of the arts. He initiated a substantial renewal of public building in Rome, including the great baths at the north-east of the Viminal Hill, the culmination of imperial bath building.
27. Cf. Harris (1990), pp. 503 ff. Soo has recently argued that this Tract of Wren's was begun in the mid-1670s: Soo (1998), pp. 119 ff.
28. Empress Helena (*c.* AD 257–337?), mother of the Emperor Constantine. She made a pilgrimage to the Holy Land in 326–27, and supported the building of a basilica and the Anastasis Rotunda (337 or after) in Jerusalem, which contained the Sepulchre of Christ on Golgotha. See Krautheimer (1986), pp. 60–63.
29. Cf. Vitruvius, *Ten Books on Architecture*, I.3.2.
30. Equicrural: having legs of equal length; isosceles (*OED*).
31. Cf. Alberti, *On the Art of Building*, IX.5, p. 302: 'When you make judgements on beauty, you do not follow mere fancy, but the workings of a reasoned faculty that is inborn in the mind.' And see the passage by Hobbes quoted above, Chapter 1, pp. 27–8.
32. Trajan's Column in the Forum of Trajan in Rome was dedicated in AD 112. It is 125 feet high and has a running spiral frieze representing the Dacian Wars.
33. Dotard: A tree that has lost its top or branches, and of which the trunk alone remains, more or less in a state of decay (*OED*).
34. Bole: the stem or trunk of a tree (*OED*).
35. According to Soo (1998), p. 288 note 24, Wren is here describing tie-beams or cross-beams, the ends of which form the triglyphs of the frieze by resting on the architrave. Cf. Vitruvius, *Ten Books on Architecture*, IV.2. There is no illustration to this passage.
36. Colvin and Newman point out in their edition of North's writings that North is here complaining of the interruption, in the interior of Saint Paul's, of the architrave and frieze of the main order by the intervening arches (North, *Of Building*, p. 116 note 139).
37. That is, flutings, which give columns the ribbed aspect that seems to have reminded North of stockings.
38. The inner façade of the tower of the Schools at Oxford, built *c.* 1613–26, onto whose five storeys the five Orders are applied.
39. According to Colvin and Newman (North, *Of Building*, p. 120 note 143) North is referring to the secret arches used by Wren at Saint Paul's to carry classical lintels and architraves across openings too wide for a single beam. The 'north and south iles' refer to the north and south transepts.
40. Sir Christopher Wren, who was Surveyor General from 1668/9 to 1718, during the reigns of Charles II and James II, William and Mary and Queen Anne.
41. Louis XIV, King of France, who had founded the Académie Royale de Peinture et de Sculpture in 1664, and the Académie Royale d'Architecture in 1671.

Bibliography

The following standard abbreviations are used in the text: *DNB* (*Dictionary of National Biography*) and *OED* (*Oxford English Dictionary*).

Primary sources

Addison, Joseph, 'Essay on the Pleasures of the Imagination' [1st publ. 1712], in J. Addison and R. Steele, *The Spectator*, ed. G. Smith with an introduction by P. Smithers, London, Melbourne, Toronto and New York: Everyman's Library, 1907 [reprinted 1979], vol. III, pp. 276–309.

Alberti, Leon Battista, *On Painting*, translated with an introduction and notes by J. R. Spencer, New Haven and London: Yale University Press, 1956.

—— *On the Art of Building in Ten Books*. Translated by J. Rykwert, N. Leach and R. Tavernor, Cambridge, MA and London: MIT Press, 1991.

[Anon.] *The Builder's Dictionary: Or, Gentleman and Architect's Companion. Explaining not only the Terms of Art In all the several Parts of Architecture, But also containing the Theory and Practice of the Various Branches thereof, requisite to be known by Masons, Carpenters, Joiners, Bricklayers, Plaisterers, Painters, Glaziers, Smiths, Turners, Carvers, Statuaries, Plumbers, &c.*, 2 vols, London: Printed for A. Bettesworth and C. Hitch, 1734.

Bacon, Francis, 'Of Building', from Bacon, *The Essays*, ed. John Pitcher, London: Penguin Books, 1985, pp. 193–6 [1st publ. 1625].

Barbon, Nicholas, *An Apology for the Builder; or a Discourse shewing the Cause and Effects of the Increase of Building*, London, printed in the Year, MDCLXXXIX [1st publ. 1685].

Bible, The: *The Holy Bible containing the old and new Testaments translated out of the original tongues; and with the former translations diligently compared and revised by his Majesty's special command. Appointed to be read in church. Authorized King James version*, Oxford, n.d. [1611].

—— *The Bible: Authorized King James Version*, ed. with introduction by R. Camoll and S. Prickett, Oxford: Oxford University Press, 1997.

Blum, Hans, *The Booke of Five Collumnes of Architecture called Tuscan, Dorica, Ionica, Corinthia & Composita Drawne and counterfeited after the right Semetry and cunning measure of Free-Masons: Gathered with great diligence by Hans Bloome out of Antiquities, for the benefit of Free-Masons, Carpenters, Goldsmiths, Painters, Carvers, In layers, Anticke Cutters, and all others that delight to practice with the Compasse and Squire*. Translated out of Latine into English by I. T., London, Printed by Simon Stafford, for the Widow of Hans Woutneell [...], 1608.

Boorde, Andrew, *The Boke for to Lerne a Man to be Wyse in Buyldyng of his howse for the helth of body & to holde quyetness for the helth of his soule, and body. The boke for a good husbande to lerne*, London: Imprynted by me Robert Wyse [1540].

—— *Thoughts Before Building*, introduction and notes by H. Edmund Poole, Canterbury: College of Arts Press, 1961.

[Browne, Isaac] *On Design and Beauty. An Epistle*, London: Printed for J. Roberts near the *Oxford-Arms* in *Warwick Lane*, MDCCXXXIV.

Campbell, Colen, *Vitruvius Britannicus or the British Architect, containing the Plans, Elevations and Sections of the Regular Buildings, both Publick and Private in Great Britain, with Variety of New Designs; in 200 large Folio Plates engraved by the best Hands; and Drawn either from the Buildings themselves, or the Original Designs of the Architects*, London, sold by the Author over against Doglas Coffee-House in St Martin's-lane [...], 1715.

Castell, Robert, *The Villas of the Ancients Illustrated*, London: printed for the Author, 1728 [actually 1729].

Colonna, Francesco (attr.), *Hypnerotomachia. The Strife of Love in a Dreame*. Translated by R. D. [Robert Dallington] [1592], repr. with introduction by Lucy Gent, Delmar, New York: Scholars' Facsimiles & Reprints, 1973.

Commission for Building Fifty New City Churches, 'Rules for the Fifty New Churches Set Down by the Commissioners and their Subcommittee', Lambeth Palace Library, London, MS 2693, fols 5–6 [meeting of the subcommittee on 11 July 1712]; repr. in P. de la Ruffinière du Prey, *Hawksmoor's London Churches: Architecture and Theology*, Chicago and London: University of Chicago Press, 2000, pp. 143–4.

Daniel, S., *Poems and a Defence of Rhyme*, ed. Arthur Colby Sprague, Chicago: Chicago University Press, 1965 [1st publ. 1930].

Dee, John, 'Preface', in *The Elements of Geometrie of the most auncient Philosopher* EUCLIDE *of Megara. Faithfoll (now first) translated into the Englishe toung, by H. Billingsley, Citizen of London. Whereunto are annexed certaine Scholies, Annotations and Inventions, of the best Mathematicians, both of time past, and in this our age. With a very fruitfull Preface made by M. I. Dee, specifying the chiefe Mathematicall Sciences, what they are, and whereunto comwodious: where, also, are disclosed certaine new Secrets Mathematicall and Mechanicall, until these our daies greatly missed*, Imprinted at London by Iohn Daye, 1570.

—— *The Private Diary of Dr. John Dee's, and the Catalogue of his Library of Manuscripts*, edited by J. O. Halliwell, printed for the Camden Society, 1842, repr. New York: AMS Press, 1968.

Digges, Leonard, *A Boke named Tectonicon. Briefly shewinge the exacte measuring, and spedye reckonynge allmaner of Lande, Squares, Tymber, Stone, Steaples, Pyllers, Globes &c. Further, declaringe the perfecte makinge and large use of the Carpenter's Ruler, contayninge a Quadrante Geometricall, comprehendinge also the rare vse of the Squire. And in thes a lytle Treatise adioyned, openinge the composition and appliancie of an instrument called the profitable Staffe. With other thinges pleasaunt and necesarye, most conducible for Surueyers, Landemeaters, Joiners, Carpenters, and Masons*, published by Leonard Digges Gentleman, in the yeare of our Lorde 1556, Imprinted at London in Fletestreate, neare to S. Dunstones Churche, by Thomas Marshe, Anno. 1570.

Donne, John, *The Sermon Preached to King Charles, At Saint James: 3°. April 1625*. London, Printed by A. M. for Thomas Jones [...] 1625.

—— *Deaths Duell, a, A Consolation to the Soule, against the dying life, and liuing Death of the Body. Deliuered in a sermon at White Hall, before the Kings Majesty, in the beginning of Lent 1630 [...] Being his last Sermon, and called by his Maiesties houshold The Doctors owne Funerall Sermon*. London, Printed by Thomas Harper, [...], 1682.

—— *A Sermon Preached at St. Dunstans, January 15, 1625. The first Sermon after our dispersion by the Sickness in XXVI. Sermons (Never before Published) Preached by that Learned and Reverend Divine John Donne [...]. The Third Volume*. London, Printed by Thomas Newcomb [...], 1660, pp. 285–90.

—— *Sermons*, ed. G. R. Potter and E. M. Simpson, Berkeley: University of California Press, 1953–62 (vol. X, pp. 230–31; vol. VI, Nr 18, pp. 356–62; vol. VI, pp. 250 and 255).

Drayton, Michael, 'To the Reader of the Barons Warres ... ', from J. W. Hebel (ed.), *The Works of Michael Drayton*, Oxford: published for the Shakespeare Head by Basil Blackwell, 1961, vol. II, pp. 3–4.

Du Bois, Nicholas, *see* Palladio, Andrea, *The Architecture of Palladio*.

Evelyn, John, *A Character of England, as it was lately presented in a Letter, to a Noble Man of France*, London: printed for Jo. Crooke, and are to be sold at the Ship in St. Paul's-yard, 1659.

—— *A Parallel of the Antient Architecture with the Modern, in a Collection of* Ten *Principal* Authors *who have written upon the Five Orders, Viz., Palladio and Scamozzi, Serlio and Vignola, D. Barbaro and Cataneo, L. B. Alberti and Viola, Bullant and De Lorme, compared with one another. Written in* French *by Roland* Fréart, Sieur de Chambray; *Made English for the Benefit of* Builders. [...] By John Evelyn, Esq; Fellow of the Royal Society, London, 1664.

—— LONDINIUM REDIVIVUM or London Restored not to its pristine, but to far greater Beauty Commodiousness and Magnificence. Humbly represented in certain proposals concerning the rebuilding of that famous and ancient Metropolis. (1666); printed in *John Evelyn: London Revived*, ed. E. S. de Beer, Oxford: Clarendon Press, 1938.

Fischer von Erlach, Johann Bernhard, *A Plan of Civil and Historical Architecture, in the Representation of the most noted Buildings of Foreign Nations* [...], *now faithfully Done into English, with Additional Notes, by Thomas Lediard*, London, 1730.

Gerbier, Sir Balthazar, *The First Lecture touching Fortifications Read Publiquely at Sir Balthazar Gerbier's Academy*, London: Gartrude Dawson, 1649.

—— *A Brief Discourse Concerning the Three Chief Principles of Magnificent Building. Viz. Solidity, Conveniency and Ornament*, London, Printed in the year, 1662.

—— *Counsel and Advise to All Builders; For the Choice of their Surveyours, Clarks of their Works, Bricklayers, Masons, Carpenters and other Work-men therein concerned. As also in respect of their works, materials and rates thereof. Together with several epistles to eminent persons, who may be concerned in building*, London: Thomas Mabb, 1663.

Gibbs, James, *Rules for Drawing the several Parts of Architecture in a more exact and easy manner than has been heretofore practised, by which all Fractions, in dividing the principal Members and their Parts, are avoided*, London: Printed by W. Bowyer for the Author, 1732.

St. Gregory 'Epistle XI.56' in: D. Norberg (ed.), *Saint Gregorii Magni Registrum Epistolarum Libri VIII–XIV*, Turnhout: Brepols, 1982.

Grataroli, Guglielmo, *The Castel of Memorie: wherein is conteyned the restoryng, augmentyng, and conservyng of the memorye and Remembraunce* [...] *by Guglielmus Gratarolus Bergamotis* [...] *Englished by William Fulwod* [...], imprinted in London in Fleetestreete by William How [...] 1572 [1st publ. 1553].

Hakewill, George, *An Apologie or Declaration of the Power and Providence of God in the Gouernment of the World*, London: Printed for Robert Allott at the Beare in Paules Churchyard, 1630 [1st publ. 1627].

Halfpenny, William, *The Art of Sound Building, Demonstrated in Geometrical Problems:*

shewing Geometrical Lines for all Kinds of Arches, Niches, Groins, and Twisted Rails, both Regular and Irregular. With several other Draughts of Buildings and Staircases all Curiously Engraven on Copper Plates. Wherein are laid down (suited to every Capacity) easy Practical Methods for Carpenters, Joiners, Masons, or Bricklayers to work by, London: Sam. Aris, for the Author […], 1725.

Hawkins, Henry, *Partheneia Sacra, or The Mysterious and Delicious Garden of the Sacred Parthenes; Symbolically set forth and enriched with Pious Deuises and Emblemes for the Entertainment of Deuout Soyles; Contriued al to the Honour of the Incomparable Virgin Marie Mother of God; for the Pleasure and Deuotion especially of the Partheneian Sodalitie of her Immaculate Conception*, Rouen: Printed by Iohn Covsturier, M.DC.XXXIII; repr. as *Partheneia Sacra*, introduction by Karl Josef Höltgen, Aldershot: Scolar Press, 1993.

Hawksmoor, Nicholas, Letter of January 7 1724 to Lord Carlisle at Castle Howard, in K. Downes, *Nicholas Hawksmoor*, London: A. Zwemmer Ltd, 1959, p. 244.

Hobbes, Thomas, 'Answer to Davenant's Preface to Gondibert' (1650), repr. in J. E. Spingarn (ed.), *Critical Essays of the Seventeenth Century*, vol. II: *1650–85*, Oxford: Oxford University Press, 1908, pp. 54–67.

Holt, Richard, *A Short Treatise of Artificial Stone, As 'tis now Made, And Converted into all Manner of Curious Embellishments, and Proper Ornaments of Architecture: Containing The most Beautiful, the Strongest, and the Cheapest Method, of Adorning Buildings of all Sorts*, London: Printed for Stephen Austen and John Brindley, 1730.

Hoppus, Edward, *see* Palladio, Andrea, *Andrea Palladio's Architecture in Four Books*.

Jones, I., 'Roman Sketchbook', manuscript in the Devonshire Collection, Chatsworth, fol. 76r–v (1614), repr. in G. Higgott, '"Varying with reason": Inigo Jones's Theory of Design', *Architectural History*, 35 (1992), pp. 51–77.

—— *The most notable antiquity of Great Britain, vulgarly called Stone-Heng, : on Salisbury plain. Restored, by Inigo Jones* […] *to which are added, the Chorea Gigantum, or, Stone-Heng restored to the Danes, by Doctor Charlton; and Mr. Webb's Vindication of Stone-Heng restored, In answer to Dr. Charleton's Reflections, with observations upon the orders and rules of architecture in use among the antient Romans. Before the whole are prefixed, certain memoirs relating to the life of Inigo Jones* […] [edited by John Webb], London: printed for D. Browne Junior, at the Black-Swan with Temple-Bar, and J. Woodman and D. Lyon, in Russel-Street, Covent-Garden, MDCCXXV.

—— *Inigo Jones on Palladio. Being the notes by Inigo Jones in the copy of I quattro Libri dell' Architettura di Andrea Palladio, 1601, in the Library of Worcester College Oxford, reproduced by Courtesy of the Provost and Fellows*, vol. 1: *Preface, Notes and Transcription* [ed. B. Allsopp], Newcastle upon Tyne: Oriel Press, 1970.

King, Peter, Lord King, *An Enquiry into the Construction, Discipline, Unity and Worship of the Primitive Church That Flourished within the First Three Hundred Years after* CHKIST [*sic*] *Faithfully Collected out of the Extant Writings of those Ages By an Impartial Hand*, London, 1691.

Knowles, C. C., and P. H. Pitt (eds), *The History of Building Regulations in London 1189–1972*, London: Architectural Press, 1972.

Langley, Batty, *Ancient Masonry, both in the Theory and Practice, Demonstrating the Useful Rules of Arithmetick, Geometry, and Architecture, in the Proportions and Orders of the Most Eminent Masters of All Nations* […], London: Printed and Sold for the Author by J. Milan and J. Huggonson, 1736.

Lecocq, A.-M. (ed.), *La Querelle des Anciens et des Modernes. XVIIe–XVIIIe Siècles. Précédé de* Les Abeilles et les araignées *essai de Marc Fumaroli, suivi d'une postface de Jean-Robert Armogathe*, Paris: Gallimard, 2001.

Lomazzo, Paolo Giovanni, *A Tracte containing the Artes of Curious Paintinge Carvinge*

& Buildinge written first in Italian by Jo: Paul Lomatius painter of Milan and Englished by R. H. student in Physik, London, 1598; repr. New York/Amsterdam: Da Capo Press Theatrum Orbis Terrarum Ltd., 1969 ('The English Experience. Its Record in Early Printed Books', vol. 171).

Marvell, A., 'Upon Appleton House: To My Lord Fairfax', repr. in A. Fowler, *The Country House Poem: A Cabinet of Seventeenth-Century Estate Poems and Related Items*, Edinburgh: Edinburgh University Press, 1994, pp. 281–304.

Mede, Joseph, 'What Holinesse' in : *Paraleipomena : remaines on some passages in the Revelations Whereunto are added Severall Discussions concerning the Holinesse of Churches*, London, John Clarke, 1650 (1st published 1638].

Montague, Walter, *Miscellanea Spiritualia or Devout Essaies*, London, printed for William Lee, Daniel Pakham and Gabriel Bedell, 1648.

More, Richard, *The Carpenters Rule, Or, A Booke Shewing Many plaine waies, truly to measure ordinarie Timber, and other extraordinaries sollids, or Timber: with a Detection of Sundrie great errors, generally committed by Carpenters and others in measuring of Timber; tending much to the buyers great losse. Published especially for the Good of the Companie of Carpenters in London, and others also; and is very necessary for Masons, Shipwrights, Ioyners, and others, using to measure Timber and Boord, and other superficies and sollids*, London, Imprinted by Felix Kyngston, 1602; repr. Amsterdam: Theatrum Orbis Terrarum, and New York: Da Capo Press, 1970.

More, Thomas, *St. Thomas More's Utopia, Latin Text and English Translation*, ed. G. M. Logan, R. M. Adams and C. H. Miller, Cambridge: Cambridge University Press, 1995.

Morris, Robert, *Lectures on Architecture, consisting of Rules founded upon Harmonick and arithmetical Proportions in a Building*, London: Printed for R. Sayer, at the Golden Buck, opposite Fetter-Lane, Fleet-Street, 1759 [1st publ. 1734].

Moxon, Joseph, *Mechanick Exercises: on the Whole Art of Printing*, ed. H. Davis and H. Carter, Oxford: Oxford University Press, 1962.

—— *Mechanick Exercises or the Doctrine of Handy-Works Applied to the Arts of Smithing, Joinery, Carpentry, Turning, Bricklaying began Jan. 1. 1677. And intended to be monthly continued*, London: Printed for Joseph Moxon at the Sign of Atlas on Ludgate-Hill, 1677–83, 2 vols [facsimile repr. ed. C. F. Montgomery, with an Introduction, Table of Contents, and captions explaining the 26 plates by Benno M. Forman, New York, Washington and London: Praeger Publishers, 1970].

—— 'To the Ingenious Artists', *see* Vignola, Giacomo Barozzi da, *VIGNOLA: or, the Compleat Architect*.

North, Roger, *Autobiography*, ed. A. Jessop, Oxford: Clarendon Press, 1887.

—— *Of Building: Roger North's Writings on Architecture*, ed. Howard Colvin and John Newman, Oxford: Clarendon Press, 1981 [includes 'Of Building', 'Of Unity and Variety', 'On Gothic Architecture' and 'The Origin and Development of Regular Architecture'].

Palladio, Andrea, *The first Book of Architecture, by Andrea Palladio. Translated out of Italian: with an Appendix Touching Doors and Windows, by P^R Le Muet Translated out of French. By G. R. To which are added Designes of Floors lately made at Somerset-House; and the Framing of Houses after the best manner of English Building, with their Proportions and Scantlings*, London, Printed by J. M. and sold by *G. Richards*, at the Peacock near the Old Exchange: and by *Simon Miller*, at the *Star* in St *Pauls* Church-yard, 1663.

—— *The Architecture of Palladio; in Four Books. Containing a Short Treatise of the Five Orders, and the most necessary Observations concerning all Sorts of Building, as also the different Construction of Private and Publick Houses, High-Ways, Bridges, Market-Places, Xystes, and Temples, with their Plans, Sections and Uprights. To which are added several Notes and Observations made by* INIGO JONES, *never printed before. Revis'd, Design'd, and Publish'd by* GIACOMO LEONI [...] *Translated from the* Italian *Original* [by Nicholas Du Bois] (*L'Architettura di A. Palladio, etc., L'Architecture de A. Palladio* [...] *Le Tout* [...] *traduit de l'Italien* [by N. Du Bois]). Italian, English and French, London: Printed by *John Watts*, for the Author, MDCCXV.

—— *Andrea Palladio's Architecture in Four Books* [...] *Carefully Revis'd and Redelineated by Edw.*[d] *Hoppus Surveyor*, London, 1735.

Papillon, David, *A Practicall Abstract of the Arts of Fortification and Assailing. Containing Foure different Methods of Fortifications* [...]. *Written for the benefit of such as delight in the Practice of these Noble Arts. By David Papillon Gent.*, London: R. Austin, 1645.

Peake, Robert, *see* Serlio, Sebastiano, *The first Booke of Architecture.*

Perrault, Claude, *A Treatise of the Five Orders of Columns in Architecture, viz. Toscan, Doric, Ionic, Corinthian and Composite, wherein the Proportions and Characters of the Members of their several Pedestals, Columns and Entablatures, are distinctly considr'd, with respect to the Practice of the Antients and Moderns* [...]. *Written in French by Claude Perrault* [...]. *Made English by John James of Greenwich*, London: printed by Benj. Motte, 1708.

Pope, Alexander, 'Epistle to Richard Boyle Earl of Burlington' (1731), in J. Butt (ed.), *The Twickenham Edition of the Poems of Alexander Pope*, vol. III, part 2: *Epistles to Several Persons (Moral Essays)*, ed. F. W. Bateson, London: Methuen & Co/New Haven: Yale University Press, 1951, pp. 131–51.

Pozzo, Andrea, *Rules and Examples of Perspective proper for Painters and Architects* [...] *In English and Latin. Containing a most easie and expeditious Method to Delineate in Perspective All Designs relating to Architecture, after a New Manner, Wholly free from the Confusion of Occult Lines: by that Great Master thereof, Andrea Pozzo, Soc. Jes.*, engraven [...] by John Sturt, done into English from the Original printed at Rome 1693 in Latin and Italian by Mr John James of Greenwich, London: printed by Benjamin Motte, 1707.

Pratt, Sir Roger, *The Architecture of Sir Roger Pratt, Charles II's Commissioner for the Re-Building of London after the Great Fire: Now printed for the first Time from his Note-Books*, ed. R. T. Gunther, Oxford: printed by John Johnson for the Author at the University Press, 1928.

Primatt, Stephen, *The City & Country Purchaser & Builder*, London: Printed for S. Speed, 1667.

R. T., *De Templis, A Treatise of Temples: Wherein is discovered the Ancient Manner of Building, Consecrating and Adorning of Churches*, London: Printed by R. Bishop, for Thomas Alchorn, at the Green Dragon in S. Paul's Church-Yard, 1638.

Ralph, James, 'Preface' to [Anon.], *The Builder's Dictionary: Or, Gentleman and Architect's Companion. Explaining not only the Terms of Art In all the several Parts of Architecture, But also containing the Theory and Practice of the Various Branches thereof, requisite to be known by Masons, Carpenters, Joiners, Bricklayers, Plaisterers, Painters, Glaziers, Smiths, Turners, Carvers, Statuaries, Plumbers, &c.*, 2 vols, London: Printed for A. Bettesworth and C. Hitch, 1734.

—— (attr.), *A Critical Review of the Publick Buildings, Statues and Ornaments, In and About London and Westminster*, London: Printed by C. Ackers, for J. Wilford, 1734.

Richards, Geoffrey ('G. R.'), *see* Palladio, Andrea, *The first Book of Architecture.*

Scamozzi, Vincenzo, *The Mirror of Architecture, Or the Ground-Rules Of The Art of*

Building, Exactly laid down by Vincent Scamozzi Mr. Builder of Venice. Reviewed and Inlarged with the Addition of a Diagonal Scale, being very useful for the dividing the Author has given parts into Minutes, whereby the Principal points of Architecture are easily and plainly demonstrated for the benefit of all Lovers and Ingenious Practitioners in the said Art. By Joachim Schuym of Amsterdam, translated out of Dutch by W. F. [...], London: Printed for William Fisher at the Postern Gate near Tower-Hill, 1676 [1669].

Serlio, Sebastiano, *The first Booke of Architecture, made by Sebastian Serly* [*sic*], *entreating of Geometrie. Translated out of Italian into Dutch, and out of Dutch into English*, London, printed for Robert Peake, and are to be sold at his shop neere Holborne conduit, next to the Sunne Taverne, Anno Dom. 1611 (includes dedication and 'To the Lovers of Architecture' by Robert Peake).

—— *S. Serlio on Architecture: Books I–V of Tutte l'Opere d'Architettura et Prospettiva*, trans. and introduced by V. Hart and P. Hicks, New Haven and London: Yale University Press, 1996.

Shaftesbury, Anthony Ashley Cooper, Lord, 'A Letter concerning Design', in his *Characteristicks of Men, Manners, Opinions and Times. The second edition corrected [with the addition of Treatise VII, viz. A Notion of the Draught or Tablature of the Judgement of Hercules and A Letter concerning the Art, or Science of Design]*, vol. III, edited by Thomas Micklethwaite, London: John Darby, 1714.

Shere, H., 'Some Directions for my Lord Nottinghams Building by S[r] H. Shere', British Library, MS Sloane 3828 fols. 176–80, dated 5 July 1695.

Shirley, Sir Robert, *Inscription over the west entrance of Staunton Harold church*, Leicestershire, 1653.

Shute, John, *The First and Chiefe Groundes of Architecture used in all the auncient and famous monymentes*, London: Thomas Marshe, 1563; repr. as *The First and Chiefe Groundes of Architecture: a Facsimile of the first Edition* with an introduction by Lawrence Weaver, London: Country Life, 1912.

Sidney, Sir Philip (1554–86), *An Apologie for Poetrie. Written by the right noble, vertuous, and learned, Sir Phillip Sidney, Knight*, At London, Printed for Henry Olney [...] Anno 1595; repr. New York/Amsterdam: Da Capo Press Theatrum Orbis Terrarum Ltd, 1971.

Stevens, Charles, and John Liebault, *Maison Rustique, Or the* COUNTRYE *Farme: Compiled in the French tongue by* Charles Stevens [*i.e. Charles l'Estienne*] *and* John Liebault *Doctors of Physicke*: And translated into English by *Richard Svrflet* Practitioner in *Physicke*. [...] LONDON. Printed by Arnold Hatfield for *Iohn Norton and Iohn Bill*. 1606 [first French edn. publ. 1598].

Stickells, Robert, 'P[ro]poc[i]tions propounded unto the Learned & Skilfull', British Library, MS Landsdowne 84, no. 10, nos i and ii, fol. 25 recto.

Strafford, Thomas (Viscount Wentworth), 'Speech when He First Sate Lord President of the North, December 1628', and 'Strafford's Last Speech in his Defence, 13 April 1641', in J. P. Kenyon (ed.), *The Stuart Constitution 1603–1688, Documents and Commentary*, 2nd edn, Cambridge: Cambridge University Press, 1986.

Stukeley, William, *Of the Roman Amphitheater at Dorchester* [1723; n.p., n.d.].

Vanbrugh, Sir John, 'Mr Van-Brugg's Proposals about Building ye New Churches' [1712], autograph version, unsigned and untitled, Oxford, Bodleian Library, MS Rawl. B 376, fols 351–2 [the title is from a contemporary copy, Oxford, Bodleian Library, MS Eng. Hist. b.2, fol. 47; repr. in K. Downes, *Sir John Vanbrugh*, London: D. Zwemmer Ltd, 1977, pp. 257–9.

—— 'Reasons Offer'd for Preserving some Part of the Old Manor [at Woodstock]',

11 June 1709, British Library, Add. MS 61353, fols 62–3; repr. in G. Webb (ed.), *The Complete Works of Sir John Vanbrugh*, vol. IV: *The Letters*, London, 1928, pp. 29–30.

Vasari, Giorgio, *Lives of the Painters, Sculptors and Architects*, translated by Gaston du C. de Vere, with an introduction and notes by David Esberdijan, London, 1996 [1st publ. 1927].

Vignola, Giacomo Barozzi da, *The Regular Architect: or the general Rule of the Five Orders of Architecture of M. Giacomo Barozzio da Vignola. With a New Addition of Michael Angelo Buonarotti. Rendred into English from the Original Italian, and Explained by John Leeke, Student in the Mathematicks, for the Use and Benefit of Free Masons, Carpenters, Joyners, Carvers, Painters, Bricklayers, Plaisterers: In General, For all Ingenious Persons that are concerned in the Famous Art of Building. London,* printed for William Sherwin, and are to be sold at his Shop next Doore to the *Star* in *Little Britain* […], MDCLXIX.

—— *VIGNOLA: or, the Compleat Architect. Shewing, in a plain and easie Way, the Rules of the Five Orders in Architecture, viz. Tuscan, Dorick, Ionick, Corinthian and Composite. Whereby, any that can but Read and Understand English, may readily learn the Proportions that all Members in a Building have one unto another, Set forth by Mr.* James Barozzio *of* Vignola, translated into *English* by *Joseph Moxon*. The fourth Edition with Additions. London, Printed and Sold by *Joseph Moxon* at the *Atlas* in *Warwick-Lane*, and at his Shop in *Westminster-hall*, right against the *Parliament Stairs*, 1694 [1st publ. 1655].

Vitruvius, *Ten Books on Architecture*, trans. I. D. Rowland, commentary and illustrations by T. N. Howe, with an additional commentary by I. D. Rowland and M. J. Dewar, Cambridge: Cambridge University Press, 1999.

Wallis, S., *A dissertation in vindication of the antiquity of Stone Henge, in answer to the treatises of Mr. Inigo Jones, Dr. Charleton, and all that have written upon that subject. By a clergyman living in the neighbourhood of that famous monument of antiquity*, Sarum: Printed by Charles Hooten, and sold by E. Easton and W. Collins, 1730.

Webb, John, 'Memoirs Relating to the Life and Writings of Inigo Jones, Esq.', in *The most notable antiquity of Great Britain, vulgarly called Stone-Heng, : on Salisbury plain. Restored, by Inigo Jones* […] *To which are added, the Chorea Gigantum, or, Stone-Heng restored to the Danes, By Doctor Charleton; and Mr. Webb's Vindication of Stone-Heng restored, In answer to Dr. Charleton's reflections; with observations upon the orders and rules of architecture in use among the antient Romans. Before the whole are prefixed, certain memoirs relating to the life of Inigo Jones* […], London: printed for D. Browne Junior, at the Black-Swan with Temple-Bar, and J. Woodman and D. Lyon, in Russel-Street, Covent-Garden, MDCCXXV.

Wheatly, Charles, *The Church of England Man's Companion; or a Rational Illustration of the Harmony and Usefulness of the Book of Common Prayer of the Church of England*, London, 1729 [1st publ. 1710].

Wheler, Sir George, *An Account of the Churches, or Places of Assembly, of the Ancient Christians from the Churches of Tyre, Jerusalem and Constantinople, described by Eusebius and Ocular Observances of several very Ancient Edifices of Churches yet Extant in those Parts with a Seasonable Application*, London, 1698.

Willis, John, *Mnemonica; or, the Art of Memory. Drained out of the pure Fountains of Art and Nature*. Digested into three books, London, printed […] by Leonard Sowersby, at the Turn-Stile, near New-Market, in Lincolns-Inn Fields, 1661.

[Wilson, John], *Trigonometry, With the Doctrine of the Sphere; Plain Dialing and Spherique Geometry, or Projection of the Sphere in Plano:* […] *To the whole is added a short Treatise of Sections of Plans, and an Introduction to Architecture*, Edinburgh, Printed by William Brown and John Mosman, 1724.

Wood, John, *The Origin of Building: or, the Plagiarism of the Heathens Detected. In Five Books*, Bath: Printed by J. Leake, 1741.

Wotton, Sir Henry, *The Elements of Architecture Collected by Henry Wotton Knight, from the best Authors and Examples*, London: printed by Iohn Bill, M.D.C.XXIV.

Wren, Sir Christopher: extracts published in this volume, as listed below, were all published in *Parentalia, or, Memoirs of the family of the Wrens; viz. Of Matthew Bishop of Ely, Christopher Dean of Windsor, &tc. but chiefly of Sir Christopher Wren,* [...] compiled by his son Christopher, now published by his grandson, Stephen Wren, Esq., with the care of Joseph Ames, F. R. S. and Secretary of the Society of Antiquaries London: Printed for T. Osborn, in Gray's-Inn, and R. Dodsley, in Pall-Mall, MDCCL [includes 'Letter of Recommendation to a Friend on the Commission for Building Fifty New Churches' [1711], pp. 318–21; 'On the Surveyor's Design for repairing the old ruinous Structure [of Saint Paul's], made (by Order of his Majesty and the Commissioner) upon an accurate Survey about four months before the Configuration' [7 May 1666], pp. 274–7; 'Tract I', pp. 351–3, and 'Tract IV: Observations on the Temple of *Peace*, built by the Emperor *Vespasian*', pp. 362–3 [both written after 1680]

Secondary literature

Addleshaw, G. W. O. (1948), *The Architectural Setting of Anglican Worship*, London: Faber & Faber.

Airs, M. (1975), *The Making of the English Country House 1500–1640*, London: Architectural Press.

—— (1995), *The Tudor and Jacobean Country House: A Building History*, Phoenix Mill: A. Sutton.

Allen, B. S. (1937), *Tides in English Taste 1619–1800*, Cambridge, MA: Harvard University Press.

Anderson, C. J. (1995), 'Learning to Read Architecture in the English Renaissance', in L. Gent (ed.), *Albion's Classicism: The Visual Arts in Britain, 1550–1660*, New Haven and London: Yale University Press, pp. 239–86.

—— (1997), 'La Lettura dei Testi come Strategia di Progettazione: Inigo Jones e la Facciata Occidentale della Chiesa di Saint Paul', *Annali di Architettura. Rivista del Centro Internazionale di Studi di Architettura Andrea Palladio*, vol. 9, pp. 245–64.

Aston, M. (1973), 'English Ruins and English History: The Dissolution and the Sense of the Past', *Journal of the Warburg and Courtauld Institutes*, vol. 36, pp. 231–55.

Auerbach, E. (1967), 'Figura', in *Gesammelte Aufsätze zur Romanischen Philologie*, Bern/Munich: Francke Verlag, pp. 55–93.

Auernhammer, A. (1973), *Johann Bernhard Fischer von Erlach*, London: A. Zwemmer Ltd.

Ayres, P. (1997), *Classical Culture and the Idea of Rome*, Cambridge: Cambridge University Press.

Barkan, L. (1975), *Nature's Work of Art: the Human Body as Image of the World*, New Haven and London: Yale University Press.

Bath, M. (1994), *Speaking Pictures: English Emblem Books and Renaissance Culture*, London: Longman.

Battisti, E. (ed.) (1996), *Andrea Pozzo*, Milan and Trento: Luni Editrice.

Baxandall, M. (1971), *Giotto and the Orators: Humanist Observers of Painting in Italy and the Discovery of Pictorial Composition, 1350–1450*, Oxford: Clarendon Press.

Beard, G. (1986), *The Work of Sir John Vanbrugh*, New York: Universe Books.

Bennett, J. A. (1972), 'Christopher Wren: The Natural Causes of Beauty', *Architectural History* 5, pp. 5–22.

—— (1993), 'Architecture and Mathematical Practice in England, 1550–1650', in J. Bold and E. Chaney (eds), *English Architecture Public and Private*, London and Rio Grande: The Hambledon Press, pp. 23–31.

Besançon, A. (2000), *The Forbidden Image: An International History of Iconoclasm*. Translated by J. M. Todd. Chicago and London: Chicago University Press.

Bold, J. (1989), *John Webb's Architecural Theory and Practice in the Seventeenth Century*, Oxford: Oxford University Press.

Bolzoni, L. (1991), 'The Play of Images: The Art of Memory from its Origins to the 17th c', in P. Corsi (ed.), *The Enchanted Loom*, Oxford: Oxford University Press.

Brewer, J. (1997), *The Pleasures of the Imagination: English Culture in the Eighteenth Century*, London: HarperCollins Publishers.

Carruthers, M. (1990), *The Book of Memory: A Study of Memory in Medieval Culture*, Cambridge: Cambridge University Press.

—— (1998), *The Craft of Thought*, Cambridge: Cambridge University Press.

Cassimatis, M. (1985), *Zur Kunsttheorie des Malers G.-P. Lomazzo (1538–1600)*, Frankfurt am Main/New York: P. Lang.

Cast, D. (1984), 'Seeing Vanbrugh and Hawksmoor', *Journal of the Society of Architectural Historians*, 43, pp. 310–27.

—— (1993), 'Speaking of Architecture: the Evolution of a Vocabulary in Vasari, Jones, and Sir John Vanbrugh', *Journal of the Society of Architectural Historians*, 52, pp. 179–88.

Chaney, E. (1998), *The Evolution of the Grand Tour*, London: Frank Cass.

Clark, I. (1982), 'Explicating the Heart and Dramatizing the Poet: Seventeenth-Century Innovations by English Dramatists and Donne', in I. Clark, *Christ Revealed: The History of the Neotypological Lyric in the English Renaissance*, Gainesville, FL: University Presses of Florida.

Clifton-Taylor, A. (1987), *The Pattern of English Building*, London: Faber & Faber [1st publ. 1962].

Colley, L. (1992), *Britons: Forging the Nation 1707–1837*, New Haven and London: Yale University Press.

Colvin, H. (1993), 'Lord Burlington and the Office of Works', in J. Bold and E. Chaney (eds), *English Architecture Public and Private*, London and Rio Grande: The Hambledon Press, pp. 263–8.

—— (1995), *A Biographical Dictionary of British Architects 1600–1840*, New Haven and London: Yale University Press [1st publ. 1954] [includes 'The Practice of Architecture, 1600–1840'].

Connor, T. P. (1984), 'Bubo's House', in *Design and Practice in British Architecture* (*Architectural History*, vol. 29), pp. 111–18.

Crinson, M., and J. Lubbock (1994), *Architecture: Art or Profession? With a Foreword by HRH The Prince of Wales*, London: The Prince of Wales's Institute of Architecture/ Manchester and New York: Manchester University Press.

Di Teodoro, F. P. (1994), *Raffaelo, Baldassare Castiglione e la lettera a Leone X*, Bologna: Nuova Alfa.
Downes, K. (1959), *Nicholas Hawksmoor*, London: D. Zwemmer Ltd.
—— (1977), *Sir John Vanbrugh*, London: D. Zwemmer Ltd, 1977.
—— (1984), 'The Publication of Shaftesbury's *Letter of Design*', in *Design and Practice in British Architecture* (*Architectural History*, vol. 29), pp. 519–24.
Eastlake, C. (1970), *History of the Gothic Revival*, New York: Humanities Press [1st publ. 1872].
van Eck, C. A. (1994), *Organicism in Nineteenth-Century Architecture: An Inquiry into its Theoretical and Philosophical Models*, Amsterdam: Architectura & Natura Press.
—— (1998), 'Giannozzo Manetti on Architecture: the *Oratio de saecularibus et pontificalibus pompis in consecratione basilicae Florentinae* of 1436', *Renaissance Studies*, 12/4, pp. 449–76.
—— (1998a), 'The Structure of *De re aedificatoria* Reconsidered', *Journal of the Society of Architectural Historians*, 57, pp. 280–97.
—— (2000), '"The splendid effects of architecture, and its power to affect the mind": the Workings of Picturesque Association', in : J. Birksted (ed.) *Landscapes of Memory and Experience*, London: SPON Press, pp. 245–59.
—— (2002), 'Rhetorical Categories in the Academy', in P. Smith and C. Wilde (eds), *The Blackwell Companion to Artistic Theory*, Oxford: Blackwell, pp. 104–16.
Eriksen, R. (2001), *The Building in the Text: Alberti to Shakespeare and Milton*, University Park: The Pennsylvania State University Press.
Evans, R. (1995), *The Projective Cast: Architecture and its Three Geometries*, Cambridge, MA, and London: MIT Press.
Farago, C. (1991), 'The Classification of the Visual Arts in the Renaissance', in D. R. Kelley and R. Popkin (eds), *The Shape of Knowledge from the Renaissance to the Enlightenment*, Dordrecht: Kluwer Academic Publishers, pp. 23–48.
de Fea, V., and V. Martinelli (eds) (1996), *Andrea Pozzo*, Milan: Electa.
Ferguson, M. W. (1990), 'Ruines of Rome', in A. C. Hamilton *et al.* (eds), *The Spenser Encyclopedia*, Toronto and Buffalo: University of Toronto Press/London: Routledge.
Fowler, A. (1964), *Spenser and the Numbers of Time*, New York: Barnes and Noble.
Freedberg, D. (1989), *The Power of Images: Studies in the History and Theory of Response*, Chicago: University of Chicago Press.
Friedman, A. T. (1989), 'Did England have a Renaissance? Classical and Anticlassical Themes in Elizabethan Culture', *Cultural Differentiation and Cultural Identity in the Visual Arts: Studies in the History of Art*, vol. 27, pp. 26–35.
Fumaroli, M. (1980), *L'Age de l'éloquence*, Geneva: Droz.
—— (1994), *L'Ecole du silence*, Paris: Flammarion.
Gent, L. (1979), 'Haydock's Copy of Lomazzo's *Trattato*', *The Library*, Sixth Series, vol. xvi, pp. 78–81.
—— (1981), *Picture and Poetry 1560–1620: Relations between Literature and the Visual Arts in the English Renaissance*, Leamington Spa: James Hall.
—— (ed.) (1995), *Albion's Classicism: The Visual Arts in Britain, 1550–1660*, New Haven and London: Yale University Press.
—— (1995a), '"The Rash Gazer": Economies of Vision in Britain, 1550–1660', in L. Gent (ed.), *Albion's Classicism: The Visual Arts in Britain, 1550–1660*, New Haven and London: Yale University Press, pp. 377–93.
Germann, G. (1972), *The Gothic Revival in Europe and Britain*, London: Lund Humphries.

Giraud, Y., and M.-R. Jung (eds) (1972), *Littérature française: la Renaissance 1480–1548*, Paris: B. Arthaud.
Goldstein, J. (1996), *Teaching Art*, Cambridge and New York: Cambridge University Press.
Gordon, D. J. (1975), 'Poet and Architect: The Intellectual Setting of the Quarrel between Ben Jonson and Inigo Jones', in Stephen Orgel (ed.), *The Renaissance Imagination: Essays and Lectures by D. J. Gordon*, Berkeley: University of California Press.
Grente, G. (ed.) (1951), *Dictionnaire des lettres françaises: le XVIe siècle*, Paris: Anthème Fayard, Editeur.
Harkness, D. E. (1999), *John Dee's Conversations with Angels: Cabala, Alchemy, and the End of Nature*, Cambridge: Cambridge University Press.
Harris, E., with N. Savage (1990), *English Architectural Books and their Writers, 1556–1780*, Cambridge: Cambridge University Press.
Harris, J. (1994), *Lord Burlington and the Making of Neo-Palladianism*, New Haven and London: Yale University Press.
——, S. Orgel and R. Strong (1973), *The King's Arcadia: Inigo Jones and the Stuart Court*, London: Arts Council of Great Britain.
Hart, V. (1993), 'Heraldry and the Architectural Orders as Joint Emblems of British Chivalry', *Res: Anthropology and Aesthetics*, 23, pp. 51–66.
—— and P. Hicks (1998), *Paper Palaces: the Rise of the Renaissance Architectural Treatise*, New Haven and London: Yale University Press.
Haskell, F. (1993), *History and Its Images: Art and the Interpretation of the Past*, New Haven and London: Yale University Press.
Hazard, M. E. (2000), *Elizabethan Silent Language*, Lincoln, NB, and London: University of Nebraska Press.
Herrmann, W. (1973), *The Theory of Claude Perrault*, London: Zwemmer.
Higgott, G. (1992), '"Varying with reason": Inigo Jones's Theory of Design', *Architectural History*, 35, pp. 51–77.
Höltgen, K. J. (1984), 'The Reformation, Images and some Jacobean Writers on Art', in U. Broick, T. Semmler and G. Stratmann (eds), *Functions of Literature: Essays presented to Erwin Wolff on his sixtieth birthday*, Tübingen: Max Niemeyer Verlag, pp. 119–46.
Howard, M. (1987), *The Early Tudor Country House: Architecture and Politics 1490–1550*, London: G. Philip.
—— (1988), 'The Ideal House and the Healthy Life: the Origins of Architectural Theory in England', in A. Chastel and J. Guillaume (eds), *Les Traités d'Architecture de la Renaissance: Actes du Colloque tenu à Tours du 1er au 11 Juillet 1981*, Paris: Picard, pp. 425–33.
—— (1990), 'Self-Fashioning and the Classical Moment in Mid-Sixteenth-Century English Architecture', in L. Gent and N. Llewellyn (eds), *Renaissance Bodies: The Human Figure in English Culture, c. 1540–1660*, London: Reaktion, pp. 198–218.
Howarth, D. (ed.) (1995), *Art and Politics in the Caroline Courts: Essays in Honour of Sir Oliver Millar*, Cambridge: Cambridge University Press.
Hulse, C. (2000), 'Tudor Aesthetics', in A. F. Kinney (ed.), *The Cambridge Companion to English Literature 1500–1600*, Cambridge: Cambridge University Press, pp. 29–64.
Hunt, John Dixon, and Peter Willis (eds) (1988), *The Genius of the Place: the English Landscape Garden 1620–1820*, Cambridge, MA, and London: MIT Press [1st publ. 1975].

Johnson, A. W. (1994), *Ben Jonson and the Poetry of Architecture*, Oxford: Clarendon Press.

Kemp, M. (1990), *The Science of Art: Optical Themes in Western Art*, New Haven and London: Yale University Press.

Kishlansky, M. (1996), *A Monarchy Transformed. Britain 1603–1715*, London: Penguin Books.

Knight, C. (2000), 'The Travels of Sir George Wheler (1650–1723)', *Georgian Group Journal*, 10, pp. 21–35.

Korshin, P. J. (1982), *Typologies in England 1650–1820*, Princeton: Princeton University Press.

Krautheimer, R. (1986), *Early Christian and Byzantine Architecture*, Harmondsworth: Penguin.

Kristeller, P. O. (1980), *Renaissance Thought and the Arts*, Princeton: Princeton University Press.

Kruft, H.-W. (1994), *A History of Architectural Theory from Vitruvius to the Present*, London: Zwemmer/New York: Princeton Architectural Press.

Lee, R. W. (1967), *Ut Pictura Poesis: The Humanistic Theory of Painting*, New York: W. W. Norton & Co.

Lefaivre, L. (1997), *Leon Battista Alberti: Recognizing the Architectural Body in the Early Italian Renaissance*, Cambridge, MA, and London: MIT Press.

Lemerle, F. (2000), *Les Annotations de Guillaume Philandrier sur le* De Architectura *de Vitruve, Livres I à IV*, Paris: Picard éditeur.

Levine, J. (1991), *The Battle of the Books: History and Literature in the Augustan Age*, Ithaca and London: Cornell University Press.

Liddell, H. G., and R. Scott (eds) (1940), *A Greek-English Lexicon*, new edition revised and augmented by H. Stuart Jones and R. Mackenzie, Oxford: Clarendon Press.

Lubbock, J. (1995), *The Tyranny of Taste: The Politics of Architecture and Design in Britain 1550–1960*, New Haven and London: Yale University Press.

McCormick, F. (1991), *Sir John Vanbrugh, The Playwright as Architect*, University Park: University of Pennsylvania Press.

McKellar, E. (1999), *The Birth of Modern London: The Development and Design of the City 1660–1720*, Manchester: Manchester University Press.

Marini, P. (1980), 'Le postille di Inigo Jones in margine a I Quattro Libri dell'Architettura: spunti critici e stimoli creativi', *Bolletino del Centro internazionale di studi di architettura Andrea Palladio*, 22, pp. 15–40.

Markus, R. A. (1997), *Gregory the Great and his World*, Cambridge: Cambridge University Press.

Mitchell, W. F. (1932), *English Pulpit Oratory from Andrewes to Tillotson: A Study of its Literary Aspects*, London: Society for the Propagation of Christian Knowledge.

Momigliano, A. (1950), 'Ancient History and the Antiquarian', *Journal of the Warburg and Courtauld Institutes*, 13, pp. 285–315.

Mowl, T., and B. Earnshaw (1988), *John Wood: Architect of Obsession*, Bath: Millstream Books.

—— (1995), *Architecture without Kings: The Rise of Puritan Classicism under Cromwell*, Manchester and New York: Manchester University Press.

Myrone, M., and L. Peltz (eds) (1999), *Producing the Past: Aspects of Antiquarian Culture and Practice, 1700–1850*, Aldershot: Ashgate.

Newman, J. (1980), 'Inigo Jones's Architectural Education before 1614', *Architectural History*, 35, pp. 18–50.

—— (1988), 'Italian Treatises in Use: The Significance of Inigo Jones's Annotations',

in J. Guillaume (ed.), *Les Traités d'Architecture de la Renaissance*, Paris: Picard, pp. 435–41.
—— (1993), 'Laudian Literature and the Interpretation of Caroline Churches in London', in D. Howarth (ed.), *Art and Patronage in the Caroline Courts: Essays in Honour of Sir Oliver Millar*, Cambridge and New York: Cambridge University Press pp. 68–88.
Nugel, B. (1980), *The Just Design: Studien zu Architekturvorstellungsweisen in der klassischen Literaturtheorie am Beispiel Englands*, Berlin/New York: Walter de Gruyter.
Onians, J. (1980), 'The Last Judgement of Renaissance Architecture', *Journal of the Royal Society of Arts*, 128, pp. 71–103.
—— (1988), *Bearers of Meaning. The Classical Orders in Antiquity, the Middle Ages, and the Renaissance*, Cambridge: Cambridge University Press.
Orgel, S. (1971), 'Inigo Jones on Stonehenge', *Prose*, 3, pp. 107–24.
Palme, P. (1959), 'Ut Architectura Poesis', in (Acta Universitatis Upsaliensis Figura Nova Series, 1). *Idea and Form, Studies in the History of Art*, Stockholm: Almquist & Wicksoll pp. 95–102.
Palmer, Rodney (2003), '"All is very plain, upon inspection of the figure": the Visual Method of Andrea Pozzo's *Perspectiva Pictorum et Architectorum*', in R. Palmer and T. Frangenberg (eds), *The Rise of the Image: Essays on the History of the Illustrated Art Book*, Aldershot: Ashgate.
Pauly, A. F. von, K. Ziegler and W. Sontheimer (eds) (1975), *Der kleine Pauly: Lexikon der Antike*, Munich: Druckmüller.
Payne, A. A. (1999), *The Architectural Treatise in the Italian Renaissance: Architectural Invention, Ornament and Literary Culture*, Cambridge: Cambridge University Press.
Peacock, J. (1990), 'Inigo Jones as a Figurative Artist', in L. Gent and N. Llewellyn (eds), *Renaissance Bodies: The Human Figure in English Culture, c. 1540–1660*, London: Reaktion, pp. 154–80.
—— (1996), *The Stage Designs of Inigo Jones: The European Context*, Cambridge: Cambridge University Press.
Pearsall Smith, L. (ed.) (1907), *The Life and Letters of Sir Henry Wotton*, Oxford: Oxford University Press.
Penny, N. (1993), *History and its Images*, New Haven and London: Yale University Press.
Pevsner, N. (1940), *Academies of Art, Past and Present*, Cambridge: Cambridge University Press.
Piggott, S. (1985), *William Stukeley, An Eighteenth-Century Antiquary*, revised and enlarged edition, London: Thames & Hudson [1st publ. 1950].
Ridgway, C. (2000), 'Rethinking the Picturesque', in C. Ridgway and R. Williams (eds), *Sir John Vanbrugh and Landscape Architecture in Baroque England 1690–1730*, Thrupp: Sutton Publishing in Association with the National Trust.
Rowan, A. (1975), 'Batty Langley's Gothic', in *Studies in Memory of David Talbot Rice*, Edinburgh: Edinburgh University Press.
Ruffinière du Prey, P. de la (2000), *Hawksmoor's London Churches Architecture and Theology*, Chicago and London: Chicago University Press.
Russell, T. M. (1997), *The Encyclopaedic Dictionary in the Eighteenth Century: Architecture, Arts and Crafts*, Vol. 3: *The Builder's Dictionary*, Aldershot: Ashgate.
Rutherford, I. (1995), 'Theoric Crisis: The Dangers of Pilgrimage in Greek Religion and Society', *Studi e Materiali di Storia delle Religione*, 61, pp. 275–92.

Saumarez Smith, C. (1997), *The Building of Castle Howard*, London: Pimlico [1st publ. 1990].
Sedlmayr, H. (1956), *Johann Bernhard Fischer von Erlach*, Vienna and Munich: Herold.
Severi, R. (1991), 'R H Traduttore di Giovan Paolo Lomazzo', *Quaderni di Lingue e Letterature*, 16, pp. 227–45.
Sherman, W. H. (1995), *John Dee: The Politics of Reading and Writing in the English Renaissance*, Amherst: University of Massachusetts Press.
Silcox-Crowe, N. (1985), 'Sir Roger Pratt, 1620–85', in R. Brown (ed.), *The Architectural Outsiders*, London: Waterstone, pp. 1–21.
Skinner, Q. (1996), *Reason and Rhetoric in the Philosophy of Hobbes*, Cambridge: Cambridge University Press.
Smick, R. (2000), 'Vivid Thinking: Word and Image in Descriptive Techniques of the Renaissance', in A. Payne, A. Kuttner and R. Smick (eds), *Antiquity and its Interpreters*, Cambridge: Cambridge University Press, pp. 159–74.
Smith, C. (1989), 'Christian Rhetoric in Eusebius' Panegyric at Tyre', *Vigiliae Christianae*, 43, pp. 226–47.
—— (1992), *Architecture in the Culture of Early Humanism: Ethics, Aesthetics and Eloquence 1400–1470*, Oxford: Oxford University Press.
Smuts, M. (1987), *Court Culture and the Origins of a Royalist Tradition in Early Stuart England*, Philadelphia: University of Pennsylvania Press.
Soo, L. (1998), *Wren's "Tracts" on Architecture and Other Writings*, Cambridge: Cambridge University Press.
Sprague, A. B. (1937), *Tides in English Taste (1619–1800)*, Cambridge, MA: Harvard University Press.
Summers, D. (1977), 'Contrapposto: Style and Meaning in Renaissance Art', *Art Bulletin*, 59, pp. 336–61.
—— (1981), *Michelangelo and the Language of Art*, Princeton: Princeton University Press.
Summerson, J. (1957), 'Three Elizabethan Architects', *Bulletin of the John Rylands Library*, 40, pp. 202–28.
—— (1978), *Georgian London*, Harmondsworth: Penguin Books, revised edn [1st publ. 1962].
—— (1980), *The Classical Language of Architecture*, London: Thames and Hudson, [1st publ. 1963].
—— (1983), *Architecture in Britain 1530–1830*, Harmondsworth: Penguin Books.
—— (2000), *Inigo Jones*, with a Foreword by Sir Howard Colvin, New Haven and London: Yale University Press [1st publ. 1966].
Szambien, W. (1995), 'Das Architekturmodell zwischen Theorie und Praxis', in B. Evers (ed.), *Architekturmodell der Renaissance. Die Harmonie des Bauens von Alberti bis Michelangelo*, Munich: Prestel, pp. 40–50.
Tait, A. A. (1978), 'Inigo Jones's "Stone-Heng"', *Burlington Magazine*, pp. 155–9.
Taylor, E. G. R. (1954), *Mathematical Practitioners in Tudor and Stuart England*, Cambridge: Cambridge University Press.
Tucker, R. (2000), '"Masculine and Unaffected" and "Varying with Reason": Decorum and the Designs of Inigo Jones', unpublished PhD Thesis, University of Bath.
Turner, J. (ed.) (1996), *Dictionary of Art*, New York: Grove.
Vendler, H. (1975), *The Poetry of George Herbert*, Cambridge, MA: Harvard University Press.

Vickers, B. (1988), *In Defence of Rhetoric*, Oxford: Clarendon Press.
Weinberg, B. (1961), *A History of Literary Criticism in the Italian Renaissance*, Chicago: Chicago University Press.
White, R. (1983), 'The Influence of Batty Langley', in *A Gothick Symposium*, Georgian Group.
Wilton-Ely, J. (1993), 'Wren, Hawksmoor and the Model', in J. Bold and E. Chaney (eds), *English Architecture Public and Private*, London and Rio Grande: The Hambledon Press, pp. 147–59.
Wittkower, R. (1971), *Architectural Principles in the Age of Humanism*, New York: W. W. Norton & Co. [1st publ. 1948].
Worsley, G. (1995), *Classical Architecture in Britain: The Heroic Age*, New Haven and London: Yale University Press.
Yates, F. (1966), *The Art of Memory*, London: Routledge and Kegan Paul.

Index

Numbers in italics indicate the page numbers of illustrations.

Academies of Art 8, 54, 71, 79, 147, 203–4, 229–30
 Academic theories of art 143
Addison, Joseph 41–4, 45
Alberti, Leon Battista 7, 15, 22, 45
 De Statua 205
 On the Art of Building 1, 3, 11, 12–14
Amsterdam 33
Ancients and Moderns
 battle between 4, 143–6
Andrewes, Lancelot 2
Andrino di Edesia 23
antithesis 9
Apollo Panionius, temple of 173
arch and vault system 161
Archer, Thomas 131, 199
Archimedes 13
architect
 as the intellectual author of a design 2, 47, 53–5, 119–21
 duties 73–7
 education 11–15, 48–9, 50–51, 59–60, 77–9, 120, 182, 205, 227–30
 God the supreme 121, 173
 introduction of the term 53
 versus master builder 53–5
architecture *see also* building
 aesthetics 10, 41–4, 105, 195–6, 197–9, 202–3 *see also* style
 and mathematics 1, 11–15, 28–9, 57–9
 Biblical 171–5
 definition 28–9
 ethics 10
 experience 106, 123, 179, 221 *see also* optics
 meaning 10, 165–6, 221
 mediaeval heritage 144 *see also* Gothic
 metaphorical use 5, 106, 111–14, 114–23, 127–9
 political aspects 178–9, 218–21, 229, 230–33
 religious meanings 114–23
architectural theory
 character of British architectural theory 1–5
  two strands in 3–4
  two varieties of 2–3
 Renaissance treatises 1, 178
 Vitruvian mould 105
Aristotle 3
 Aristotelian division of the arts and crafts 7–9
Associationism 41–4, 144, 165–6
Aubrey, John
 'Chronologia Architecturae' 161

Bacon, Sir Francis
 Of Building 87
Barbaro, Daniel 25
Barbon, Nicholas 10, 29–34
 see also economical aspects of building
beauty 34, 39–41, 144, 218–21, 225
Bedlam (London) 40
Bellarmine 124
Bernini, Gianlorenzo 231
Bible 106, 144, 172
 Authorized (King James) Version 107–10
Binet, Etienne
 Essay des Merveilles de la Nature et des plus nobles Edifices 118
Blenheim Palace 136, 166
Blum, Hans
 Quinque Columnarum (*Booke of Five Collumnes*) 21, 59
Bodleian Library (Oxford) 22
Boorde, Andrew 2, 55–7
Borromini, Francesco 201, 231

Builder's Dictionary
Frontispiece 47
building
country houses 91–7
economical aspects 10, 29–34
farms 62–7
financial aspects 76, 77–9, 86–8, 134–5
measurements 86–8
moral aspects 34–9, 106
organization 55
practice 53–55
social aspects 10
traditional English views 8
Burlington, 3rd Earl of 53, 98, 101, 167, 178, 200, 233

Campbell, Colen 203
Vitruvius Britannicus 1, 2, 54, 178, 201, 230–33, *231*
Cambridge Platonists 227
Camden, William 145, 147
Caron, Noel de 71
carpentry 60–62, 90–91, 91–7
Castell, Robert 167–71
Castle Howard 44, 136
Cato 66, 168
Cawdrey, Robert
Table Alphabeticall of English Words 2
Chambers, Sir William
Treatise of Civil Architecture 2, 3, 5
Charles I 71, 99
Charles II 44, 79, 203
Charleton, Walter
Chorea Gigantum 146
Charterhouse (London) 56
Chelsea College (London) 40
chimnies 194
church
burial 131–2, 138
Catholic 105, 114, 177
character 106, 124–5, 133
Christian doctrine 106
design 126–7, 131–5, 135–6, 136–9
early Christian 106, 123–7, 129–30, 139–41
interiors 134, 138, 139–40
spires 137
Cicero
De Oratore 17
Partitiones Oratoriae 17
[attr.] *Rhetorica ad Herennium* 17
City Companies 53
Company of Carpenters 61
Civil War 100
classical style 177–9, 224–7
aesthetics of 4 *see also* nature, imitation of *and* architecture, aesthetics of
pagan associations 105
classifications of arts and crafts 7–9, 11–15, 25–7, 48–9
Clemens Alexandrinus 139
Le Clerc, Sébastien 200
Coecke van Aelst, Pieter 185
Coelus 154
Colonna, Francesco 9, 15
contrapposto 9
see also antithesis
Columella 168
Commission for Building Fifty New City Churches 106, 131–5, 135–6
communication
persuasive 9
see also rhetoric
Constantine (Emperor) 124, 139, 154
Constantine VII Porpyrogennetos 168
Constantinople 81, 139
Sancta Sophia 124, 164
corona 4, 182, 184, 221
see also orders of architecture
crafts 89
criticism 27–8
Counter-Reformation 22
court 119, 128
Cryptoporticus 169–70, *170*
Ctesibus 13
Cuṣanus (Nicholas of Cusa) 3

Dallington, Robert 16
Daniel, Samuel
Defence of Rhyme 177
D'Avenant, Sir William 27, 99
decorum 10, 148, 154, 183, 206
Dee, John
'Mathematicall Preface' 8
Denham, Sir John 205
Desgodets, Antoine 217
design 8, 10, 11, 20–21, 24–5, 25–7, 46–9, 75, 192–5
Dickinson, William 131
Dietterlin, Wendel 189

Architecturae 189
Digge, Leonard 57–9
Tectonicon 3, 60
Diocletian (Emperor)
Baths 212, *214*, 215, *216*
Dissenters 130
Donne, John 5, 106, 110–14
Dudley, John, 1st Duke of Northumberland 59
Dudley, Lord Robert 16
Dugdale, Sir William 144
History of Saint Paul's Cathedral 156–7
Durham Cathedral 161

Elizabeth I 59
portrait by Crispin de Passe 178
emblematists 15
empiricism 44
enargeia 118
Epiphanius
Eusebius
description of church at Tyre 129, 139–41
Evelyn, Sir John 45
Idea of Perfection in Painting 205
Londinium Redivivum 79–86
Parallel of the Antient Architecture with the Modern 2, 3, 178, 203–15, *211*, *213–4*, *216*
Sculptura 205
Sylva 205

Fairfax, Sir Thomas 67, 192
fancy 9–10, 24–5, 27–8, 42, 44–5, 219
Félibien, André
Des Principes de l'Architecture et de la Sculpture 89
figural interpretation 107, 127–9, 139–40
Filarete 15
Fisher, William 215–17
Florio, John
Worlde of Words 2
Fortification 67–71
religious aspects 71–3
foundations 111–14
Fréart de Chambray, Roland
Parallèle de l'Architecture antique et de la moderne 3, 199–202
freemasonry 49
St Fulgentius 128
Fulwod, William 16
The Enemie of Idlenesse 16

geometry 60–62, 89, 185, 205, 218–19
Gerbier, Sir Balthazar 71–3
A Brief Discourse 71, 192–5
Counsell and Advice to all Builders 71, 77–9, 87
Hampstead Marshall (Berkshire) 71, 192
New Hall (Essex) 71
York House (London) 71
greatness 43
Gibbs, James 49
Giotto 23
Gloucester Cathedral 162
Golding, Arthur 148
Gothic 43, 49, 144, 155–60, 161–5, 171, 177, 220, 231, 234
opposition between 'Gothick and Regular' architecture 161, 226
Grataroli, Guglielmo 9, 16–17
St Gregory 3, 123
Gribelin, Simon 100

Hakewill, George
Apologie or Declaration … 4, 143–6
Halfpenny, William 54
Hampton Court (London) 40, 228
Hawkins, Henry
Partheneia Sacra 3, 106, 114–23, *115–17*
Hawksmoor, Nicholas 10, 44–5, 49, 98, 131, 136, 178, 199
designs for All Soul's College, Oxford 144
St Anne, Limehouse (London) 234
Christ Church (London) 234
Haydocke, Robert 24
health 56–7
Henry VI 145
Henry VII 145
Henry VIII 145
Henry, Prince of Wales 185
Hercules Farnese 174
Hiram 107–110
Hobbes, Thomas 9, 27–8, 44
Holland 195
Hollar, Wenceslas *149*, *151–2*, *156–7*
Holt, Richard 101–4
house 111–13, 114–23

humanism 2, 167

icnography 28
iconoclasm 140–41
imagination 9 *see also* fancy
Iupiter
  temple at Olympia 123

James I 99–100, 107, 110, 143, 146, 161, 226
James, John
  Translation of Perrault's *Ordonnance* 3, 144, 178
  Translation of Pozzo's *Prospettiva* 97–8
St John 129
Jones, Inigo 3, 9, 10, 54, 55, 177–8, 192, 230
  annotations to Renaissance treatises 177
  Banqueting House (London) 99, 230, 231–2
  Covent Garden 100
  Designs of Inigo Jones 146
  life 99–101
  Old St Paul's (London) 162, 178
  Queen's House (Greenwich) 232
  'Roman Sketchbook' 24–5
  Somerset House 100
  Stone-Heng Restor'd 100–101, 143, 146–55
  'Plant of the whole work' *149*
  'The Upright of the work' *151*
  'The Profyle' *151*
  'The whole work in Perspective' *152*
  'The Ruine yet remaining' *152*
Jonson, Ben 99
judgement 9, 24–5, 27–8

Kent, William 55
Kip, William
  Britannia Illustrata 230
King's College Chapel, Cambridge 145, 163

Langeren, P. van 114, *115*
Langley, Batty 49–51, 54, 101, 233
Laud, Archbishop 123
Laurentinum *168*, *170*
Leland, John 146
L'Estienne, Charles [Stevens] 54–5, 62–7
Liebault, Jean 62
Locke, John 227
Lomazzo, Giovanni Paolo
  A Tracte containing the curious Artes … 8, 21–4, 59
London 29–34, 146, 195, 234–6
  Great Fire 29, 53, 55, 57, 79, 101
liberal arts 1, 7–9

magnificence 194
Marlborough, 1st Duke of 165
Martianus Capella
  De Nuptiis Philologiae et Mercurii 7
Marvell, Andrew
  'Upon Appleton House' 118
masculinity 10
materials 74, 77–9, 91–7, 132–3, 189, 196
May, Sir Hugh 205
Mede, Joseph
  'What is Holinesse?' 106
memory 27–8
Merchant Taylors' School (London) 98
Michelangelo 24
microcosm
  analogy with macrocosm 8, 20–21, 21–4
    see also proportion
mnemonics 9, 16–20, 62 *see also* rhetoric
Monmouth, Geoffrey 155
Montague, Walter 5, 106–7, 127–9
More, Richard 60–62
More, Sir Thomas 4
  Utopia 126
Morris, Robert 45–6, 233
Moses 128
  Tabernacle 171–3
Moxon, Joseph
  Mechanick Exercises 3, 89–91
  Vignola; or the Compleat Architect 189–92, *190*
Le Muet, Pierre 189, 195–9
music 45–6

nature
  imitation 197–9, 202–3
Neo-Platonism 8, 21–4
Newton, Sir Isaac
  Chronology of Ancient Kingdoms amended 171, 173
Noah's Ark 173
None-Such Palace 4, 143, 145

North, Roger 3, 9, 34–41
'On Gothic Architecture' 161–5
'The Origin and Development of Regular Architecture' 178, 224–7
Norwich Cathedral 162

Office of the King's Works 54
optics 26–7, 41–4, 218–19, 221
orders of architecture 105, 186–9, 189–92, *196–8*, 206–15, 218–21
capitals 126
Corinthian 178, *204*, 223
Corinthian pediment 114
design 224–7
Doric 123, 173–4, 178, 179–81, *181*, 182, 209–12, *211*, *213–14*, 220
Gothique order 215
Ionic 183, 212, 215, *216*
origins 171–5, 220, 226
Tuscan 153, *190*
Origen
Homily on Genesis 140
ornament 10, 24–5, 96, 101–4, 120, 183, 219, 226
orthogonal projection 143
orthography 29, 72
Ovid
Metamorphoses 121, 148

Paine, James 55
painting 26 *see also* scenography
Palladianism 45–6, 49, 195–9, 199–202, 230–33, 233–6
Palladio, Andrea 3, 54, 143, 154, 195–9, 210, 212, 222–3, 231
atrium graecum 189
edition by Giacomo Leoni 199–202, 203
translation by Edward Hoppus 202, *204*
translation by Geoffrey Richards 195–9, *196–8*
Palladius 168
Pantheon (Rome) 4, 43, 124, 143, 146
Papillon, David 67–71
Several Political and Military Observations 67
The Vanity of the Lives and Passions of Men 67
patron 54
patronage 185
St Paul's Cathedral 134, 224, 228, 234–5
Peake, Robert 184–5
Pembroke, William Earl of
Perrault, Claude
edition of Vitruvius 217
Ordonnance 3, 144, 217
perspective 97–8, 143, 219
persuasion 9, 27
see also rhetoric
St Peter's (Rome) 165, 235
Philandrier, Guillaume 186
Pliny the Younger 168–71
St Paul's (London) 165
Pheidias 22
Picturesque 144
Pincot, Daniel 101
poetics 8
Pope, Alexander 45
Pozzo, Andrea
Prospettiva 55, 97–8
Pratt, Sir Roger 28–9, 55, 73–7
Primatt, Stephen 55, 86–8
proportion 21–4, 51, 105, 108–10, 120, 144, 171–3, 191, 192–5, 200, 208, 220
Protagoras 187
public
relation between a building and its public 10 *see also* architecture, experience of
pupillage 55

Quintilian 3

Ralph, James 10, 46–9
Critical Review 49, 233–6
reason 10, 44–5
rhetoric 1–2, 8–9
rhetorical art of memory 9 *see also* enargeia; architecture, experience of
Richards, Geoffrey 195–9
Rococo 49
Romans 153–5, 177
Royal Academy of Arts 55
Royal Society 44, 55, 79, 161, 205
R.T.
De Templis 3, 106, 123–7
Rubens, Sir Peter Paul 99

Salisbury Cathedral 163
Scamozzi, Vincenzo 3, 210, 212, 215, 217
scenography 28, 72

Schools (Oxford) 226
Schuym, Joachim 215
sculpture 26
Serlio, Sebastiano 3, 59, 143, 146, 184–6
Shaftesbury (Anthony Ashley Cooper, Lord) 45, 227–30
Shere, Sir H. 3, 54–5, 91–7
Shute, John 3, 53–5, 59–60, 177
  First and Chief Groundes 21, 179–81, *181*
Simonides 8
Sirach, song of 44
Sister Arts, doctrine of 8–9, 25–7, 39–41, 45–6
situation 26, 76, 94, 120, 126, 131–2, 135, 137
Smirke, Sidney 77
Smith, James 230
Society of Antiquaries 55
Solomon's Temple 106–110, 121–2, 124, 171, 173, 193
The Spectator 41–4
Spon, James
  Voyage d'Italie, de Dalmatie, de Grèce 129
statics 218–19
Stickells, Robert 9, 19–21
Steele, Sir Richard 41
stone 101–4
Stone-Henge 143, 146–55, 171 *see also* Inigo Jones
style 105
Suratt 138
surveying 57–9, 60–62, 77–9, 86–8
symmetry 14

Talman, William 55
taste 234
tectonic principles 161
  approach to architecture 178, 224–7
Temple-Bar (London) 235
theoria 2
Tacitus 143
Taylor, Sir Robert 55
Temple Church (London) 163
Temple of Peace (Rome) 4, 184, 222–3
Tresham, Sir Thomas 19

ut pictura poesis 8

Vanbrugh, Sir John 44, 54, 98, 131, 178, 199
  on church building 106, 136–9
  on Woodstock Manor 144, 165–6
Varro 168
Vasari, Giorgio 7, 145
Vergil
  Georgica 63
Vesta, Temple of (Rome) 124
Vignola (Giacomo Barozzi da) 54
Villa urbana 169
Villiers, George, Duke of Buckingham 71, 127
Virtuosi of St Luke 55
Vitruvius
  Ten Books on Architecture 1, 12–14, 22, 45, 54, 59, 144, 167, 169, 171–5, 177–8, 187, 220
Vitruvian tradition 2, 143
  assimilation of Stone-Henge 146–55
  dissemination in England 184–6, 189–92, 203–15, 215–17
Vredeman de Vries, Hans 49

Ware, Isaac
  Complete Body of Architecture 2, 3, 5
Webb, John 55, 98, 143
  'Memoirs Relating to the Life and Writings of Inigo Jones, Esq.' 98–101
  The Most Notable Antiquity of Great Britain, vulgarly called Stone-Heng 98
  'Vindication of Stone-Heng Restored' 146
Westminster Abbey 162–3
Westminster Chapel 145, 161
Wheatly, Charles
  The Church of England Man's Companion 139–41
Wheler, Sir George 129–30
  Journey into Greece 129
  reconstruction of primitive Christian church *130*
Whitehall 228
William III 220
Willis, John 9, 17–20
Willsford, Thomas
  Architectonice 66
Wood, Anthony 100
Wood, John 144, 171–5
  An Essay towards a Description of Bath 171
  The Origin of Building 171–5

Woodstock Manor 144
Wotton, Sir Henry
  Elements of Architecture 3, 25–7, 87, 126, 186–9, 195
Wren, Sir Christopher 1, 3, 4, 34, 38, 44, 54, 55, 79, 98, 217–23, 224
  City churches 53
  on church building 106, 131–5
  designs for Christ Church College, Oxford 144
  on Old St Paul's, London 144, 155–61, 156–7
  St. James, Westminster 134
  on Temple of Peace, Rome 179, 221–4
  on Westminster Abbey 144
Wren, Christopher jr 131
Wren, Stephen
  Parentalia 217

Zeuxis 22